Melancholia of Freedom

Melancholia of Freedom

SOCIAL LIFE IN AN INDIAN TOWNSHIP
IN SOUTH AFRICA

Thomas Blom Hansen

PRINCETON UNIVERSITY PRESS

Princeton & Oxford

Published by Princeton University Press, 41 William Street,
  Princeton, New Jersey 08540
In the United Kingdom: Princeton University Press,
  6 Oxford Street, Woodstock, Oxfordshire OX20 1TW

Jacket art: *Unit 3* © Riason Naidoo. Courtesy of the Durban Art Gallery/South Africa

press.princeton.edu

LIBRARY OF CONGRESS CATALOGING-IN-PUBLICATION DATA
Hansen, Thomas Blom, 1958–
  Melancholia of freedom : social life in an Indian township in South Africa / Thomas
Blom Hansen.
    p. cm.
  Includes bibliographical references and index.
  ISBN 978-0-691-15295-0 (hardcover : alk. paper) — ISBN 978-0-691-15296-7 (pbk. :
alk. paper) 1. East Indians—South Africa—Durban. 2. Chatsworth (Durban, South
Africa)—Race relations. 3. Chatsworth (Durban, South Africa)—Social conditions.
4. Chatsworth (Durban, South Africa)—Religion. 5. Durban (South Africa)—Race
relations. 6. Durban (South Africa)—Social conditions. 7. Durban (South Africa)—Religion. I. Title.
    DT2405.D889E3735 2012
    305.891'41068455—dc23   2011041406

British Library Cataloging-in-Publication Data is available

This book has been composed in Baskerville 120 Pro

10 9 8 7 6 5 4 3 2 1

Contents

Illustrations

Preface and Acknowledgments

LIKE MANY OTHERS OF MY GENERATION, THE YOUTH REVOLT IN SOWETO IN 1976 made me a committed antiapartheid activist. Less than two years later, I found myself in South Africa along with other young activists who were documenting international investments in the country while posing as innocent travelers. Those months taught me much about the starkness of everyday apartheid. One of the startling experiences was that my own skin color immediately placed me, even implicated me, in the structural logic of race that was defined though the administration of space. I felt somehow violated by this de-individualization. Months later, I became friendly with exiled activists from Soweto who were now eking out an existence in Gaborone in Botswana. De-individualization of a far more brutal kind than anything a white person would experience, violence at home and in public spaces, and a bleak future had been their world. Their anger and their incredibly high spirits were instantly infectious and humbling for a middle-class boy from northern Europe. My somewhat formulaic idea of the antiapartheid struggle changed as I began to understand that their anger was directed against the very form of life that apartheid has assigned them to. They were angry at the passivity of their parents' generation, angry at the African National Congress (ANC), which they saw as a haughty and distant organization, and they adored the free spirit of Steve Biko. They had nothing but contempt for what they called the "commissars," those who tried to recruit them for the ANC in exile. Their fear of the apartheid state was gone and they wanted to defeat it at home, inside the country, and in communities and townships. Many of them did return to South Africa where their example set the tone for the protracted but also bloody modes of protest that eventually brought the regime to its knees. Many of them perished in the brutal internecine warfare between supporters of Black Consciousness and those supporting the ANC. Today, this ambiguous chapter of recent history is largely forgotten. In the early 1990s, the ANC emerged as the main author of the postapartheid society, and the organization could not resist rewriting history as well. In the Hector Peterson Museum in Soweto, the rebellious "comrades" of 1976 are largely incorporated into a self-serving story of the ANC as the general commander of the antiapartheid struggle, globally and at home.

Twenty years later I returned to South Africa, and to Durban, as a visiting scholar at the University of Natal. It was a different country in many respects, but most things were still recognizable. Before returning, I had devoted a decade and a half to studying modern India. I was quickly drawn to Durban's Indian worlds, which were so conspicuous in the city and on campus. Soon I found myself spending most of my time in Chatsworth, the oldest and most consolidated township for Indians in the city. I attended theater and music performances and religious functions, and I befriended an ever-growing circle of people in the sprawling township. Many were puzzled and surprised by the fact that I had lived in India for several years. I was often asked to be a (reluctant) adjudicator of the authenticity and quality of everything from wedding rituals to food and music compared to what I knew from India. Many took pleasure in assuring me that they were actually "bad Indians" who had been corrupted by the lifestyle in South Africa. Most people I met were entirely absorbed by their own ethnic world and decidedly uninterested in politics. They looked at the emerging new South Africa from a slight distance, mainly as spectators, thinking themselves disempowered and marginal and keeping their heads down.

How different this was from the environments and atmosphere I had encountered two decades earlier—and how different from the images, reporting, and academic writing in the intervening decades, which had depicted South Africa as a country where everything happened under the sign of political conflict! I was intrigued by this, and also drawn to the plainspoken, garrulous, and humorous world of Chatsworth. It was clear at the time that South Africa was beginning to abandon its status as a global exception and entering the ranks of ordinary—if troubled— countries in the global south. I sensed that in this township there would be many cues that would help me to begin to understand another reality, and to ask questions that were more compelling to the social scientist I had become than to the political activist I used to be: How did the decades of apartheid and its reorganization of social life shape communities and everyday subjectivities? What horizons of family life, morality, and personal and collective history were being enabled, and disabled, in apartheid's vast township spaces? How were these forms of social life and cultural sensibility shaping the way people interpreted and inhabited the new institutional, physical, and discursive realities of the postapartheid republic?

I set out to explore these questions in a series of fieldwork studies from 1999 to 2007. Initial funding was provided by a generous grant from the Danish Social Science Research Council for fieldwork in 1999 and 2001. In 2007 my fieldwork was supported by a grant from the Ford Foundation in a collaborative project on religion and migration that was organized and funded by the Social Science Research Council in New York. I am grateful to these funding bodies for their support.

The debts I have incurred during the process of researching and writing this book are innumerable, and I can only mention the most important here. In Durban, my warmest thanks go to the Sahadeo family in Chatsworth who were my warm and lively hosts for many months during several periods of time since 2001. Their friendship and generosity made their home, their neighborhood, and their social world a welcoming and genial environment for me. My late friend Kas Lalla, always enthusiastic and unfailingly in the know, was another dear friend who was a fantastic guide to Chatsworth's social worlds and history. Another friend was the late "Yanks," who was also a valuable friend and guide in the beginning of my fieldwork and whose family extended their friendship to me in the years after his premature death. In addition, I spent time and shared meals with dozens and dozens of ordinary people in the township over the years: members of prayer groups, da'wah (conversion/preaching) organizations and church communities, political workers and social activists, social workers, schoolteachers, students, taxi drivers—the list is endless. Their warmth, hospitality, and good humor made my fieldwork in Chatsworth one of the most rewarding experiences of my life.

Naresh Veeran became a friend and a guide to the world of music and media in Durban, and his parents, Denny and Christina Veeran, were superb hosts in their Chatsworth home. Rajesh Gopie, the late Kessie Govender, Ronnie Govender, and Jay Pather educated me in the Indian theater tradition in South Africa. Intellectuals and academics like Brij Maharaj, Bill Freund, Ashwin Desai, the late Fatima Meer, Vishnu Padayachee, Ian Edwards, Goolam Vahed, Anand Singh, and many others educated me in the history of Durban and the Indian community. At the University of KwaZulu-Natal, the Department of History and its lively seminar became my institutional home in 1998–99. Here, Jeff Guy, Keith Breckenridge, Catherine Burns, and many others provided a most inspiring education in South African history. Daniel Herwitz and Lucia Saks opened their house, lives, and intellects to me, and we became friends for life. Preben Kaarsholm generously shared his many academic contacts and his knowledge of the province.

From 2001, Wits Institute for Social and Economic Research (WISER) in Johannesburg became my academic home in South Africa. I am grateful for the inspiring conversations during many seminars and conferences throughout the years. I would like to extend special thanks to Achille Mbembe, Sarah Nuttall, Deborah Posel, Jonathan

Hyslop, Liz Gunner, and the staff at WISER for their friendship, engagement, and generosity. I am also grateful to Rehana Ebr.-Vally, Peter Alexander, Isabel Hofmeyr, Loren Landau, Hylton White, Eric Worby, Dilip Menon, Jon Soske, and other scholars in the Johannesburg region for their kind invitations and sustained intellectual engagement.

My work has benefited from discussions with many colleagues in my various workplaces and friends and interlocutors at seminars and conferences over the years: Arjun Appadurai, Janaki Bahkle, Barney Bate, Gerd Baumann, Carol Breckenridge, Wendy Brown, Gabi vom Bruck, José Casanova, Partha Chatterjee, Kamari Clarke, Jean Comaroff, John Comaroff, Vilashini Cooppan, Val Daniel, Faisal Devji, Nicholas Dirks, Jacob Dlamini, John Eade, Patrick Eisenlohr, Marc Gaborieau, Peter Geschiere, James Ferguson, Ulf Hannerz, Susan Harding, Christophe Jaffrelot, Steffen Jensen, Bruce Kapferer, John Kelly, Raminder Kaur, Peggy Levitt, Lisa Malkki, Saba Mahmood, William Mazzarella, Birgit Meyer, Yael Navaro-Yashin, Chris Pinney, Mattijs van de Port, Dhooleka Raj, Arvind Rajagopal, Lisa Rofel, Peter van Rooden, Danilyn Rutherford, David Scott, William Sewell, Jonathan Spencer, Finn Stepputat, Dimitri Tsintjilonis, Manuel Vásquez, Ravi Vasudevan, Peter van der Veer, Oskar Verkaik, Lisa Wedeen, and many, many others.

I would like to extend a special thanks to the Department of Anthropology at the University of Edinburgh, and to my dear friend, the late Charles "Chuck" Jedrej, who generously facilitated a research leave in 2001–2 that made all the difference. A warm thanks to Janaki Bahkle, Nicholas Dirks, and Brinkley Messick for facilitating my academic year at the Department of Anthropology and the South Asia Institute at Columbia University in 2009–10. Bill Carrick, Annapurna Potluri, and Sabrina Buckwalter provided a most congenial work environment, which allowed me to finish this book during that year. They also rescued my boxes of material that went missing in postal mishaps between Amsterdam and New York.

Ajay Gandhi helped me organize my archival material in 2006. Doug Hill cleaned up my manuscript in 2010. Fred Appel, Cathy Slovensky, and Natalie Baan at Princeton University Press shepherded my manuscript with professionalism and consistent support. Anonymous reviewers provided incredibly helpful and constructive comments on my manuscript. Thanks to all of you.

My daughter Laerke and son Malte came with me to Durban in 1998–99, and again as teenagers in 2007. Durban left a mark on them and became a much-loved reference point in our shared lives. They spent most of their adolescence hearing about how their father was "about to finish his book"! The most consistent support and encouragement have come from Sharika Thiranagama, my lovely wife, my best friend, and my partner in life, love, and work. She read, commented, encouraged, and pushed me toward the finish line. Our little son Mirak provided the daily sunshine that puts life in proper perspective.

Thomas Blom Hansen
Stanford, March 2011

Melancholia of Freedom

As South Africa celebrated its first decade of freedom and democracy in 2004, a film called *Broken Promises* (Kumaran Naidoo, 2004) became a craze in Durban's formerly Indian townships. A slapstick family comedy about a Hindi-speaking girl who marries into a Tamil family, the film followed a long tradition of local theater in these townships. The acting, story, and dialogue had a semi-amateur style that was instantly recognizable from many plays I had attended in the Indian townships. The film was packed with fast-paced dialogue that was sprinkled with vernacular abuse. It was an instant hit and sold about 150,000 copies within a year, almost exclusively among the 1.3 million South Africans of Indian origin who lived mainly in Durban and Johannesburg. In 2005 this success was followed by the sequel, *Broken Promises 2*; in 2006, *Run for Your Life* debuted, which had a similar cast and story line, and this was followed by *Run for Your Life 2*.

I watched *Broken Promises 2* in Durban in June 2007 when it was featured at the Durban International Film Festival as a local contribution to an impressive list of international quality productions. The venue was small and the audience was limited that evening, with no more than three dozen people in the hall. I chatted briefly with a number of people as we waited outside the hall. An elderly American couple who were film enthusiasts looked forward to this local production and clearly expected something between a quality Bollywood movie and the art house genre that dominated the festival. Behind me sat a group of young, smartly dressed couples who spoke a mixture of Zulu and English, which was characteristic of Durban's new African elite. A few rows down sat a conservatively dressed Indian couple of Gujarati descent with their young son.

Half an hour into the film, the American man leaned over and asked me, "Is this some spoof? Is there something else coming after?" I told him that what appeared to him as a spoof was indeed the film. Somewhat embarrassed, he smiled and said, "I think we are leaving . . . this was not what we expected." The Gujarati man got up fifteen minutes later, cursing through his teeth that "one was supposed to pay for such garbage," and dragged his disappointed family with him. The young couples behind me were loudly discussing what the film was about and started laughing in disbelief at some of the exaggerated sound effects and the quality of acting. Soon they also left the hall, while making jokes about how this film was indeed a broken promise. I soon found myself in the hall with a handful of local Indians who were laughing heartily while also sending me, the only outsider left, occasional glances and slightly nervous smiles as they watched my reactions.

This slight measure of unease, or mild embarrassment, in my friends and informants was well known to me. When watching a performance, or partaking in this aspect of the cultural life of the Indian townships, I often felt that I was watching something that was not meant for me, as if I represented a gaze that was out of place. This film was clearly neither meant for me nor made for my eyes. The unease was not born of hostility or protectiveness but rather from a sense of embarrassment: now I could see for myself how things really were with them. These films, as most of the popular culture among South African Indians (which I will return to later in this book), revolve around an internal gaze that is making what people often refer to as "the community" (of Indians in the country) visible to itself through jokes and self-deprecating humor. This is where a "we" is generated and reproduced, a sense of who we really are, where we came from, and how foolish we are. This is neither the official story nor any authorized representation of the community. It is the informal inner space that most of my informants in the township, and many who have left the township, know very intimately. It is also a side of the community that appears silly and unrefined to those who have climbed into the middle class or have constituted its historical elite since the nineteenth century. Yet it is also funny because it mocks a past that was shared in the face of systematic discrimination and historical exclusion from institutional and public spaces in the country. What unifies the South African Indians today are the laugh and the self-deprecating joke.

This embarrassment vis-à-vis an outside gaze indicates one of the most difficult problematics across postapartheid South Africa: to redefine identities, communities, and selves within a new economy of recognition; that is, to live under a new and differentiated gaze that feels unfamiliar and never fully intelligible. This differentiated gaze marks new horizons of recognition—some local, some national, and others global. In the cinema hall that evening, we, the audience, represented several forms of gaze—the foreign visitors, the new black middle class, the local Indian elite—all of whom were puzzled or even disappointed at the obvious banality of the film on display. This small event was but one example of the daily misrecognitions that mark postapartheid South Africa.

Under the Gaze: Freedom and Race after Apartheid

To live under the gaze is fundamental to human consciousness. To be seen is a physical and palpable sensation, an ontological ground of being human. The gaze is neither restricted to people one knows nor to recognizable beings. The gaze is constitutive, fundamental to being, or as Merleau-Ponty puts it in his reflections on visibility, "As soon as I see it is necessary that the vision be doubled with a complimentary vision or with another vision: myself seen from without, such as another world would see me, installed in the midst of the visible, occupied in considering it from a certain spot" (1968, 142). Consciousness emerges from the assumption of a preexisting gaze that comes from all sides, a strange, unfathomable force that can never be entirely reduced to the specific social or cultural context in question, and can never be reduced to sets of eyes that can be known: "it is not I who sees, not he who sees, because an anonymous visibility inhabits both of us, a vision in general . . . being here and now, of radiating everywhere and forever, being an individual and also a dimension and a universal" (ibid., 142). In *The Phenomenology of Perception* (1945/2002), Merleau-Ponty reflects at length on the enigma of seeing: "Nothing is more difficult than to understand *what we see*," as he proposes (2002, 17; italics in the original). What appears as immediately visible to the eye is but one dimension of what we perceive. What we actually see is culturally and socially conditioned by received frames and formats. When we see the front of a house, we also "see" its full form and begin to assume its functions, and even its people. The visible is always supported and supplemented by a range of social conventions and tacit, embodied forms of knowledge of how objects look from other sides, as such, in their totality (ibid., 172).

This is analogous with Merleau-Ponty's idea of language as a form of embodied convention, a structure that helps a subject speak herself into existence as a person. As the uttering of the sound of a word only acquires meaning within a certain community of embodied speech practices, the physical sensing and seeing of an object is also embedded in a thick context of shared assumptions about how things and people look and act, however historically provisional these may be. In this, the most common and fundamental dimension of being, we always assume and impute a larger and more abstract gaze that beholds objects in their entirety, and for which these objects exist *as such*, regardless of our particular gaze. This imputed gaze is a form of phantasmic regulator that provides an ontological guarantee of the veracity of the world as it appears to us in our social imagination.[1] This labor of the guarantee also includes an embodied experience of one's self that always depends on the constitution of corporeality—the social existence of the body, seen, objectified, and vulnerable to the world, as "flesh constituted by the other." The relationship between embodiment (a sense of one's body) and corporeality (the body constituted by the gaze) is always asymmetrical, if not discrepant.[2] Both Sartre and Merleau-Ponty were undoubtedly inspired by Simmel's reflections on the mutual exchange of gazes in the modern city, where the inability to fathom and read the face and gaze of the other and where the categorization and "de-individualization" of strangers assume critical and foundational importance for production of sociality as such.[3]

Lacan, more than any other theorist, elaborates the perspective of a split between the (actual/physical) eye and the (phantasmic) gaze into a theory of the barred subject, subjectivity perpetually haunted by constitutive blockages and illegitimate desires and unable to complete itself. What appears as a familiar gaze of actual people looking also stands for what Merleau-Ponty called "vision in general," a generalized gaze that splits the subject: on the one hand, the regulating assumption of social conventions and injunctions (the symbolic order) that regulates behavior even when no one is looking, and on the other hand, a fuzzy, unfathomable, demanding, yet enticing and durable other gaze that has no language or stable form, just pure presence. The latter, qua its lack of intelligibility, can appear as a radical void of nothingness, even as something nonhuman, uncanny, or perhaps divine. This unfathomable—and sometimes abject—underside of that which is visible and conventional never fails to unsettle and puncture subjectivity as such.

The result is a perpetual economy of misrecognition where subjectivities are formed in anticipation of a regulating and desiring gaze but fail to fully embrace what they are supposed to be or become, because this second unfathomable gaze can never be fully understood or gauged. Lacan's formula for this perpetual misrecognition and "economy of lack" is: "You never look at me from the place from which I see you . . . conversely what I look at is never what I wish to see" (1977, 103). Lacan's fundamental position is that misrecognition is constitutive because the gaze always trumps the eye. The most powerful desires and anxieties are always phantasmic, circling around a more powerful truth that is believed to stand behind any face or appearance. This split gaze constitutes, on the one hand, a (phantasmic) guarantee of an ontological order, and, on the other hand, a field of vision and experience fraught with instability, doubt, and anxieties of incompleteness.

Situations of great social upheaval always undermine the visual regimes of recognition and fantasy that govern social life. That was certainly true of the transition from apartheid to a new liberal-democratic order. Let me sketch why the relationship between gaze, anticipation, and failed subjectification are so important in postapartheid South Africa.

The nexus between a racialized social order and the privileging of the visible reached a historical climax in Nazism. Films, public spectacles, and body aesthetic were designed to provide a firm ontological ground of unambiguous categories: the true German people and their multiple enemies (Gilroy 2002, 137–77). The privileging of the visible in South Africa was historically more widespread, naturalized, and insidious. While race thinking was embedded in every aspect of the economic order, it also found strong expression in scientific racism, which always privileged physical appearance in the absence of any firm genetic, objective proof of linkages between phenotypical and socio-cultural qualities (Dubow 1995). Race thinking became a hegemonic political common sense (Norval 1996) and acquired a reality of its own, a widespread and deeply embedded popular economy of belief that invariably embedded behavior and social practice in phenotypically marked bodies. Today, no statement, no sentence, and no gesture can acquire its full meaning and significance in South Africa without being linked to, and invariably qualified by, the phenotypical classification of the speaker. An individual's pigmentation is what can be seen by the eye but is also always/already inserted and framed by a larger gaze, a schema of racial ideology that makes bodily pigmentation the very root cause of intrinsic social qualities and cultural propensities.

Fanon begins his *Black Skin, White Masks* by discussing the body: first, the scandal of sexual unions between racially defined groups, and second, the deprivation of people of color of the ability to have authentic embodied selves, culture, and historicity. According to Fanon, the imposition of an all-important "racial epidermal schema" meant that "I was responsible at the same time for my body, for my race and for my ancestors" (111). He continues by comparing himself to a Jew: "All the same, the Jew can be unknown in his Jewishness. He is not wholly what he is. His actions, his behavior are the final determinant . . . [but] I am given no chance. I am overdetermined from without. I am a slave not of the 'idea' that others have of me but of my own appearance" (116). Thus a larger racialized gaze always trumps, structures, and gives meaning to that which is actual and visible—an individual being or a singular event. Such a complex gaze prestructures any subjectivity. "In this country we are imprisoned in our bodies; we cannot escape" was how a friend in Durban described racialization in South Africa. This fundamentally corporeal and racial structure of the gaze has durably shaped common-sense perceptions of race among a majority of South Africans.

While I cannot disagree with Gilroy's penetrating critique of the utterly senseless and illogical basis of contemporary racism (2002, 11–53), and his description of race as "an impersonal, discursive arrangement, the brutal result of the raciological ordering of the world, not its cause" (2005, 39), I believe that the institutional force of this "discursive arrangement" has produced entire social worlds. Every ethnographer of South Africa will have to reckon with this social fact in order to understand and describe contemporary social and cultural life in the country.

The existence over decades of a repressive state apparatus whose multiple institutions tried to monitor, make visible, and police racial boundaries created an acute consciousness of being watched by the authorities. This gaze was panoptic, disciplining, and regulative by making objects and bodies visible and intelligible in the full sense of biopolitical rationalities that were entirely structured by racial categories. Despite its totalizing intentions, the apartheid state was far from always effective in regulating social practices, yet governmental practices created an acute sense of watching and being watched, albeit with different intensity. A constant second-guessing of the gaze of the state produced fine-grained readings, mostly imaginary in nature, of different degrees of freedom and physical security in different locations. Spatial limits were policed with utmost severity and violence with respect to African populations, while other population groups were regulated less violently but in greater and more intrusive detail. Almost every South African had to viscerally internalize the tacit boundaries of the permissible and conventional with respect to the surveillance by the state whether real or not. Such a life under the gaze of the law and the state did indeed create what Crossley has called an "anxious awareness."[4] It also allowed the carving out of less-visible spaces where furtive enjoyment and unique social rules thrived, often semisecret and rarely shared freely with others. The strictures on social and political life have changed profoundly within the last fifteen years, but the legacy of this gaze of the state and the social attitudes, predilections, and lasting inequalities it shaped (MacDonald 2006) continue to exert enormous influence in the lives of ordinary people.

Because life during apartheid became so rigidly divided along race lines, and yet remained intimate and close in workplaces and homes, every South African had to learn to live according to a complex cultural economy that was structured by several forms of (imputed) gaze. Racialized identities and anxieties were played out at every level of social and intimate life. The result was a set of complex, performative anxieties that are by no means unique to South Africa but became more developed there than in most other societies. No matter who and where one is, one is always being watched and looked at through the eyes of someone who represents another social and racial category, and thus a different world, maybe even a different ontological horizon: the live-in maid, the employer, the man in a passing car, the neighbor, the walkers on the street, the official, the policeman, and so on. The unique feature of South Africa is that every physical space remains historically marked and defined by a single racial category—rarely two or more. Social spaces are marked by calculations of physical danger, appropriateness, and risk. Every act and individual utterance is always/already doubled as a representation of a racial category that "acts" through the act or utterance. In other words, the eye of any onlooker is also always the gaze of the category. One is always potentially doubled by the category; one's actions can always be interpreted as a category that is acting through one's body; one is always potentially reducible to a phenotype, a cultural cipher, or a racialized shadow or doppelgänger. The category functions as a constant shadow; every action takes place in the gaze of the other, even when that other is not physically watching. With Merleau-Ponty, one can say that forms of embodiment, understood as the subjective inhabitation of a body, always/already coexisted in an irrevocable tension with the racialized categories of corporeality that were constituted and reproduced from without.

Racialization of every dimension of social life produced a peculiar "flatness of public perception," by which I mean that the categorical doppelgänger, the stereotype, provided the script and the interpretive grid within which individual action—and anxiety—was situated. This de-individualization and anxious flatness of public perception continue to haunt virtually every corner of South African society. The peculiarly commanding and yet ineffective gaze of the apartheid state rendered spaces of private and cultural intimacy somehow pleasurable and safe. The flatness of public representation has perpetuated a structure of social life in which an actual sense of individuality, depth, and completeness only seem possible, comforting, and attractive *within* the intimacy of one's own racial-cultural world, because only there can one merge with one's racial shadow and make it less intrusive and obvious.

The seismic shift in the political order of South Africa since 1994 has been experienced first and foremost in a profound transformation of the social imaginary, and a transformation of the order of the gaze. Apartheid tried to structure social practices of all kinds under a unified gaze of the state that purported to stand for and represent Western civilization as a form of universality. For people of color, apartheid institutionalized the idea of the customary and traditional as a form of internal gaze enforced by political-cultural elites and institutions within each racial and ethnic community.

The postapartheid scenario was equally enticing and confusing on both of these dimensions. On the one hand, the events of 1994 created a strong sense of the country becoming readmitted into the larger universal history and into a postcolonial and globalizing present. Now, South Africa was no longer the exception, the anachronistic remainder of colonial violence that for decades made the country and its social order a central object in a universal and global condemnation of racism as an absolute evil. Condemnation of apartheid unified postcolonial governments and progressive forces across the world in a common moral and political front. In the 1990s, the new South Africa was to enjoy the fruits of that global visibility and global moral stature.

However, apart from iconic people like Mandela or Tutu, it was unclear who could represent or embody this imputed global universality. It soon became obvious that the celebrated nonracial doctrine of the African National Congress amounted to nothing more than a poetic vision of a rainbow nation. In his famous inaugural address in 1994, Mandela said, "We enter into a covenant that we shall build the society in which all South Africans, both black and white, will be able to walk tall, without any fear in their hearts, assured of their inalienable right to human dignity—a rainbow nation at peace with itself and the world."

Nonracialism now became an injunction to find authentic expression within the multicultural nation: now that you are free, define yourself as you truly are, define your own culture and your own history. Many South Africans embraced the promises of hope and redemption within the peculiar postauthoritarian "millennial capitalism" that arose in the 1990s across the globe (Comaroff and Comaroff 2001). Aspirations toward self-making within a global horizon also found strong articulations in the gospel of health, wealth, and self-improvement within the global Pentecostal movement, and in the self-respect, purity, and strength promised by globalized Islam.

On the other hand, it remained unclear who was looking and who was listening. Who was evaluating and appreciating me as I truly am? Who was the community of new South Africans? The indisputable emotional strength of African nationalism notwithstanding, no credible and legitimate formulation of what constitutes the South African nation and people had been produced. South Africans do not exist as "a people" (Chipkin 2007, 1–15), only as discrete groups sharing a territory and a history of deep segmentation and bloody antagonism. Although many discrete struggles against the state had been loosely confederated under the sign of a future freedom from minority rule, no compelling idea of a unified "people" had emerged. The question of who was an entitled citizen was still framed in racial terms. Truly shared public spaces where nonanxious mixing of communities may occur remain scarce and have been provided mainly by new commercial media and new commercial spaces and shopping malls across the country.

A central proposition in this book is that the legacy of colonial and apartheid regulation and cultural policy has made the embodied imagination of a range of imputed gazes extraordinarily compelling and complex in everyday life. The authority and compulsion of these gazes, the recognition they elicit and demand, and the anxieties they instill have been in rapid flux over the past fifteen to twenty years. The deeper theme of this book—how the meanings and spaces of freedom and democracy are perceived and inhabited by nonprivileged South African Indians—reveal contradictory sentiments that are shared across many other communities in the country.

Freedom and Sovereignty after Apartheid

The antiapartheid movement was driven by two not always compatible desires: freedom and sovereignty. On the face of it these two desires are eminently compatible as goals for a modern and autonomous self that is embedded in, and empowered by, a sovereign nation. The equation of personal freedom and national self-realization is perhaps the single most suggestive and influential idea of the past century.[5] The equation is heavily indebted to a classical Kantian understanding of freedom as the primacy of an inner and autonomous capacity for judgment, the capacity to impose a moral law on oneself, and an inner freedom that enables the release of the free will as the source of true freedom.[6] Freedom is measured by the ability to realize a true and autonomous self, a self that matures and outgrows its need for tutelage, a self that trusts itself and its own judgments (Kant 1963).

Many critiques of the implicit political theology of the idea of inner emancipation of the human will, with all its Christian baggage, have demonstrated that freedom of the modern self was not a self-evident universality.[7] The imagining of free selves was always shaped by the specific structure of unfreedom they arose from, and the national and cultural community they claimed as their sovereign vehicle. With this in mind, let us begin with a few reflections on the structure of unfreedom in South Africa and the racially differentiated ideas of personhood and sovereignty it gave rise to.

Although violent and authoritarian, the apartheid state never depended on the regimentation of speech, text, and language, which is so ably analyzed by Alexei Yurchak in the case of the Soviet Union (2005). The power of the apartheid regime depended exactly on the reverse, on a robust body politics that governed, categorized, and separated on the basis of "objective" phenotypical marks that determined everything:

dwelling, types of work, education, income level, range of mobility, and forms of information and styles of speech available to different groups. Apartheid recruited visceral fears and relied on what the regime saw as natural, prelinguistic, and affective ties, which emerged from shared phenotypical marks. Through infrastructure and biopolitical engineering, apartheid made a racialized world appear natural and a given. It was the structure of everyday life and the reproduction of easy entitlement and privilege that kept apartheid going rather than any ritualized public commitment to an idea. De facto acceptance of this structure of life counted for support for apartheid rather than any overt statements or special effort. The perfect white citizen moved among her own kind, consumed, mowed her lawn, and enjoyed life without too much reflection.

Even those critical of this structure of body politics were forced to, and indeed invited to, partake in the easy life of relative privilege and considerable freedom for those classified as whites. In this Athenian democracy there was considerable freedom of movement and speech for the fully entitled white citizen.[8] The included but less entitled (Indians and colored) had to live with severe restrictions on movement and life opportunities but were relatively secure within the boundaries of their racially defined world. The nonentitled (Africans) were seen as wholly outside, forever destined to live in their traditional life worlds in Bantustans, submitting to the yoke of the *nkosi* (chief), and only visiting the republic as temporary guest workers.[9]

There was indeed censorship and surveillance, but its main target was seditious activity and actual organization among people of color in the country. The enemy was first and foremost the communist organizer, not necessarily the critical intellectual. Physical repression was also carefully calibrated. Routinized categorical brutality was meted out to Africans, while other race groups were disciplined by exemplary incarcerations or occasional eliminations of individual "enemies of the state." The preferred site of the apartheid planner was the regulation of everyday practices. The target was the predilections and habits of ordinary life that enabled its language games, little comforts, and sense of knowability in racial enclaves and townships. Apartheid's attempts at ideological persuasion of people of color were generally clumsy and ill-fated.

In this world of authoritarian rule by a highly visible minority, and deep racial-spatial segmentation of everyday life, the idea of freedom and autonomous self-making gradually split into two discrete horizons. On the one hand, there was a strong desire for majority rule and the resurrection of the sovereignty of African people and communities, the horizon presented by the now-exiled ANC, whose position was strongly supported by large sections of the international community.[10] On the other hand, there was the more mundane desire for further autonomy in everyday life, for enjoying moments of sociality, dignity, and cohesion around community events, in community spaces. Cultural and social autonomy, and a measure of self-governance, were actively promoted by the apartheid state as a way of deflecting political energies away from the question of sovereignty and majority rule. More important, community spaces and townships also became the primary horizons of social life and shaped social identities and political action. Local protests were loosely connected with other political actions elsewhere in the country, particularly under the umbrella of the United Democratic Front (UDF) in the 1980s, but rarely under the sign of a unified national aspiration.

The fall of apartheid produced a strong sense of an epochal event that turned entire social worlds, languages, and imaginaries into anachronisms. Freedom had been yearned for, and apartheid had been globally represented as an anachronistic settler state that delayed South Africa in emerging as a free and sovereign African nation. Yet no one had fully anticipated how quickly the particular affective ties that had formed meaningful communities during the decades of apartheid— township cultures, the lingo of the comrades, aesthetic production opposed to the state, and so on—lost public validity and ethical coherence after 1994. As ANC rapidly adopted a technocratic language of service delivery and stakeholders, the heroic pathos of the struggle rhetoric was rendered evermore anachronistic.

The new official policy of multiculturalism spurred an unprecedented revival of cultural and religious identities across the country. They were all attempts to embrace a newfound freedom, often by recovering older registers of cultural memory. As we will see in this book, some of these registers were haunted by the perpetual embarrassment caused by the recent past and by the pleasures and memories of community life during apartheid that had so pervasively shaped ordinary life in townships across the country, including during the years of militant struggle. In his reflexive memoir on the moral communities that structured his childhood township in Johannesburg, Jacob Dlamini writes, "there is nothing wrong with native nostalgia, a longing for a lost home set in a politically problematic time and place . . . I attempt to seize hold of memories without which we cannot understand why apartheid suffered the kind of moral defeat that led to its demise" (2009, 152). It was in fact the strength of ordinary township life rather than the rhetoric of its anomie that ultimately broke apartheid, Dlamini suggests. The current popularity of Jacob Zuma and his election to become president of ANC in 2007, and later president of the country in 2008, was based on a heterogeneous range of affective political registers that had lain dormant in the townships for more than a decade—hypermasculine Zulu identity, labor militancy, struggle rhetoric, and anticapitalist advocacy of nationalization and social redistribution.[11]

Similar configurations of hope, and the contradictory recollection of a past that cannot be openly yearned for, characterize many other segments of South African society. The injunction to acquire a new kind of past is intrinsic to the moment of new sovereign self-making as free subjects: recast the past as nothing but a gradual yearning and struggle for freedom; critique the recalcitrance of the older social habits and comforts of unfreedom; but celebrate the past in a way that permanently relegates it to anachronistic oblivion and cuddly irrelevance.

In order to understand the continuing emotional attachments to the habits and spaces of unfreedom that I explore in this book, let us turn to the theme of melancholia and loss through Hegel's reflections on the dialectic between the lord and the bondsman in the *Phenomenology of Spirit* (1977). Hegel suggests that while the lord is the site of pure desire and consumption of the world and its goods, the bondsman achieves a sense of himself through labor. Labor is a manifestation of negativity, both in its ability to transform objects and in its marking of an irreducible difference vis-à-vis the lord. The bondsman's desire is expressed in the ability to produce and shape things, although the enjoyment of these things remains reserved for the lord. The recognition taking place between the two is actually a perpetual misrecognition: the lord believes himself to be autonomous, but this autonomy depends entirely on the labor of the bondsman whose desire he needs but cannot desire because it has no value for him. The bondsman derives a sense of himself and dignity of labor from being able to leave a mark on the world, a "signature," as Butler puts it (1997, 37–40). Yet his autonomy is illusory inasmuch as he only desires through the lord's desire and thus can be nothing without the lord. The larger point is, of course, that this dialectic marks a single but irrevocably divided consciousness (Hegel 1977, 104–12).

With the *Aufhebung* (elevation/cancellation/overcoming) of this contradiction and the delivery of the bondsman into a state of freedom, something curious, if entirely logical, happens: the consciousness of the former bondsman splits into two as he produces an ethical law of the community that becomes the source of the regulation of his desires, of prohibition, and the injunctions to work and leave signatures on the world. This leads to the birth of what Hegel famously called an "unhappy consciousness"—a consciousness divided within itself and never fully identical with itself (127–28).

The unhappy consciousness is marked by a loss of certainty that was secured by the negativity of the other, and a loss of the (often malevolent) sure-handedness imputed to the lord. As the question "Who am I?" or rather "What am I for you?" is no longer answered by the lord, the free subject has to figure out whose desires it wants to desire, and what in the subject others may want to desire. The question that is opened, and that can never be fully answered, is: On which ontological ground can the subject imagine itself as striving to become a free and reflexive being?

The usefulness of this formal model for historical moments of liberation should be obvious.[12] But it is also insufficient because it does not in itself account for the marking of the bondsmen as racialized bodies bearing bodily marks that demand complex re-signification as marks of freedom and sovereignty. In her analysis of Hegel's relationship to the victorious slave revolution in Haiti, which was unfolding as *The Phenomenology* was written, Buck-Morss argues that Hegel was most probably a cultural racist. He took inspiration from the events in Haiti but discarded the capacity of black slaves to develop true interiority and true freedom (2009, 21–77). However, as Buck-Morss also acknowledges, this civilizational racism did not diminish the momentous influence of Hegelian notions of struggles for self-realization as authentic history on nationalist, revolutionary, and anticolonial thought and practice for two centuries.[13]

In Arendt's famous essay on freedom, she engages the limits of Hegelian thought and suggests that the only proper form of freedom lies beyond "the social" (and its unhappy consciousness) as a horizon. Freedom only appears through true political action, by which she means acts that create something new, that enact a beginning as such—not for instrumental gain, securing sovereign rule, or protecting property or other rationalities of "the social," but for their very opposite: to show fidelity to a principle or to create a new society or new social form. Freedom is nothing but the wages of political courage, and without courage there is no real politics: "It takes courage to leave the protective security of our four walls and enter the public realm, not because of particular dangers which may lie in wait for us but because we have arrived in a realm where concern for life has lost its validity. Courage liberates men from their worry about life for the freedom of the world" (Arendt 2000, 448). This leads Arendt to a conceptualization of true political action as a form of miracle, analogous with the logic of organic and natural processes of birth and gestation that rely on "infinite improbabilities": "In the realm of human affairs we know the author of 'miracles.' It is men who perform them" (460).[14]

Such a heroic concept of politics corresponds quite directly with the horizon of revolutionary transformation that was promoted by an exiled ANC for decades. When South African transition eventually did take place, it was widely referred to as a form of miracle strangely removed from the flow of everyday life.[15] A set of fortuitous events emerged from bloody street fights and from courageous opposition in thousands of battles for rights, but the result was nonetheless a negotiated solution of a radically different order than that of daily existence. In popular political imagination, freedom was made possible in large measure by the presence of one man: Mandela. Force and circumstance had removed him from the grit, violence, and meanness of late apartheid, which in turn allowed him to appear as an author of the new society. The script and the excitement of the new possibilities after apartheid were exhilarating and unnerving at the same time. It is telling that this new and still alien order was widely referred to as the "postapartheid dispensation." Dispensation is a term with theological roots and means an order handed down by supreme authority (e.g., by God, the church, or by law), but it can simultaneously refer to an exemption, a temporal phase bracketed by exceptional circumstances. The "dispensation" was soon given form and body in the new constitution in 1996, a farsighted and progressive document that expresses the spirit and aspiration of postapartheid freedom while also being at odds with many prevailing social norms in the country. The constitution was produced as a small pocket-sized book with the subtitle "one *law* for one *nation*" (emphasis in original), and millions of copies were distributed across the country in an attempt to make it "the property of the people," as a high-ranking ANC member put it to me in 1998. However, in order to retain its foundational and quasi-magical force as a symbol of sovereign, collective freedom, the constitution and the new Constitutional Court had to remain elevated above the flow of ordinary life and what soon became "ordinary" politics.[16]

When "the thrill was gone" and heroic struggle politics gave way to gradual administrative change and a liberal regime of rights,[17] it became clear that the resistance to apartheid in the 1980s had indeed been forged within political and social horizons that were strongly lodged in "the social" produced by apartheid in localities and specific communities.[18]

For the majority, freedom had not been imagined as individual self-expression or revolutionary transformation but as collective and constructive acts that secured community and dignity as it was known and lived. Or, as Simmel argues about modern freedom, "Freedom consists in a process of liberation, it rises above a bond, [but] finds its meaning, consciousness and value only as a reaction to it . . . the individual is tied to others, and ties others" (1950, 121–22). The problem was to acknowledge precisely what freedom entailed. Hegel describes the moment of freedom as one of alienation. It is marked by an inability to fully recognize that its very own essence lies in the mere effort at "desiring and working" in everyday life itself: "Where that 'other' is sought, it cannot be found, for it is supposed to be just a *beyond*, something that can *not* be found . . . Consciousness, therefore, can only find as a present reality the *grave* of its life . . . the Unhappy Consciousness merely finds itself *desiring* and *working*; it is not aware that to find itself active in this way implies that it is in fact certain of itself, and that its feeling of the alien existence is this self-feeling" (1977, 131–32; emphasis in original).

To understand work and life, the old categories of unfreedom, as the very sites of a new freedom, turned out to be particularly difficult in South Africa. The apartheid governance through biopolitics, space, and everyday routines meant that when freedom arrived it could barely be recognized as a new horizon but instead appeared as a continuation of the old. For some, freedom signified a redemptive dream of radical change in life circumstances and futures and a complete break with the apartheid past. For most people, however, the idea of freedom revolved around more modest and concrete aspirations: a new house, a secure job, education, and securing of their enclaves of relatively autonomous life. At the level of locality and community, the transition from "revolution to rights" (Robins 2008) turned out to be more seamless than many an ANC functionary had imagined. Now it was ANC cadres turned bureaucrats and ministers that were expected to deliver the daily wages of liberal freedom.

Melancholia of Freedom

Anxiety, embarrassment, and obsessions with the gaze and visibility may be particularly pronounced among South African Indians. The forging of this category of people from many discrete and disparate parts of the Indian subcontinent into a single racial and cultural category was accompanied by constant charges of being culturally alien people. The position of Indians in the economy and the political structure in South Africa as an intermediate group of "quasi citizens" between white privilege and African disenfranchisement only heightened the sense of perpetual marginality. Yet the story that follows could have been told about many other groups in South Africa, a country whose society is deeply segmented and internally separated. A society of migrants and recent urbanites, the majority of South Africans live far away from anything they can call their proper home in a cultural or historical sense. Just like the people of Chatsworth who appear in this book, most

South Africans struggle to inhabit their urban spaces, their history, and their new political and cultural freedoms.

As I began fieldwork, I was immediately struck by a pervasive sense of loss and displacement. The transformation of the South African economy has resulted in an economic marginalization of the Indian working class. The township has also changed. Today, thousands of Africans live in informal shacks or in newly built government houses in Chatsworth and in other formerly Indian areas. The effect of these changes has been a multilayered sense of loss: loss of economic security, loss of the township as "our place," loss of perceived existential and physical safety, and a loss of what Hegel called the "loss of the loss," that is, the disappearance of the blockage—unfreedom and apartheid—that prevented true self-realization and thus explained most problems and shortcomings in everyday life.

The second remarkable feature of life in Chatsworth was the ubiquity of the self-deprecating humor that made *Broken Promises* such a roaring success. Jokes, stories, and everyday mockery of the *charou* (local slang for nonrespectable Indians) way of life constituted an important medium for reflection on a very uncertain future. I realized that self-deprecating humor and stinging satire had been central to Indian life in South Africa for many decades (Hansen 2000). In his well-known essay *Mourning and Melancholia*, Freud argues that while mourning expresses the feeling of loss of a loved object, melancholia may be "a reaction to the loss of a loved object" (1969, 245) when one cannot see clearly what it is that has been lost. The patient knows whom he has lost but not what he has lost as a result. The symptoms of this condition are often difficult to gauge and understand, for both the melancholic and those around him. Yet one symptom is clear: self-reproach and self-reviling. Freud continues, "The melancholic displays something else besides which is lacking in mourning—an extraordinary diminution in his self-regard, an impoverishment of his ego on a grand scale" (246). In mourning, it is the world that has become poor and empty; in melancholia it is the ego itself.[19] Freud argues that the melancholic incorporates the unrecognizable loss into her own self, where it reemerges as a peculiar enjoyment in reviling the self as flawed and imperfect.

This formulation of melancholia resonates with the multilayered sense of loss and the representations of everyday life in this particular community. Much public debate, many performances, and much informal conversation are organized around an oscillation between intense self-reproach regarding the past, conservatism, tradition, of introversion, and loving self-absorption and idealization of family life, culture, and sociality. This oscillation is marked by melancholia rather than nostalgia.[20] Melancholia arises from a deep anxiety regarding how the identity and history can be represented and enunciated. The attachment to the recent past during apartheid, where community life flourished in the racial enclave, cannot be publicly enunciated at this point except as narratives of struggles to defy the state. The emotional attachments to this period and its forms of life must remain repressed and can only be referred to in intimate and informal settings. Like in other sections of South African society, the loss of this deeply problematic past, its plea-sures, and its forms of life cannot be acknowledged. The past is tense, and the experience of freedom becomes melancholic.

BETWEEN IRRELEVANCE AND IRREVERENCE: "OUR CULTURE" AFTER APARTHEID

The end of apartheid entailed a challenge to everyday life and revisions of many social practices and forms of everyday speech. Many ordinary people retained their attachments to the community life of the town-ship, imperfect but intimate, known and comforting. Others reached out and beyond the township in search of larger global and diasporic identities or universal religious communities. Immersing myself in the township, I found myself confronted with two analytical rubrics. The first was the concept of "diaspora." Most of my initial assumptions were shaped by a tacit understanding that South African Indians were at-tached to a deep and affective sense of cultural practices that tied them to South Asia. Many local organizations, much local scholarship, and a good chunk of public discourse, including a resurgent interest in Bol-lywood aesthetics and stars, seemed to confirm the existence of such a durable link.

I soon realized that such a perspective locked me into an interpre-tive frame that elided the deep entanglements and profound shaping of social life in the city and the township. Chatsworth must be seen as a moment in the history of a "permanent minority" that is embedded in a colonial and postcolonial territory where every claim to belong-ing, land, and livelihood has been contested for a century. The anti-immigrant violence in May 2008, which affected migrants from Africa and also people of Asian origin,[21] instantly reactualized the deep sense of alienation and questioned the status of Indians as true citizens, as had been the case during anti-Indian riots in 1949 and 1985. Diaspora is, in other words, not a condition that applies permanently to cultural minorities anywhere but is a particular framing of a "call of history" and a particular framework for cultural self-making that people respond to according to class position, alienating political events, and their local political imagination. I will explore this problem and the cultural at-tachments to South Asia, be they virtual or concrete, toward the end of his book.

The second analytical rubric was that of everyday life. Many progressive and left-leaning intellectuals in South Africa assume that "the only good Indian is a poor Indian"—the still powerful idea that ordinary and poor Indians in the township harbor genuinely nonracial ideas of solidarity and justice as opposed to the culturally conservative and race-conscious Indian middle class.[22] There is a deep romantic nexus between everyday life and the supposed authenticity of the poor and marginalized that has exerted considerable influence in political practice here, as in many other parts of the world, and indeed in the theory and practice of anthropology.

Everyday life, understood as the institutionalized and highly structured routines of movement, work, leisure, and dwelling characteristic of modern societies,[23] was the preferred site of apartheid's robust biopolitical interventions. For generations of Africans and other people of color, the dull disciplinary routines of work, township, and trains were sites of violent subjection and occasional heroic bursts of defiance. These were key institutions in what Will Glover in his work on urban planning has called a "materialist pedagogy"; that is, "the ordinary material fabric of a modern city would continuously irrigate its residents with a flow of salutary effects" (2008, xxi). These effects were imagined to instill in the natives what they were lacking: an interiorized self-discipline, capacity for work, and practical appreciation of the ordered aesthetics of modern life. This form of material government relied on daily material routines and diminished the reliance on ideological persuasion. This had important precedents in the mission stations and the early colonial state in South Africa. In a set of incisive reflections on the analogous interests in the everyday by Christian missionaries and social theorists, Jean and John Comaroff note, "a crucial goal of the Protestant outreach was to implant the methodical habits that produced civil, self-disciplined Christian subjects . . . [both missionaries and social theorists of practice] evince a distrust of contemplative truths, opting instead for a vision of *homo faber*, of human life as the product of instrumental action" (1997, 30). This identification of everyday life as a site of virtue has roots in a wider Protestant celebration of the lay, of ordinary speech, of work, and of thrift and modesty (Taylor 1989, 211–303). It also marks a fundamental acceptance of the leveling and objectifying effects of modernity on the modern self: "its double life as subject and object. This being was, at once, unique and faceless, a self-conscious individual and an impersonal noun . . . at once 'somebody,' a named mortal, and 'anybody,' the generic man in the street" (Comaroff and Comaroff 1997, 32).

As we will see later, everyday and ordinary life as a set of material disciplines—erasing the old while shaping the recalcitrant or unwilling native mind—assumed a central place in twentieth-century governmentality in South Africa and elsewhere in the (post)colonial world. This obvious fact has had surprisingly little impact on how anthropology constructs the everyday and the ordinary as its new privileged place of investigation. Anthropology abounds with submerged assumptions about the autonomy, discrete ontologies, and moral force assumed to be intrinsic to this realm of life. De Certeau, Deleuze, Foucault, James Scott, and even the notion of "subalternity," understood as a relatively uncolonized form of life, serve as standard references. But neither colonial governmentality nor Protestant ideology make regular appearances in this work, not even in work that critically assesses and questions the force of the everyday as an analytical optic.[24]

In Veena Das's recent foregrounding of the "ordinary" as the privileged site of anthropological intervention and knowledge, this blind spot is particularly obvious (2007). Das's main inspiration is the late Wittgenstein's (and Stanley Cavell's) view of the world as constituted through series of provisional, inadequate, but nonetheless functioning language games that in their turn produce both selves and sociality (neither of these being whole or complete) as "forms of life" (*lebensformen*) (Wittgenstein 1953, 19–23). Cavell accepts the assertion that there are indeed ordinary language games that can provide proper "homes" for words, places where words and their referents actually mean something— that is, have a certain stability and real meaning within certain communities—as forms of life. These are the spaces where "acknowledgment" is found—of oneself and of others. By acknowledgment, Cavell means not just to recognize the other in the Hegelian sense but to make an attempt to see the other person as she/he actually dwells in the world. I understand this to be a more intense, if not intimate, striving than that of neighborliness. It is, in fact, a desire to understand the very subjectivity of the other.[25]

The ordinary plays a double role in Das's work, and both of them are redemptive: first, as the limit of language understood as a set of nondiscursive and mundane practices, mostly illustrated as forms of life among slum-dwellers and victims of violence in India who are capable of overcoming pain and of "pick[ing] up the pieces . . . to find out whether and how to go on" (2007, 6); and second, as the very opposite; namely, the true origin and referent of language in a more authentic or original sense, as when she writes on the very last page of the book that the role of anthropologists is "witnessing the descent into the everyday through which victims and survivors affirm the possibility of life by removing it from circulation of words gone wild— leading words home, so to speak" (221). I take this to mean that words come home to those who properly own them but are unable to utter them without the aid of anthropologists or other interlocutors. In this move, actual speech, public statements, and ritualized conduct by those who claim social or cultural authority in the communities studied, or those who may just speak and banter, may be relegated to a realm of the mediated, even not-so-ordinary. Only those properly equipped (with Cavell, or anthropology?) seem able to decipher the whispers and murmurs of the ordinary.

Against such an obliquely moralizing perspective, this book focuses on the everyday as a site of open conflict and moral debate. The everyday culture I document and analyze in detail is not merely the somehow inexplicable preserve of those who are poor, marginal, silent, or without the capacity to express themselves in public speech. The everyday practices of ordinary people, youth, newcomers, women, and religious people are indeed the manifest object of much worry, reflection, and joking in homes and cars, in markets and newspaper columns, and in taxis and talk shows. The local terms for this shared object vary from generalized notions of kinship, the idea of the "Indian family," or to the colloquial notion of being charou. Much of this charou culture is regarded as embarrassing, inappropriate, and outright ridiculous—and even a blockage to the full embrace of freedom. The status of the everyday is, in other words, not a semivisible ontology waiting to be divined. The status of everyday life as a space of meaning and "our culture" is a problem right at the heart of life as it is lived in Chatsworth—a life that is irrevocably split between an external and an internal view of oneself, strung between several gazes and marked by highly flexible modes of self-presentation. It is a life that is reflexive and worldly but also suffused by intimate and intensely self-absorbed forms of enjoyment. Prior to 1994, much political rhetoric posited the "inner" community life as the source of moral cohesion and even as containing the seeds of a future redemption and renewal.[26] This powerful political fiction of cultural unity, pride, and even purity was shared from parts of the ANC to the conservative right, but soon splintered into many discrete parts in the 1990s. In its stead emerged an anxious life in freedom and a split gaze that was very pronounced among the people I studied, but also paradigmatic of many other segments of South African society.

STRUCTURE OF THE BOOK

I have structured the book around three major themes: (1) the vexed and morally complex question of the constitution and practices of life in unfreedom and of ordinary life in the apartheid township; (2) the hopes, pleasures, anxieties, and alienations that erupted in the 1990s as a new postapartheid society invited everybody to embrace freedom and reinvent themselves; and (3) the process of reimagining oneself, claiming identities, and recasting historical narratives and collective memories in a present torn between a commitment to a contested and feeble South African nationalism and a variety of global and diasporic desires.

These three broad themes do not suggest any inevitable flow from unfreedom into self-invention. The problem of rewriting the past became more urgent as the new society and its freedoms emerged. Everything became illuminated and inflected but never redeemed by history, and each chapter incorporates the echoes of this celebrated and also disavowed past that is so omnipresent in the lives of the people I am describing.

Chapter 1, "Ethnicity by Fiat: The Remaking of Indian Life in South Africa," forms the foundation for subsequent chapters by telling the story of how the Asiatic question was configured in South Africa from the 1860s to the present as a question of necessary containment of culturally alien people. I tell the story of how the township of Chatsworth was set up, imagined, and framed as a purely Indian space over decades of tense and often antagonistic tussle between policy makers and social activists. I look at how specific methods of policing contributed to the current mythology of the Indian township during apartheid as fundamentally safe, as a place where "we never locked our doors." This chapter draws on official documents, newspapers, and governmental publications, as well as a range of narratives by older residents of Chatsworth.

Chapter 2, "Domesticity and Cultural Intimacy," explores how the space of the township gradually became marked and coded as a space that was interior to Indian life. I chart the emergence of the figure of the charou in the township as the constant other of the emergent, respectable Indian community in Chatsworth. Mainly based on archival material, narratives, and ethnographic material, this chapter shows how the older figure of the "coolie"—the stereotyped, lower-caste plantation worker—gives way to a new and deracinated menace and irritant within the township that is equated with "backwardness" and stubborn, traditional conservatism, which needs to be reformed in order for the community to fully evolve. I trace various genres of joking and argue that older forms of joking have been recalibrated to address the radical sense of discontinuity and also loss of a relevant past, or even present, which has become so prominent not only in Durban but across South Africa.

I tackle the difficult and controversial theme of racism and fear of Africans among people of Indian origin in chapter 3, "Charous and Ravans: A Story of Mutual Nonrecognition." The relationship between indentured Indians and Zulu speakers in the province of Natal was tense and contentious throughout the twentieth century. The large riots in

1949 in Durban when Indian homes were attacked by African workers, as well as subsequent conflicts in 1985 and after apartheid, left a legacy of apprehension and suspicion between the two communities that periodically erupt in racist allegations from both sides. I explore this history and the mythologies of Cato Manor, the Indian-African neighborhood that was the epicenter of the 1949 riots. I draw on narratives I collected, as well as the representation of this area and the relationship with Africans in plays and fiction. The last part of the chapter explores the tension between what I call "racism's two bodies"—notions of surface and substance—in racial practices among Indians. Finally, I explore the circulation of racialized fear among young people in schools and on street corners, and argue that the influx of large numbers of Africans in Chatsworth has fundamentally transformed the cherished idea of the area as a knowable site of cultural intimacy.

Chapter 4, "Autonomy, Freedom, and Political Speech," explores the development of political institutions of autonomy that were designed for Indians during the apartheid years. I try to flesh out the pervasive sense of unreality and absurdity that accompanied the heavily circumscribed functions of these bodies and how this consolidated an already pervasive disengagement from the world of politics in the township. I argue that from the 1980s, representative politics became subsumed under a larger imperative of enjoyment and self-deprecating humor. Political figures and their speech are still not read literally but are transposed into a form of entertainment and performance that is enjoyed at a distance. This apprehension vis-à-vis the world of politics is clearly more pronounced among non-African communities in South Africa but still defines an important and ill-understood dimension of the postapartheid "unhappy consciousness."

In chapter 5, "Movement, Sound, and Body in the Postapartheid City," I investigate the rise of new forms of physical, social, and cultural mobility in the postapartheid city, in particular, the rise of the kombi taxi and its massive sound system as the most striking innovation in the urban landscape. While the private taxi industry has been at the center of much violence and criminal networks, it has also been important in providing new forms of agile physical mobility across the erstwhile fixed boundaries in the city. More important, the taxis have also been the vehicles and symbols of a new type of music and youth culture that begins to cut across boundaries of class and race. I explore the particular form of taxi industry in Chatsworth and look at the wider phenomenon of the new sonic taste alliances forged by *kwaito* (a form of South African pop music) and other forms of urban music after apartheid.

Chapter 6, "The Unwieldy Fetish: Desi Fantasies, Roots Tourism, and Diasporic Desires," looks at the new economy of diasporic imagination that hit South Africa after 1994. I begin by exploring a range of narratives of roots tourism whereby thousands of South African Indians each year travel to India in search of the village of their ancestors and for shopping and/or spiritual purification. These journeys are often complex discoveries of both the real and the imaginary India, and are almost invariably linked to desires for purification and "proper" Indianness and "culture," which, in their turn, are spawned by social mobility and ambition. The other side of this new fascination with India's past and its emerging power as a nation is an intense interest in Bollywood films and their songs, stars, and aesthetics. The revival of the interest in Indian films dates to the arrival of a new type of teenage flick that catered to a diasporic market and sensibility. I explore this moment in 1998 and the discussion of Indianness and the global standing of Indian culture it gave rise to.

Chapter 7, "Global Hindus and Pure Muslims: Universalist Aspirations and Territorialized Lives," explores the quest for religious purification that has arisen from the Indian middle class in South Africa since the 1980s. I look at the power and attractiveness of neo-Hindu movements in South Africa and how new and more standardized Brahmanical forms of Hinduism today clash with the popular customs and traditions that still inform weddings and ideas of belief and rituals in the Indian townships. A strikingly similar logic of purification is at work among the Muslims of Indian origin, only even more so. Apartheid forced forms of social and ritual sharing upon communities that despite their common religious orientation have little desire or inclination to share social spaces or mosques. The postapartheid society has made it possible for the traditional Muslim elite, the merchant communities of Gujarati origin, to embrace global piety movements and to reimagine their own genealogies as somehow "Arab" and thus not South Asian. The theological schism between scripturally oriented purists and the proponents of traditional Sunni Islam of a more Sufi-oriented popular South Asian variety has been mapped onto long-standing class differences between Gujarati-speaking elites and predominantly Urdu-speaking working-class Muslims. In both cases, South Africa has become yet another field wherein global conflicts play out in complex local configurations.

In chapter 8, "The Saved and the Backsliders: The Charou Soul and the Instability of Belief," I explore how the process of reevaluating one's past and reaching for a future beyond a clear ethnoracial definition is played out among the thousands of ordinary working-class Indians in Chatsworth and elsewhere who convert to Pentecostal Christianity. I argue that these conversions, which have gathered significant force since 1994, reflect a desire for respectability and purity, but even more so a powerful attempt to find a religious identity that seems both intelligible and in tune with the culture of the larger South Africa society. I look at how these church communities, among many other things, negotiate new forms of inclusion and embody a promise of being both included in the new nation and global yet decidedly and conspicuously nonpolitical. Like governmental interventions and most political and cultural activism, the multiple churches identify the charou home and the charou soul as the main targets of reform and purification.

In the postscript, I reflect on how much of the situation I describe in this book may have wider applicability across community, location, and class in South Africa. I also speculate briefly on how Zuma's presidency is altering predominant styles of politics and public culture toward a more ordinary, imperfect, but also culturally intimate style of political performance that may lead to naked majoritarianism but that also may prove hospitable to the country's many minorities.

METHODS AND MATERIAL

The deep segmentation of South African society has resulted in a certain insidious segmentation of scholarship and ethnographic work along racial lines that carries on to this day. Writing the new South Africa across these lines, and understanding the complex links across and between racially defined groups, is one of the biggest challenges facing anyone writing about contemporary South Africa. I cannot claim that I have overcome this problem in this book, which draws the main bulk of its material from areas and people that were classified as Indian. Many of my interlocutors and informants over the years have assumed that I was writing an Indian community history, as this is indeed the common formula of the vast majority of local studies and local perceptions of history and heritage. I do, however, pay as much attention as I can throughout the text to the many entanglements, encounters, tensions, and confrontations with other worlds, and other people, that shaped the social world of my informants.

The material I draw on in the following has been collected over nearly a decade and spans extensive ethnographic field notes, hundreds of interviews, cultural and media products, archives of government institutions, and multiple local, cultural, religious, and civic institutions. The magnitude of my material and the limitations of what one can do in a single book means that I do not do full justice to many details or events that I touch on. Fieldwork was conducted for a year in 1998–99, for six months in 2001, three months in 2002, annual or biannual visits in the following years, and then another three months in 2007. In keeping with standard anthropological practice, most of my informants appear under pseudonyms, while those holding public office have been mentioned by their proper names. I hope that my friends will forgive this adherence to a convention that still serves the discipline as a whole quite well. This is an academic book, not written for a lay audience but hopefully not inaccessible to students and interested readers outside the academy. To my many friends and informants in Durban and Johannesburg, you may find much of what I am arguing somewhat outdated already, you will surely find much to disagree with, some recognizable figures and events, but hopefully also a thing or two to appreciate. I hope you will read this work as one that opens the world of the charous to a wider world of discussion within South Africa and in the world of global scholarship. It is also an invitation to continue our enjoyable banter and debate that we began more than a decade ago about charous, South Africa, and the world.

CHAPTER 1

Ethnicity by Fiat

THE REMAKING OF INDIAN LIFE IN SOUTH AFRICA

"WHY CAN'T YOU JUST CALL YOURSELF AFRICAN INDIANS?" ASKED THEN PRESIDENT-elect Thabo Mbeki in May 1999 at a large meeting with self-styled community leaders drawn from the Indian community in Durban. Mbeki's entourage consisted of a high-powered group of ANC ministers and advisers, many of Indian origin. ANC leaders hoped that the meeting could broker an electoral breakthrough among the resourceful Indians in the city, a group that had largely turned its back on the ANC since the early 1990s.

After listening to what his advisers dismissed as "perceptions, not rooted in facts," Mbeki lost his patience with what he saw as a privileged group of people who wanted unambiguous public recognition in the postapartheid order, but only as Indians. Mbeki continued, "If you called yourself African Indians it would make a major difference in how you are perceived. In this way you'd say to your fellow South Africans, 'This is my country, I am an African first, but I am also an Indian because my forefathers came here to work.' . . . after all, what is wrong with being an African?"

Mbeki's remarks were clearly informed by the broader project of an "African Renaissance," which he had made his trademark through high-profile conferences and nebulous rhetoric.[1] The remarks also sought to define the terms of incorporation of people of Indian origin into the new political order in South Africa. The imperative of putting "African" first signified the overriding emphasis on autochthonous origin as a crucial defining feature of the true citizens of the new South Africa. The struggle against the illegitimacy of white, culturally alien minority rule and privilege meant that the antiapartheid movement constructed the true, sovereign people of South Africa as the black, autochthonous, and poor majority.[2] The perception of Indians as a culturally alien, unreliable, and opportunistic minority has a long history among both white and African communities in South Africa. The accompanying desire to either deport or properly domesticate the range of communities origi-

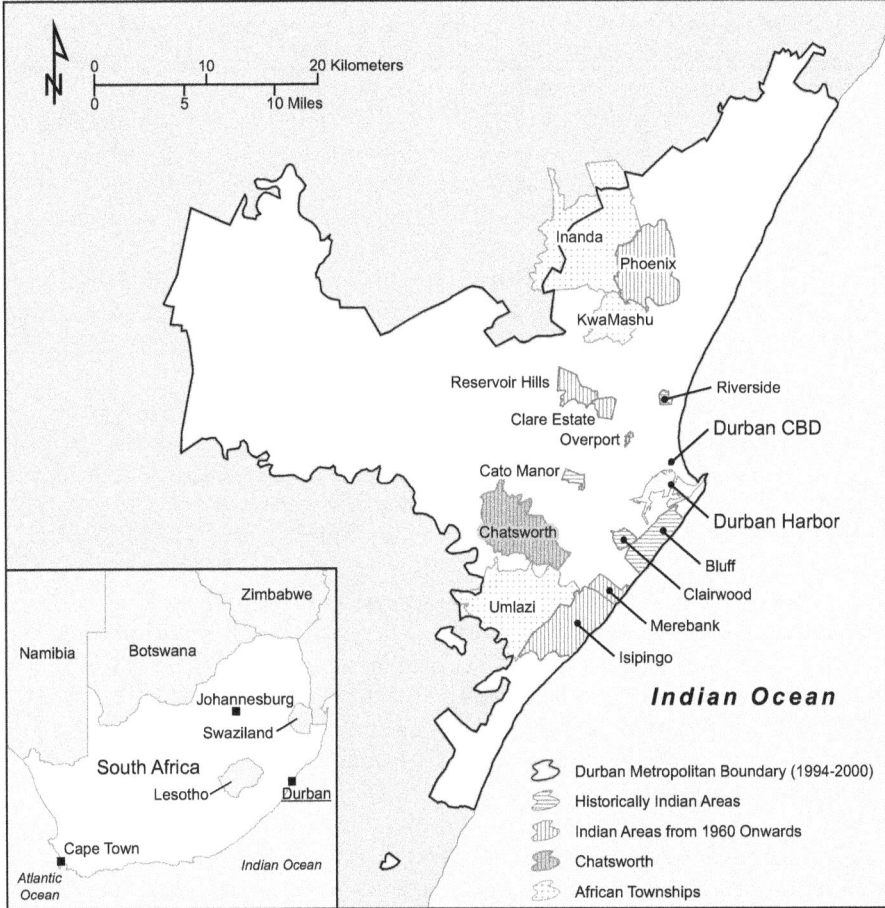

MAP 1. DURBAN

nating in the Indian subcontinent has a long history of Durban and in what today is the province of KwaZulu-Natal.

THE ASIATIC QUESTION

Indians came to South Africa in two ways. The vast majority came between 1860 and 1890 as indentured laborers to work in the sugarcane plantations in the fertile coastal land of Natal. Most laborers belonged to lower-caste communities from the northern districts of present-day Tamil Nadu, the southern districts of contemporary Andhra Pradesh, and the Bhojpuri region in northern India. These heterogeneous groups of people spoke Tamil, Telugu, Bhojpuri, Hindi, Urdu, and Bengali (Ebr.-Vally 2001). After terminating their indenture contract, many laborers bought or leased small patches of land and began farming or market gardening in and around Durban and along the coast. By the 1940s, most of their descendants had moved to Durban and other cities. This period saw the formation of large Indian working-class neighborhoods with a rich popular culture in Durban. During the 1940s, a decade of political unrest and mass mobilization across South Africa, this Indian working class was at the forefront of labor organization and the struggle against the new racist legislation that culminated in the apartheid policies from 1948 onward (Freund 1995, 54–63).

The numerically much smaller group of so-called passenger Indians (around 15 percent of the total Indian population in the country) arrived during the 1880s from Gujarat and North India in search of trade and business opportunities. The majority were Gujarati-speaking Muslims (Memons and Surtees), as well as North Indian and Gujarati Hindus. This resourceful group established the entire Grey Street commercial area in Durban and quickly spread into the interior, particularly to the towns and villages in the Transvaal Province and around the goldfields in Johannesburg. The Indian commercial elite was incessantly in conflict with white settlers and businesspeople, particularly in Durban, where the success of Indians in commercial life was regarded as a threat to white business and social respectability. This was the immediate background of why prominent Indian businessmen in 1893 hired a young lawyer, proficient in Gujarati and competent in British law, to fight for Indian interests. This young lawyer, Mohandas Gandhi, not only transformed the fight for narrow sectional interest into a wider struggle for Indian rights in South Africa but produced one of the founding gestures of subsequent anticolonial thought and political strategy (Swan 1985; Bhana 1997, 9–31).[3]

The passenger Indians provided political and cultural leadership for the wider Indian community for many decades. Wealthy Gujarati businessmen sponsored educational institutions, religious sites, and cultural events, and were instrumental in maintaining links between South Africa and India through trade, family relations, and cultural exchanges. The cultural and social unity of the "Indian community" was far from self-evident, however. Wealthy Muslims were colloquially known as "Arabs" and, like other "free Indians," were regarded "with suspicion, fear and disgust" (Palmer 1957, 47) by white settlers and planters in the province. These sections petitioned, in vain, for reclassification as Arabs in order to distance themselves from the mass of dark-skinned Asiatic laborers and gardeners, and to avoid the threat of repatriation to South Asia. Instead, white protests against the presence of Indian traders and misgivings about their alleged "unfair competition" intensified. Intense debates arose on the manner in which Asiatics could be repatriated to the Indian subcontinent. A commission headed by Sir John Lange was set up in 1919 to investigate the allegations from white settlers that "Asiatics send their money out of the country"; their allegedly "unclean habits"; the complaint "that their methods of business are different from those of the Europeans"; and finally, the warning that "they become too familiar with Europeans, especially females . . . and thus destroy the respect of Natives for Europeans."[4] In what today appears like a colonial Freudian slip, the problem became known henceforth as one of "Indian penetration."

The commission made a string of recommendations pertaining to the question of creating separate residential areas. It suggested that each town and city should have its own "Asiatic bazaar" area where Indian traders could be accommodated. Many of these ideas went into the later Areas Class Bill of 1922, which recommended separation of white from "non-European" residential areas and predated apartheid's more infamous schemes by three decades. This was far from enough, however, in the eyes of the Nationalist Party/Labor Party government that came to power in 1924 and began initiatives to prepare for large-scale repatriation of Indians. The minister of the interior, Dr. Malan, stated, "the Indian, as a race in this country, is an alien element in the population, and no solution will be acceptable to the country unless it results in a very considerable reduction of the Indian population in this country."[5]

In February 1926, the government introduced new policies that stripped property-owning Indians of their municipal franchise (Padayachee and Morrell 1991). In response, mass meetings and a "National Day of Prayer" was called among Indians throughout the country on February 23, 1926. The South African Indian Congress sent a deputation to India to mobilize political support for the cause of the Indians in South Africa. Mass meetings were held in various parts of India, and the viceroy of India, Lord Reading, felt pressured to send an official note of protest against the legislation to the South African authorities. Acting as an advocate of broader interests of colonial India and its imperial subjects throughout the world, the government of India pressed for a roundtable conference where the issue could be negotiated between the two governments within the empire.

A roundtable conference began in late 1926 in Cape Town. The Indian delegation consisted of six civil servants (three Indian and three British) and was led by Sir Mahomed Habibullah. The South African delegation was all white. After protracted negotiations the so-called

Cape Town Agreement was signed in 1927. It stipulated a new voluntary repatriation scheme that built certain financial incentives (free tickets, a fixed sum per adult and child) into the repatriation procedure.[6] However, the more remarkable part of the agreement was that a review of Indian education was to be undertaken with the assistance of experts in education from India; the South African government was forced to promise to provide better housing and living conditions for Indians; it was agreed that Indians should receive "equal pay for equal work"; and it was resolved that no unreasonable obstacles should be put in the way of Indian business initiatives. As part of the agreement, a permanent agent-general of the government of India was to be posted in South Africa to oversee the implementation of the agreement (Joshi 1942, 127–37).

The repatriation scheme had some effect in the first five years after its implementation, but the worldwide economic crisis slowed down the pace. As stories of terrible hardship among repatriates in India filtered back into South Africa, the numbers applying for repatriation fell dramatically in the early 1930s (Palmer 1957, 105). The other parts of the Cape Town Agreement concerning the provision of suitable residential land for Indians and their orderly integration into the labor market had only limited effects. By the late 1930s, the specter of "Indian penetration" once again appeared on the political agenda in Durban and Johannesburg. The so-called Indian Penetration Commission was appointed in 1940 to investigate the matter. After several reports it was concluded that the population increase in the Indian community and the economic prosperity of parts of the community, along with its "desire to demonstrate equality with Europeans or to make defiance against segregation," indeed meant that more Indians bought property in white residential areas.[7] These findings further animated anti-Indian sentiments among whites, particularly in the Durban area. A series of new regulations limiting Indian purchase of land came into existence in 1944, of which the provisional Pegging Act was the most controversial.

The outrage against these strictures generated massive protests from Indian organizations, which at this point were powerfully represented by the Natal Indian Congress (NIC). Unprecedented levels of Indian mobilization and assertiveness unified whites throughout the country across the usual divides between Afrikaners and English speakers. In 1946, the Union government passed the highly controversial Asiatic Land Tenure and Indian Representation Act. The act limited the land tenure of Indians to certain zones in urban areas and formalized measures to avoid what at the time was termed "the risk of residential juxtaposition"—the possibility of Indians and whites living next door to each other. The act also granted Indians a so-called communal representation in the House of Assembly. This merely amounted to the representation of the entire Indian population through three appointed European representatives.

The reaction against this openly racist and discriminatory legislation was strong and vehement. Indian organizations termed it the Ghetto Act and pointed out that it violated even the highly paternalist terms stipulated by the Cape Town Agreement. The government of India, still under British administration, protested strongly and withdrew its high commissioner in South Africa. This reaction was prompted in part by the strong opinion in India on this question and the priority that prominent leaders of Congress in India gave to it. An Indian delegation from South Africa met Gandhi in Pune in March 1946. Gandhi assured the delegation of the unconditional support of the Indian National Congress and vowed that the matter would be taken up in the newly formed United Nations.[8] On behalf of the government of India, the issue was put before the General Assembly in 1946 as a clear example of discrimination on the basis of race and culture. A lengthy debate ensued wherein the Indian delegates eloquently defended a universalist agenda of human rights and accused South Africa of practicing racial supremacy. In response, the South African prime minister dismissed the United Nations as "a body dominated by colored peoples."[9] The South African delegation unsuccessfully asserted its right to treat the matter as one of "domestic jurisdiction." In December 1946, the vote in the General Assembly went against the South African government—the first in a long series of international condemnations.[10]

In South Africa, the international condemnation infuriated many whites. Many boycotted Indian shops and enterprises and resumed the campaigns for repatriation of Indians. The large riots in Durban in 1949, where African workers attacked Indian shops and neighborhoods, took place in a climate of extreme stigmatization of Indians in the white-owned press and among the white population. Even liberal forces within the white political establishment blamed the escalation of the conflict on the left-wing leadership of the Natal Indian Congress. Many whites saw the appeal to India and the United Nations as proof of the fundamental lack of loyalty to South Africa among Indians, and saw it as nothing short of an act of treason.[11]

This protracted conflict over land, residential patterns, and sociopolitical recognition made many whites in Natal more amenable to the Nationalist Party's new agenda of apartheid, which became official policy after the elections in 1948. The Asiatic Land Tenure Act was a precursor of the later infamous Group Areas Act, one of the cornerstones of apartheid's management of urban space. The paradoxical effect of the international condemnation was that the government of South

Africa was henceforth forced to treat the "Asiatic question" as a strictly domestic problem that could not be solved through repatriation. This paved the way for granting Indians de facto rights to remain in South Africa, and later formal citizenship rights in the new constitution in 1961, albeit as a form of *capitis deminutio*, political minors.

In 1963, the government set up a new Department of Indian Affairs that was to oversee and administer what was now called "the Indian community" in the following three decades. Three years later, it launched its official mouthpiece, *Fiat Lux* (literally, "light by decree"), a glossy monthly magazine that in the decades to follow was offered to every Indian household in the country. In one of the first issues, a Mr. Prinsloo, who chaired the Festival Committee, encouraged "Indian South Africans to commemorate . . . the quinquennium of their acceptance as South Africans."[12] In the following section, I will explore how biopolitical engineering, civic activism, and policing practices decisively changed the face, social structures, and self-understanding of what became known as "the community."

THE NEW HYGIENIC INDIAN

The political climate created by apartheid's many new and draconian laws meant that the city council in Durban felt emboldened to begin a large-scale clearing of established settlements of Indians and Africans within the city proper. The impact of the clearings and removals was proportionally higher among Indians who had overwhelmingly settled within the city limits—in pockets and enclaves around industrial estates, markets, as market gardeners along the Umgeni River, and elsewhere.[13] In the early years of this policy (1958–63) the city council forced more than sixty thousand Indians to leave their homes. The majority was rehoused in the new Chatsworth Township, which was built on farmland expropriated from Indian freehold farmers at a nominal compensation (Desai 2000, 13). Many more were to follow in the next decade as Cato Manor and other major areas, such as Clairwood, Riverside, parts of Springfield, and the (in)famous area called Magazine Barracks, were cleared and turned into industrial estates and residential and recreational areas for the city's white middle and working classes.

The relocations were at times haphazard and ill prepared. The new houses were hastily erected, of poor quality, and offered at rents that were often several times higher than what residents had previously paid. Water connections and transport facilities were underdeveloped, and this remained a bone of contention between the predominantly working-class residents of the township and the city authorities throughout the first decade of the existence of Chatsworth and other townships in Durban.[14] Many residents complained about the modest size of the new one-family houses they were offered. Most of these were one-family dwellings in row houses, each of them with two small rooms. Even smaller dwellings, so-called subeconomic units in blocks of flats, were offered to the poorest sections from the slums around the harbor. An oft-repeated complaint I heard from the older generation was that the houses were too small to house the large *almirahs* (wardrobes) that were essential to many families, both as symbolic and practical signifiers of Indian life. Women's saris, jewelry, and other essential parts of dowry gifts were kept in them. The *almirahs* would often be transferred intergenerationally and were preeminent symbols of a marriage bond and proper kin sociality in a household. The design and layout of the houses were, however, central to the promotion of new family structures and of the authorities' attempt to modernize kinship practices and obligations among Indians. Another complaint was that the distance to places of work was greatly increased and that the opportunities for casual employment were next to nonexistent in what many described as the "bush" of the new township.

By the early 1970s, the population of Chatsworth was substantial (160,000) and grew to at least 250,000 by the end of the decade. Fears developed that the new modernist township would turn into a slum area where older "insanitary habits" that were routinely associated with Indians would proliferate. One of the city's newspapers that catered to affluent whites reported in 1964 that the "concentration of dormitory types of dwellings" and generally "unpleasant surroundings" would depreciate the price of houses and deter settlement of anyone from the "professional class."[15] In response, the city council began the development of slightly upgraded zones within the township that were designated for middle-class habitation. These were laid out near nature reserves, had larger plots, and carried more poetic names (Umhlatuzana, Silverglen, etc.) than the prosaically named Unit 1 through Unit 11 that constituted the basic grid of the township. New elite and middle-class areas like Reservoir Hills were added to the new Indian geography of Durban. The city council entertained the vain hope that these new middle-class suburbs would deplete the population in older Indian-owned neighborhoods such as Overport and Clare Estate, which were both built on old Indian freehold land closer to the city center.

However, the following decades of unprecedented economic growth and prosperity in South Africa meant that a significant proportion of the fast-growing Indian population in the country began to aspire to a lifestyle akin to that of their immediate neighbors, the white working class and lower middle class. As a result, the demand for houses, space, education, and improved services in Indian areas continued to outgrow

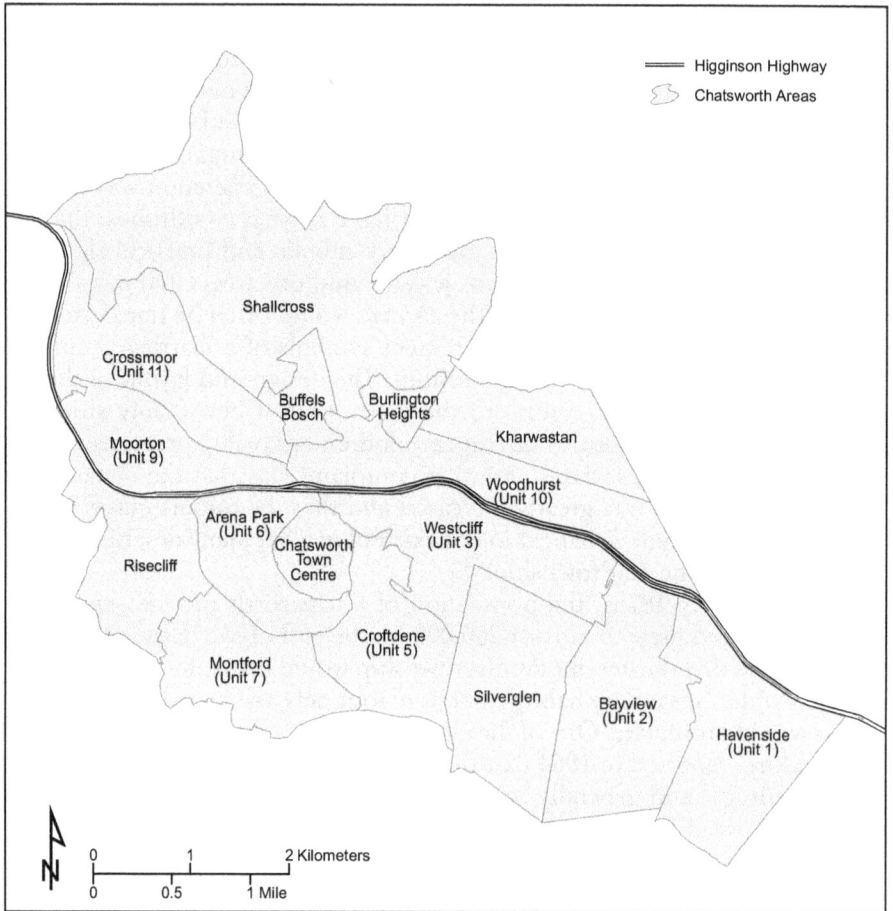

Map 2. Chatsworth

the allocations provided by the authorities. In response, the city hiked up the level of rates, rent, and other payments in Indian areas in order to avoid what would appear as a net burden on the white taxpayers of Durban. The anti-Indian sentiments among whites ran as deep as ever, despite the fact that Indians provided an essential backbone to the city's economy. This structural imbalance between high levels of rates and rents and relatively paltry urban services defined political conflicts and identity questions among Indians for decades to come.

In spite of all these misgivings, the heart of the Indian world in Durban gradually relocated from the downtown Grey Street area, which was dominated by Gujarati commercial interests, to the burgeoning township area of Chatsworth, and later the township of Phoenix. This gradual remaking of the Indian world of the city was a project eagerly promoted by the city council. This project was constantly contested, debated, and contributed to by a flurry of new and emerging social and cultural organizations, which were mushrooming across the township.

Census et Censura

In the new apartheid order, the role of the government and the police was indeed to collect information, enforce morality, and protect domestic life among those who were included in the political community, whether as fully entitled white citizens or Indian and colored "quasi citizens." The broad support among whites for the violent methods of repression and government—spying, surveillance, use of informers, heavy-handed policing—corresponded with Pascale Pasquino's definition of the eighteenth-century concept of police as a form of government: "If you want to be protected, assisted, taken charge of—if in other words you want happiness and well-being—we must know and you must pay: *census et censura*" (1991, 113).

While Indians and coloreds became formally included in the city from 1961 onward, they were never regarded as proper citizens but as "minors" in need of paternalistic care and education in order to evolve more fully. The mass of Indians were included in the realm of what Hannah Arendt called "the social"; that is, the socioeconomic realm of interdependence dominated by administrative and biopolitical rationalities but removed from the realm of politics (2005, 129). In this modality of urban governance neither Indian nor colored areas were explicitly mentioned as separate "racial" problems. The areas were merely singled out as being in need of biosocial intervention. In the paper trail left behind in the municipal archives,[16] from the Department of Health and Welfare, these areas of special intervention were merely mentioned by their name. In the annual reports called Mayor's Minutes, the entries under the Department of Health and Welfare had special sections on "Health education," "Milk supply," "Food hygiene," and "Community liaison," where activities were listed under specific areas, invariably all defined as Indian or colored. The unstated premise was, of course, that the proper white citizens needed none of these services and that "community" itself was intrinsic to the minor social body of Indians and coloreds. On the rare occasion that activities targeted the white population as well, these would be listed under the heading "General," a nomenclature that mirrored a wider public practice during the apartheid era.

A recurrent feature under health education was the screening of the department's heavily didactic documentary *Silent Guardian,* which portrayed the discreet and benevolent work of educating and helping the city's nonwhite population take care of their own health.[17] Other related programs addressed child care ("Tips for Toddlers"), extermination of rodents, prenatal and infant care, food hygiene, sexually transmitted diseases, alcoholism, smoking, and anticholera drives, among others. The scale of the operation was carefully listed, and in 1982–83 alone, the department held 9,533 educational sessions and recorded more than eight thousand home visits.[18] In the course of the 1980s the paper trail in the archive indicated that the gradual influx of impoverished Zulu speakers from the countryside into informal shack settlements within the city limits was becoming a growing concern. More programs were now conducted in isiZulu, and in 1981–82 an impending cholera epidemic among the city's poorest demanded action. The registered households received pamphlets about preventive measures while "methods of cholera prevention were communicated to inhabitants of shack settlements by means of loudspeaker and by practical water purification demonstrations."[19]

Community liaison activities were permanently understaffed. In 1979 the department boasted of having undertaken more than one hundred projects but admitted that "the section is presently working at 75% under strength,"[20] and in subsequent years many large areas of the city with Indian and colored populations had no permanent liaison officer assigned to them. Initially, all liaison officers were white, but by the end of the 1970s most officials posted to Indian areas were Indian. Most of the projects targeted pensioners, children, and women. Women's clubs, in particular, were promoted and offered courses on hygiene, child rearing, home decoration, and so on. These groups were often called Women's Improvement Groups (WIGs) and the philosophy behind them was to mobilize the "caring instinct of women" in order to "benefit the area as a whole," as stated in connection with a newly formed group in the Indian area of Newlands East.[21] The more successful groups mentioned were often sponsored and aided by so-called general (white) welfare organizations and society clubs such as Rotary Club, Women Who Care, and Durban Round Table.

The mobilization of women aimed at making them coresponsible for the care of the elderly, maintaining recreational spaces such as parks and playgrounds, and setting up nursery schools. The aim was to make the "communities" in question more autonomous and self-sufficient in taking care of their own deserving sections. A report stated that the "women's clubs in Merebank [Indian area] are making noticeable and progressive steps toward self-sufficiency . . . so successful have they been that both senior citizens clubs have now become autonomous and wish to run their own clubs without assistance."[22]

In the mid-1980s, at the height of the conflicts between the very active Indian civic organizations and the city council, the Department of Health and Welfare felt the need to impose more discipline on its encounters with the community. It was reported, somewhat laconically, that as a response the department had produced a video "highlighting some of the problems experienced by community groups at meetings and specifically demonstrating the value of effective meeting procedures."[23] Later in the report it was admitted that "the increased level of political consciousness at the community level and the rapidly changing state structures have made the function of Community Workers both difficult and demanding."[24]

The increased tension across the country, including a number of bombings of government installations in and around Pretoria and Johannesburg in 1983–84, prompted the city council to securitize a range of different public services. The city and its people were potentially under attack by "subversive forces," and the population had to be mobilized. Hundreds of security guards were posted at municipal facilities across the city, and a special Municipal Industrial Commando was set up in 1984 to attract volunteers with some prior military experience (i.e., white males) to be given "counterinsurgency courses" and to serve as guards at vital industrial complexes.[25]

Another initiative was the creation of a Civil Defense Corps designed to attract volunteers across the city and impart training in firefighting, first aid, and so on. The response among Indians was lackluster: "Regrettably only a small number of persons volunteered to join the Corps," the annual report stated, but emphasized that three hundred volunteers (including municipal employees who were also "volunteered") had been trained and mobilized in the course of the year. The annual report gives a painstakingly detailed breakdown of this volunteer force by gender and race. The most striking thing is that the two largest groups of volunteers enumerated were white women (29 percent) and Indian men (33 percent), while white men constituted just over 20 percent of the volunteers. Chatsworth alone contributed a quarter of all municipal "volunteers" in the city.[26]

The multiple interventions over decades by the Department of Health and Welfare into family life and intimate habits, the building of schools and decreeing of compulsory education for Indians from 1960 on, and the general prosperity in the city and the country after the 1960s all remade life in the township. By the 1980s, the extended family had more or less vanished, English was the all-dominant home language, divorce rates were up, sexual mores had changed, a majority of women had joined the workforce, and the general structure of everyday life resembled that of the white working class more than the more "traditional" lifestyles that were still maintained among the mainly Gujarati elite.

The New Indian Social Body

This effective remaking of Indian life all but happened in the name of maintaining the supposedly naturally existing Indian propensity to nurture strong kin and community ties. However, this innate propensity had to be properly educated, channeled, and aided for it to come into itself as a properly modern and autonomous community; hence, the constant references in official prose to, for instance, "diminish the dependency on Community Liaison Officers" among women's groups and other social bodies, the openly absurd attempts to teach modern cooking to people whose culinary skills were renowned, the attempts to teach the descendants of the city's market gardeners how to grow vegetables, and the constant worries in the city council that the Indian townships could become burdens on the city's economy.

The picture of the Indian townships that emerges from the municipal archive is one of a slightly passive, compliant, and feminized community whose women, elders, and children were grateful recipients of the new regime of social engineering. However, this can only really be understood against the backdrop of the simultaneous reality of a diverse, recalcitrant, and argumentative culture of activism and association that sprouted across the townships from the 1960s onward and that was dominated by Indian men who wished to speak for—and give a public face to—the new, emerging community.

The physical fact of the forced removals in the late 1950s and early '60s had not been opposed in any systematic fashion. For the residents of the cramped neighborhoods near the Durban harbor and elsewhere, the promise of a modern house and a small garden in a "modern suburb" was embraced with cautious optimism. In 1949, simmering tensions between Indians and Zulu speakers in the sprawling area of Cato Manor had culminated in deadly riots that affected thousands of Indian homes and lives. In that light, the promise of a new and purely Indian living space appeared as both safe and attractive. The promise of a certain measure of safety and new dignity in a properly "Indian" area came to inform the new civic life—a plethora of associations that was almost completely dominated by men. These associations came to play an essential role in remaking the Indian community. However divergent their agendas were, all these associations were compelled to operate in a field defined by the multiple interventions by the city in the social and intimate life of the community.[27]

The first major social organization to emerge was the Chatsworth Township Association, which became an umbrella for the many local ratepayers associations in the township. Its main focus was to represent the interests of the township vis-à-vis the city council concerning issues of fees (rent, utilities, property taxes, etc.). This organization held mass meetings as early as 1968 and was later a powerful force behind the 1980s rate boycotts and the campaigns for upgrading roads and public facilities in the township in the 1970s and '80s. Another important association was the Durban Indian Child and Welfare Society, which was set up in 1968 and later developed more than twenty-five local branches across the township. In 1972, the Chatsworth Community and Research Center was initiated by the city council in collaboration with students and teachers at the new University of Durban-Westville, which was designated for Indians. Despite its official origin and design as a form of field laboratory for students in the social sciences, it soon became a central source of knowledge and advocacy in matters of public health, education, delinquency, drug use, and much more. In the 1980s, it took the name Community Research Unit and became tightly aligned with the powerful and effective Durban Housing Action Committee, which assumed a leading role in the rate boycotts. This campaign gained force in the 1980s across the Indian areas and was fueled by the relative overpayment of rates by Indian households, which on the whole were much poorer than the average white household. One of the seminal reports written by researchers from the center and leading housing activists in 1986 concluded that levels of poverty were consistently high in Indian and colored areas. The report concluded in dramatic tones that social and political unrest was brewing: "Let none say 'we did not know' when the Sowetos of South Africa explode in a demonstration of our people's will to change their South Africa for the better."[28]

The branches of Chatsworth Child and Family Welfare Society soon developed its own cadre of volunteer social workers who worked in parallel with the city's official machinery, often criticizing and outdoing the city in its efforts and quality of data and access to families.[29] The activists volunteering in these organizations easily outnumbered the volunteers that had been mobilized by the city's community liaison officers. Most were young, well educated, and highly critical of ineffective and halfhearted official policies, and equally critical of religious traditions and social customs within the community. The society conducted its own biopolitical program—surveys, house visits, counseling sessions, advisement on removing children from violent homes, campaigns against excessive use of alcohol, and so on. The close affinity of aims, rationales, and background meant that volunteers and the municipal workers developed close relations and saw themselves as working toward the same overall goal: that the affairs and problems of "the community" could, and should, be run and addressed by Indians themselves. Both shared the view of the need to reform the "Indian mind-set," the need to improve the situation for women and children, to improve education, and much more. Both groups shared the view that the people of Chatsworth should not slide back into the "slum conditions" that many had known before. The target of most campaigns was the obvious fact that the city governed Indians as second-class citizens, and that the services and infrastructure extended to Indians were substandard and inadequate. By virtue of being legally included in the city, the civic activism among Indians differed substantially from that of many African townships and locations where the very right to live in the city was in question, and where the threat of removal loomed as large in the collective imagination as the threat of arrests and deportations did for individuals.[30]

Lal, now well into his sixties, was typical of the young progressives that emerged from schools and colleges for Indians in Durban and who in large numbers joined these social organizations from the late 1960s onward. Lal was born in a working-class home in Cato Manor, and the family had to move to Chatsworth when he was a teenager. He had supported the Natal Indian Congress and the ANC's broader goals as long as he could remember. As a student, he had been intensely interested in radical politics, Marxism, and the anticolonial struggle. He had joined a small group of radical students who were almost all from wealthy Gujarati backgrounds. They were discussing political strategy, the working class, and much more. Initially, Lal had been warmly welcomed as a representative of not only the working class but also of what Lal now ironically called the "charou proletariat" in Chatsworth. He always felt there was a strange disconnect between the discussions in his group and the people he lived among. He told me:

> For these guys I was some sort of freak. I talked in a funny way and they often made little remarks or jokes about me, not in a hostile way but they made me feel strange and as if I was never at their level. . . . Their idea of the working class was completely unrealistic, as if you want the revolution just because you join the union. . . . I always tried to say that first we had to change our mind-sets and how we lived before we could do anything like getting rid of apartheid. . . . What does it help if you talk big at a meeting in the union and then come home drunk, without money, and trash your wife and kids?

After some years, Lal got married and decided to devote himself to volunteer work closer to home, and within an environment in which he was more at ease. He became a trusted volunteer in the Chatsworth Child and Family Welfare Society for more than two decades. For him, this was the best way to fight for what he called self-respect. He had studied Indian history and had concluded:

> If you begin to respect yourself and behave with dignity, you cannot be kept down forever. Here in Durban the whites always hated Indians more than anyone else. They thought they could do without us, but show me a single business in this city that does not depend on Indians running the show. . . . We had the power but were too afraid to use it. I think that was because we did not respect ourselves. . . . That begins at home, with your wife, your children, your neighbors. . . . too many charou guys drink and talk loud, but when some white guy shows up they are all, "oh baas, yes baas."

For men of Lal's generation, the apartheid state seemed unjust but also an invincible fact, solidly and assertively planted in the midst of the Indian world. Accommodation without submission became the key to the form of activism that also thrived inside the structures of state and municipal institutions. Many of the employees of the municipal services designated for Indians saw it as their task and opportunity "to work for the community," as Brij, a former policeman turned social work volunteer after his retirement, put it to me.

> When I left school there were few jobs available, and I managed to get casual construction jobs in the 1960s. We were more carefree then and the money was good. . . . My parents had a new house in Chatsworth and they were happy with it. One day, my mother told me that the police advertised for volunteers to become Indian policemen. "You are big and strong," she told me, "You should apply." I got in and all of us in the first batch did not really think of this new job as anything else than keeping our own area safe. I knew the social workers and the teachers, and we all felt that we worked for our community. . . . we could not oppose the whites then and instead we wanted to make the most of it for ourselves.

Not everybody shared Brij's relatively harmonious view of the past. For the more politically active, it was a question of "beating the system from within." Krish, a retired principal of a secondary school in Chatsworth and a long-standing supporter of the ANC, told me:

> In the 1960s all these new schools were built and Indians had more opportunities than before. But we knew that the plan was to make

sure that Indians never really excelled or go to the highest level of achievement. Medical school, engineering, and the sciences were very hard for us to get into. The Indian was supposed to become a teacher and an accountant, and that was it! . . . I can tell you that the curriculum for Indian schools was much harder than in white schools. That is why many decided to beat the system from within. . . . We wanted to outdo everybody else in the city, in the country. . . . Teachers, parents, and students worked on this together. . . . And we did it. You can check it—from the 1970s, Indian high schools in Durban topped the list of achievement in the country. That is still true, even now [2002]. The top of the list in South Africa this year were two Muslim schools, one in Johannesburg and the new one for girls, here in Durban.

The understanding of the concerted effort at educational achievement as a form of collective political statement is today an integral part of the story of the township's journey from dusty bush to a thriving and upwardly mobile community. It is one of many interrelated stories of the Indian townships that are woven around the central theme of working the system from within: making the most of it in adverse circumstances of strictures and racial discrimination, demonstrating that Indians could outdo whites in any field, and showing that Indian activists could wrestle the project of building a new Indian social body out of the clutches of the city authorities. Krish was well aware that "beating the system" was not opposition in any meaningful sense. His brother was one of the very small number of Indians who were directly involved in the armed struggle and who was killed by the security forces. His family home was under surveillance for years, and his parents were interrogated by the Special Branch on many occasions. Yet it amounted to something, he said.

> Our community is not like the people in Soweto or even Umlazi. Indians are more timid, you can say, but very proud, and we do speak up for ourselves. . . . We all tried to make the most of it, you can say, to make this place [Chatsworth] into a nice place to live, with good schools and all facilities. That was our way of showing that we were as capable as anyone and that we deserved to be treated with respect.

This will among Indians to work for themselves, to be heard, to be counted, and to reconstitute a new Indian social body, albeit in a field defined by others, is captured well by Foucault's remarks on how modern disciplinary power presupposes a field of already acting and desiring subjects:

To govern is to structure the field of possible action of others. . . . Power is exercised only over free subjects . . . since without the possibility of recalcitrance power would [merely] be equivalent to a physical determination . . . at the heart of every power relationship, and constantly provoking it, are the recalcitrance of the will and the intransigence of freedom. (1982, 221–22)

This project of responding to, and working within, the parameters of the biopolitics of the city with stubbornness and recalcitrance was spearheaded by the broadly progressive forces that were as critical of apartheid as they were of the conservative defenders of Indian tradition and ethnicity. Their practical critique of apartheid governance was not aimed at its underlying rationalities of modernizing Indian social mores but rather the ineffective and incoherent implementation of government policies. The underlying question of sovereignty (who was to legitimately govern whom?) was rarely addressed directly, partly out of fear of repression. In this light, the intense efforts of many progressive activists toward a de facto self-governance of the new Indian social world stood in an intimate and tense relationship with the parallel efforts by local politicians, cultural activists, and businessmen at consolidating a measure of cultural autonomy and self-government within the new institutions of apartheid.

A part of this more conservative activism emerged from traditionally inclined men for whom retention of Indian religious forms and ethics was the most pressing concern in the face of displacements and forced removals. The planners of the township had set aside designated areas for religious sites, which were available for purchase from the city. Most of the new inhabitants of the township retained their attachments to the older temples across the now-abandoned Indian areas of Cato Manor, Clairwood, Umgeni Road, Riverside, and many other sites. While houses were generally removed unceremoniously, older religious structures were generally retained. For decades after the forced removals, devotees of Lord Muruga (or Subrahmanya) would flock to the old Tamil temples that were devoted to Muruga and Mariammen in the industrial areas of Jacobs Circle and Clairwood for fire-walking ceremonies and other rituals.[31] It was only from the late 1960s on that smaller committees came together in Chatsworth to raise funds to begin the building of small temples in the township. Today, a range of smaller temples, some mosques, and an increasing number of churches dot the expanse of the township. Yet even relatively recent publications on Hindu temples in the country (e.g., Diesel and Maxwell 1993) never mention any of the newer temples in Chatsworth, some of which are very substantial in size and popularity. The importance assigned to temples generally depends on their age and history, and the older temples built by the first generations of Indian migrant laborers count as the more authentic, as being closer to the ancestral tradition.

Similarly, today the smaller mosques in the township are rarely visited by anyone outside the local community. It is only with the intensification of conversion to Christianity in the 1990s, and the emergence of dozens of smaller Pentecostal churches and many more congregations, that the townships became real battlefields of cultural attachment and practices. Allan, a building contractor and devout Tamil Hindu, explained to me that it was the setting up of a whole new community in the township that diverted the attention away from religion for decades:

> All the men in my family were temple musicians in India. My grandfather also played many instruments. They lived in Clairwood and kept the tradition alive. When we were all moved out here, I think something broke in him. He more or less stopped playing his music and, well, I think we all forgot about our tradition. We went to the Mariammen temple every now and then, but I never cared much when I was younger. My father was just making money and going out drinking with his friends. My mother always shouted at him that he should think more of Lord Muruga than Lord Rum!

"I discovered that I was a Hindu," Allan told me, when he and a network of men from his locality in Chatsworth started an informal neighborhood watch in the mid-1990s. Crime was out of control, they felt, and "we decided to take turns watching our houses and cars at night." They were all Hindus, and most of them came from a Tamil background. "One evening we decided to begin to collect funds for a temple in the street. We got closer to each other and felt that we wanted to have a small place for worship, to show that we are Tamils."

The small committee could not afford one of the larger plots that were vacant in the neighborhood, although they really wanted to purchase a plot "just to make a point," as Allan said. The reason was that one of the large and successful of Chatsworth's Pentecostal churches was located a few hundred yards down the thoroughfare from Allan's house. Allan looked at the hundreds of cars and the milling crowds in and around the large church every day. He could not help but admire the enterprise of the pastor behind the church, but he also felt sad. "I often think, *This is what Chatsworth has done to us.* We have forgotten our tradition and have become like everybody else. I look at the girls going to church in their tight jeans and I think, *Why did we let this happen?*" In response, he had acquired permission to have the small temple structure built in his garden, "because it is right on the corner for all to see, to remind them all [the Christians] of where they came from." The architecture and carvings on the small structure were all made by him and his friends because they could not afford artists from India. However, that was less important to him than the strategic location of the temple. His daughters were studying classical Carnatic music, and he insists that they dress "like Indian girls, at least when we have functions here."

Allan was not the only activist for whom the Hindu tradition had assumed new significance as a way of asserting a specifically religious identity after the end of apartheid. Lal continued his work as a volunteer in various social organizations after 1994. However, he became increasingly dismayed with the local ANC branch and felt that many of the Indian supporters of the ANC were ignored, if not looked down upon, by the new ANC-dominated municipal administration (now mostly isiZulu speakers), which came into office in the mid-1990s. He turned to what he called his "ancestral tradition" after a holiday trip to Mauritius. "There I saw the beautiful way people lived with their language and traditions, without being ashamed of it, and not even in a land that was their own. . . . *Why can we not do that as well?* I thought." He quit smoking, gave up drinking, and also decided to embrace vegetarianism mainly for health reasons. "I returned to being a Hindu on my doctor's advice," as he jokingly put it to me on more than one occasion. He reconnected with the Sri Luxmi Narayan Temple, which had been important to his family for several generations. This rather large temple was also located in Clairwood but was torn down to make way for a new highway in the 1960s. The city had offered meager compensation, and it was only in 1979 that a new and modern version of the temple was consecrated in the southernmost part of Chatsworth. On the current temple's website, the history of the temple from its founding in 1916 till the present is presented, and the destruction and relocation plays a major part in the narrative: "The hearts of every Hindu bled at the thought that after all the sweat, toil, and sacrifices, the buildings and the Temple was going to be destroyed."[32] Today, the temple offers classes in Hindi and classical dance, and it finances its activities by running a large wedding hall next to the temple proper. For Lal, this was the place to serve the community in the way he knew best: organization and logistics. Volunteering in the temple was also about self-respect:

> For me this work I do is more about preserving our tradition. I cannot say that I am religious like my wife or her sister. They come to the temple to sing *bhajans* [Indian devotional songs] and all that. I think we should remember where we came from, that our ancestors were humble and hardworking people who managed to survive also here. . . . Think of it, the whites here always chased us around, blamed us for not being loyal. . . . To whom, to them? Why should we? We

are loyal to our own community and to this country. That is what Mandela always practiced. Is that not enough?

Lal was definitely one of the most humorous and also recalcitrant of the people I got to know in Chatsworth. He was a uniquely energetic and gregarious person. His ethical stance of gaining self-respect by working for one's own community summed up a very broad opinion among the generation that were moved to Chatsworth and were forced to remake their lives by engaging creatively and critically with the urban governance structures of the apartheid state. As I will explore later, the attitude of "my community first" was also premised on a sense of anxiety and unknowability of the African neighbors that to this day remains one of the sorest points of life in Chatsworth and other formerly Indian townships. Let me turn to another field where the township has been remade and made inhabitable in equally ambivalent terms from the 1960s onward.

POLICING THE INTERNAL FRONTIER

As I began my work in Chatsworth in 1999, I encountered a world inundated by stories and rumors of accidents, sudden death, and misfortune. Crime, real and spectral, has historically been understood in very different ways within the racially segregated social worlds of South Africa. In the African townships high levels of violence and physical insecurity had been the norm since the early 1980s, when the permanent youth rebellion in the townships that brought down apartheid also created an enormously dangerous and violent environment.[33] After 1994, township youths and *tsotsis* (gang members or street thugs) entered the main urban environment and the crime statistics.[34] The fact that crime became the primary symptom of fear of a new democratic era betrayed a deeper truth about South African society. A settler society, white society in South Africa was always bedeviled by fears of the natives, a fear underlain by the colonial view of Africans as a form of nature, as people who were in the thrall of elemental drives. Only the combination of the word of the Bible and a firm, punishing hand of the state could control the otherwise natural desire to consume and devour the white world of order and plenty. This belief was stated clearly by the minister of law and order in 1977: "Evil and permissive force are almost unstoppably at work in the process of destroying authority in nearly every sphere [but] timely and responsible action has, fortunately, always controlled this degeneration of life."[35]

The obsession with crime after 1994 derived its force from the ability of ubiquitous stories of victimization, supported by crime statistics, to become truths beyond falsification. Jean and John Comaroff have recently described this complex as one of "sovereign statistics" that sustain the picture of the (white) "citizen-victim" through cascades of deeply flawed numbers, or "mythostats" (2006). A closer look at crime figures and policing during apartheid and before shows that the fear of potential crime has been a constitutive ground of state formation throughout the twentieth century in South Africa. What changed was the way in which the state was, and could be, imagined. The democratic elections in 1994 began to erode the long-standing illusion of state power as having a clear center. In spite of its inefficiency and endemic corruption, the apartheid state had managed to portray itself as powerful, dangerous, and omnipotent to the oppressed majority, as well as to the privileged groups it protected.

It was a police state in two senses of the term. First, it was a police state in the more conventional sense of being preoccupied with security and political crimes. It saw itself as engaged in a perpetual war against communism and subversive elements. The South African Police Force was organized as an army; the titles were those of generals, colonels, and so on; and its operations to "clean up" townships or quell protests had an entirely military character. During the final decades of apartheid, the heart of the police force became the Special Branch who hunted "terrorists." The maintenance of order in the townships took place in armored vehicles (Casspirs) and largely followed the formula *skop, skiet, en donder* (kick, shoot, and hammer).[36] Increasingly, African policemen and auxiliary forces were deployed to quell unrest and run a regime of everyday harassment and terror in townships. Crime fighting and investigative police work was mainly given priority in the white neighborhoods.

Second, the apartheid state was a police state in the early modern sense of the term: integral to the "science of government," which aimed at maintaining order, and the "science of happiness," which promoted the prosperity and health of the population (Pasquino 1991). In the eyes of the apartheid planners, such order and prosperity could only be achieved if the populations of the country were managed separately. The object of policing Africans was first and foremost to control the movement and reproduction of labor. The bodies of African workers were reduced to matters external to the political community, a form of purely economic and functional life that never could become included as citizens in the white republic and yet were vital to the reproduction of the most intimate details of white households and enterprises.[37] Africans were never "bare life" (Agamben 1998) within this order of things. Africans simply belonged to another realm, subjects of their own authorities, but if they strayed outside the predefined spaces, laws, and boundaries, African bodies were indeed treated with brutality and impunity. The African townships were never policed in any great detail from within, but mainly at a distance and by figures whose authority was brittle even at the best of times.[38]

In his powerful description of the high levels of insecurity in Soweto, Ashforth writes, "The aura surrounding the police, dominated in the apartheid era by Afrikaners, was that of arbitrariness and brutality . . . no one expects truth to emerge from the course of criminal investigations" (2005, 37–38). In Benjamin's famous formulation, the law rests upon "a mythical violence" that only appears as a faint echo in routinized forms of law preservation, such as the death penalty (1978, 286). Law-preserving violence, on the other hand, has as its rationale the reproduction of a visible order and legitimacy. In order to uphold the illusion of the law being omnipresent and effective, law enforcement must appear as predictable, procedural, regulated, and, above all, visible to the public. It must bear in public what Jean Bodin (1992), in his classical treatise on state power, called "the marks of sovereignty," which are unique to the ruler but in the modern nation-state must become signs of the state (letterheads, uniforms, stamps, licenses, etc.). The interrogation room, the torture chamber, and the random arrest have to be supplemented by the courtroom, the hygienic and monitored detention cell, and orderly arrests. The police have to be visible and uniformed, and must appear to work with restraint and some accountability. They must be seen to be part of everyday life and yet stand out, be ordinary and yet bear the mark of something more—the inscrutable potential for unleashing overwhelming force.

The apartheid state and its ruling party consistently tried to present its own actions as legal, transparent, and visible in law and regulations. A social order based on racial categories necessarily needed to privilege the visual in order to establish the "phenotypical certainty" that, in its turn, determined in which spaces specific bodies could work, sleep, procreate, and enjoy themselves. Though every native in South Africa had to carry a passbook, widely decried as the *Dompas* (stupid pass), the object of policing was always groups and communities. This produced a quintessential sociological form of policing that was interested in broader tendencies within the group and larger causes of crime and unrest. Crime and felonies among average people of color were seen as symptoms of social problems, not primarily as issues of individual culpability. This would have presupposed recognition of the interior life, conscience, and capacity for choice that was generally believed not to exist in the average uneducated person of color;[39] hence, the birth of what locally became known as "confession-based" policing, which relied on forced confessions.[40] Actual proof of individual guilt was less important than the performance of a severe punishment of a black or brown body.

Indian townships were generally separated from white and African areas by stretches of bush and wilderness but were never fenced in or subjected to the degree of surveillance applied to African townships. The tacit contract was that Indians were supposed to enjoy a certain measure of protection and relative freedom in their own areas in return for loyalty, or at least nonresistance to the state. It was clear, however, that this loyalty could only be retained as long as Indians saw themselves as protected by the state in the face of a potential all-out racial conflict that haunted political thinking in apartheid South Africa. The South African Navy had started recruiting Indian volunteers in 1975 for a "training battalion" stationed in Durban. *Fiat Lux* praised the attractive career opportunities for young Indian men in the armed forces. Under the heading "Message to Parents," the text reads as a promise and an injunction to the community as a whole to take responsibility: "The Battalion asks parents to give their sons to it, and it will give them back a man who can stand on his own feet and look the world in the face. He will return to them a responsible adult and better able to manage his own affairs."[41]

In 1978, the official Institute for Sociological, Demographic, and Criminological Research, conducted a survey among 3,500 randomly selected Indian households in Natal and Transvaal regarding the attitudes among Indians to undergo compulsory military service. The findings were conclusive: "87.6 % of the men and 79.1 % of the women were of the opinion that Indian men, just like their white counterparts, should undergo compulsory military training." The report goes on to state, "It is consequently apparent that the Indian population of South Africa is willing to serve in certain conflict regulating structures in order to maintain the equilibrium. This points to the probable polarization of the Indians on the side of the Whites in an acute conflict situation" (my translation from Afrikaans).[42]

Compulsory military service was never implemented for Indians but recruitment of volunteers for the navy's facility S.A.S. Jalsena was stepped up significantly in the following years. *Fiat Lux* boasted that "nearly 2,000" young men had shown interest in the training, and the navy was able to recruit 150 volunteers from among them. The magazine praised Indians as "descendants of an ancient seafaring people" but could not help poking fun at possessive Indian mothers who would not let go of their sons. Assuring the readers that most of the volunteers would probably never have to take up arms in "an all-out conflict," the magazine quotes an officer for saying that, "many of the recruit's worst enemy was his mother."[43] A decade later, a platoon from the Durban North Commando, Indian volunteers trained in counterinsurgency techniques, were sent to the northern border of Namibia. It was stressed that their training and qualifications were on a par with other volunteer forces (mainly white) in the country. Such "demonstrated commitment to defend our beloved country from the Communist terrorist threat" was a double-edged sword.[44] It served to strengthen the argument that Indians indeed should enjoy citizenship rights along with whites and others.

Policing was carried out by a growing cadre of Indian policemen who were commanded by senior white officers.[45] In 1970 alone thirty-five new recruits were added to the force in Chatsworth. A decade and a half later, Indians held ranks as major and colonel. In 1985, there were eleven police stations in Indian areas that were almost exclusively manned by Indians, and seven of them were under the command of Indian officers.[46]

In spite of allegations of endemic corruption in the police force and their close ties with local businesspeople, Indian policemen were rarely portrayed as traitors who were attacked and killed, as was routinely the case in African townships. This was rooted in a mixture of general political apathy and a measure of tacit support of the apartheid regime that had enabled Indians to win some improvements in their material life. The dominant idea of "Indian" crimes was that they stemmed from "social evils," which were concentrated in certain areas, and that they were symptoms of the charou culture, which was rooted in the old "coolie" neighborhoods. The charou was more vulnerable to the anomic effects of rapid "Westernization," which had to be tempered in order not to affect the larger Indian community. Policing dealt mainly with crime, drugs, and drunkenness *within* the community and mainly targeted the poorest council housing estates. Many older residents in the township, and many older policemen, recalled the period as harmonious and secure.

However, even the most cursory look at local newspaper reporting from the 1960s and 1970s makes it abundantly clear that murders, robberies, and gang-related violence were constant concerns from the 1960s to the 1980s.[47] Crime rates and the poor quality of policing were recurrent points on the meeting agendas of official political bodies. One document submitted to the city council in 1982 from Indian ratepayers in the middle-class area of Clare Estate demanded more patrolling and a "massive clean-up operation in the township, especially in the flat areas" to crack down on drug-trading, illegal shebeens, and the informal shacks (inhabited by Africans), which were claimed to be "the headquarters of burglars and thugs who roam the streets of Chatsworth."

Finally, the document recommends that more "people of colour" (Africans) be introduced into the local (Indian) police force to improve policing. "One gets the impression that some of the officers [Indians] are afraid to apprehend suspects."[48]

In the retrospective version of events one encounters today, however, the criminality of those decades appeared less threatening to many Indians because it only concerned "bad elements from our own community," as a retired police officer put it to me. The real extent of criminality and feelings of threat have today been completely overshadowed by the idea of crime as a new and mainly postapartheid phenomenon. When comparing crime statistics for Chatsworth in 1987 to those in 2007 (when the population is significantly higher), the differences are much smaller than the general public discourse makes one believe. Murders and homicides stood at 53 in 1987 (80 in 2007), common assaults were 895 in 1987 (1,181 in 2007), and "assaults with intent to do grievous bodily harm" stood at 417 in 1987 (857 in 2007).[49]

In the 1970s and '80s, policing of the township relied on both an extensive network of informers and on an unstated ethnic/racial solidarity that made the "fact of brownness" of the policeman's face into a sign of relative familiarity and security in a world marked by escalating and bloody unrest across the country. Many informants would defend the policemen, however corrupt, because they were "Indians, local boys . . . they never roughed us up." The selection of Chatsworth in the mid-1980s as the first township in the country that was enjoying complete "own area" policing, which was carried out by locally recruited Indian policemen, gave substance to this sentiment.

The uniform was indeed a mark of state sovereignty, but it was always supplemented by the color of the face. This secondary mark invoked tacit assumptions of solidarity (among one's own), as well as stereotyped fears of whites and Africans. These were—and remain—powerful and real images that are based on a widespread internalization of the apartheid notion of racial solidarity as a natural and fundamental form of sociality.

CONTAINING THE BUSH: CRIME AND VIGILANTES IN THE AGE OF DEMOCRATIC POLICING

The first democratic elections in 1994 had little immediate impact on police practices across South Africa. Fearing a backlash among the security forces, the ANC postponed reform of the police force for a decade. A key problem was a very low recruitment for the police force for almost a decade. Pay scales were left unaltered and advancement possibilities and resource allocation remained unchanged. A logistical implosion ensued: the equipment of the police—weapons, vehicles, radios, computers, training, and so on—quickly became hopelessly inadequate.

Renaming the force to the South African Police Service was indicative of the inauguration of a style of policing that was to be based on human rights, evidence-based detective work, and community service. Within the force, there was scarcely any comprehension of this style of policing. To many officers I talked to, abandoning the old-style "confession-based" policing, that is, beating a suspect until he confesses, was tantamount to allowing criminals to rob and kill with impunity.

Combined with institutional stasis, this police culture produced disillusionment and massive corruption. Many younger policemen left the corps to seek employment in the burgeoning private security industry. Among the remaining officers, many took long-term sick leave, which the new Employment Act made possible, while others slid into a destructive cycle of alcohol and corruption.

As a result, for years the main police station in Chatsworth, which covered more than three hundred thousand people, had only two functioning vehicles (one of them with a dysfunctional radio), and of the ten officers on each shift, half would be on sick leave or too drunk to perform their duties, while the remaining officers would only reluctantly respond to calls or leave the station. Emergency calls concerning serious shoot-outs or murders would be attended—if at all—by the Flying Squad, a unit comprised almost exclusively of white officers who were often drawn from the former Security Forces that had been created by the Durban Police to service the city as a whole. In practice, Chatsworth was hardly policed for years.

The regular police force reduced itself to the role of record keeping. They would arrive late at crime scenes, record names and events, write sloppy reports, and return to the station—or to their flourishing side businesses—as soon as they could. Private companies and shopping malls used private security guards who, in the case of robberies or assaults, would only get in touch with the police after the fact to record shootings, deaths, and damages—mainly for insurance purposes.

Democratic policing requires a high degree of visibility and a new form of participation, a voluntary participation whereby citizens actually inform on themselves in order to be included in the community and submit in exchange for protection: *census et censura*. In spite of all these expectations of democratic policing, actual policing, as Benjamin argues, inevitably unfolds in a gray zone "where no clear legal situation exists" (1978, 287). Police officers are always testing, and often violating, the boundaries of what is legal, appropriate, and politically acceptable. Police forces always seek to prove their efficiency to the public through highly visible crackdowns on "suspects," by "cleaning up" notorious neighborhoods, by ubiquitous patrolling, and "zero-tolerance" policies. In this effort, police routinely break the law and kill innocent people, often in covert and less visible ways. The suspension of the law by the police, in the name of enforcing the law and protecting the public, happens all the time across the world.[50]

The tension between the two forms of legal violence, or between visibility and invisibility, assumed a more complex form after the end of apartheid. The enemies of the apartheid state had been seen as "terrorists," sly and strategic individuals moving stealthily and under cover. By contrast, the enemy of the postapartheid society is conceptualized as the ordinary, undereducated, and impatient young man of color who is emerging from an anomic and morally distorted township culture armed with lethal weapons and imagined to be aligned with crime syndicates. This popular and official view of "the criminal" as a morally inferior person who is beyond redemption and reform, and only amenable to punishment and incarceration, suddenly seemed to be in tune with a broader global trend, particularly in neoliberal "risk societies."[51]

In Chatsworth the presence of young African men in the streets was translated into a sign of danger and insecurity that quickly gripped the township in the 1990s. In informal settlements and across the township, African residents began to exact punishment to rapists and other offenders through "kangaroo courts" and mob violence. For Indians, this unfolded as a spectacle of extreme violence emerging from "the bush," seemingly internal to the African mobs that they watched in horror from inside their increasingly fortified houses. On several occasions, the mostly Indian police were reluctant to rescue victims of these forms of justice or even to get involved. On one occasion in Chatsworth, two young Indian brothers found an African man banging on their door and begging to be let in so he could be saved from three dozen men from a nearby settlement who besieged the house outside the gates and the perimeter of its tall fence. The brothers did not let the man in, and the situation was only resolved as a security company showed up with a policeman in order to "disperse the crowd which disappeared and hid in the nearby bush," as a reporter wrote in the local weekly.[52]

From 1997 onward, Community Policing Forums (CPFs) began to be established throughout South Africa. The idea was that policing was now to be carried out in collaboration between local "communities" and the police. Local residents were to assist the police and act as their ears and eyes but also work together as "partners." This initiative rested on two assumptions: first, that only the mobilization of the local communities could check the crime rate, check the excesses of the police, and force the police to actually carry out their duties; second, that the CPFs would carry out the fundamental symbolic task of constituting "the people" and the body of citizens as the new sovereign power on whose behalf the police should work.

The many meetings of the Chatsworth Community Policing Forum were never a great success. Police officers were reluctant to come and found it extremely difficult to sit through long sessions while patiently listening to the barrage of complaints and demands that came from a range of people who claimed to represent the community. Some were the former foes of the police—ANC activists and others active in the antiapartheid movement; others were local self-styled leaders and religious figures whose claims to leadership and local authority were often extremely tenuous.

The meetings soon turned into arenas where the very right to represent the community, and in which style, became the bone of contention. The ANC was listened to more attentively by the police officers than the many local leaders, yet their authority was far from uncontested. Soon, ongoing debates about the changing character of the township, the influx of Africans, the large number of African children at local schools, and general anxieties about Indian identity in postapartheid South Africa also began to dominate the agenda of these meetings.

In 2000, a new station commander who had recently converted to a Pentecostal church began to decorate his office with Christian symbols. It became known as the "station church." He would pray loudly and publicly, also at roll calls, and it was alleged that he discriminated against non-Christian policemen. For more than a year, members of the CPF (predominantly middle-class, mostly Hindu) were up in arms against what they saw as an undue mixing of religion and public office. They found it objectionable that the commander was overtly Christian and thus not a proper Indian in their view. The crisis came to a head when irate residents in Chatsworth demonstrated in front of the police station and blocked roads in protest against the corruption and incompetence reigning at the station.[53]

The issue at stake was who was a citizen? Who constituted the sovereign community that had the right to protect itself and be protected by the police in the name of democracy and rights? Was the average working-class charou also a citizen and a member of the community? Could an African be considered a citizen at all in this township? Who should the community protect itself against and by what means? These questions became actualized as the issue of citizens' patrols was raised—based on successful experiences from predominantly white areas. It was clear to most members of the CPF that the police force itself was unable and unwilling to carry out the task of policing at night, and it was decided to call upon volunteers to sign up for night shifts. Civil patrols were not supposed to carry firearms and should just alert the police in case of house break-ins or suspicious activity; in other words, act like the ears and eyes of the police. Many of those who signed up had very definite and set ideas of what and where they were policing: the target was young black men who were threatening middle-class homes and Indian women. There was a distinct reluctance among the volunteers to police and patrol in poor Indian areas that were already known as centers of drug trading. In practice, the citizen-vigilantes merely put into practice the widespread idea of the proper Indian community: respectable, taxpaying owners of property. The responsibility for organizing these patrols was indeed left to the ratepayers associations—the spearheads of the old "civics movement" that had successfully boycotted and obstructed the workings of the municipal authorities for years prior to 1994.

The patrols quickly attracted a mixed group of volunteers—some with questionable motives and a history of encounters with the police—and others who were driven by strong religious and ethical motives of revenge and violent protection of family and property. A number of radicalized Muslims, many of whom had been involved in the short-lived launching of People Against Gangsterism and Drugs (PAGAD), a vigilante group formed in Cape Town in the mid-1990s in Durban, now got involved in the neighborhood policing. One of them was Ahmed, the owner of a small workshop, and his son Shahid. Ahmed described himself as a member of the Muslim lay movement Tablighi Jamaat (see chapter 7). Ahmed had a weapons license and felt strongly about defending the community and his family. He said, "In Islam the man is expected to defend his family and to protect women and children. A man who fails to do that is a man without honor, a man without courage, someone who cannot be trusted. . . . In doing this I show my son what it means to be a Muslim."

Father and son would show up in their 2.5-ton truck, in boots, camouflage trousers, black jackets, and caps with *La ilaha illa Allah* (there is no deity but God) written in golden Arabic letters. Shahid, who studied Arabic every day after college, was excited about these night patrols and managed to get a number of his friends involved as well, most of whom belonged to the same class in his local madrassa.

Another new recruit was Shaun, a young man from a Tamil family who converted to Christianity some years back. There were several members of Shaun's church (he insisted on never using his Tamil name) who were active in the patrols, but Shaun was the most articulate with regard to the duty of defending the neighborhood:

> There is so much evil in this world, not least in South Africa at the moment . . . the people we arrest are not evil people but I believe that

they are possessed by evil forces and demons that make them steal and rape. They don't steal because they are poor—most poor people are good people, they steal because they have lost their will and sense of pride. . . . We have to stop them and detain them. People say that we should not beat them up, but you have seen in our church what people do when the demons take them. . . . we have to be firm and strong and show the demons who are the strongest. That is the only way we can help the criminals.

The net result of the influx of these new, overly keen vigilantes was not a sense of security but rather a new insecurity. Visible policing or flaunting of public authority had vanished and self-styled defenders of the community had taken over. Some volunteers were highly unreliable and often risk-averse, while others armed themselves and went into situations and attempted arrests that resulted in shoot-outs and beatings of young Africans. Law enforcement was rapidly disentangling itself from even nominal oversight by the police and slipping into the hands of what resembled vigilante groups.[54]

For some residents, this amounted to a form of category confusion—a mixing and conflation of worlds and realms of experience that should be kept separate. Remarks like "This is not a job for ordinary citizens," "They don't have the training to do this," and "We need to be protected by professional people" abounded in everyday conversations on security. The sight of your neighbor or uncle on patrol in the evenings did not necessarily produce a sense of security. On the contrary, it was almost as if it profaned an activity that many people preferred to be left somewhat opaque and handled by more anonymous professionals. Characteristically, it was not the police that called for an end to this short-lived experiment, but rather ANC members who were alarmed by the potential emergence of a regime of random terror that was exercised by fear-stricken, angry, and inexperienced family fathers.[55]

The alternative was tailor-made. A number of private security firms were already operating across the city, and most of their employees were former policemen who had left the force. On the recommendation of the CPF, the ratepayers associations in various parts of Chatsworth signed contracts with security firms.[56] Their job was to provide protection at night, visible policing in the daytime (in distinctive uniforms and in fast and flashy cars), and a visible presence that included patrolling around schools to prevent drug dealers from entering through holes in the fences. This supports the Comaroffs' argument that South Africa is facing a "metaphysics of disorder," which in turn impels the police to perform their presence and capacity in highly theatrical and often profoundly absurd ways,[57] or, as in this case, to outsource the necessary performance of a fiction of security.

During their operations in the township, the security guards "withheld" or "detained" the suspects and collected "evidence"—that is, quick notes on the damage done, the effects stolen, and the possession of any weapons. In the morning, they delivered the suspects to the police station fully "prepared" (the term that was used for beaten and threatened). The policemen would then record the facts and decide whether to formally arrest the suspects. In most cases, there was insufficient evidence or reluctance on the part of the police to detain suspects, as this required more elaborate paperwork, justification, collection of evidence, calling of witnesses, and, later, probing questions from the public prosecutor's office.

The security guards worked as legally licensed firms. They were heavily armed and schooled in the old style of policing in South Africa. Like their former colleagues in the police force, they felt that arrest and formal prosecutions had become much too cumbersome. One of the security guards told me, "The police are not allowed to do the work they should do. How can we get them to confess their crimes if we can't lay our hands on them?"

Instead of formal punishment, the security firms administered their own form of violent justice on the spot or in their vans. "We have to show them who is the boss around here, that they can't get away with anything . . . someone has to do the dirty work and the police aren't capable of it anymore," a guard told me. The beatings went on with complete impunity, were condoned and encouraged by the police, and tacitly approved by the local community organizations, which mainly took action if Indians were wrongfully harassed by the firms. The local homeowners encouraged the security firms to punish young housebreakers, or those merely picked up on suspicion of crimes, and withhold them on the "assumption of criminal intent," as a new operative quasi-legal category went.

The security firms had offices and control rooms that received emergency calls from customers and from people in the neighborhood. Every night shift saw several alarm calls and frequent shoot-outs, either inside houses or outside houses, as burglars fled the premises and were pursued by the security personnel. Most of the guards were seasoned, cynical, and battle-hardened former policemen. I befriended a group of guards in one of the local gyms. They proudly showed me gunshot wounds and boasted about their role as local warriors who defended the community against attack and literally defended the border between the Indian and the African world. Few of them thought much about the causes of the crime they dealt with. For them, crime was entirely naturalized and racialized; black bodies were seen as inherently criminal and naturally unrestrained. The widespread fact that many violent crimes were committed by local Indians was almost written out of the picture. "Most of the crimes among Indians happen in homes and we don't deal with domestic disturbances," the chief security officer of one of the firms explained.[58] These crimes, many of which involved firearms and severe abuse of women and children, were simply seen as domestic in a double sense: inside homes and inside the community. The real violence and source of fear now came, as before, from the categorical other, who was lurking in the bush.

Let us now turn to how the Indian home and the space of the township had merged into a single, seemingly unbroken site of a cultural intimacy and solidarity.

CHAPTER 2

Domesticity and Cultural Intimacy

At the end of June 1999, yet another grisly murder occurred when an Indian policeman gunned down his fiancée and then turned the gun on himself in downtown Durban. So-called love-murders have become more common as ownership of guns among Indians has skyrocketed in recent years. Under the headline "TV and the West Stand to Blame," the weekly *Post* reported answers to the question, "Has our culture and society gone horribly wrong?" The answers ranged from people calling for counseling for young families to those blaming the new global television landscape for glorifying violence. A man stated a widespread opinion: "Indian people have lost their sense of who they are. . . . The Indian family is no longer what it used to be."[1]

The crisis of the coherence of "the Indian family" and its associated moral values is today the single most shared concern among Indians in South Africa across class and linguistic backgrounds. A feeling of impending sociomoral disaster became widespread after apartheid among many communities in the country. This crisis and its associated dramas are played out in domestic and intimate settings: as proliferating witchcraft accusations within households in Soweto (Ashforth 2005); as estrangement from the ancestors in Zululand (White 2011); as displacement of the authority of older men by the new generation of "com-tsotsis" in the 1980s in African townships (Bank 2011; Bozzoli 2004); and as worries about the proliferation of multigenerational female-headed households in Cape Town (Lee 2009). This chapter explores how Indian concerns became uniquely centered on the particular construction of the Indian family and intimate life as a space of traditional patriarchy shattered by the emergence of new nuclear families and modern selves.

From Kinship to Family

The nineteenth-century system of indenture brought together extremely heterogeneous populations on plantations and colonial estates in Natal. Most arrived alone, some as groups of friends, and much fewer as married couples. Some had married or cohabited on the ships across the Indian Ocean, probably to minimize sexual harassment by crew and other passengers. The sex ratio was extremely skewed, and the dearth of women on the sugar estates was a major worry among the colonial authorities in Natal, as elsewhere across the colonial world of indenture.[2] Women were routinely accused of loose morals and adultery, and most of the conflicts, murders, and suicides on the sugar estates revolved around love, jealousy, and fraught sexual unions.

One of the many unresolved issues was the validity and legal status of religious marriage ceremonies performed in India or after arrival in Natal. On the recommendation of the Coolie Commission, a string of laws emerged from the late 1870s onward that aimed at stabilizing proper families and legitimate unions.[3] This was part of the larger colonial project of creating legibility through legal fiat but also an initiative heavily inflected by the quest for moral reform and codification of what in nineteenth-century Britain was seen as generally depraved and immoral South Asian sexual practices: polygamy, child brides, and concubines.[4]

On the sugar estates, most of those whom Desai and Vahed call the new "moral families" were small and generally nuclear units.[5] As Indians bought land and settled across Natal, they adopted extended family practices in an attempt to reinvent customs and norms from "back home" in "a new and creolized world" (Freund 1991, 420). The period from 1910 to the 1950s saw a certain "retraditionalization" of Indians. The enforced mixing and cross-community marriages from the era of indenture were papered over as a shameful chapter born out of material necessity. New syndicated identities arose that were mainly grouped along lines of language and class in homes, religious associations, and in a growing range of educational institutions that provided training in both English and Indian languages. By 1950, this new world was well established in three major segments: a Gujarati-speaking elite and landholding middle class dominated by Muslims; a substantial Hindi/Urdu-speaking segment mainly comprised of small farmers, artisans, and the working class; and the largest group, a Telugu/Tamil-speaking working-class and urban subproletariat.

In her classic study *Indian People in Natal* from 1960, Hilda Kuper described an ostensibly self-contained urban world. In a remarkably depoliticized tone, Kuper described customs, habits, and cultural dispositions among Indians, with due respect to the differences between the three main segments mentioned above. Although peppered with incisive vignettes of individuals and families, Kuper relied largely on a systemic view of what she earlier called "The South African Indian Family and Kinship System" (1956). Kuper asserted that this system mostly relied on the "original matrix" among Hindus, which was the most relevant considering that both Christian and Muslim Indians were shaped by a culture that was dominated by Hindu practices (1960, 95). The distinct features of this system were those of a preponderance of patrilineal extended families (*kutum/kudumbam*), arranged marriages, extended families living under the same roof, and the virtual absence of individuals living alone. Throughout her analysis, Kuper reproduced the idealized kinship models that prevailed among her informants: well-defined roles for parents and elders, brothers ranked in a defined seniority system, functional separation of men and women, strong notions of female purity and modesty, and the emphasis on the family home as an ever-growing compound of adjoined or adjacent units of couples and their children.

The Indian freehold farmhouse, and the sprawling compounds of the urban trading family, provided the models and examples in Kuper's sympathetic account of a culturally cohesive and self-conscious community. Yet her account suggests that the cultural models described were already under pressure at the time of her fieldwork (1950s), or maybe were never consolidated. She observed that the joint family system was under pressure because of the lack of housing (caused by the severe limits put on Indians by the city council but never spelled out by Kuper) and a declining willingness to pool resources and live under the same roof in the younger generations (104); the fine-grained vernacular classificatory naming system for relatives on the maternal and paternal side, which was giving way to general English terms like "uncle" and "aunty" (99); and that the positions of the mother-in-law and grand-mother, which were so central to the joint family system, were becoming increasingly contested, if not detested, among younger women (116–20). Moreover, her survey data from 1953 showed that less than half the households were joint families (48 percent), while 42 percent were nuclear units (107).

A mere decade later the terms of discourse and the reality on the ground had changed irrevocably. Chatsworth was emerging as the largest concentration of Indians in the country. Thousands of homes had been razed to the ground and their inhabitants had been rehoused in the generally small units in the townships. Indian women entered the industrial workforce in Durban in substantial numbers, accompanied by anxieties about the allegedly loose morals and new independence of the "factory girls" (Freund 1991; 1995, 80–82). Indian kinship ceased to be a valid reference, and a new breed of sociologists and social workers, employed by the new Department of Indian Affairs and research institutes, began analyzing the changing intimate and domestic practices of Indians.

Figure 1. Mr. Govender and his house in Chatsworth, where he has lived
since 1961

At a symposium organized by the liberal South African Institute
of Race Relations in 1966, a Mrs. Ramasar, a psychologist and social
worker, reported a steep increase in the number of Indians suffering
from "personality defects," "unmodified attitudes of rebelliousness
against elders," and rising marital problems caused by the new independence of women, which in turn resulted in "male passivity" and
withdrawal—and sometimes domestic violence (1967, 24–25). The author attributed many of these ills to the new but insecure embrace of
romantic love as a basis for family life. The cases of men leaving families
and refusing to pay alimony more than doubled in one year, Ramasar
reported, which suggested that an older sense of obligation had given
way to a new and aimless selfishness. Painting a romantic picture of
the older joint family, Ramasar noted that "children no longer grow up
in piety and obedience taught by the eloquent silence of example and
expected not to stray away from the family tradition" (29). She argued
that the township's new "closely packed geographical areas [were] lacking all the throbbing consensus of living neighborhoods" (34). One
could only expect growing juvenile delinquency, alcoholism, divorce,
and "mental disorganization."[6]

Here we see the seeds of what in the following decades became a truism and widespread opinion among educated and concerned Indians: the townships created a new breed of culturally deracinated individuals who were devoid of proper cultural values and not yet fully acculturated into the new emotional disciplines of the modern family. The result was uprooted, in-between people who were deprived of the social and cultural leadership of the Indian elite and middle class and vulnerable to further deracination by the onslaught of the new consumer- and lifestyle-oriented modernity of the fast-growing South African economy in the 1960s and '70s. An important part of this new common sense was the idealization of the joint family and of the pure and strong Indian values of the 1940s, which had been bred in Cato Manor and other Indian freehold areas, as a golden age of Indianness. These older places of dwelling, and their supposedly more organic culture, were becoming the mythological sites of authentic Indianness in Durban and were often celebrated by critical Indian intellectuals as the now-lost bedrock of social cohesion and cultural pride.

In the 1970s and 1980s a new type of sociology emerged that sought to understand the realities of the "new" Indian township as a world ravaged by a conflict between backward Indian "tradition" and modern Western cultural forms and lifestyles. Daniel Lerner's well-known idea of the pathologies of "transitional man" (1958), as well as Marxist social theory, was invoked by local sociologists during these decades. Based on large-scale surveys, they concluded that the ongoing Westernization of family patterns (nuclear families, women's emancipation, individualization, etc.) was seen as a problem and a threat by most Indians. However, older, less-educated, and poorer respondents coped less well with the changes than did the younger and educated sections (Jithoo 1975; Schoombee and Mantzaris 1985).

A mental health study assessed the functioning of twenty-seven Indian families and divided them into three groups: dysfunctional families, in-between families, and adequate families. The key problem studied was the relationship between the parental unit and the wider kin group. The conclusions were crystal clear: the dysfunctional families suffered because "the extended family seemed to prevent rather than facilitate long-term problem solving . . . the alliances with the extended family resulted in the less effective spouse becoming even more powerless in the relationship." In addition, the dysfunctional families were generally poor, uneducated, and bedeviled by alcohol problems. By contrast, the adequate families were generally well educated and Westernized, and the problem of the extended kin was solved. The author concluded, in an almost militarized terminology, "There were clear boundaries between generations. Parental coalitions were well-defined, with a clear hierarchy of power and leadership in the hands of the parents. In the two families where a grandmother was living in the family, her role was clearly defined and she did not intrude on the parental coalition" (Mason 1985, 46–48).

In this rendition, the extended family represented an echo of an incompatible and irrelevant past and would be disruptive and dysfunctional if allowed to contaminate the new and natural unit of the nuclear family.[7] Only when the past—represented by the extended kin—had been properly disciplined and "clearly defined" in a "hierarchy of power and leadership" could it be harmoniously incorporated into a fully modern Indian family. Only those with enough education and emotional discipline could make the past into a sentimentalized object that no longer intruded in everyday life but could be enjoyed in its objectified form as a proper myth of "our culture." This overcoming of a past marked by cultural alterity (the extended family) and excess (lower-class habits) was at the heart of transforming the townships as a new social body (self-)governed by disciplines conducive to a modern and industrious life.

The making of new Indian families faced further obstacles, however. One was how Indian cultural life and moral families could be recreated in the new stripped-down, largely nuclear households and homes in the townships. Another was the persistence and reinvention of prejudices along lines of caste and language. As we will see, the sociologists and governmental officials who grappled with these questions in the 1980s were joined by playwrights and comedians.

The New Indian Woman and the Family House

The new township spaces and their various houses were designed to encourage modern and clean living. Neither the row houses nor the smaller flats could accommodate a larger extended family, and the plots laid out for self-built bungalows were generally too small to have more than a small main house and an outbuilding in a corner of the plot. If the new Indian family was to resemble the "Western biological family," the responsibility for emotional management of romantic love between parents,[8] children, and kin relations should fall more clearly on the woman in the household. Unshackled from earlier dependence on the male head of the *kutum* and the watchful eye of the mother-in-law, but also better educated and more independent, the "new Indian woman" became the focus of much writing and governmental intervention from the 1960s onward.

Fatima Meer's classic study *Portrait of South African Indians* devoted much attention to the shift in marriage patterns and the new and often difficult position of Indian women. The new nuclear families were relatively large (between seven and nine people on average) and lived in small houses (Meer 1969, 65), and the extended kin was now often grouped across the township, which left the work of maintaining kin contacts more complex than before. Social attitudes did not always follow the new physical realities and social imperatives, which meant that young women were often the victims of male condescension and gossip from elder relatives, Meer argued. A prominent intellectual and critic of apartheid, Meer asserted that despite the odds, Indians "project an image of greater integration than would be expected in a community exposed to intensive urbanization" (72).

Apartheid officials and many intellectuals celebrated the emancipation of the Indian woman due to her exposure to Western culture. *Fiat Lux* ran multiple articles praising the new and educated Indian women who were adopting Western habits in their homes and communities. The inspector of education, M. G. Pillay, praised the new assertiveness of Indian women and added, "The fact that Indian girls now take part in beauty contests is an indication that our Venuses refuse to be cloistered any longer" (*Fiat Lux,* October 1967, 181). K. P. Naidoo wrote in 1973, "Some Indian women cling tenaciously to the Eastern way of life. Religious ceremonies are still practiced by Indian women in a traditional manner but they are now considerably modified." Naidoo further reported that "rings were replacing the wedding *thali* [traditional Indian meal], and wedding cakes were introduced." Indian women now wore Western clothes "for the sake of convenience" and were "using cutlery, crockery and laying the table with linen and also western table manners" (*Fiat Lux,* May 1973, 23). The most important step, according to Naidoo, was that Indian women now "speak English without a trace of an Indian accent which is usually associated with their Indian forebears" (25).

A senior education official, Mr. Osman, argued in 1975 that the advances in lifestyle required more education and thus more independence of women: "The role of the girl could no longer be confined to simple home affairs . . . the Indian mother now has to cope with a conglomeration of things which require decision making like choosing the family car, designing the new home, buying the right food mixer, planning a holiday, directing the interests and hobbies of the children. Without education she cannot fulfill that role" (*Fiat Lux*, April 1975, 6). In an article celebrating Indian women's progress, a staff writer waxed lyrical: "They are rebelling but without noise or fuss. Theirs is a silent revolution, an unfolding experience more like a lotus flower quietly emerging to freedom from centuries of restrictive prejudices."[9]

Governmental authorities and volunteers from Chatsworth's thriving milieu of social work organizations were keenly aware of what they saw as emerging pathologies of the new township culture. The key problem was the poor Indians who were unable to cope with modernity and its choices and vices. The deficiencies of the township household became a staple of research and studies among Indians. The consensus, then as now, was that the reconstitution of Indian family life from the traditional to the modern form had severe effects, especially on men and young boys, many of whom displayed signs of excessive consumption of *dagga* (local hashish), drugs, and alcohol. Study after study by Indian research students in sociology, education, and social work identified the broken family structure, lack of parental attention, and rampant drug culture that ravaged the poorer parts of the Indian townships.[10] The chief of social development pointed out in 1975 that, "alcoholism has become a problem of no mean measure pertaining almost exclusively to Indian Males" (*Fiat Lux*, September 1973, 26). In the same issue, an official from the Health Department pointed out that the new protein- and fat-laden Western diet would not be feasible for Indians because it would make them more prone to diabetes and obesity (24).

At a seminar for social workers in 1975, speakers warned that the combination of broken families and the new "rebellious attitudes of the youth," and the many films and advertisements coming from the West that celebrated drinking and smoking, could have detrimental effects among Indians.[11] A study of rising divorce rates in 1984 found that alcoholism was cited as the main cause of marital discord in 53 percent of all cases (Ramphal 1989); in Meer's 1976 study of suicide, she found that the suicide rate among adolescent Indians was alarmingly high.[12]

Yet not all was lost. The Indian townships were indeed still described by local intellectuals and political activists as sites of intense and warm sociality, much of which was ascribed to the endurance of social ties and affection beyond the nuclear household. The townships had a rich array of cultural institutions and a new political life wherein debates on the nature of "the community" and the meanings of "our culture" became deeply polarized. On one side stood the conservative and cautious forces who were collaborating with the white authorities, celebrating and retaining Indian cultural forms, and reiterating the attachment to the extended family as the proper cultural form of the family; on the other side, a new and radicalized younger generation saw Indian family forms and traditions as redundant and as obstacles to real emancipation.

In this process the notion of the proper Indian family was increasingly becoming projected onto the multilinguistic Indian community that was coming into being in the townships. The Indian family, now emerging as an enduring mythical structure, hovered over the vast township as a cultural matrix of how families really were: intense, warm, and inclusive, whether based on a nuclear or an extended kin structure.

Regardless of actual practices, this matrix enabled ordinary families to define their own ordinary practices, food, love for one another, and their form of life as somehow "Indian." Otherwise mundane modern practices—shopping in shopping centers, entertaining friends, neighborly commensality, watching television and films, going on outings, and so on—were now all coded as specifically Indian.

Let me illustrate the workings of this mythical structure by how homes were constructed, imagined, and improved. The prefabricated houses in apartheid's townships were all heirs to the long history of reform of native dwellings in the colonial world. On the colonial frontier, native dwellings were models of the native souls: sunk in a morass of unhygienic and immoral habits that blocked the development of any civilization. The answer was windows (inviting light and enlightenment) and cleanliness but also separate rooms, rectangular layouts, and straight lines, which would encourage a more systematic and civilized interior life of the mind and the house (Comaroff and Comaroff 1997, 287–310).[13] The new township houses for Indians were indeed designed to produce modern families, proper everyday disciplines, and to lift Indians out of their intrinsically "insanitary habits."

These houses have hardly any history, little relationship with the land they sit on, and none of the deep organic features and functions that is the assumed ground for most anthropological reflections on "the house," its memories, and so on.[14] These were houses and structures of dwellings that bore the indelible marks of governmental fiat. The modern houses were framed by planners as a form of "emancipatory machines" that would break young women's reliance on kin and extended family and in the process produce a new kind of Indian. This presupposed a break with an older model of domesticity as a site of complex intra- and intergenerational relationships between women, and shared memories among women of different generations.[15]

The forced removals in South Africa turned out to reconfigure social life more decisively than in many other cases of draconian biopolitical interventions.[16] The houses in the townships were, in short, neither dwellings nor habitations but mere sites that gradually, and sometimes painfully, had to become inhabited and enculturated, and turned into "lived space" or represented space, Lefebvre's category for the unruly inhabitation of places whose layout and functions were already defined (1974). The mode of habitation of these new dwellings was neither particularly unruly nor subversive, however, and far from unique to the Indian townships. In Soweto, the "matchbox houses" were improved and altered by their residents in order to consolidate their claim on urban residence (Ginsburg 1996); in Gugulethu, home improvements became a means to consolidate respectability, as well as residential rights

Figure 2. MR. PILLAY IN FRONT OF THE HOUSE HE MOVED INTO IN 1962 IN UNIT 3, CHATSWORTH

to dwellings by female heads of households (Lee 2009, 81–105); and in East London home improvements were central to the consolidation of new modern families in the apartheid townships, which in the 1960s replaced the earlier "locations" (Bank 2011, 175–81). In the African township, the improved house was a site of new urban respectability, while "tradition" and ancestors remained tied to the rural homestead (White 2010). In the Indian township, "our culture" also needed to find a new home.

In Chatsworth, the large areas of council flats housing the very poorest families did not allow for many individual improvements. The same was true for decades of the thousands of standard row houses until the 1980s when the city council began to sell these in a bid to encourage homeownership and individual responsibility. However, already from the 1960s the distinctive "Indian home," marked by exterior and highly visible adornment and to some extent by their interior decoration, began to emerge. The idea of a "typical" Indian home became one that is incessantly improved and decorated by the men in the household, their male relatives, and friends, most of whom belong to the large skilled working class in Durban. The most basic improvement and mark of individuality of most houses was paint and outside decoration on windows, gardens, and fences. These are often painted in strong colors and sometimes decorated with versions of Asoka's wheel, decorations that imitate details from Hindu temples, or green colors and mosque aesthetics referring to Islam. In many cases, the original small standard house form had been extended into the front and the back. Some houses had been covered with a larger roof, and a layer of new bricks had been added to the outside to cover the standard plastered concrete walls. Other houses proudly displayed ornately carved wooden doors and windowpanes, which signaled taste and also a vague, if not always discernible, Indian aesthetic.

In other words, the houses were made into testaments to the dedication of the men in a household who built and defended their domestic life. The individual houses ranged from the small and modest rectangular houses, originally designed in the 1960s, to the flamboyant multilevel houses with small terraces, walls around the compound, and one or more tiny outbuildings that were more or less incorporated within or connected to the main house. Many families had built outbuildings to accommodate their aging parents or their children. Today, the typical pattern is that outbuildings are rented out to tenants in order to generate additional income. Other families have started small businesses—garages, sewing shops, electronics repair, and so on.

My host family was a typical example. They had bought the plot of land with a small house on it three decades ago. As the family grew, they extended the house gradually with extra rooms in the back, then a new roof, and later a small covered terrace overlooking the steep slopes and extending down toward the Umlaas River. Gopal, my host, said that all of this had been done incrementally by using materials that had been bought and gathered over the years and not by taking out loans. The work was usually done with the help of work colleagues, neighbors, and family members. Later they added a small outbuilding where Rekha, the wife, did some of her commercial sewing work. It housed the *almirah* that Rekha had brought from her home and later became the home of a visiting anthropologist for some time. Subsequently, the eldest son of the household returned from Johannesburg to live there while saving up money for a new home for himself and his wife. The interior of the house was also rather typical in its layout. The largest room had big sofas that accommodated the guests and friends who passed in and out of the house on a regular basis. The sofas were facing the television, which was turned on most of the time and broadcast local news programs, Hindi channels, or Bollywood movies. There were

Figure 3. The Sahadeo home in Chatsworth with a view of Umlazi in the background

simple decorations, school certificates, a sports trophy, a calendar art poster from India, and several photos of children, relatives, and family gatherings.

The dining room was small and adjacent to the kitchen where Rekha and the grown-up daughter reigned supreme. Just next to the table, and usually covered by a cloth, was a corner with small images of favorite deities, such as Ganesh and Shiva, incense sticks, and a *jyoti* (oil lamp). Here *pujas* (religious rituals) were performed regularly and in more elaborate ways during festival times and other auspicious occasions. However, on a daily basis this was not a conspicuous part of the interior of the house. The most visible sign marking the house as a Hindu household was the *jhanda* pole (a bamboo pole with Hanuman's red flag on top), which was planted on top of a small concrete structure near the entrance to the house that also served as a site for pujas and offerings during times of major festivals.

The more extended and elaborate houses in the area were often proudly presented as particularly typical "Indian" because they could accommodate many people of different ages and generations. They could serve their appropriate cultural function as sites of large family

Figure 4. THE SAHADEOS' PRAYER ROOM

gatherings and social and religious functions. Despite the burgeoning construction of smaller temples in the township, most religious activities still took place in homes. The now inhabited and enculturated houses in the townships acquired new and more poignant meaning as the true containers and expressions of "tradition" and "our culture." The ma-

Figure 5. The Sahadeo family

jority of religious activity, prayer groups, and many of the neo-Hindu movements operating in the area were located in ordinary houses. Their functions were typically held in gardens and compounds rather than in the spaces designated for public use.

The ability to display and inhabit a house that was "properly Indian" slowly emerged as a new and visible distinction that reflected status and social aspiration. However, in its discursive form, the urge to visibly assert "culture" appeared as a willful enactment of cultural tradition akin to what the Comaroffs in the context of the colonization of the Tswana called "primal sovereignty."[17] In the township, this manifested itself as Indian culture being a force that was welling up in people, becoming an urge, also in adverse circumstances, and defying reason and material possibilities. This force and disposition could not be kept down or away for too long except at one's own peril.

Naidoo saw himself as torn between this urge and his inability to accommodate and express it in his material practice. Naidoo was a skilled worker in a large factory south of the city. He had worked there for many years and things were going well for him and his wife and two daughters. They had been renting a small row house in a slightly run-down part of Chatsworth for decades. In the late 1980s they bought it from the city at a concessional rate. They began improving the house, put in a small bathroom, and even got permission to extend the house toward the street. Naidoo planned on redecorating the whole house and building a shrine in the garden. However, he fell ill and lost his job after six months of absence. "They just gave it to a black fellow who did not know the job at all," Naidoo told me. Now in his late fifties, Naidoo had been managing with odd jobs ever since, and he and his wife were struggling. Their daughters helped them, but their new families were not so keen on supporting them. "You know what Indian families are like with the daughter-in-law—she must always look after her mother-in-law before her own mother. . . . The mind-set is still there."

He felt stuck and unhappy. He had become a devout Hindu and went to Tamil temples as often as he could. He wanted to decorate his house in a way that he found pleasing, to build a shrine, but he could not: "Now at my age, I feel strongly about being Tamil. My wife and I try to speak it at home but our daughters are not interested. I want to live like a Tamil, like an Indian, you can say . . . but it is difficult in this small house and in this area. No one cares around here . . . where would we do pujas or have people for functions? We don't even have the money to build a shrine outside! . . . I don't know how to say this, but I feel like I am in prison in a way . . . as if I am not free to be a Tamil." Naidoo's sense of incarceration gave voice to the way in which "our culture" had become deeply interiorized in some people. It was an inert urge, an ego-ideal in Freudian terms, as well as an exteriorized, shared, social ideal that required physical expression and manifestation in order to reaffirm its existence and credibility in everyday life.

The spatial and aesthetic layout of many houses, large and small, thus signified a desire to construct a proper Indian household—sprawling, multigenerational, and visibly Indian. This was essentially a form of memory work, where the ideal Indian homes of an earlier era were re-created and remembered, albeit within the strictures and confines imposed by the density and lack of space in the township. The performative urge folded into these aesthetic practices aimed at visibly marking the space of the township as loudly "Indian," as if to compensate for the fact that the extended family, traditional practices, and vernaculars had vanished in these new spaces. The decoration and marking of homes as visibly Indian signified a longing for houses that one had never lived in. It was a longing to be connected with a more unadulterated Indian world of the past, a life among those who were never displaced and huddled together in the townships. The "Indian family" and "our culture" could not grow unaided within the homes and dwellings of the deracinated charou families. It needed the supplement of the fantasy of respectable, proper Indianness of the multigenerational homes that now only existed in elite areas. This phantasmic, proper Indianness was constantly invoked metonymically through colors and decorations. It was called upon as a phantasmic gaze and asked to behold the outward signs of the fidelity of the charou household to "our culture." For those who, like Naidoo, felt this "call of culture" as an inert, sovereign force, the inability to live in a properly marked house was experienced as a loss—not of the past per se but of the illocutionary force of the visible sign. It marked a loss of the fantasy of living in an approving and authorizing gaze that enabled one to be a true Indian.

Tongues without Speech: Caste as Language Community

The question of how indenture and subsequent life in multiracial and multicultural societies affected ancestral caste identities has been debated extensively in the literature on the indenture system in Fiji, Trinidad, Guyana, and also South Africa.[18] Marxist historians have argued that the spontaneous camaraderie among coolies on ships and as labor on the colonial plantations forged a spirit of the *jahajibhais* (shipmates) across other cultural markers. This thesis appears inadequate in the light of recent scholarship.[19] Caste was not reproduced in the same forms as in India, but caste consciousness remained strong. By this I mean there was a common-sense ranking of groups and individuals in a hierarchy of distinct and largely closed segments that were defined by blood and inheritance, which in turn governed appropriate social contacts, commensality, and marriage partners. As in other sites of indenture, language and religion emerged in South Africa as the main vehicle for collective identification. Linguistic identification tended to cluster around the Kalkatias (those who spoke Hindi, Bhojpuri, Urdu, Bengali, and other North Indian languages) and the Madrasis (those who spoke Telugu, Tamil, and other South Indian languages). The third major grouping, the Gujaratis (who spoke various Gujarati dialects), was a socially and culturally distinctive group that had limited contact with indentured laborers. By the early twentieth century, this segmentation along linguistic lines was further consolidated by the formation of educational societies and schools that were devoted to teaching vernaculars and ancestral culture.

There are many examples of the maintenance of discrete, supposedly endogamous, *jati* (endogamous caste group) boundaries within each of these clusters in the early decades of indenture, especially among those who claimed higher-caste status. Those named Maharaj soon became vaguely identified with being of clean and North Indian background (see Kuper 1960, 18–43). Today in Durban many carrying the name Maharaj believe themselves to be of Brahmanical descent, or at least heirs to a somewhat purer interpretation of North Indian Hindu culture. The provenance of the name is contested, and in India it was historically used as an honorific title (it literally means "great ruler"). The modernist Hindu reform organization Arya Samaj promoted the use of the name to efface traditional caste names. However, distinct caste names were rapidly disappearing already by the mid-twentieth century. In a survey conducted by Kuper in the 1950s, only 23 percent of students in an Indian school knew their proper caste name (1960, 39).

Language groups gradually consolidated as the castelike affiliations that governed marriage practices and broader social ties. The older Indian settlements around Durban often saw clusters of houses or localities dominated by one or the other language group. This was broken up and dispersed as the forced removals began. Already in the 1950s, practices associated with high caste and piety—chaste (*shuddh*) Hindi, learning, and vegetarianism—had been translated into more serviceable practices of "fasting days": observance of a vegetarian diet and abstinence from alcohol and sex days before and during important festivals (Kuper 1960, 35). Today, these practices are widespread among Hindus in Chatsworth as a sign of respect for "our culture" more than as a set of systematically observed religious practices.

In his sociolinguistic study of Bhojpuri, the dialect spoken by the majority of those known as Hindi speakers in South Africa, Meshtrie found that around 1940 more than half of all daily activities (including dreaming!) were undertaken in Bhojpuri or standard Hindi. Four decades later only religious activity was undertaken in Hindi, and Bhojpuri was only used occasionally in homes (Meshtrie 1991, 117–25). By 1980, the vast majority of Indian homes (except the Gujarati homes) used English as their home language, and the vernaculars were all but extinct except for ritualized spaces and among the older generation.

Yet the attachment to linguistic identities has persisted long after the vernaculars fell out of daily use. The formation of a new life in the townships and the establishment of schools for Indians across the city in the 1960s were accompanied by generational tensions regarding language practices. Just like the extended family and its associated obligations, vernaculars became signs of the past and thus purely of sentimental value. A new generation spoke English at home and in the street. Distinct language practices developed rapidly into a new colloquial English tongue full of expressions from Hindi, Tamil, and Afrikaans. This was less true of the Gujarati-speaking community, which had retained lively connections with the subcontinent, including importing marriage partners, and for whom the use of Gujarati or one of its regional accents was intimately tied to networks of trust and credit that governed the prosperous economic life of this community.

In 1979, government schools made a range of the so-called Eastern languages available at the secondary level and at teacher training colleges. As early as 1972, the minister of Indian Affairs stated that "other languages of high cultural value will be accepted and offered as third languages," and he mentioned Arabic and Hindi as eligible for recognition. The final implementation of regular teaching of Indian languages was celebrated as an opening to "the inherent richness of Indian religious and cultural heritage."[20]

The actual spoken English among Indians was often derided as impure, an impediment and a sign of imperfect modernity: "The South African Indian cannot speak, read or write his own language as well as his brothers in India, nor can he speak, read or write English as well as the white English-speaking South African. He is neither one nor truly the other" (Ramphal 1989, 74). The meaning of linguistic community now became governed by notions of purity and cultural "comfort." The command of standard Hindi and Tamil, as opposed to the spoken vernacular of the older generation, became a mark of education and social aspiration. Within each group, it was class background, education, the reputation of the family, and also physical appearance—especially complexion—that in practice regulated and determined the appropriateness of marriage partners. However, every single family I encountered over nearly a decade had stories of exceptions, of love marriages across boundaries of language and religion. The severity of sanctions applied to such cases reported by Kuper from the 1950s has all but disappeared. Today, strong sanctions are only contemplated in cases of conversion to Christianity because of the historical connotations of Christianity with lower-caste Hindus. The logic of ranking communities in segmented but incompatible communities has been transferred from caste to religious and linguistic community and from notions of incompatible bodily essences to notions of differing beliefs and performances of identity.

Today, mastering the vernaculars is seen as evidence of a sincere commitment to "our culture" but is also at times a showy and somewhat superfluous sign of middle-class aspiration toward pure Hinduism. Most prayer groups and local temples are actively encouraging the teaching of Hindi and Tamil as a way of generating interest in Hindu religious practices and Indian culture as such. As I will show in chapter 7, the mastery of vernaculars is like the practice of vegetarianism: often intimately connected with a striving for respectability. The older colloquial parole of the vernacular dialects of the forefathers has now given way to a more studied embrace of the grammatically proper langue.

"Our Culture" as Embarrassment

In the 1970s, many younger and educated Indians began to view attachments to Indian culture with profound suspicion, as signs of a conservative and now corrupted past that would continue to enthrall Indians to introverted and myopic forms of life and judgment. As in the case of the extended family, linguistic community and cultural traditions were only truly valued if they were projected as a conscious and reflexive lifestyle choice based on conviction, rather than on nonreflexive adherence to tradition without understanding its inner values. Let me illustrate how caste had become subsumed under a larger category of tradition and "our culture" by turning to the genre of family comedies, which came into being in the 1970s. This genre derived its enormous popularity among Indians from constantly returning to vexed questions of caste and prejudice in a manner both critical and lighthearted.

Kessie Govender's *On the Fence* (1978) launched the genre of the Indian family drama as a critique of snobbery, opportunism, and prejudice within an Indian middle-class family. The drama revolves around the reactions of an Indian family when the educated and radicalized daughter (Sita, preeminent symbol of virtuous womanhood) announces that she is going out with a colored man whom she intends to marry. The father says angrily in colloquial South African Indian English: "Now she doing this things. Not going by one suleman fella; not going by one porridge fella, must going by one bushman fella."[21] The family mobilizes a friend of Sita's brother, a successful doctor from a respectable family, who volunteers to marry Sita, believing that he, the incarnation of the desire of every Indian woman and mother-in-law, can persuade Sita to come to her (cultural) senses. But she refuses, leaving her parents devastated.

The family drama continued as a genre into the 1980s when the disappearance of the Immorality Act and the incipient mixing across color made the moral challenges more complex. In the face of this, the genre as a whole tended to slide toward that of comedy. In 1988, the popular actor Essop Khan staged the successful comedy *The Jamal Syndrome*, which dealt with a conservative Muslim family facing a new white daughter-in-law and the many absurdities this gives rise to. Shortly after, Essop Khan and his cowriter Mahomed Ali staged a sequel, *Jamal 2*, which was more slapstick in form and revolved around internal family quarrels and stereotyped fights between troubled mothers and rebellious daughters (always more educated than their mothers), mach-inations of cunning grandmothers and evil mother-in-laws, and other stock characters well known from Bollywood films. In *My Second Wife*, Ali and Khan were poking fun at the mother-in-law and portrayed In-dian men as hapless props in the machinations of the female members of the households. All of these plays ran for many months in Indian community halls in townships and Indian enclaves all over the country.

Ali and Khan deplored being regarded as mere producers of light-hearted, popular "low art" but also took pride in the fact that they, as Muslim actors, had drawn the substantial Muslim community into theater halls: "To many Muslims theatre is *haram* [unclean/forbidden] but we actually got them out, we made them laugh at themselves, their ways, their marriages and families and all that. That is our lasting con-tribution and we are proud of it."

In April 1999 the duo staged another play, *Coconut Busters*, in their trademark genre. The main theme of the play—how parents and in-laws interfere in the marriages and family life of the younger generation—remains a site of explosive conflicts, yet the tone was cozy and dis-armingly over-the-top, full of Indian colloquialisms and exaggerated accents. It was good, clean family entertainment and intended to be so. Judging from reactions and comments from the audience in the com-munity hall in Chatsworth where I watched the play, it was received as somewhat predictable among an audience that was clearly literate in this genre. "Oh, but it was not as good as *My Second Wife*," said one man, "too much of the same, man," said another. "But I really liked *Jamal 2*," said a third man in a conversation during the intermission. Upon see-ing me, as always the only white person in the audience, some became apologetic and explained to me that the play really was "very Indian" and "maybe you don't find it so funny." When I asked a group of men if they could recognize themselves or families they knew in the play, one man said, "Oh sure, man, we are worse—but the only problem is that our families are not so funny," and they all roared with laughter.[22]

Interestingly, these plays and their many imitations—among them the *Broken Promises* series—have managed to compress the question of attachment to caste, extended families, religious convention, and even linguistic community into one form: the cunning but myopic female family members and their willy-nilly accomplices among the older men who ineffectively attempt to hold on to remnants of an already dying patriarchal tradition. Caste and linguistic community are by now cul-tural echoes without clear-cut practical implications—no unanimity on the ranking of caste and few speakers of the vernacular. Despite asser-tions of culture as an inert force, Indianness no longer knows itself in an organic way and no longer speaks effortlessly as itself. Indians and

Indianness must always be produced and projected. This production always happens in a tense conversation with the most disavowed and yet celebrated figure of everyday life in the township: the charou.

Cultural Intimacy and Embarrassment: Charous and Lahnees

The unreflexive attachment to parochial cultural forms, and imperfect ways of speaking English, are sure signs of a deracinated township Indian who is unable to understand his or her own culture. In his hands, traditional practice, or even the vernacular parole, turns what was once meaningful and purposeful practice into a dysfunctional impediment to achieving full modernity and complete personhood. The name for this figure is a "charou," a term of unclear origins but all of which relate to being "minor" and brown.[23]

While never as derogatory as the older colonial term "coolie," it has today acquired a wide range of rather ambivalent connotations that range from disdain to affection. It is first and foremost a signifier of cultural intimacy, which Herzfeld usefully defines as " the recognition of these aspects of cultural identity that are considered a source of external embarrassment but that nevertheless provide insiders with their assurance of common sociality . . . these are the self-stereotypes that insiders express ostensibly at their own expense" (1997, 3). To Herzfeld this is an intrinsic part of marginalized cultural identity. Here, embarrassment is not the interpersonal awkwardness that Goffmann (1982) identified as companions to the breaking of tacit rules of interaction. What Herzfeld has in mind is a more fundamental underside, or inside, of cultural identities that are seeking to shield themselves: "Embarrassment, rueful self-recognition: these are the key markers of what cultural intimacy is all about. They are not solely personal feelings but describe the collective representation of intimacy" (6). Embarrassment is linked to public behavior and an imputed gaze upon one's conduct as a stereotyped category. The intensity of this type of collective, "categorical" embarrassment is (re-)produced by the real and deeply institutionalized social distance between groups and communities, or as Michael Billig puts it, "the looser the social bond, the greater the potential for embarrassment" (2001).

When people in Chatsworth describe someone as "a real charou," they are referring to a certain way of speaking, joking, eating (and drinking), and comportment that is characteristic of working-class life. Wealthy and upwardly mobile Indians are, in other words, decidedly not charou. They seek to purge everything charou—cheap liquor, traces of colloquial South African Indian English, eating of meat, cracking (coarse) jokes, and enjoyment of low-grade Bollywood film songs. The colloquial name for this type of person and behavior is a *lahnee* (meaning "fancy" or "boss"), a term historically used for white people but that has become a commonplace endearment/abuse for any Indian that is doing well, is educated, has good manners, and so on.[24] A nice house, car, neighborhood, and so on can be lahnee as well. This continuous distinction between that which is charou and that which is lahnee is driven by the fact that the features of charou culture are both intimate and well known among most Indians in South Africa, however lahnee they may appear.

Four decades of township life created a space of experience, predicament, and possibility that was shared by the middle class and the unemployed alike, by Hindus, Christian, and Muslims, and by Tamil, Gujarati, and Hindi speakers. The social horizon of the ordinary person in the township, his or her patterns of movement, and social imagination became deeply affected, and often determined, by this sociospatial regime. One became an Indian because one lived an Indian life—went to Indian schools, shopped in Indian shops, went to Indian cinema halls and Indian beaches, and visited family in other parts of the country who also lived in enclaves designated for Indians. The charou culture was, and remains, interior to this everyday form of life, a social and linguistic code one could switch back to and a mode of being and speaking that was a part of the everyday experiences of most Indians, however morally ambiguous or even shameful it was in the eyes of those striving for respectability. Their striving to become lahnees was, in other words, interior to the charou world.

Many ordinary Indians are somewhat embarrassed about this inner "truth" of the community, a truth very far removed from the classicized idea of the Indian that is espoused by the cultural and political leaders of the community. The charou register marks a zone of cultural intimacy, a zero-point from where cultural capital and respectability can be built and developed, but therefore also a register one can slip back into if not carefully purging charou ways from one's home and family. The embarrassment that always seems to accompany the charou culture remains intimately tied to the importance of an imagined external gaze in performance of public cultural practices. This amounts to what Žižek has called a logic of "anticipatory identification": the desire to perform the part one already has been assigned by powerful modalities of external gaze (1994, 73–80).

Seen from Chatsworth there are two powerful external gazes in which Indianness must be performed. One is the general so-called mainstream hierarchy of accents, styles of consumption, dress, forms of domesticity, styles of Christianity, and global commercial trends and popular culture, which remain the yardstick of public normality whether inhabited by white or black bodies and persons. This general public gaze is marked by condescending and orientalist assumptions about the overriding importance of religion and spirituality, a strong family life, and the colorful and exotic customs among Indians. The other powerful gaze has historically been that of the Indian elite and middle classes, the lahnees, for whom India appeared as a cultural homeland, and to whom appropriate representation of Indian culture in South Africa was a matter of great pride and public importance. The Indian elite strive to purify Hindu practices and retain Indian vernaculars, and many community leaders are worried about increasing Westernization and conversion to Christianity.

Squeezed between these powerful gazes, the language and practices of the charou inevitably appear imperfect, if not morally deficient. Although firmly nested in the working-class culture of the townships, charouness is also a performative category that does not just disappear with education or a new house. Many of the successful Indians who have left the townships to live in formerly white areas, and who are often dismissed as arrogant lahnees, have a nostalgic recollection of the township and their childhood, and of the comfortable and easygoing life they spent there. This is similar to Jacob Dlamini's recent recollection of growing up in Katlehong Township outside of Johannesburg during the same tumultuous decades (2009). Like Dlamini's depiction of an ordinary life of neighborliness and intense sociality, many of those who were raised in Chatsworth recall a haven of mutual support, care, and security, where people did not have to lock their doors all the time. There was crime and violence, but it mainly happened elsewhere, and one heard rumors of these other and more dramatic townships like Soweto or Umlazi in Durban. This sense of the pure Indian township of the apartheid era as a more idyllic past that is now irrevocably lost is probably the most widely shared sentiment in and about Chatsworth. Advertising newspaper columnists and talk show hosts refer to the charou life as something simple, crude, or even quaint, yet honest and unpretentious. In a playful reversal, they depict their own middle-class lives through a charou lens that is charmed but hypocritical, with their own accents and behavior inauthentic when purged of every trace of charoudom.

For the aspiring middle classes, as well as for most people I met in the townships, the charou culture thus holds a deeply ambivalent position—denounced, despised, and ridiculed in much standup comedy and community theater when it appears in glimpses in the behavior or speech of educated people. At the same time, charou culture is also half secretly enjoyed and even celebrated as "our" past, the authentic, ethnic thing that is truly ours; an object of ambivalent rejection and enjoyment, a jouissance of an embarrassing past.

Another central attraction of "charou" ways is that it is a semisecret set of codes and references that unlike high Indian culture cannot be learned and known by outsiders. It is a part of the environment one dwells in, a form of disavowed surplus that can never be fully domesticated.[25] The term "charou" is often used in the third person as if it is something anonymous and latent that is living out there in the community, traces of which may suddenly show up in people, such as cheating, stealing, wicked ways, gossip, superstition, and so on. When it was revealed in the 1990s that the largest robbery in South Africa—31 million rand (about $4.6 million in U.S. dollars)—had been carried out by a group of policemen from the local police station in Chatsworth, the local reaction was, "Ah, the charous did it." It was surprising that "such people" could pull it off, but also unsurprising because it merely demonstrated that these policemen were indeed irredeemably charou.[26] In everyday conversations, people may warn you, "Don't carry that cell phone—the charous might take it," or if someone gets robbed by an Indian, it is always said that "a charou did it" or "the charous did it."

For all its despised and disavowed features, the charou culture was in fact the very stuff of cultural intimacy, the shared secret that enabled a sense of community, and the much-cherished informality that marks the memory of the township in its heyday—open doors, permeable houses, fluid sociality, and easygoing banter. This trace of the charou inside every Indian, however lahnee the accent and comportment, lives on but now as a shared loss that has become available to popular comedy, as we will see below.

CLASS AND CHAROU NAMES

The use of multiple personal names in Chatsworth illustrates another aspect of the interior and familiar status of the charou. From the 1960s on, the use of English names became widespread among working-class Indians. Names like Johnny, Steve, Alan, and Billy became popular among boys, while girls generally retained Indian names, although names like Donna, Orlean, Dorothy, and Daisy began to appear. Indian surnames were generally retained because local authorities were reluctant to allow Indians to abandon an obvious ethnic mark without which they would be indistinguishable from whites in official and commercial interactions.[27] The use of anglicized first names were often attempts to preempt humiliating nicknaming by white superiors who generally refused to pronounce Indian names. The Tamil name Munasammi, for instance, became "Sammy," which in turn became a generic nickname used by whites for any Indian waiter or worker.

A system of double or parallel naming thus developed in the townships. Most Indian men and boys who were part of the charou culture were given, or invented for themselves, an English-sounding first name or a cool-sounding nickname. Their more elaborate Indian name was mainly used in connection with official transactions with authorities, banks, and so on. The "outside" world of work and wider urban space was defined as male and anglicized, part and parcel of the tense and uncertain existence as quasi citizens of the city. Officially registered Indian names were used in the most intimate situations, between man and wife or between parents and children. These names were signifiers of affection and intimacy in a domestic structure wherein women were the keepers and custodians of Indianness—vernaculars, cooking, dress, and so on. Age played a crucial role in terms of how men addressed and named themselves. Retirement and the status as grandfathers did in some cases mark a "return" to the community, to religion, to family, and to tradition—and would imply the public use of Indian names. In public addresses, letters, and meetings involving "the community" as such, older men used their full Indian names, while their anglicized nicknames, which grew out of male peer groups and work life, remained in use in informal interactions among their peers.

I only discovered that my long-standing friend Trevor actually had a Tamil name when he asked for my help to file an affidavit in connection with a court case he was involved in. Trev, as he was called among friends, never used his Tamil name, and he was just given it because "you need to have some name," as he said. When I asked him if he thought that was his real name, he said, "Trevor is my real name because that is how people know me. If you walked into our block and called for Tungasamy—and that is such an old-fashioned name—people wouldn't know who you were talking about. . . . It is written on my ID, but even my pay-slip says Trevor. It is not that I want to be like a Christian or anything, but Trevor *is* my real name, I feel." Many of his neighbors had converted to Christianity quite recently, but their English names had been used for as long as Trevor could remember.

Billy was only known as Badri or Badrinath in his own household, which consisted of his wife, his aging mother, and three daughters. A portly builder with a weather-beaten face, he was known as Billy in his working life and among friends and neighbors. Inside his house, he assumed a different role as the gentle patriarch, pampered as Badri by three generations of women. There was nothing secret or unusual about it, as many of his friends who would call him Billy were also known by their "proper" Indian names among their relatives. For Billy, however, the use of his Indian name in public would be "what lahnees do," as he jokingly told me, and not something he felt comfortable with.

A friend and informant worked as an attendant in a kombi taxi. He liked to be called Rocky. He was a Hindu and given the name Rama-chandra, which he found awful. "My name is too long; no one can say it. It is also an old type of name, and it was my Granny who wanted me to be called that . . . but people don't like long names; they like them short and easy. It is better to shout, don't you think?" he laughed. His reply confirmed the power of anticipatory identification: "Ram is a god, right, and I don't want to be called something like that. It is also too . . . eh . . . Indian in a way, you know, as if I'm the type going to temples and all that. I go sometimes but, hey, what is the point in splashing 'I am a Hindu' all over in that way. We get most of our customers in the city. Some are Indian but many are black or colored people and a white man sometimes. I like to joke with them. They call me Rocky and I don't think they'd like Ram." Another informant was known as Yanks because of his characteristic drawl. Yanks, a Muslim, assured me that it was all about self-confidence: "You will see that it is all the Tamil people who are ashamed of their names and they don't know their religion anymore. You will not find a Muslim who will call himself by an English name, not if he is a good believer and proud of being a Muslim. . . . But then our Muslim names are shorter and easier to say for the *witous* [whites]." His own nickname was just for fun, he claimed, but it did fit seamlessly into the lively street culture and naming practices in his neighborhood.

Performing in the Gaze: The Indian Public Sphere

Despite the active promotion of African vernaculars by television and radio stations after 1994, the two official languages of the apartheid state, Afrikaans and English, remain the preferred public languages. A racial-cultural segmentation of readership and audiences persists between newspapers that are seen as "white" (e.g., *Sunday Times*, *Mail and Guardian*, *Cape Times*) and African or Indian newspapers, such as the *Sowetan* or the *Post*, respectively. A similar segmentation applies to radio stations that cater to different audiences via accents, music styles, and the themes debated.

While nonwhite publics have historically been subordinated and marginalized, they remain important arenas for the play of cultural in-timacy and are deeply structured by class, emotion, and memory. The "ethnic" or vernacular public remains a site of pleasure as well as embar-rassment, with localized and more intimate and informal news, gossip, and events. It is a space occupied and consumed primarily by those whose lives are mainly lived on "the inside" of the community—women, children, older people, and the marginalized and poorer sections. For the educated, whose general orientation in terms of work, education, and leisure is directed toward wider South African or global publics, the "ethnic" publics appear as conservative remnants of the past.

Nowhere is this ambivalence more clearly articulated than in the case of the "Indian public" in South Africa, especially because its all-dominant language is English. This public is constituted by a number of newspapers, radio stations, and art circuits that are defined by particular accents, names, aesthetics, and musical styles. The Indian public is not closed to the gaze of other groups but is generally not considered interesting, let alone appealing, to people outside it. To many whites, it remains an exotic world of alien customs and practices, while to most Africans the world of the Indian appears neither friendly nor of relevance. Surrounded by this dismissive indifference, Indians have developed traditions, musical forms, and a unique vernacular. The leading Indian newspaper in the country, the *Post*, started in the 1950s as the *Natal Post*, a hard-hitting tabloid with crime, sensation, and pinup girls, which catered mainly to the white working class. Immensely popular with Indian workers, it gradually metamorphosed into an Indian family newspaper in the 1980s.

In the 1990s, the Indian public sphere has been supplemented by the so-called extras—inserts in the mainstream papers on Sundays that follow along the lines of the *Post* in terms of style, advertising, and themes discussed (Bollywood music, food, social problems, cultural events, etc.). The extras are arresting metaphors for the status of Indians as a permanent minority that is effectively appended to a white world. At the same time, they have expanded the Indian public and opened it to an imaginary white gaze that derives its main force from being potential rather than actual audiences. The "Indian public" is neither the ideal "self-organized relationship among strangers" nor the "counterpublic" that is defined in opposition to a mainstream evoked by Michael Warner.[28] South African publics are without exception shaped by a century of institutionalized regulation of bodies, languages, dispositions, tastes, and desires.

In 1999 when I wanted to subscribe to the *Post*, the saleswoman (of Indian origin) was convinced I had made a mistake. "You will find it very Indian, sir—you know, dance, films, recipes, and all." "Yes, exactly," I said. She smiled, half embarrassed, and accepted my money, but she clearly had doubts about my mental condition. The *Post* advertises itself as a weekly "paper for the family." Like Radio Lotus, it holds a position of interiority among most Indians in Durban—an unavoidable and necessary reference, not always loved or admired but accepted as a screen upon which the community gets written and invoked every week. The

Post is a place where one sees oneself and where the gaze of the community becomes literal. Every week, the paper carries a full photo page covering minor and major events either in Indian areas or involving Indians: concerts, sports events, galas, meetings, and conferences. Photos are arranged to contain as many faces and names as possible. Those being photographed are given due time to arrange their clothes, put on a tie, extra lipstick, and so on to get ready for the shot. The two photographers covering these events try to give as many people as possible the opportunity to get their photo in the *Post* in this characteristic family album style of representation.

Many homes are adorned by little cuttings of *Post* photos taken of family members, sometimes framed and hung on the wall. The community is also made visible by the ubiquitous vox-pop with pictures, names, and sections of the township. Questions run along the lines of "Are Indians being discriminated against?" or "Indian schools—how to rescue education?" or more predictable, "Are Indian beauties the best in the world?" The chances of being asked these questions in workplaces or in a shopping mall are quite high. On certain issues deemed of broader interest, such as the beauty issue, a black or white person (man) may be asked, but respondents are almost exclusively Indian.

An important attraction of the *Post* is the update on crimes, murders, and scandals in the community. Like everything else, death is profoundly racialized in South Africa. So-called mainstream newspapers run laconic updates in side columns on the shocking death toll of the preceding days or weekend in the African townships. No names are mentioned, just the arid prose of the police report. Only murders of whites, and occasionally Indians, receive real attention in these papers. Likewise, the *Post* carries stories of Indian murders or crimes no matter where they take place. The weekly column Court Update has been an established part of reporting since the 1960s. Reporters always make sure that the personal details of the involved parties are precisely reported. Each week, one can read detailed reports of planned murders, extortion, illicit sexual liaisons, crimes of passion, divorces, and so on, as they transpire in the courtroom. Needless to say, this column is a cherished source of gossip and fantastic elaboration of stories of excess and conspiracy, of deviant behavior among the small Indian elite and local celebrities.

These widely savored stories of misdeeds and scandals are printed side by side with regular columns and op-eds in the *Post* by a few dozen intellectuals and writers who, week after week, in a systematic and rather ritualized manner, evoke the history of the community, the moral basis of Indianness, the need to restore family values and have the community's heroes respected, to preserve the essential spirituality of the community, and so on. These are the gatekeepers of the community talking inward, talking the community into existence, a creation upon which their own positions depend.[29]

What emerges from this specific public is a deeply divided consciousness. On the one hand, a strong narrative emerges of the community as a unit and a space of moral experience and unique cultural values that are centered on spirituality and family values. On the other hand, there exists a constant awareness of a continuing and deepening cycle of domestic violence, divorces, delinquency, corruption, conversions to Christianity, deep running racism toward Africans, and so on. The function of cultural intimacy is, in other words, that the community's secrets generate a bond of "bad faith." Andrew Shryock has argued that minorities under pressure are constituted through a double discourse on identity: "Identity 1," which is the official and onstage story of who we are and how we live that is presented to a wider and dominant world; and "Identity 2," which is the real and embarrassing story of how we actually are and how we do things—an offstage version that is strictly for internal circulation. Outsiders may be accepted if they master the first version and also demonstrate that they can administer the knowledge of the second in an appropriate and measured way (2004, 279–314). While this distinction is crucial to the Indian community in Durban, it is equally striking how porous the boundary between the two registers is. This porosity has generated a vigorous and inventive space of the comic and joking more generally.

JOKE-WORK ON A SATURDAY MORNING

A decade ago, Radio Lotus developed a distinctly commercial profile as Lotus FM by appealing to younger listeners and promoting DJs and contemporary Indian dance music. The station's website tried to appeal to a modern diasporic sensibility by running small fact sheets about the phenomenal success of Indian entrepreneurs across the world. The news items from India were regarded as quite irrelevant—except for the gossip about Bollywood stars. Like many other radio stations across the world and in South Africa, talk radio—the contemporary blend of strongly opinionated talk-show hosts and phone-in programs—became central to the new format. Lotus's most popular item was the phone-in talk show *Viewpoint*, which took up new issues that were briefly and provocatively presented by the host for an hour every day. *Viewpoint*, nicknamed "Spewpoint," emerged in the late 1990s as the most controversial program on Lotus, not least because of the long-term presenter, Devi Sankaree Govender. She insisted on taking up thorny issues like teenage pregnancies, infidelity, AIDS, Indian racism, the persistence of a subservient "coolie" attitude to whites, conversions to Christianity, domestic violence, the role of accents, and so on. Govender made women's issues a part of her trademark. A clear preference for women and younger listeners was exercised. Men who tried to capture or dominate the program—often men with strong charou accents—were cut short.

Most of the media personalities have a rather clear perception of "the community" as being conservative, timid, narrow-minded, and unwilling to confront its own vices and problems. Like so many other educated Indians, Govender saw herself as liberal, broad-minded, and ahead of "the community," which needed to be "shaken up," as she put it to me. Devi Sankaree readily admitted that there were issues that were too difficult to talk about and that no callers responded to readily, however prominent they loomed in families and everyday gossip: domestic violence, incest, racism, interracial marriages and liaisons, and the universe of demons and evil eyes. These issues—based on rumors, stories, and parables—were discussed in vague and general terms, but very rarely in discussions that were based on personal accounts or examples.[30] These themes are so sensitive that they have to be left to the comedians.

The comedy and talk show *The Weekend Lift-Off* was created by Ray Maharaj and Vikash Mathura a decade ago as a mixture of light news, phone-in sessions, music, and weekly parodies performed by the two fictional figures, Bala and Peru—two pensioners from the town of Verulam, the only town in South Africa with a distinctly Indian (Tamil) name. Set in the heart of the sugar belt north of Durban, Verulam is widely seen as predominantly Tamil (as were the majority of indentured laborers), provincial, and backward, and the seat of an older rustic and uncouth charou culture. Peru and Bala were portrayed as out of place and funny in every possible way: they were old and did not quite understand all the changes in the country, their command of English was lacking in many ways, they were misogynist and talked about women in ways that mocked and ridiculed any attempt at producing a new role for women, and they were Tamil and from Verulam. They represented, in essence, the embarrassing past of the community, the unreformed charou, and the Tamil core of working-class culture—innocent, simple-minded, and myopic but also endearing.

Over the period of time the show has been running, Peru and Bala have "gone to India," where they behaved in ways that were distinctly nonspiritual and petty-minded, and constantly made abusive remarks about the place for which they are supposed to have some veneration. They have "been to" Johannesburg, where they behaved like country bumpkins and made uncouth remarks about women, modern life, and Africans on the streets. They frequently go to the seaside (to look at skimpily clad women) and to the doctor, where they complain and talk about their failing health. They go to African healers, where they are tricked while making uncouth remarks about African medicine. The funny element throughout was, of course, that they persisted in seeing the world from their limited perspective and never got the larger picture: they misunderstood things, displayed all kinds of prejudice, had a misplaced sense of superiority, and could only comprehend the most immediate things and phenomena, and only within their own limited horizon. They were provincial in every sense and therefore deeply embarrassing. Bala and Peru were not merely on radio but appeared at stage shows throughout the country and appeared as a comic strip on the station's website and elsewhere, albeit in a tamer and more family-friendly version than when on the air. They have become immensely popular in many quarters, especially with men and younger people, because of their risqué transgression of the boundaries as to how misogynist jokes and sexually explicit language can be articulated in public.

Other sketches performed on *The Weekend Lift-Off* have taken up current events or common frames (like "This is not the 8:45 news") and make fun of public figures. The well-known Indian strongman and politician Amichand Rajbansi's very public divorce and remarriage was depicted Bollywood-style with badly performed songs. In another sketch, an Indian man described a recipe for rum pudding and got drunker as he made the pudding. His accent went from neat and lahnee to a broad charou accent, implying that beneath the cultivated exterior of a respectable Indian always lies an uncouth charou. Here it was the rum, made with sugarcane, that referred to the coolie and plantation past and to the vice of heavy drinking, which is widely associated with the charou man. As he ingested the rum (the past) it possessed him, took him over, and unmasked him as nothing but a charou. As the sketch progressed, the ridiculous figure was no longer the charou per se but the very attempt to literally put charou life on "a recipe"—that is, to present it in a cultured and cohesive way as an origin of ethnic cuisine. The two comedians normally stayed away from politics and contentious issues, and the only African figures they have made fun of have been Mandela (his life story told Bollywood-style) and Desmond Tutu, both of whom are universally loved and respected and made fun of in a loving and respectful way.

It is no mere coincidence that both the comedians are Hindi speakers and that they used Hindi and Hindi film songs in other sketches, and also used Hindi terms for sexual acts and organs (*danda, choot, ganda-ganda*), as if to conceal them and yet pronounce them, thus making signifiers of physical intimacy into transmitters of cultural intimacy. But there was also more than a trace of disdain running through this mockery and self-deprecation—disdain of Tamil and charou culture by

Hindi speakers, who have historically regarded themselves as more or-ganized, purer Hindus, and better Indians.

The talk-show hosts also displayed a different form of disdain that was based on class and articulated through accent and the power of language. When receiving calls from listeners or reading news, they used almost "white" accents in order to demonstrate their competence and worthiness. The barely disguised element of disdain showed itself in interactions with listeners whose accents and imperfect English be-trayed them as uneducated charous. The hosts would make fun of them, ridicule them in ways they often did not quite understand, and often made fun of letters they received, reading out their spelling mistakes and broken grammar.

There were multiple complaints from Tamil speakers about this pro-gram, but they were generally brushed aside as indications of a lack of a sense of humor and/or an inability to join in the self-deprecation that is the dominant form of humor in this community space. Opinions on the program were wildly divided. Many educated Indians found the program offensive and a disgrace—ostensibly because it portrayed In-dians as stupid and gullible—but as much because it foregrounded and represented the charou culture that middle-class Indians generally dis-avow. Yet, as was the case with Lotus during the apartheid years, many ordinary working-class people tuned in to *The Weekend Lift-Off* to laugh and listen to Hindi pop. In 2002, the station manager estimated that the show had 700,000 listeners—something like 70 percent of adult In-dians in the country and nothing less than an astounding success. The program could be heard from most houses, in taxis, shops, and at the outdoor markets in Chatsworth and Phoenix, where it was the source of intense and unapologetic collective enjoyment. Phrases and ways of speaking from the program proliferated among young people, such as when Peru yells "Baaalaa" or the ironic use of the formal Tamil greeting *Vanakkam* among those who do not speak the vernacular.

The success of this program suggests that the culture of self-deprecation—of making fun of the charou, of the past, and of the pro-vincial mind-set of Indians—remains not only the dominant genre of fun and entertainment within the community but also the dominant mode of self-representation more generally. Although a whole range of problems internal to the community were incessantly debated on *View-point*, the larger and thornier issues, such as the future of Indians in the country and the relationship with Africans and the ANC government, remained difficult to discuss. Most Indians shied away from these sub-jects, even in informal conversations. Such questions were clearly left to spaces and genres defined by comedy. The question of why humor has assumed such a prominent place in the everyday life of Indians in South Africa calls for a slightly deeper set of reflections.

Comic Belief? Laughter and Cultural Intimacy

"Humor is local and a sense of humor is usually highly context-specific," Simon Critchley points out in his crisp review of theories of humor (2002, 67). The relative untranslatability of humor makes it a form of "insider knowledge" or a "linguistic defense mechanism" that is comforting and produces an intense *sensus communis* among those who share the joke and the laughter (79–91). This constitutes an ethical community of laughter by sharing an implicit range of meanings and presuppositions. But such ethos often shares ground with ethnos, as Critchley points out (68).

Ridiculing and celebrating parochial mind-sets and "our stupidity" has a long and deep history among many communities in South Africa. It thrived during apartheid where the enforced isolation of South Africa by apartheid was often processed in everyday life through the half-embarrassed sharing of jokes and colloquial abuse in Afrikaans. To this day, crude Afrikaans expressions remain a stock of common currency that can be shared and exchanged among those who grew up during apartheid, regardless of race and language. These phrases refer to an embarrassing past, a language forced upon the public sphere, but also the pleasures of sharing this past and its absurdities. Among Afrikaans speakers, the comedian Leon Schuster has made a long career based on celebrating and poking fun at the determined parochialism of Afrikaners. Irony, self-deprecation, and embarrassment are also key sentiments that pervade contemporary colored fiction,[31] and the thriving stand-up comedy scene is transacted in coarse and highly idiomatic *kaaps*, the colored Capetonian variety of Afrikaans. One of the most widely acclaimed popular books in South Africa in recent years is the satirical *Some of My Best Friends Are White: Subversive Thoughts from an Urban Zulu Warrior* by Ndumiso Ngcobo (2007). In short vignettes Ngcobo makes fun of other race groups in a style where self-deprecating riffs on Zuluness and the new black middle class constantly mitigate what otherwise could have been read as abusive slurs.

In Chatsworth, the effect of sharing comic performances clearly produces a form of "ethnic closure." By this, I mean two things: first, closure as in *closing ranks*. The knowledge of the follies of the charou world and the comical effects of exaggerated accents and well-known stock characters presuppose a sharing of the spaces of cultural intimacy where these accents and their connotations exist.[32] Second, I mean closure in the *ordinary therapeutic sense*, as reconciling oneself with a certain traumatic event or process. The key here is what Freud, in many places in his early work on jokes and the unconscious, calls "economy in psychical expenditure," that is, the exchange of energy between inhibitions (consuming energy) and their release in the laugh or the comical pleasure. What Freud calls "joke-work" basically consists in providing mechanisms for discharge; that is, exchange between pent-up inhibitions/repressions—that which one cannot say or even think—and the preconscious, that which becomes sayable in the specifically condensed and always displaced form, which Freud argued was a central feature of jokes as well as dreams (1989, 143–93).

The social settings of laughter—sitting in an audience, sharing a joke, listening to the radio—adds to the experience of ethnic closure. The laughter reaffirms a "we" and provides emotional discharge and enjoyment of an imperfect form of life in a situation that is fraught with anxieties. The space created by the laughter is thus redemptive, if in an intrinsically limited fashion. The moment of ethnic closure is clearly a moment of "anachronistic enjoyment" that is despised by many educated Indians. Yet these community spaces are seen by many charous to be exactly moments of momentary freedom wherein one can be "Indian without apologies," as it was often put to me, and to imagine a form of nonalienated consciousness wholly identical to itself.

This corresponds with what Alenka Zupančič calls "conservative comedy": the procedures expose the follies of a character (of ourselves) but redeem them by showing that they are merely human and thus fallible and prone to mistakes (2008, 30–33). This is the essence of the feel-good family comedies of Ali and Khan that I discussed earlier, where there is always a happy ending and forgiveness all around. Such comedies leave the fundamental characters untouched by criticism—the mother-in-law, the clumsy husband, and so on—as mere ossified traditional roles that good-hearted people have to perform.

As we will see, there exists a long-standing tradition of political satire and stinging critique of conservative social mores. However, the primary object of fun and ridicule during apartheid was rarely white people (although there was plenty to laugh about) but invariably the puffed-up Identity 1 enunciators of the truth of "our culture" and collaborationist politicians such as Rajbansi and others. Despite its political nature, this form of satire and comical characters hardly conforms to the well-known image associated with Bakhtin of popular wit and satire as carnivalesque and subversive genres that contain a measure of emancipatory potential. The target of derision remains firmly within the Indian world itself. Such forms of comedy are in some senses "rites of expiation, [where] laughter and derision give way to imaginary well-being; they allow for distance between the subject who laughs and the object of mockery . . . that is[,] to become a stranger to this 'thing' that exercises domination" (Mbembe and Roitman 1999, 186). Yet, the "thing" that exercises domination remains within ourselves.

Let me illustrate this with regards to the play on accents, which is *the* central device in community theater and on radio shows. Accents are used as comical devices by exaggeration or discrepancy. Exaggeration is the most widely used technique by which a typical charou, often an elderly person, is depicted as both naive/endearing and ridiculous. Similarly, exaggerated "white" accents are deployed to portray the typical overambitious lahnee who tries to expunge every trace of his Indianness but is betrayed by the exaggerated gesture itself. The other technique is to create a discrepancy between a person's appearance/race/class position and her accent in order to generate a comical effect: for example, an expensively dressed Indian with a broad charou accent, or conversely, a character whose comportment and dress signals a charou but who, nonetheless, has a clipped lahnee accent. These two techniques are often combined to generate a comical situation. It is, argues Bergson, the elementary separation of gesture from action that allows gesture to assume its own and often absurd form qua alienation from conscious intent: "we may allow our sympathy or our aversion to glide along the line running from feeling to action and become increasingly interested. About gesture, however, there is something explosive, which awakes our sensibility when on the point of being lulled to sleep and, by thus rousing us up, prevents our taking matters seriously. Thus, as soon as our attention is fixed on gesture and not on action, we are in the realm of comedy" (2007, 45).

The comic effect of both these techniques draw on what Freud, in his work on jokes and humor, calls "difference [*Differenz*] between the two cathectic expenditures—one's own and the other person's as estimated by empathy" (1989, 242). Freud continues, "[A] person appears comic to us if, in comparison with ourselves, he makes too great an expenditure on his bodily functions and too little on his mental ones . . . our laughter expresses a pleasurable sense of the superiority we feel in relation to him" (242). These performances of an open discrepancy between the person and the gesture affords the ordinary township dweller the possibility of inhabiting two simultaneous positions: first, the position of the enlightened and educated Indian who can feel "a sense of superiority" when charou ways and accents are ridiculed; second, the position of the charou laughing at herself and at the absurdities of family conflicts, petty jealousies, narrow-mindedness, and the ridiculous ambition of the lahnee. This in turn allows for two simultaneous pleasures: the ridiculing of the charou as the past and the concomitant celebration of the achievements of the community away from charoudom, and the mourning of the loss of that same past and its more innocent and authentic pleasures.

Let us take a final step in order to properly assess the function of the comical in charou life. Ridicule and derision are not just (self-)redemptive acts, as Billig points out; they are also driven by a genuine enjoyment of seeing someone else being humiliated (2001, 27). Zupančič argues that the central pivot of the comic is when someone fools herself into sincerely believing in something utterly false and behaving in accordance with this deception. Here it is not the falsity of belief, but the sincerity of belief, the full identification with a gesture or a posture and the lack of consciousness of self-deception, which is comical (2008, 43–60).

In contemporary South Africa, comedy has become a new kind of exchangeable currency and a shorthand way of dealing with otherwise unspeakable "truths" about the other. The comic is the de-masking of the pretense of being something other than what you actually are—something different from your own body and appearance—and to laugh at the way the past, the primitive, the venal, and the outright lie literally sticks out of people and reveals itself almost as a mechanical dimension of human conduct.[33]

When a charou tries to behave as if he is actually a proper Indian, or merely an elderly human being, as with Bala and Peru, these inhabitations inevitably fail because a "stereotyped content" acts almost as a mechanical doll inside the human frame. The comical element is that none of these figures are actually in control of themselves. They are not even fully human but are moved by forces and desires far beyond, behind, and outside of themselves. Charou ways keep coming up in them and expose them as fundamentally not in control of their own selves. The theme that "I am not me" or that "the Other (which in fact is my own past) acts in me in spite of myself" are very strong themes in current Indian comedy and joking in Durban.

Charou humor, in short, revolves around a basic theme of alienation from, and aspiration toward, a sovereign cultural self that one never possessed. The comical lies in the obvious enjoyment of this alienation, the full and blinkered identification with the less-than-perfect being known as a charou, who is cohabiting with constant and naive aspirations to actually be a proper Indian. The humor is, in other words, deeply melancholic in nature. The laugh stands in for the act of mourning, as if both gestures are unsure of their legitimacy. Here we are back in the realm of the everyday as a surreptitious, alienated, and non-ontological space where words have no home as such. In the charou world, the home of words consists not in being connected with others, but in the bittersweet laugh that follows any sincere attempt of words and their enunciators to pretend to be at home.

Charou 4 Eva: Domesticity Lost and Refound

Today, the township and the figure of the charou have been transformed from a space of incomplete modernity and deracination to a space of nostalgia, of the "hood" remembered with all its quaint and funny characters. As in the case of Cato Manor, which was lost to Africans and subsequent removals, today the space of Chatsworth as the home of the charou is gradually being lost. This time the cause is migration of Africans into the area, and to the exodus of most of the younger and successful members of the Indian community. The original houses and the extended families were lost during the forced removals and thus reenacted in Chatsworth. Today, the charou, his jokes, and his style are being lost and remembered in multiple ways. The recently launched website Chatsworth Live has a large number of links and sections—community forum, complaints, debates, notice boards—but it is the section with jokes that takes up the most space and has the most hits. Not all the jokes are original and far from all deal with charous. But it is significant that the most recurrent reference to Chatsworth and charoudom is through the trope of the risqué joke.

Another website called Proudly Indian explains under the entry "charou": "A Charou refers to an Indian. Mainly a South African Indian in this case. The name charou is derived from 'char,' a slang meaning 'brown.' The term charou in fact is a slang in itself." This is followed by a dictionary of charou slang with key terms explained in Standard English.[34] Another recent website is called Charou 4 Eva and is run by a South African Indian who recently migrated to Australia. The site states, "This website is dedicated to everything Charou. Since I left South Africa I missed what I call 'The Charou Life.' So I decided to create a webpage with all Charou content. This is dedicated to all the charous who left South Africa and are feeling homesick. Remember, never ever forget your roots!" This website also has a dictionary of Chatsworth expressions and a long explanation of what is typically *char*:

> But we charous would prefer some thitha mutton curry and roti OR sugar beans and roti. MMMMMMmmmm . . . Lucker Chow! . . . We have our boxers underneath our Le-Vi's jeans and a facecloth and gonie in our back pocket. . . . Our accent is unlike any other in the world. We speak English, but very different from these vettoes. . . . We charous have a lot of respect for adults, mainly our Mother and Father. No matter what we think of an adult we respect and obey

them. The biggest insult that u can tell a charou is to swear his mother. If you do, consider yourself dead.

Charoudom is in the process of becoming one of several vanishing objects among Indians in South Africa; it is no longer the unreflexive, popular practices of yesteryear, but is now a fully sublated and sentimentalized, even cuddly, street version of "our culture." However, as we will see in the following chapters, the actual practices of charous constantly get in the way of this procedure.

CHAPTER 3

Charous and Ravans

A STORY OF MUTUAL NONRECOGNITION

THE RELATIONSHIP BETWEEN INDIANS AND AFRICANS IN SOUTH AFRICA, AND IN particular in the province of KwaZulu-Natal, is a strange story of mutual nonrecognition. It is neither misrecognition nor lack of presence but nonrecognition, by which I mean a willed incomprehension derived from a lack of desire, intimacy, and respect. In Hegelian terms, I propose that Indians and Zulus in this colonial province never constituted their identities through actually "seeing" each other, by deciphering each other's gaze, or by "desiring the desire of the other." Despite 150 years of "apprehensive coexistence," these communities never developed regular forms of conviviality or commensality, not to mention intermarriage.

To put it starkly, the relations between Zulus and Indians have historically been mediated through white power, gaze, and presence, despite the starkly anti-Indian sentiments that to this day pervade the white population of the province. This relative invisibility and nonrecognition of other dominated groups, except through (hostile) colonial mediations and their apportioning of patronage and punishment, is intrinsic to most forms of colonialism but particularly striking in this case. In a brief section on Hegel in *Black Skin, White Masks*, Fanon presents a surprisingly conciliatory version of the dialectic of recognition: "At the foundation of Hegelian dialectic, there is an absolute reciprocity which must be emphasized. . . . It is in the degree to which I go beyond my own immediate being that I apprehend the other . . . as more than a natural reality." Only by an active act of recognition can one restore to the other "human reality in-itself-for-itself" (1967, 217–18). Such active acts were not only absent in Natal but they seemed to be blocked by the very structure of colonial rule. Both Africans and Indians were locked in intense battles of recognition with the colonial master in distinct ways, but neither could recognize each other directly, only as categorical strangers. To the African, the Indian was a form of impostor, an undeserving accomplice of colonial rule, a man of color trying to assert his place in a land that was not his own. To Indians, the Zulus were of the land but incomprehensible, an unnerving gaze and presence that framed and also disturbed their constant struggle to be recognized by the colonial masters as belonging to the land that they lived on. In both cases, it was only the white gaze, whether paternalistic or antagonistic, that was able to accord to each group a sense of recognition, however incomplete.

Among Indians, a commonly used term for Africans is *ravans*, referring to the black demon king of the South, Ravana, who kidnapped Lord Ram's wife Sita in the epic Ramayana. Ravana is big, fearsome, and proud, and belongs to another world: his kingdom in the South. The term captures the sense of the African world as alien, distant, threatening, violent, and peopled by strong and violent sexual predators who are consumed by uncontrolled bodily drives. It is a world that appears unrefined in terms of food, rituals, and custom—a world often described as intertwined with an awesome but dangerous African nature.[1] While derived from European forms of exoticism and primitivism, Indian views of Africans seem devoid of the attraction toward nature and the innocence of the primitive that was at the heart of the white colonial paternalist relationship with African culture and customs. Wealthier Indians have engaged in a certain paternalistic care for their African employees, but most Indians see the African worlds as unfathomable, a form of dark matter where the dialectic of recognition stops as it reflects nothing; the gaze is simply absorbed and disappears.

Africans represent a compelling and omnipresent gaze, an uncanny shadow, a constant reminder of the precariousness of an existence literally at the edge of the bush. The identity of Africans and nature literally merged when areas of bush or dense vegetation along the slopes at the edge of the township were described to me as uncanny places where criminals lurk and where informal settlements of Africans were likely to appear.

Such ideas resonate strikingly well with widespread hostility and nonrecognition of Indians among many Zulus. Here, Indians were often referred to as parasites and thieves, as people who pretended to be white but did not deserve the respect given to whites, as aliens, and as gluttonous, unmanly cowards who did not even deserve to be properly looked at or recognized. When an editorial in the largest Zulu daily *Illanga* in February 1999 called for "a new Idi Amin to be born from the womb of a Zulu woman," it reflected a sentiment more widespread than the official denials would have it; a sentiment that resonated with a long history of apprehension vis-à-vis the figure of the Indian trader (a figure that remains a dominant metaphor of Indianness), and a widely shared view of Indians as opportunistic "fence-sitters" and people who lived off the land without having rights to it. Over the years, many

Zulu friends and acquaintances expressed reservations about my study. Why Indians? Were they not a form of parasites and collaborators with whites? Why not real South Africans?

Through an account of the long-standing structure of the appre-hensive coexistence, as well as violent conflicts between Africans and Indians in the twentieth century, I try to arrive at a diagnosis of the specificities of Indian race thinking in everyday life. In the second half of the chapter I explore how racialized anxieties are reproduced in pub-lic spaces in the postapartheid city.

AMAKULA AND AMAZULU ON THE COLONIAL ESTATES

In their fine documentary study of the lives of indentured laborers in South Africa, Ashwin Desai and Goolam Vahed argue that the contacts between Indian and Zulu laborers on the vast sugar estates of colonial Natal were scarce and often hostile.[2] Indentured labor had been re-cruited to improve productivity and weaken the bargaining position of the local Zulus, who the planters saw as a proud and "martial race" unfit for the dullness of manual labor. J. R. Wilson, who came from a sugar estate north of Durban, was thrilled with the arrival of Indian labor in 1860: "The Coolies, although not as physically strong as the kaffirs, do on the whole a better day's work, as they are not only diligent and regu-lar, but they economise their strength, and finish their appointed task in a much more satisfactory manner . . . their capacities for devouring food are happily much less than the Zulus."[3]

There is also substantial evidence that mutual hostility between Indians and Zulus was encouraged and deployed by planters who in keeping with the prevailing prejudice in the Indian colony generally regarded Indians as "cowardly" and "weak" but also scheming and con-niving (Desai and Vahed 2007, 179). Africans were seen as strong and proud but primitive and in need of constant surveillance and a firm hand. Foremen and *sirdars* (overseers) on the plantations were recruited among the indentured Indians, while Zulus were recruited as police-men and watchmen. Planters encouraged, or turned a blind eye to, the brutal punishment of Indian laborers meted out by these policemen, sometimes called whipping boys, which in turn further consolidated the Indian perception of Zulus as intrinsically violent.

There were a few intimate liaisons and marriages between Indians and Zulus in the early decades of the indenture system, but this virtu-ally ceased with the arrival of more Indian women at the end of the century. Tensions and competition between Zulu and Indian labor also persisted in urban areas. Several instances of violent clashes between the two groups in Durban were recorded, such as a bloody brawl in

1890 in the Railway Barracks of Durban that left deaths on both sides (Desai and Vahed 2007, 182).

As Indians spread throughout the province from the 1880s, they developed a variety of neighborly relations with Zulus as traders, employers, and fellow workers. Many of these relations were embedded in routines of everyday life and by physical proximity but rarely included affection or respect. There were misgivings about Indian traders in Zululand who exchanged liquor for sex with African women, and there were persistent suspicions among Zulus that the *amaKula* (coolies/Indians) *dukawallahs* (shopkeepers) overcharged and cheated their customers. The disdain for the Indian trader was widely shared by white planters and farmers, and was fueled by the broader antipathy against commerce and other "parasites" that was strong throughout South Africa and other parts of the imperial world at the time.[4] Indian traders inside the African reserves and settlements were generally fluent in isiZulu. There is no evidence, however, of an Indian embrace of Zulu customs and culture akin to the patronizing love for the purity and pride of Zulu culture among white planters and officials, and the affection many whites professed for the childlike simplicity of their African workers.[5] This combination of everyday proximity and continuing cultural distance, framed by the white sentimental embrace of Zuluness at a patronizing distance and their intense dislike of the Indian trader and the "coolies," marked the subsequent development of Zulu and Indian relations in the twentieth century.

A striking illustration was found in the Inanda area north of Durban where two pioneering institutions emerged in the early twentieth century within less than five miles' distance. John L. Dube, the first president of the ANC, who was educated at Oberlin College in Ohio, was, like Gandhi, an admirer of the industrial school of Booker T. Washington at Tuskegee Institute. In 1901, he established the Ohlange Institute in Inanda along similar lines.[6] Two years later, Gandhi created his Tolstoy-inspired Phoenix settlement on a nearby hilltop. Both institutions fought for the recognition of the rights of colonized people of color, and both of them were to exert seminal influence on the political consciousness among Indians and Zulus, respectively. While both men were acquainted and praised each other publicly, there was neither regular contact between the two institutions nor attempts at cooperation or alignments in the impending confrontation with the colonial government of Natal. Dube favored a gradual and cautious attitude vis-à-vis the colonial state, while Gandhi asserted the rights of Indians as subjects of the British Crown, thus fundamentally different in civilizational level and political aspiration from the African "natives." When he arrived in Durban in 1893, Gandhi's original assignment as a lawyer was to defend the commercial interests and the property-based voting rights of a few hundred prosperous Gujarati trading families. In his critical account of Gandhi's career in South Africa, the American historian James D. Hunt (who is extensively referenced on the ANC's website) quotes a speech made by Gandhi in 1896 in Bombay, in which he stated, "Ours is one continual struggle against a degradation sought to be inflicted upon us by the Europeans, who desire to degrade us to the level of the raw Kaffir whose occupation is hunting, and whose sole ambition is to collect a certain number of cattle to buy a wife with and, then, pass his life in indolence and nakedness."

Gandhi gradually broadened his ideas into a fully-fledged anticolonial program for India and Indians. There is little evidence, however, that Gandhi sought to forge broader alliances except with the organizations of coloreds in the Cape Province. In Natal and the Transvaal, he ceaselessly worked for separate treatment of Indians—initially the trading class and only later the so-called colonial-born and indentured laborers. In practice this meant separation from Africans, and it included a demonstrative loyalty to the British Crown. He organized an ambulance corps of Indians that assisted the British government during the Boer War, and in 1906 he set up a similar corps to assist the white authorities in Natal in their bloody repression of the Bambatha rebellion, the last Zulu resistance against colonial domination.[7]

The political and cultural horizon of both Gandhi and the founders of the ANC were firmly centered on seeking recognition and concessions from the colonial state. A horizontal alliance with other colonized people was simply not yet a part of political consciousness. Hunt concludes, "Gandhi began as a very conventional Victorian Indian, seeking accommodation and personal success within the British Empire. He shared the prejudices of his class concerning Black people, and his lifestyle and work kept him isolated from them. In this respect he became a segregationist, albeit a liberal one, arguing for a special status for his own people while objecting to the treatment given to the Black Africans."[8] Decades later, in his reflections on his experiences in South Africa, Gandhi portrayed African culture as simple and pure, but this never amounted to recognition of Africans as allies and equals in the quest for self-determination.[9]

It was only in the 1950s that more regular forms of alliances and cooperation between Indian and African organizations emerged in Natal and elsewhere in South Africa. As we will see, these strategic alliances, which were forged by the ANC and the two main Indian organizations in 1947,[10] happened against a backdrop of increasing political and social tension between whites, Africans, and Indians in and around Durban.[11]

DURBAN, JANUARY 1949: "THE LARGEST RACE RIOT IN THE WORLD"

At the heart of the rising tension between Zulus and Indians in Natal in the 1940s lay unresolved questions of land and dwelling. The city administration was not well prepared for the rapid growth of the city, and the large number of Africans working in the city faced hopelessly inadequate housing and transport facilities. They relied on a range of informal arrangements that were mainly provided by the Indian landowners at the outskirts of the city. Many Indians rented out land, shacks, and small houses to Africans and set up shops in informal settlements. Indians also began a range of bus and transport services across the city. Whites were employers, policemen, and overseers in full control of the city, but for needs such as housing, water, transport, and daily amenities, Zulu speakers encountered mainly Indians who controlled the lower end of the market. This gave rise to conflicts, particularly around the issue of the pricing of goods and services.

These tensions, triggered by a minor scuffle in an Indian-owned shop in the busy Victoria Street market, came to a head in mid-January 1949. An African boy was injured, and soon rumors spread among the thousands of Africans waiting for buses that he had been killed by the shopkeeper. Crowds began to attack Indians and to loot and burn Indian shops in the entire commercial area around Grey Street (*Daily News*, January 14, 1949). The police controlled the situation by evening but tension continued to simmer as rumors spread across the city. The next day thousands of African men armed with sticks, clubs, and spears gathered in large groups in the Grey Street area, Cato Manor, Clairwood, and many other areas dominated by Indians. Many of these men were mobilized through social networks such as boxing clubs, workers' hostels, and local ANC-affiliated activists.[12] In the following forty-eight hours, Indian homes and shops were attacked and burned, many people were killed, women and young girls were raped, and property was looted. The *Sunday Tribune* reporter wrote on January 16, "On the verandah of the Cato Manor police station yesterday lay a pile of corpses, grotesquely frozen into the positions in which they have died. Their contorted faces told me of their terror and agony when death came upon them. Some were burned, all were battered and mutilated. . . . As busloads of Natives passed the station the passengers leaned out, laughing and taunting the Indians. 'Just you wait,' they shouted in Zulu, 'we'll get you; you will die.'"[13]

The police reacted very slowly and regained control only two days later when reinforcements from the navy were brought in to quell the unrest. A policeman complained that "Natives resort to guerilla tactics . . . when the police arrive, the Natives flee, dropping their sticks.

They then appear to be peaceful bystanders until we leave. Then they renew their attacks."[14] In keeping with the general philosophy of colonial policing, the methods were brutal. The majority of the African casualties occurred as policemen opened fire on crowds and on looters in a deliberate attempt to demonstrate the overwhelming power and determination of the government. Several days after, smaller and scattered incidents occurred across the city, such as the killing of three unarmed Zulus by a group of Indians in a belated act of retribution in Clairwood.[15]

The scale and seriousness of the riots, which at the time were labeled the largest race riots ever in South Africa if not the world,[16] shocked and surprised everybody: 142 casualties, 1,087 seriously wounded, and thousands more bruised and traumatized, and almost 2,500 buildings and shops destroyed or damaged. Twenty-five thousand Indians gathered in refugee camps for months after the riots. Thousands had been involved across the city, and it was clear that the police and many whites in the city had actively encouraged the rioters. An eyewitness stated, "Europeans gather in office windows and on balconies watching the scene, regarding it with amusement. On the pavement a European comments: 'I am all for the Natives. Serves the Coolies right.' Europeans stand aside, spectators. They do not go to the aid of the Indians or try to restrain the natives" (Webb and Kirkwood, 1949). Another contemporary observer gave the following assessment to the official commission of inquiry into the riots: "The majority of Europeans took no active part in the incitement of Natives. Theirs was a passive role but it was a passive role having the most powerful positive consequences. The feeling was, and still is, very strong and articulate that Indians deserved what they got, and this feeling at the same time, and more especially since, has been translated to the Native mind" (van den Heever report 1949, 9; see also Calpin 1949).

The general anti-Indian atmosphere among many whites clearly played a part in creating a perception of impunity among many Africans. The local reporting of the riots in white-owned and controlled newspapers shows many forms of ambivalence at work. On the one hand, the conservative *Natal Mercury* reported with a certain satisfaction, "There was no animosity towards Europeans throughout the rioting" (January 17, 1949). The city authorities expected white sympathy for the rioters and a special order closed all bars and bottle stores in the city "to prevent young European men and women drinking and then visiting the disturbed areas and provoking fights and interfering with the police."[17]

At the same time, the rioters were represented in text and in photos as crazed savages who were out of control, and as a natural fury that the Indians had unleashed upon themselves by overcharging the natives and imprudently insulting the "Native pride" while also refusing to accept white rule and superiority. The Indian victims were portrayed as "pitiful," panic-stricken, and humiliated, but the major part of the coverage was devoted to the police, with admiring portraits of the heavily armed naval forces in dapper white uniforms. The *Sunday Post* showed a picture of a column of naval troops moving through the hilly terrain in the suburbs—reminiscent of similar pictures of European troops in punitive action in Zululand during the Bambatha rebellion in 1906— to track down "Native rioters." The same issue showed several pictures of young African men who had been shot dead by the troops. One of the captions read, with righteous satisfaction, "He joined the rioters, caught in the madness that infects a mob. But for him there will no more such moments of wild excitement. For him, this is the end."[18]

Immediately after the riots, a commission of inquiry was established to determine the course of events and assess the causes of the conflagration. The procedures adopted and the skewed nature of evidence drew much criticism, and none of the major Indian political organizations wanted to give evidence. Their critique of the mandate of the commission had led the chairman, F. P. van den Heever, to exclude them altogether and to dismiss their motives as that of "making propaganda—not to shed light but to engender heat" (1949, 2). The report of the commission revealed the depth of anti-Indian feeling and self-serving paternalism that pervaded the white elite at the time. The commission admitted that certain elements among whites had taken an active role in inciting riots, but refused to attribute this to racial bigotry. The commission stated, "During times of civil commotion one sees the same kinds of expression on the faces of spectators in Chicago, London or Paris. Most people love sensation and spectacle: to impute racial antagonism to those who watch any commotion would be to lose perspective . . . it must be clear that the women who went dancing up the street were degraded specimens of their race" (8).

The report also dismissed the allegations that anti-Indian statements and the campaign to expel Indians had played any role: "From their evidence [natives] it is clear that they were not motivated by outside influences" (10). Instead the commission took the line that many of the native grievances regarding overpricing, living conditions, and bad and overcrowded transport were indeed valid and that Indian "arrogance" and bad business practices were to blame for this. "The Native has always regarded the Indian as a stranger . . . but he regarded himself as the son of the soil. . . . Events in India had repercussions here. A certain type of Indian began to ride the high horse. [The Natives] keenly resented the air of superiority adopted toward them by the younger generation of Indians. Their comment upon the riots was: 'the Indians died cruelly, but, oh they had become so arrogant'" (12).

Predictably, the commission blamed the tsotsis and other antisocial elements, who they believed played a disproportional role in the "increasing lack of discipline" among the "urban Natives" (12). The commission also blamed the Indian organizations for "causing a feeling of unrest and dissatisfaction to stir among the Natives, always a dangerous course with a section of the community not yet ripe for responsibility. In the result, the Indians were hoist with their own petard" (12).

A major area of concern for the commission was the allegation of miscegenation. It was alleged that Indian men were taking advantage of Zulu women, using their superior monetary situation to seduce them "with motorcars and money." The commission accepted that this amounted to an insult to the "Zulu race pride" and turned this into an argument for a stricter policing, if not prohibition, of interracial liaisons in the future: "We have found this grievance to be one of the most powerful motives of anti-Indian feeling on the part of the Natives. If the provisions of the Immorality Act could be extended to illicit carnal intercourse between Natives and Indians it would in some measure repress this evil" (14). The report concluded by turning to the negative portrayal of South African race policies in the foreign press. The contemporary coverage of the riots was already keenly aware, and somewhat irked by, the general criticism of South African policies throughout the world. The commission concluded that the Durban riots pointed to the necessity of further segregation: "Contrary to the prevalent opinion abroad, the average Native is a keen supporter of segregation. He realizes that he is ill-equipped in the fight for survival which has become so sharp in recent times. Consequently he demands residential, racial and economic segregation" (21).

The very last paragraph of the report purported to represent the views of the impoverished Indian majority who was also in favor of segregation but whose authentic voices were silenced by the wealthy Indians. As a result they "were afraid to give evidence, even in camera." In spite of this van den Heever did not hesitate to paraphrase their alleged position (or perhaps merely the commission's own fantasy of the average obedient Indian) and blamed the well-to-do Indians—the always-reviled trading classes—for being above their station: "'The privileged 30 percent made all the noise and stirred sleeping forces. They exploit us like they exploit the Natives. They have the motorcars and the wealth . . . they fired revolvers at the natives and further infuriated the mob against us.' These things are muttered by less privileged Indians, and they are talking of lynching those of their race who overcharge or associate with Native women" (21).

The Durban riots were complex, both in their causes and consequences. Jan Smuts, who had lost the election to the National Party
(NP) the year before, was quick to call it the "First fruits of the new
Government's policy,"[19] while the National Party asserted that the riots
proved the necessity of permanent segregation as hammered out in the
Group Areas Act of 1950. The minister of the interior, T. E. Donges,
stated, "The Durban riots of last year . . . show the dangers of residential
juxtaposition for the peace and quiet of the country. Consequently, the
solution of separate areas for different races, compulsorily enforced if
necessary, is not a novel idea."[20]

Separation of Africans and Indians did indeed happen after the
riots, particularly in Cato Manor where much of the looted property
was taken over by Africans, but none of the contentious issues of land,
trade, and transport had disappeared. Many Indian families returned to
their land and property and rebuilt their lives, but now with more care
and apprehension. Shops had armed watchmen, and African customers
were rare in the first years after the riots.[21] Another significant change
was that the number of African residents in Cato Manor increased dramatically, and the area began to be seen as the African heart of Durban.
The city council was quick to grant a number of new trading and transport licenses to Africans, who by 1952 numbered 105, while the Indian
licenses remained at 26, as before the riots.

One of the factors behind this was the strong anti-Indian opinion
that emerged among urban Zulus and in the more radical ANC Youth
League, both during and after the riots. This opinion was firmly focused
on the Indian trader as the focus of resentment. The Zulu-language
publication *Inkundla ya Bantu* had celebrated the "Heroes of the Riots"
at the time. In the aftermath, the events were widely referred to as *impi*,
a war that the Zulus had won (Soske 2009, 120–23). In subsequent debates between Indian and African intellectuals, strong voices, such as
the influential editor of *Ilanga*, H.I.E. Dhlomo, portrayed the riots as
a form of logical historical justice visited upon the parasitical Indian
trader (129–32). The ANC and other organizations helped set up co-
operatives and so-called buying clubs. One of the more high-profile
ones was named Zondizitha (Hate the Enemies), which promoted the
stores that had been taken over from Indians. Another and more important organization was the Hlanganani (literally, "get together") Association, which organized annual commemorations of the riots as a
victory for Zulus, in particular, and Africans more generally (Kirk 1983,
133). Leading members of the ANC supported these initiatives with a
fervor that indicated the depth of anti-Indian feeling among many Zulu
speakers at the time.

The claiming of Cato Manor as the heart of a new urban Zulu culture also proved a major obstacle in the attempts to coordinate African and Indian political campaigns throughout the 1950s. Almost thirty years later, then president of the ANC Youth League, C. A. Champion, revealed this attitude in an interview: "I had two minds but I supported it [the Doctors' Pact of 1947] because it was supported by the ANC . . . in 1949 the Indians deserved to be assaulted. They had become too big for their shoes. They were too proud. They looked upon us as nothing except a laborer and a kaffir" (Webster 1977, 51–52). To this day, the 1949 riots and Cato Manor continue to be a controversial and touchy subject, because the relations between the two groups and their historical memories are so separated and contradictory that they have emerged into two separate mytho-historical complexes.

CATO MANOR AND THE URBAN ZULU

In the 1950s Cato Manor developed into a vibrant home for a mainly Zulu urban culture in which the ANC enjoyed increasing influence and support. The neighborliness with Indians remained distant and the number of residents big enough to sustain a range of informal institutions, such as the profitable brewing of beer sold by women in local shebeens. The shebeen became a central node in ongoing debates and controversies around family forms, love, style, and relationships in Cato Manor. With access to money and a measure of educational facilities, women gained a new and stronger position than in the rural kraals. In his incisive cultural history of Cato Manor in the 1950s, Edwards argues, "Women had ambivalent attitudes towards shebeen queens; while scorning them for trading in liquor and keeping their husbands and lovers in debt, they would also laugh admiringly at the shebeen queen's ability to keep their husbands thin, cowardly and dominated" (1996, 120).

The city authorities wanted to dismantle and discourage the relatively autonomous urban life in Cato Manor. The Group Areas Act involved construction of new African townships farther away from the city, in KwaMashu and Umlazi. Cato Manor, or Mkhumbane as it was called in isiZulu, called for a solution. One method was to undermine the shebeen economy. In the late 1950s, a range of men-only beer halls had been opened and licensed by the city council across Durban in an attempt to rein in the shebeen economy.[22] This sharpened already existing tensions around the growing independence of women. The initiative aided a reassertion of male authority in the new township spaces that promised a new and exclusively African urban modernity: "To the men, the beer-hall offered the prospect of drunken male solitude. The she-been was the public reminder of the sexual and emotional gender pattern of the shacklands. In the late 1950s all the symbolic rituals of the shebeen were stripped away. Drinking did this" (Edwards 1996, 126).

Mkhumbane was indeed the heart of a new urban Zulu culture, and its dislocating effects on gender hierarchies and cultural mores had profoundly unnerved many intellectuals for several decades prior to the riots. Soske shows that anxieties about the uncontrolled sexuality of the new urban Zulu woman had occupied Zulu writers and preachers, such as Isaiah Shembe, Sithole, and Dhlomo since the 1930s. Their supposed liaisons with wealthy Indian men, and rumors of widespread miscegenation, were symptoms of this new state of immorality. This was seen as a stain on the honor of Zulu culture, which collectively humiliated Zulu men (Soske 2009, 149–70). The sexual violence against Indian women during the riots must be understood in the light of this atmosphere.

These many long-simmering conflicts came to a head in June 1959 when the municipal authorities responded to a typhoid epidemic by clearing a large number of shebeens in Cato Manor. In response, hundreds of women armed with sticks and other weapons invaded a beer hall to chase out the men. Later, a larger beer boycott was initiated with support from ANC and affiliated organizations, and attacks on beer halls began across the city. Events escalated and culminated in massive police actions in Cato Manor in which several people were killed and hundreds arrested. This sealed the fate of Cato Manor and the forced removals proceeded swiftly in the following years. By 1960, thousands of informal shacks had been cleared. The brick houses were gradually cleared of their mainly Indian owners, most of whom never received compensation for their houses and landholdings. A total of 160,000 people were removed in a few years. Of these, at least a third were Indians.[23]

The vast area was never redeveloped. For three decades it remained an empty void of hilly grassland that separated the city center from its western and southern suburbs and townships. Around this void emerged a range of memories and popular mythologies. Cato Manor had indeed had two parallel worlds that coexisted with mutual apprehension, if not incomprehension. With the structural violence of forced removals, a traumatic wound and loss was inflicted, but this loss could never be fully shared. The radically differential readings of the events in January 1949 blocked any shared Indian-African myth from emerging. Instead, two parallel interpretations, both of them mixing living memory, political fantasy, and popular mythology, were projected onto the grassy, undulating hills that cut through the city.

For the Africans, it was the loss of the (ancestral) land of Mkhumbane, which had gradually been won back from illegitimate Indian landowners during the heady days of January 1949. It was also the loss of a vibrant urban culture and the mythical home of the large ANC-initiated resistance campaigns in the 1950s, including the beer hall riots. The African narrative of Cato Manor begins in the 1930s and ends in 1960, and barely recognizes the presence of Indians. This is also true of scholarly work and official representations. Edwards's extremely well-informed work on the area barely mentions the presence of Indians.[24] In an entire volume describing Durban as the "People's City," there is not a single mention of Indian presence in Durban. The role of Indians in the city's history is also conspicuously downplayed in the official history of apartheid that is represented at the KwaMuhle Museum in Durban. This dovetails in the 1990s with a larger effort toward Africanization of the city, its street names, its history, and its memory and character.

In the past decade Cato Manor has played an important role in this effort to reclaim Durban as an African space. Informal settlements sprang up in the area in the 1990s, and there were extended and difficult negotiations between some Indian landowners and the city council about the future of the area. The question of entitlement to land and the tense relationship between African tenants and Indian landowners came up in the adjacent area of Clare Estate. Here, the long-standing practice of "shack-farming" on old Indian freehold plots, which was so central to Cato Manor, was reenacted from the late 1980s onward. This had generated explosive conflicts concerning soaring crime rates and the question of whether the thousands of informal shacks should be legalized or simply removed. A high-ranking ANC man who was campaigning in the shack-lands in the run-up to the general elections in May 1999 told me that this was not a legal issue, only a political one: "These Indians say they own this land, but that is only true according to the white man's law. In reality, we don't recognize this law and none of the people living here in these degrading conditions deserve to live like that. This is our land; this is their land [the shack-dwellers] and these Indians have no business taking money from them."

The highly charged and symbolic weight of Cato Manor made it perfect for a high-profile launch of the ANC's new development program for both the city and the nation. It became the first area in the city to see large-scale building of the so-called RDP houses, the modest houses designed to replace informal settlements that were the most visible part of the ambitious Reconstruction and Development Plan (RDP) adopted by the ANC in 1995. Later, private investments flowed into various high-profile housing schemes, the new Luthuli Central Hospital,

Figure 6. CATO MANOR TODAY

radio station Siyaya FM, and a range of cultural institutions. Cato Manor has also become part of the "township tourism" projects that have proliferated across the country. In 2003, Mandela inaugurated the so-called Umkhumbane Urban Reality Tourism Trail, which takes tourists through the history and legacy of Cato Manor.

Indians are briefly mentioned on the glossy website's bullet-point history of the area, which mentions "a hybrid, vibrant culture developed in the 1940s" but also speaks about the riots of 1949 as an "anti-Indian war" wherein Indians lost their property to Africans, and only returned later as "landlords collecting rent." The timeline ends somewhat hyperbolically with the "2052: Umkhumbane Centenary is broadcast to a global audience of billions to celebrate World Peace day."[25] In this version of the Cato Manor mytho-history, its real existence only began in 1952, three years after the riots.

THE INDIAN "1949 SYNDROME" AS A SOCIAL TEXT

The Indian mythology of Cato Manor is that of the single most traumatic event among South African Indians. The central theme is the white betrayal that unleashed the uncanny and unintelligible force of African wrath and violence on them. In this version, an idealized and proper "Indian culture" had supposedly existed in organic community spaces where people had built houses and compounds for their large extended families, as in Clairwood, Point, and around Durban harbor. At the height of apartheid rule, Durban's authorities considered the possibility of resettling Indians in Cato Manor, but no decisive moves were made and the area remained largely empty. This in turn only cemented the sense of white betrayal and duplicity.[26]

Early on in my fieldwork, a young Indian professional, Satish, offered to take me through the area. He was personally and professionally vested in retrieving the history of Indians in Durban. The crime wave in South Africa was at its peak. Stories of hijackings and murders in and around the deserted grasslands of Cato Manor abounded. Satish was nervous and locked the car doors as we made our way through the hilly terrain while he told me about the dense and lively Indian life that had once unfolded here. Clusters of old and derelict houses were still inhabited by a few hundred Indian families. The houses were formally owned by the city's Department of Community, and the occupants had become tenants in the houses they often built themselves. There were also patches of informal shack settlements at the very entrance to the area. Along the highway that was cut through Cato Manor in the 1960s, foundations for the new RDP houses were being laid.

Everything else was empty on that sunny afternoon, with no people in sight, apart from an old woman carrying firewood. Only tall grass and bushes were to be seen. We stopped by one of the old temples that had been spared when the bulldozers had moved in. It was in a state of disrepair, and I asked Satish why people were afraid to come here. "It is very dangerous. People are killed on this road, and if we start rebuilding this temple or reclaiming all the land we owned, they will attack us. The Africans say they own this place and they have the support of the government." I remarked that everything seemed empty, almost like a nature reserve. As I began to get out of the car, he vehemently told me, "But they are hiding in the bush. If we get out, someone will come, don't do it."

It was clear from Satish's reaction, and that of many others I met, that the area itself had become imbued with danger, a looming fear of death and violence that was lurking in the bush and the grass in the form of African men who were supposedly ready to attack. Africans were equated with nature as such, but also with the form of an uncanny spirit of looming revenge and sudden attack that was devoid of reason or clear cause.

The coexistence with Africans remains the unstable heart of the Indian narratives of Cato Manor. Over the years, many intellectuals and political activists have held forth Cato Manor as an example of the

Figure 7. Old temple in Cato Manor

harmonious relationship between Indians and Africans before apartheid. Yet the split memories of 1949 block any attempt at framing the story of Cato Manor as analogous to the mixing and tolerance of the famous District Six in Cape Town, the "Ur-home" of modern colored culture in South Africa (Coombes 2003). Cato Manor has not seen a concerted attempt at recuperating property and a shared past, as in the case of District Six (Beyers 2009).

Cato Manor and African Indian relations also appear in the rich archive of popular theater. The most well-known example is the popular play called *1949 and Other Cato Manor Stories*, which was staged in 1990 by Ronnie Govender, one of Durban's foremost and popular playwrights and writers. The play, which is based on short stories of Govender's experiences of growing up in Cato Manor in the 1950s (1996), has become iconic of a certain genre of memory of Cato Manor among Indians. Like Govender's other stories, it is marked by two recurrent features: first, they unfold in an entirely Indian milieu, and the main characters are funny, over-the-top, and charming Indians in all their eccentricity. The setting is an entirely Indian geography of Durban and includes other Indian areas such as Isipingo and Grey Street. Second, white people appear as powerful figures—policemen, employers, and officials—while in most cases Africans appear as quite distant figures who are devoid of real individuality.

The protagonist of the story *1949* is a young Zulu-speaking man, Dumisane, who rents a small outbuilding from an Indian, Mr. Maniram. We follow him on his happy morning walk to the garage where he works for a white man, Osborne. On the way he passes the house of the garrulous and Zulu-speaking Naidoo, the Jewish shop, and so on. Dumisane is a good worker who enjoys the kind, paternalist care of his employer, as when he is invited to Osborne's big house to sing for his guests. We only see a glimpse of another and unkind Osborne when a Muslim family moves into a house opposite the garage: "Osborne was livid, 'Why, in God's name, don't these people go and live with the rest in their own areas? Why do they insist on living with us?' . . . it was the only time Dumi had heard him swearing, 'Bloody bastards! Give them an inch and they will take a yard. They should send them all back to India. They breed like damn flies'" (Govender 1996, 113). On this particular morning, lots of Africans are waiting to buy kerosene. An Indian customer with whom Dumisane is friendly tells him in isiZulu that there is trouble in town, that Indian shops had been attacked, and that the whites are helping by ferrying tsotsis armed with sticks and kerosene out to Cato Manor and Riverside. Later in the day, Osborne calls his staff together and tells them in isiZulu, "This is your country. We white people have come to improve it for you. We have built hospitals, roads and shops. These people have only come to make money. They have houses. You haven't. You can tell your friends that they can have all the paraffin they want, free of charge" (115).

As Dumisane returns home, he is shattered by the events and finds his Indian landlords "huddled together in their bedroom," scared by the fires and the sound of Zulu war chants. Dumisane offers to hide the Maniram family in their small outbuilding while he waits outside for the crowd to approach. He tells the crowd that the *amaKula* have fled but they do not believe him, and the Indian family is found in the outbuilding. The mob, gripped by the "savagery that lurks eternally in the human heart" attacks and kills everybody, including Dumisane and his family. "There was no pity, no reason in the hearts of these malleable souls, held captive by minds more savage in their cunning—the cunning on which empires have been built" (Govender 1996, 117).

This interpretation reiterated the long-established notion of white betrayal and incitement as the cause of the riots, and redeemed Africans of real responsibility, as mere "malleable souls" who were manipulated to do the dirty work. Dumisane is also a malleable soul, simple and quite naive in his understanding of the world, but basically a good and moral human being who risks and loses his life by acting as a true neighbor. Yet the drama and the struggle are never about Africans. For Govender, it is between Indians and whites, a struggle for space, dignity, and recognition. In 1980, Govender described how after a happy and carefree childhood, where he felt at one with "my native hearth," he discovered that he was a "strange animal officially referred to as an 'Indian' South African. . . . I was an outsider in the land of my birth . . . the need for an identity, for a pride in my being became urgent and I discovered the glories of Dravidian civilization."[27] Yet he rejected cultural chauvinism on the part of any group ("those smug little Indians with their Ravi Shankar records") and concluded his essay by asserting that all he wanted to claim was that "this land is mine."

In many of the modern Indian plays and writing, the African appears as a mere bystander, an innocent, authenticating, but fundamentally inscrutable presence. In Hegelian terms, the African does not exist as himself in his full individuality and unfolded desire for the Indian. He can be recognized in his humanity only through the actions of the master—as a fellow victim or as a duped and manipulated instrument for others. The question that remains unanswered at the end of *1949* is why Dumisane risks his life. Because of the friendship and respect accorded to him by Indians? Or, more likely, because of his simple humanity, untainted by cunning or reason?

In Kriben Pillay's play *Looking for Muruga* from 1994, the accent shifted toward explaining racism as a form of class alienation. The play is set in a bar around the barman Muruga, the proverbial Indian waiter, full of small jokes, wisecracks, and stories. The central dialogue is between Sherwin, an aspiring writer and intellectual who becomes fascinated with Muruga's earthy wisdom, lightness of being, and capacity to understand and deal with the world through wit. Dante, a student of Indian dance, is the African in the play, but he is marginal to the dialogue and merely appears at the beginning and the end of the play. Yet, Dante is a crucial "absent presence" whose sentences in isiZulu and jovial conversations with Muruga permeate the entire setup as a form of background canvas. Sherwin, the intellectual, has lost the ability to connect with his own past—which is why he wants to write about Muruga, the quintessential charou—but he has also lost the ability to effortlessly relate to the African world, which is represented by Dante.

At this point, the supposedly organic connections between working-class Indians and Africans in the past (such as in Cato Manor) had become a firm, underlying assumption for playwrights and public intellectuals. Yet the work of translation of Africans into intelligible humanity still had to take firm root. Previous African figures were made intelligible through conditions of exploitation, or Dumisane's naive humanity. In *Looking for Muruga*, Dante, the Zulu, demonstrates his capacity for full humanity by submitting to the disciplines of an intricate Indian art form mastered by very few.

There is a remarkable correspondence between this canon of plays and writing, and the personal narratives I encountered from older Indians who had grown up in Cato Manor. Few of those stories ever mentioned the presence of Africans, unless specifically asked. The following fragments, told by two middle-aged men, are quite typical of the way the supposed racial harmony is remembered:

> We lived in this kind of compound with a number of houses where my uncles, aunties, and brothers lived around a little yard. There the women would cook and we children would play. In one corner, but outside the yard, there was an African family living. They rented the house and the man worked for my uncle in his little shop. We never had any problems with them—in fact we children were sometimes sent to their house with food and sweets if we had a celebration or a festival. But I remember that I thought this black man and some of the friends that came to him were very big. I guess that we boys were a little afraid of them. I did not like going down to that corner in the evening when you could hear them sing and sometimes shout very loudly.

Another man who grew up in Cato Manor related the following:

> My father was a gardener, and every Saturday he would go to Crawford market with my uncle in their old van. I remember sitting in the front with them while our laborers, Africans, would sit on top of all the boxes with vegetables while they would sing in their language. My father would speak to them in Fanagalo, ask them to unload the van, and carry stuff around at the market. All day they would sit next to the stall waiting for the next order . . . I did not speak to them; I did not know their language. But I liked their way of laughing, and sometimes we played mischief and played football with old cabbages and things like that.

Most of the stories I have heard from Cato Manor seem to repeat this pattern of Africans being "intimate strangers"—living next to Indians, working for them, renting from them, or being customers in Indian shops—but never being familiar or being invited into Indian homes or social gatherings. Soske suggests that the events of 1949 changed the relationships between Indians and Africans within the Indian households. African men were now kept out of houses, away from Indian women, and generally treated with contempt. "You were served your food like a dog," one of Soske's sources put it (2009, 189).

The memories of 1949 are still in circulation and are now settled as narrative frames that externalize the event by making it into the doings of anonymous tsotsis, "people from outside," not "our blacks" or "our workers" who were involved in the attacks. These forms of externalization, like that of white instigation, may be motivated by an avoidance of a personal story—too painful or intimate to narrate—or simply that the personal narrative over time has been subsumed by the larger standard narrative.[28]

The combination of intimacy and distance in the relationship between Africans and Indians undoubtedly reflects that the significant relationships in Cato Manor were overwhelmingly economic and unequal: African workers and Indian employers, Indian shopkeepers and African customers, cleaners, assistants, and so on. The distance was reflected in the use of Fanagalo—the command language that developed in the mines of Johannesburg—which is made up of Tswana, Zulu, Xhosa, and Afrikaans words in a simple and unkind command language without nuances or room for complex sensibilities.

The "1949 syndrome" was a term that was used in newspapers and public debates in the 1990s to refer to a collective psychological condition of the Indian community as a whole in its response to the conservative warnings of *swaart gevaar* (black danger) in the dying days of apartheid. However, the fear of sudden and irrational African violence had been stoked in a variety of ways over decades. Idi Amin's expulsion of Indians in 1971–72 from Uganda reverberated among Indian communities across Africa. In Natal, the long-standing leader of the conservative Zulu party Inkatha, Gatsha Buthelezi, had caused consternation among Indian leaders and activists on numerous occasions during the 1970s by questioning Gandhi's pro-British role in the Bambatha rebellion and by issuing thinly veiled threats that 1949 could repeat itself if Indians "lost their balance."[29]

THE SYNDROME AFFIRMED: INANDA 1985

In August 1985, thousands of Zulus invaded the old Indian freehold settlement in Inanda, burned and looted houses, and destroyed Gandhi's Phoenix settlement and the area around it known as Bambaiya (Bombay). Hundreds of Indian families lost everything and were put up in camps in nearby Phoenix Township for several months after. The area remained a highly volatile informal settlement that was marred by bloody factional fighting and clashes between Inkatha and the ANC until the early 1990s.

The sudden invasion was related to long-standing tensions over land and the so-called shack-farming—renting land and providing basic amenities to shack-dwellers—that Indian and African landowners had practiced for years. Factional fighting between ANC and Inkatha-affiliated groups and the constant jockeying for space in the vast shack-lands of Inanda only added to the underlying tensions. In addition, the area had officially been declared as "African," and the authorities asserted that the presence of non-African landowners (Indians) blocked any further development of the area (Hughes 1987, 345–46).

Three Indians, and many more Africans, were killed and hundreds wounded in the conflagration, which lasted almost a week. Contrary to 1949, the target of the attack was initially property, shops, land, and houses rather than people. Casualties and severe violence only occurred on the third and fourth day of the riots when a self-styled Indian vigilante group, the Phoenix Boys, mounted a counterattack in order to take back the Phoenix settlement. Later the same day, a large Inkatha *impi* attacked the area, ostensibly to resolve the situation by establishing their superiority. Bloody infighting between the UDF and Inkatha factions ensued throughout the following day (Hughes 1987, 347–52).

Two days after the initial attacks, groups of Indians tried to return with a fleet of trucks to retrieve possessions from their homes. They were met by a large stone-throwing crowd at the entrance to Inanda and were forced to return.[30] The chairman of the House of Delegates, Amichand Rajbansi, was heavily criticized for not making good on his promise of escorting the evicted people back to their homes. Later that day, escorted by heavily armed police, some dozen families did return, only to find their homes completely burned and gutted. Their African neighbors claimed that the attack had been launched by tsotsis from outside and told reporters and policemen that their relations with their Indian neighbors had always been cordial (ibid.).

Among most Indians, however, the attack was seen as a replay of 1949, and the feverish reactions suggested the force of a deep and shared archive of fear. In the township of Phoenix, there were scenes of panic when rumors spread that gangs of marauding African thugs were about to attack the sprawling township. Thousands of panic-stricken residents gathered around the police station where heavily armed police with Casspirs and machine guns tried to assure the crowd that they would be protected against African attacks. In Indian areas south of the city, such as Chatsworth and Isipingo, and in the predominantly Indian towns of Tongaat and Verulam on the north coast, groups of Indian men armed themselves with firearms and began patrolling their neighborhoods in tense anticipation of an all-out replay of 1949.[31]

As the riots died down and the permanent Indian displacement from Inanda had become an indisputable fact, the expelled families questioned the conduct of the security forces in Inanda. Compared to the extremely harsh approach in Umlazi south of Durban during the same days, where security forces killed thirty-seven protesters, the approach in Inanda seemed "soft." It was soon assumed among most Indians that the government acted in accordance with an understanding with Inkatha, who tried to establish its superiority in the area.[32] This assumption of white instigation was supported by the perception among many Indians that it was Inkatha *impis* (traditional regiments), rather than police squads, that ultimately dispersed the rampaging crowds. Once again, African violence was interpreted as a wild and destructive force that had been unleashed and instigated by the superior cunning of the white regime.

This particular incident has received only cursory attention from intellectuals. It seemed to lend itself easily to a solidifying fear and racial prejudice amid the more conservative elements among Indians. Only in 2002 was the incident taken up explicitly by Rajesh Gopie in his play *Out of Bounds*, probably the most popular Indian play in South Africa ever. It was performed for Mandela in his residence and ran for years across the country and at theater festivals and venues in Europe and North America. The play tells the story of a boy's journey from an innocent childhood in Inanda through the township of Phoenix and eventually through university, to middle-class respectability and a white accent, and finally to the United States and an American girlfriend. His childhood is set within a noisy, warm, multigenerational household in Inanda that is organized around three brothers. The household and the narrator's world revolve around the grandmother and her beloved mango tree in the garden, and also around the much-loved African maid Togo.

Gopie movingly depicts how the boy experiences a painful contradiction between the brothers' idea of themselves as strong and brave at home and their repeated emasculation in the wider world. The outside world intervenes mercilessly in a few short but poignant moments that demonstrate that the narrator's aspirations and subjectivity matter precious little. One of these moments is the 1985 riots in Inanda that force the family off their land and into the desolate township of Phoenix. The riots, and the African rioters, are depicted as a natural force, a furious storm with no apparent cause that is unleashed upon a harmonious and wholesome Indian community life, uprooting and destroying it, a destruction poignantly symbolized by the falling mango tree, a preeminent symbol of reproduction, comfort, and fecundity outside the house.

Gandhi's settlement has recently been reconstructed and made into a national monument. Mandela decided to cast his vote there in 1999 to emphasize the ANC's indebtedness to Gandhi. The settlement features in what is now called the Inanda Heritage Trail, which also includes

Dube's Ohlange Institute. Today the Phoenix settlement is managed by a Zulu caretaker with a broad knowledge of Gandhi's life in South Africa. The area is a well-maintained and highly securitized island with massive steel gates and fences, and sits in the middle of the vast, informal settlement that has changed very little in the past decades. "For these people, and also for the local Indians, Gandhi means nothing today," the caretaker told me in 2007, "our visitors are Indian school children in buses and people from abroad like yourself."

RACISM'S TWO BODIES

It should be clear by now that the archive of Indian African hostility and mutual apprehension in KwaZulu-Natal is deep and consistent in both themes and structure. This prompts two questions: (1) to which extent can one describe the Indian racial prejudices and fears as specific products of the history of Natal and South Africa; and (2) to which extent is this Indian modality of race thinking structured by South Asian cultural paradigms of hierarchy and caste segmentation?

Let us begin with race thinking as it developed into a consolidated body of thought, scientific rationality, and global colonial culture in the nineteenth century. Here it was held that the body is the site of both biological and historical truth and destiny: one can speak many languages, change religion, nationality, and habits, and one can imagine oneself into a new community, but one cannot change one's race. Race is embodied, objective, and genetic—the ultimate fixation of identity.[33] Schemes of racial classification were, nonetheless, always haunted by the impossible fixation of pure types and by worries about miscegenation and its outcomes: the mestizo, the quadroon, the Creole. Ideologues and administrators of racial orders, from Gobineau to colonial officials, doctors, and scientists, were always obsessed with sexuality, desire, and the dangers of racial mixture that would weaken and question the self-evidence of whiteness as the governing norm. Anxious (colonial) whiteness was the "structuring principle of racial meaning . . . that subjects individuals to a phantasmic identification that the body's surface seems to literalize" (Seshadri-Crooks 1998, 355; see also Stoler 1995, 2002; Young 1995).

Scientific race thinking foregrounded race as a biological fact, something fundamental in the blood and the body, traces of which could never be fully concealed, erased, or changed by speech, education, or bodily comportment. This was the basis of colonial race policies in South Africa (Dubow 1995) and the foundation of the official classification of four race groups in South Africa during apartheid. However, practical perceptions of race were always suspended between two deeply interdependent registers, both located in and written upon the body as notions of substance (blood) and notions of conduct.[34] On the one hand, there were naturalized notions of blood and physical inheritances that were assumed to generate and transmit enduring, if not entirely immutable, intellectual and bodily dispositions. On the other hand, there was a performative register of clothing, comportment, speech, hairstyles, skin coloring, tanning, and bleaching that could package, pronounce, or conceal the supposedly natural "facts" of hair, bodily form, and pigmentation. Let us call this the two bodies of race thinking—surface and substance—that are conjoined and indivisible, like two sides of the same coin.

The distinction between that which is immediately visible (and possibly deceptive) and that which is hidden (and thus more true) is, argues Sander Gilman, the very axis around which anti-Semitism developed, particularly in nineteenth-century Europe. Mental and cultural differences could be disguised, but the racially distinct body of the Jew would always betray itself and shine through in various bodily and gestural symptoms. With the advent of modern medicine, eugenics, psychiatry, and associated disciplines, the older Christian/Western matrix of racial difference gained a new and medicalized language. Gilman convincingly shows how the anxieties about the true, if often cleverly concealed, nature of the Jew—his excessive impulses, nervousness, sexuality, and avarice—were constantly projected onto visible, mostly pathological symptoms: the Jewish stare, the Jewish foot, the Jewish nose, Jewish speech, and so on (1991).

Colonization involved the education and cultivation of new types of bodily dispositions through countless microdisciplines of clothing, comportment, gestures, diet, and sexual conduct. The native body had to learn to maintain and produce its own physical boundaries and orifices through hygiene, health, and "proper" and practical clothing. Only when possessing a properly self-contained body, protected from contagious disease and immoral conduct, would the soul, interiority, and essence of the Christian convert begin to improve—albeit in a constant struggle—against slipping back into the older habits that their bodily essence still predisposed them to (Comaroff and Comaroff 1997, 323–64). Like the Jews who revealed their (perverted) bodily nature by being too clever, too urban, and too modern, the labor of colonial reform was also premised on the distinction between surface and substance, although in a reversed form. By changing the bodily surface and conduct of the inferior native, their soul and inner life could, perhaps, with arduous effort, become moral and proper, if always in danger of slipping back into the primitive disposition inherent in the substance of the black body.

Over time, the colonial distinction between surface and substance gradually overlaid and even replaced preexisting and less dualistic notions of the body that were attuned to periodic flows and sharing that did not necessarily equate the physical skin of an individual with the social skin of the person. Today's racialized cultures in South Africa are deeply informed by the duality of surface and substance. They have become undeniable sociological and political facts that are reproduced in all their contradictions through countless institutional structures and procedures. As Deborah Posel has convincingly argued, race became the common sense by which South Africans lived:

> these categories were powerfully rooted in the materiality of everyday life. The ubiquity of the state's racial designations, and the extent to which they meshed with lived hierarchies of class and status, meant that apartheid's racial grid was strongly imprinted in the subjective experience of race . . . it would be difficult to deny the extent to which the demarcation of South African society into whites, Indians, coloureds, and Africans has been normalized, for many, a "fact of life." (2001, 109)

Nowhere have the practical difficulties and arbitrariness of the determination of "proper" race through physical appearance been more glaringly absurd than in the case of the category of coloreds in South Africa, a group that by definition was of "mixed blood." In some cases the "pencil test" in the hair (will it sit or will it fall?) was supposed to determine the degree of blackness, while individuals in other cases managed to "pass as whites" through a carefully accumulated portfolio of papers and public social practices (Western 1981; Jensen 2008). It was ultimately administrative classification that fixed racial identity of any individual and thus determined place of dwelling, education, and life chances. The racialized cultures in South Africa, including the Indian world I describe in this book, are thus social and bodily dispositions that were produced and embraced over time as administrative categories were turned into lived space and everyday practices, all specific to South Africa.[35]

If practical determination of race as "common sense" is the work of sustained administrative fiat, the question of how racial identities, anxieties, and racialized bodies are perceived and made into subjectivities remain to be addressed. Racism has not merely produced two conjoined bodies of surface and substance but also complex psychic, sexual, and moral dimensions. The deep cultural archives of racialized bodies as split between the visible and the hidden dimensions means that any bodily appearance and performance always/already is co-constituted by endless fantasies of the essential and intrinsic dispositions, dangers, afflictions, sexual allure, and secrets of that same body. To use Merleau-Ponty's distinction, corporeality understood as objectified and socially constituted schemas of perception and classification impinge on how the subjective sense of being a body of a certain kind is experienced. As Fanon pointed out so forcefully, the way a racially marked body must be inhabited, the relationship between its surface and its supposed essences is not a matter of free choice but an existential condition one must live with in different ways: as pride, enjoyment, disavowal, shame, or bewilderment. In deeply racialized cultures, indifference is foreclosed, it is not an option.

In the context of such habitations of one's body, the color of the skin, phenotypical appearance, and other surfaces become much more than mere indicators of one hidden truth of a body. Bodily appearance and comportment, as well as forms of speech, all work together as what Lacan called *objet petit a*—signs that acquire their force because they refer to registers of cultural fantasy of irreducible difference, radical and perhaps uncanny alterities, and bodies governed by unknowable forces and logics. Skin color and physical appearance have historically been sites of countless forms of fear, enjoyment, and fantasy, a surplus of signification that never could be closed or fully fixed. The physical body is always shadowed by a phantasmic body, or a social corporeality, the "truth" of which is constituted by a huge archive of "mytho-knowledge" beyond falsification. By this term I mean the complex archive of "scientific facts," personal stories, and collective cultural fantasies about "racial essences" that always have specific historical forms but are irreducible and globally circulating social facts that structure conduct and desire in innumerable ways.

One example of this was the Immorality Act enforced by the apartheid state. It aimed at separating white women from the dangers and temptations of the supposedly oversexed black male body. The key problem for the state was historically the figure of the urban African male. In this figure the tension between the two dimensions of race thinking were condensed: the African male body was regarded as naturally "primitive," but at the same time thousands of African men were mastering the codes and comportments of urban modernity. The tsotsi and the rebellious comrade, simultaneously urbane and "wild," were two sides of the same ungovernable figure. The youth revolt and the associated criminalization of the townships in the 1980s reconfigured the long-standing complex of fears surrounding the black male body into an essential locus of danger and violence that no amount of "acculturation" could transform. The performative repertoire adopted by the comrades (and the tsotsis) played on these registers, most poignantly in the practice of toyi-toying. The rhythmic dancing and singing in rows and crowds drew on the long tradition of rhythmic singing in church choirs and at mining compounds, where drumming was banned because it was assumed to excite the native body too much. It also referenced the long precolonial tradition of war songs and war dances among Zulus and many others. The performance of toyi-toying, often in large groups, became the most important physical-tactile signature of the antiapartheid struggle. Like the older war dances, toyi-toying was designed to intimidate the enemy by its condensation of sound and rhythm, which emanated from a dense compact of hundreds or thousands of singing bodies moving in sync—often chanting militant slogans. The other effect was the internal somatic dynamic of crowds, which strengthens a sense of group cohesion and harnesses courage and determination. Such physical manifestations reversed the stereotype of the black body by making it into a political weapon of great precision and poignancy. Since 1994, toyi-toying has also become something of a political cliché, a somatic reference to the glory of the struggle, and is occasionally performed by white politicians in feeble efforts to perform their fidelity to the legacy of the struggle. Yet, when a suit-clad Jacob Zuma began his signature dance on stages around the country a few years ago, the cultural force of racism's two bodies was unmistakable. The message was lost on no one: here was the self-consciously defiant (and oversexed) African male body asserting itself and mobilizing its essentialized mythos and its more recent political history in a single, poignant gesture.

Racial Practice, Indian-Style

Among Indians, racial fear does indeed circle around the purity of the female Indian body. Ideas of female purity, which Indians brought with them from the subcontinent, were central to ideas of pollution and a preference for endogamous marriages. On the Indian subcontinent, caste is also based on strongly gendered ideologies of the transfer of blood and essences, and accompanied by elaborate, popular ideas of the correlation between surface/appearance and assumed substance.

Across South Asia one finds a complex tension between notions of bodily essences, which are graded on a hierarchical scale of purity and impurity, and bodily appearance, which is graded on an aesthetic scale from fair to dark. Both scales are generally supposed to coincide with caste status: fair skin equals a high status, while a darker complexion equals a lower-caste status. These scales are embedded in an economy of phantasmic enjoyment and sexualized anxiety. Fair skin is valued as a sign of beauty, chastity, and high status in women, while darker women are often seen as "wild" and sexy, because the complexion refers to (but is not always identical to) the assumed qualities of lower-caste women.

In men, a dark complexion can also signify strength and virility (as in the lower-caste male) as opposed to the cultural refinement and higher status that is routinely attributed to fair males.[36] In practice, however, actual skin complexion of individuals is widely regarded as somewhat random within families—from "wheatish" to dark—a fact that affects marriage prospects for women in particular but never affects fundamental inclusion within a family or community. Only uncertainty regarding actual "blood" inheritance—in the case of children, for instance—may cause enduring anxieties. In other words, surface is neither directly nor necessarily connected to assumed essences and enduring dispositions. Acquired skills, knowledge, sophistication, and achievement, but also maintenance of strict bodily regimes of ritual purity and diet, will almost always trump immediate appearance.

To complicate matters further, there is a strong categorical distinction between those who are "within" a Hindu system of differentials and those who are outside, but the boundaries are complex. Untouchable communities are traditionally regarded as so impure that they are categorically different, yet they are within a Hindu social order as a form of included exclusion. This caste matrix, including untouchability, also pervades Muslim and Christian communities in the subcontinent. Within this order, and certainly within the proper *savarna* castes, practices of purification, vegetarianism, education, and strict discipline can purify bodily essences and can lead to a higher status over several generations, a practice that M. N. Srinivas famously named "Sanskritization" (1962). This limited fluidity, which is internal to the caste order, stands opposed to the tribal populations of India, who are regarded as "wild," primitive, and completely outside civilized society.[37] Descendants of African slaves and soldiers in South Asia were regarded, and indeed officially classified, as tribals, such as the Sidis of Gujarat, black Muslims who descend from slaves brought by Muslim traders in Gujarat from East Africa in the sixteenth century.[38] However, as in South Africa, firm categorical determination of belonging was never possible on the basis of genealogy or physical appearance in South Asia. Since the nineteenth century, the effective determination of boundaries and substances of caste groupings became a question of administrative fiat and legal ruling across the subcontinent (Dirks 2001).

As I discussed above, caste practices among Indians in South Africa had been transformed and consolidated in a new hierarchy along linguistic lines. The broad linguistic groups of Tamil, Telugu, Hindi, and Gujarati emerged as the decisive categories governing marriage practices for many decades while internally divided along cross-cutting religious lines. Marriages across these lines have become more common but are still conceptualized as crossing both aesthetic lines of color and cultural habits, as well as more essential lines of food and bodily essence. Yet, the negotiability of boundaries remains in constant flux. Unions between Tamils and Hindi speakers were relatively rare until the 1980s, while marriages between Muslim, Hindus, and Christians within the same linguistic group were regarded as less controversial. This has changed in the last few decades as religious identities are asserted much more forcefully in a new and globalized context, as we will see in the final section of this book. Marriages between Hindus and Muslims, and between Hindus and Christians, are more prone to familial conflict than just a decade ago.

Practices of caste and endogamy undoubtedly reinforced and recalibrated existing ideas of categorical distinctions between bodies, dispositions, and morality among Indians. If Africans could interpret white exclusivity and endogamy as signs of dominance and hierarchy, the even more fine-grained systems of endogamy and social segmentation among people of South Asian origin came across as inexplicable hostility and poor neighborliness. Questions of marriage, purity, and status were, however, decidedly inward-looking and directed at the world of South Asian communities. Internal gradation of differences in complexion, language, and religion continued but were structurally similar to caste in India—one's status could improve with education and lifestyle, which in turn could compensate for a less-respectable background, a dark complexion, or a different religion. However, turning one's back on categorical others was historically a sine qua non to any attempt at gaining respectability. Interactions with these categorical others were—and remain to this day—structured by a deep and long archive of colonial racial prejudice that is expressed in widely accepted hierarchies of status, wealth, and color. Relations and marriages outside one's community were generally discouraged but most effortlessly accepted with whites, less so with coloreds, while distinct hostility and fear govern most everyday relationships vis-à-vis Africans.[39]

Apartheid's spatial regime placed coloreds and Indians in adjacent areas. Lively interactions and many sexual unions across boundaries ensued from the 1960s onward. While Indians were generally seen as acceptable marriage partners among coloreds, the situation among Indians was more complex. Marriage with coloreds was not generally approved of among Hindus, while these unions have been on the rise among both Muslims and Christians. Indian women marrying white men, especially foreigners, were routinely warned of sexual exploitation because white men are only "after one thing," as the phrase commonly goes. As the Mixed Marriages Act was repealed in the mid-1980s, the Indian press ran many stories about the difficulties of mixed marriages and cautioned young people against "adventures."[40]

During my fieldwork, I met a number of older white working-class men who had married Indian women and had settled in the township during the 1980s after rules had been eased. Susie, a quiet Indian woman in her late fifties, told me how she ended up marrying Rob, a retired construction worker, now in his early seventies: "Rob and I worked in the same company for more than twenty-five years. I was a secretary and Rob was a foreman. When I was widowed, we started seeing each other, but it was not easy. Rob's children and family did not like me, and Rob said to me that he would rather live in Chatsworth than anywhere else. He liked it here, and my family accepted him after some time."

Rob and I later shared many stories of how people always assumed we were employees of public services companies who were just visiting the township rather than residents. "When I *chune* [talk] like a charou they just laugh; they never thought I could I live here, but they never gave me a hard time," he told me. In these cases the assumed essence of whiteness could never be trumped by performative competence in charou registers.

If unions involve an Indian woman and a colored man, and even more so, an African man, such marriages invariably elicited qualifying or apologetic comments, such as "he is very fair-skinned," "he is very well educated," "he is tall and handsome," as if to generate performative and aesthetic qualities that could mitigate the transgression of category and substance. Cases of Indian men marrying colored women were generally regarded as relatively uncontroversial, especially if the girl was beautiful and the man was educated or of financial means. Among Muslims of Indian origin, Cape Malay women were seen as "wild" and exotic yet acceptable as marriage partners.[41] Finally, Indian men who married white women were almost unequivocally regarded as determined social climbers and rarely commented on in negative ways.

However, in everyday life, physical proximity to Africans remains suffused with a fear of contamination. This is connected to the older archive of physical fear of Africans and of African men in particular. A young woman, a primary schoolteacher, told me:

> You must understand that from early childhood we were always told that Africans were dangerous and that we should stay away from them. I was never afraid of the women, but I never had an African friend . . . when I was in town and there was a group of African men on the sidewalk, we would cross over to the other side. . . . We also never met Africans except as workers or people who were cleaning and things like that. Here in Chatsworth we never saw a black face except for the work gangs that were brought in to do various jobs. . . .

So most of us here know nothing about Africans, how they live, and what they think. I have never been to Umlazi, and to be honest, I don't feel like going there.

I only met a few people who had Indian and African parents. Zach was a high school dropout and aspiring R & B singer. As a child he was told that his father, whom he had never met, was Tamil. "I was so much darker than my mom, and I have curly hair, but I looked like a Tamil so I never worried about it." As a teenager he developed a strong body and very curly hair. He was teased and called a "darkie" and a "bushman." When he was eighteen his mother told him that his father was a Muslim man from Malawi, and initially Zach was shocked. "I knew I was a bit different, but I never knew why," he told me. Since then he started embracing a more African identity; he was performing hip-hop and was developing a new set of friends in the adjacent colored township: "I am not one of *de bruine mensen* [the brown people], but I like these guys, I like their style . . . I still live here in Chatsworth and I am still a charou, but it is not like it used to be. I have changed. All I want to do is to sing." For Zach, who had been accepted as a charou throughout his life and behaved like one, the revelation of his African parentage meant that the new truth of his body had to be inhabited and made his own all over again. He now assumed that his musical talent, which he saw as his true self, was intrinsically connected to his African blood.

While the relationship between substance and surface is somewhat more fluid inside the social category of "Indians," it is very rigid when pertaining to other racial categories. In the latter case, substance almost invariably trumps surface. Wealthier Indian families had employed African domestic workers for generations, and this practice continued, albeit on a limited scale in the new Indian areas from the 1960s. However, live-in maids were never common as in white suburbs. It was difficult for Africans to get a permit to live in an Indian township during apartheid, and many Indians disliked having Africans living in their homes. Anxieties of pollution by African "beef eaters," and a general disdain for Africans as entities who belonged to the bush, meant that African domestic workers often slept outside Indian households and ate from separate plates and utensils. In the new and domesticated township space of the 1970s, many Indians preferred to not even see Africans on the streets of their "own" ethnic-racial space.

Africans at Our Doorsteps

In the 1970s, a few thousand "Zanzibaris," black Muslims who were descendant of slaves brought from Zanzibar in the nineteenth century, were moved to Chatsworth after sustained pressure from elite Muslim circles in Durban. The Zanzibaris were settled in the poorest area in Chatsworth, which was a center for drug trade and the home of many of the Urdu-speaking Muslims in the township. A number of residents argued that the Zanzibaris were incompatible with the culture of the township because they were "negroid."[42] Several local organizations, sports clubs, and others also opposed the settlement "not because we are racialist, but because we are realistic."[43] In February 1970, two sociologists undertook a survey that revealed that the group was "physically mixed . . . mainly negroid but also with members with straight hair." The report found that the "educational and social level was similar to that of Indians in the area," and foresaw that the sharing of food habits and religion with their neighbors would ease integration.[44]

However, the rhetoric of Islamic brotherhood could not transcend entrenched racial and cultural prejudice. In the 1980s, the wealthy Juma Masjid Trust in Grey Street built a separate mosque for the Zanzibaris at a hilltop overlooking the river and neighboring Umlazi. An imam from Malawi was hired in order to create a separate congregation. The Zanzibari community retained a strong internal organization for many years. The few educated men and the local imam attempted to regulate the behavior of the younger men who continued to be a matter of concern. Abobaker, an elderly community leader, told me:

> We came as guests to this place. The community here had accommodated us, so we felt we had to fit in and behave properly. Now we feel more at home, but we have lost some of the respect that we enjoyed among the younger generation. But that is the same all over Chatsworth—the policeman, the teacher, the imam—no one is respected these days. So many people now stay in this area, people who are not Muslims, they just come over from Umlazi and hide among our black people—but what can we do about it?

Abobaker referred to the massive growth in the number of Africans living in Chatsworth. Already in the 1980s, smaller groups of squatters began to appear in various parts of the township. I lived in a neighborhood that housed a small industrial area with workshops and some warehouses. In the late 1980s, some of the Indian employers in the area had given several of their workers permission to build little shacks on an empty lot between two warehouses. The families of the workers came to live with them, and some of the women began to work as domestics in the nearby houses. By 1993, the little colony had grown to about two hundred families. In 1994 the city authorities decided to act on the many complaints about African "vagrants" at night in the streets. The murder of a customer in the local bottle store confirmed the idea of Africans as the origin of violence and crime. Bulldozers were brought in and the stage was set for a showdown. However, inspired by the heady atmosphere of transformation and change of 1994, and a desire to keep their employees nearby, local Indian residents formed pickets and prevented the bulldozers from clearing the area. The administration decided not to escalate the conflict. ANC won the national election a few months later and forced removals came to a standstill. Since then the settlement grew bigger. Most of the people in the streets of this locality were Africans, and the local residents complained even more than before. A local man told me: "It has become a transit-camp—people move in and out all the time. They bring in their relatives, and once they are here they find a job or somewhere else to live in Chatsworth. That way more and more people are coming. We can't keep track of who is coming and going. They all look the same, especially at night when all this happens."

After I had walked the relatively short distance to his house, a friend told me off: "You should not walk in the streets here. Use your car, then you won't be bothered by the dogs." I had indeed been harassed, not by Africans, but by big dogs trained to be hostile to everything walking the streets. Many local residents now regretted their action in 1994 and feared further depreciation of property values.

The local shopping complex had two general stores, a bottle store, a video shop, and a pawnbroker. All of the shops were heavily fortified, and the shop attendants and shopkeepers worked behind two sets of iron bars. Mr. Moodley served his customers through a little opening, less than a foot square, while customers, mostly Africans, looked at the goods through the sturdy grid of his security fence. "I have been robbed more often than I can remember," Mr. Moodley said. "I never keep much money here . . . but as you can see, these people never buy for more than five or ten rand [about 75 cents to $1.50 in U.S. dollars]. My Indian customers don't come anymore; they go to the big supermarkets, and you only have these youngsters buying cold drinks and cigarettes."

The parking lot in front of the shops was a favorite place for African men to gather after work to have a drink and a chat. On the weekends, it often became a rather volatile place with fistfights, broken bottles, and occasional shoot-outs. Mr. Moodley continued, "It is all because of these bottle stores. Where you sell booze you have problems . . . and these darkies. . . . Well, our own people are no angels, but if these people make twenty rand one day, they will go and spend it on their friends in the evening. That is why they are so poor; they never think of tomorrow. At least our Indians have the decency to feed their children and keep a nice house . . . but these people, I don't understand them."

The playground on the other side of the road had also become a popular place for African workers to rest in the shade. In the daytime, groups of women and schoolgirls would rest in the midday heat, while at night young men would drink, chat, and smoke dagga on the playground. The local ratepayers association demanded, in vain, that the liquor shops should close down. Rumor had it that the owner, a retired policeman, paid off his former colleagues to leave him alone. In 2007, the residents of the colony were rehoused and the area was cleared, but crime rates were only marginally improved. A few years later, Mr. Moodley died and his shop, as well as the bottle store, was taken over by an enterprising Pakistani family who saw physical risk and crime as part of a general business climate in the country.

This was but a microcosm of the situation around the edges of the big township where large informal settlements with thousands of huts and informal dwellings emerged. Street corners, local shopping complexes, and the small patches of playground and recreational space that used to be the pride of many people in Chatsworth became a battleground where civic organizations, security companies, and the city council fought over the future character of the township. Two competing understandings of what the township signified were in direct collision. The most common understanding was that Chatsworth was and should remain a proper Indian space—transformed from barren land and domesticated to "our place" as the result of the initiative and self-help of its residents, often in the face of adverse conditions. The older residents felt that they had earned the right to enjoy the relative safety and pleasure they associated with living in an "Indian" space. In this generation, one found a distinct unease with the presence of Africans in public spaces of the township and a pronounced fear of crime and car hijackings, which had become part of everyday life in Chatsworth. This was widely perceived as a result of Africans targeting Indians—"We are soft targets; Indians don't put up a fight, not like the whites," as a standard saying went. This version of Chatsworth's history was also essentially the tale of charou culture—how the move to Chatsworth enabled a working-class family to get its own house, expand it, make it their own place, and enjoy life in relative security in the ethnic-racial enclave.

The ANC and left-leaning, well-educated Indians argued, on the other hand, that the residents of Chatsworth and other formerly Indian townships should be prepared to share some of their amenities and resources with the hugely deprived majority population. This was indeed the policy of the government and the city council. Schools were open to all, and many informal settlements were gradually becoming regularized and replaced by little brick houses that were set up on patches of vacant land, which made thousands of Africans legitimate residents in the township, with access to water, sanitation, and transport. Many Indian residents saw this policy as a pure party-political move that was sponsored by the ANC in order for the party to gain an electoral foothold in the township, and in order to deliver some of the promises to their African supporters at the expense of hapless charous. "Why don't they move them into white neighborhoods?" people would ask in informal conversations. "There is more space." My informants answered these questions themselves by pointing out that effective vigilante groups patrolled white neighborhoods with the sole purpose of keeping Africans out. They also suspected that the new African elites in the country had no interest in changing the character of the leafy upmarket suburbs they now resided in.

In an attempt to attract support for the ANC, the stadium in Chatsworth was chosen as the location for the celebration of Mandela's eightieth birthday in 2001. The organizers hoped that the epic scenes of 1994, when thousands of Indians almost stampeded to see Mandela at the same location, would be repeated. They had underestimated the depth of the fear most Indians have of being in a crowd of thousands of Africans. The result was a half-empty stadium that was mainly filled with Africans who had come from the settlements and nearby Umlazi. Although Mandela is almost universally loved and respected in Chatsworth, most of my friends and informants did not even consider attending the free program of music and entertainment at the stadium. They knew it would be a predominantly black audience. "You may get killed in a crowd like that," I was told by a friend. "To be honest I don't feel comfortable when they start dancing and toyi-toying . . . they also speak at the top of their voices and the music is loud . . . it is too much for me," said another Indian, a long-standing ANC member. The idea of the physical danger associated with large numbers of African bodies remained a decisive factor. Most local residents stayed away.

Somatic Anxieties

By the 1980s, Chatsworth and Phoenix had a comprehensive system of municipal schools. Many committed teachers in these schools saw the challenge of managing a multilingual and multiracial classroom as a way of contributing to a new society after apartheid. However, less than a decade later there was a marked change in attitude among both students and parents. A teacher in Chatsworth told me: "Before 1994 both teachers and students felt that we were trying to beat the system from within. It was as if students wanted to make the most of the few openings there were. . . . Now the attitude is more 'I want it all now,' but students no longer care about their studies." Other teachers echoed the sentiment. Many described African students as rude, aggressive, and destructive in their behavior. Another teacher said, "It may sound racist to you, but these people don't have the same culture as us; they want an exam but don't work hard. They also don't have good English, and how can you teach a child that only speaks isiZulu?"

By the mid-1990s, concerns about falling standards in schools, and alleged destruction of classrooms and intimidation of teachers, had become one of the greatest concerns in the Indian newspapers and public debates.[45] In May 1999, violent episodes at several schools across Durban prompted the authorities to dispatch special teams of investigators to probe into the problem.[46]

One of the biggest secondary schools in the area where I stayed was Chatsworth High. The school was previously known as one of the best Indian high schools in Durban, with highly motivated teachers and equally motivated parents, many of whom were climbing the social ladder. After the last racial strictures on schools were lifted by the early 1990s, a large number of middle-class children moved to the formerly white schools across the city. Chatsworth High now received students mainly from its local catchment area, mostly very poor Indian families in the council housing estates, from the Zanzibari section, and from the informal settlements where most of the African children hardly have any knowledge of English. African students now counted for more than 50 percent in the school, which was close to the average for the township schools as a whole. Many of the African students told me that they had been sent from Umlazi, or even from Zululand, to live with relatives in Chatsworth because of the attractions of education. Indian schools were still considered some of the best in the city; Indian teachers were highly respected, and the schools in Chatsworth generally charged modest school fees.

The school was now riddled by massive social and disciplinary problems. In spite of a tall fence with barbed wire around the entire compound, a massive gate, and multiple security guards, burglaries and vandalism had become common. A few computers had been stolen, many windows were broken, and the run-down state of the solid buildings bore witness to the effects of drastically reduced budgets for such "historically advantaged institutions," as all formerly Indian schools have been classified. The school had massive disciplinary problems, and the local police carried out frequent surprise searches for guns, knives, and drugs. Male teachers admitted that they were afraid of confronting some of the older African boys out of fear of being overpowered. They even found it difficult to discipline younger African boys in physical education classes.

Several of the female teachers related their difficulties in dealing with the sexually charged atmosphere in the school yard and in classrooms. Many girls, both Indian and African, wore their school uniform dresses as very short miniskirts, and jokes and contact between the sexes were very direct. Challenges were many and complex: often students would disappear for hours, going to bars, having sex, or watching X-rated movies; some girls were known to be prostitutes from the age of fourteen or fifteen; and drug dealing in the school was rampant and difficult to control.

Based on conversations with students and my frequent visits to the school, it became clear to me that very little of this sexualized youth culture involved interracial relations. Students would indeed establish friendships in school across the racial boundaries, but it would rarely develop into friendships outside the gate, and even more rarely into interracial relationships of love or sex. Outside the school gates, lives became largely separate in terms of which street corners students were hanging out on, the fashion in clothes, and the style of music. A sixteen-year-old girl explained to me, "It is hard to say why it is, but we feel more at ease with Indians—it is the Indian thing—you know the way of *chuning* [talking], our jokes, our food and spices, *bhangra* ["and the film stars!" another girl chipped in]. How can they understand any of that? It is a charou thing!" All the other Indian students standing around laughed at the punch line. The interest in the African worlds in which they lived so closely was minimal among the Indian students, except for kwaito and soccer. Even the discos and clubs in downtown Durban remained almost completely racially divided, except for incipient mixing between whites and Indians.

Many teachers and parents saw the changes in the schools, the disciplinary problems, and the sexualization of the teenage culture as a direct result of the entry of African students into Indian schools. They saw it as a threat to Indian girls and saw the sexualization as something utterly alien to "Indian culture." However, as a group of Indian students from the school explained to me in the most disarming manner, it is all happening because "there are too many charous in the school." One of the boys, a seventeen-year-old with two gold teeth and a firm resolve to own his own nightclub one day, and who proudly defined himself as a charou, put it succinctly:

We always blame the darkies, but they work harder in school than most of the Indians. I live in the flats. I know these charous; they just want to cheat, to get by without work, to drink and do drugs. In my block there are twelve families and I only know one *ou* [guy] there who has a regular job. If you have anything and are doing good, they will pull you down, cast a spell on you or something. . . . We charous always pull each other down. So why study and get a job if you get by in other ways . . . I ask myself, why am I here? My friends have money but I don't.

The presence of large numbers of Africans created spontaneous anxieties in many Indians. Most of these revolved around a notion of the naturally strong, aggressive African body, which was seen as superior to soft and weak Indian bodies. A constant displacement between race and class also seemed to be at work. The ongoing "charoufication" of Chatsworth, and the general liberalization of laws and cultural attitudes in postapartheid South Africa, were squarely attributed to the presence of Africans.

Such anxieties converged in repeated rumors in February 1999 over alleged attacks by African students on Indian students in Chatsworth with syringes filled with HIV-positive blood. By 1998, the full-scale AIDS pandemic was becoming clear, with the province of KwaZulu-Natal and the city of Durban as its epicenter. Infection rates among pregnant women were reported to run as high as a staggering 45 to 50 percent. In the same year, a number of stories began to emerge in the city's newspapers about young HIV-positive Africans roaming the city. They had told a journalist "they did not care anymore, and that if they were going to die, they would take others with them."[47] This theme of a dreaded African revenge combined with a general white and Indian anxiety about walking in the city center of Durban, which was now widely regarded as black territory, led to the circulation of rumors of random white women being stabbed with AIDS-infected needles. These stories instantly became urban legends. They were never corroborated, and the police identified neither perpetrators nor syringes.

In May 1999, one such "stabbing incident" was reported at a school in Chatsworth. In the days to follow, students from many schools, almost exclusively girls, reported that they too had been stabbed, or that they had felt a certain pain in their neck or arms. It seemed as if a concerted attack on Indian girls had been launched. The *Post* ran the story on the front page, and parents, school principals, and chairmen of the governing bodies all over Chatsworth demanded swift action from the authorities.[48] Several school principals called in the police to make searches for syringes, and a number of male African students were suspended from schools on suspicions of having carried out these "racially motivated attacks," as they were called in the Indian newspapers. Concerned parents kept their children away from school for days and weeks.

Chatsworth High also experienced an incident, but the principal did not panic. A doctor was called in, and after an examination of the girl who claimed to have been stabbed, the doctor found a tiny little spot on her shoulder that seemed to have been made by a sharpened pencil. Investigations were carried out at several schools, but no syringe was ever found, no students were ever identified with marks from a syringe or with a sudden HIV infection (which could have other causes), and no students were ever identified as culprits. The affair died as quickly as it had risen and is today referred to with half-embarrassed smiles from teachers and principals, some of whom maintained that "some kind of stabbing must have occurred in the first place."

The whole affair seemed to be generated from conjecture, a somatic effect (the sting felt by students) generated by compounded fears of the threat of contamination by the black bodies in the school and the general black presence in the township. It is probably no coincidence that the affair unfolded during the election campaign in 1999, at a time when the incoming president Thabo Mbeki, under the slogans of an African renaissance, promised to speed up transformation of all aspects of life in South Africa. The affair also indicated how the widespread notion of AIDS as a "black thing" confirmed and recycled ideas of the black body as not only unrestrained and oversexualized but also medically contaminated and polluting.

The racial categories as a site of public recognition and visibility continue to generate heated emotions if transgressed. This became clear in July 2007 when a Xhosa-speaking girl entered and won the local Miss Teen Indian South Africa Pageant in Port Elizabeth. The winner was dressed in an Indian dress and performed a Bollywood dance routine to perfection. "I love Bollywood, have many Indian friends, and have a flair for dancing." The audience protested vehemently, and the judges had to be physically protected as they left the venue. The protesters argued that the winner, Anelisa Willem, could not enter because she was not Indian. The judges insisted that they only looked at how "our Indian culture was being celebrated . . . anyone can enter the pageant."[49] This insistence on race as a performative quality that is akin to culture collided head-on with the deep-seated idea of race as embedded in two conjoined bodies of surface and substance.

As Africans have become a very visible presence in everyday life in the township, the importance of the boundaries of the house and the boundaries of the self have become increasingly "securitized" and moralized. The height of walls and securitization of houses are increasingly indexical of the moral quality of its people. The older habits of maintaining fluid social relationships with kin and neighbors, and living in socially permeable houses in the township, are giving way to a distinction between closed and open houses that are inhabited by moral and immoral people. For those who live respectably behind walls, the outside is categorically different and dangerous. Status depends on maintaining a proper Indian house and a properly bounded and moral Indian body. For those who live in the old-style township houses, the openness to the street, the school, and other public spaces is maintained and constantly negotiated, often out of material necessity. This proximity and suspected openness to a sexualized African outside is today the most poignant marker of low class and low status in the township.

Nonrecognition and the Elusive Master

Let me draw together the main pattern that emerges from the long history of African Indian encounters and apprehensive coexistence. My main proposition is that Africans and Indians have only been able to properly see and recognize each other through the mediation of a white colonial gaze, a master that distributed violence, care, desire, and partial recognition, as well as a hegemonic language of what I called racism's two bodies. In this perspective, the transformation after 1994 was doubly perplexing to the Indians and other minorities in the country. Where, and who, was the new master who could protect, redeem, recognize, and "see" us? The structure of recognition of groups, memories, and identities was now fragmented and unclear. There had been many examples of Indians, especially professionals, activists, and artists, who had been a part of the defiant and creative black milieus in Johannesburg in the 1940s and '50s (Naidoo 2009). A determined nonracial ethos had also pervaded sports like cricket and soccer in KwaZulu-Natal for most of the twentieth century (Desai 2002; 2010). However, none of this had changed the dominant racial perceptions and anxieties among the vast majority of Indians. The Truth and Reconciliation Commission (TRC) played a key role in one of these respects: the recasting of the past and producing visible and legitimate victims of apartheid. However, the status of Indians remained ambiguous.

As the TRC hearings got under way in 1997, two different calls emerged from Indian leaders. First, the conservative strongman Rajbansi called for an investigation into the 1949 riots and the 1985 violence in Inanda. He wanted the TRC to investigate the role of the police and whites in "fanning racial hatred and violence against Indians. . . . How did trouble break out in so many parts of Durban at the same time?" he asked.[50] This was seconded by several leading intellectuals in Durban but never picked up by the commission. However, six months later another call came, this time from Gandhi's granddaughter Ela Gandhi, MP for the ANC. She asked Indians to apologize for having benefited during apartheid. This was seconded by the ANC's Youth League and African student leaders. One of them, Dumisane Ngcobo, put the matter bluntly: "It is true that Indians take the initiative and prosper but our argument is that they have prospered because they have suppressed African people."[51] The call elicited a flurry of responses and reactions from leaders and ordinary Indians who felt hurt and offended.[52] The general assertion was that Indians, too, were victims of apartheid and had also been active in the antiapartheid struggle. Ela Gandhi backtracked but added, "The ANC is not calling for an apology from the Indian community . . . people must decide as individuals" (ibid.).

In the ensuing debate it was asserted that although the community had been victimized,[53] individuals could well be guilty of moral wrongdoing. This indicated that identities and stereotyped anxieties could no longer be merged into a categorical and collective form. A new demand was emerging that full humanity was to be accorded to those who had until now been faceless, distant, and inferior others. Indians were now called upon to begin to "see" Africans not merely as a category but in their full individuality. Contacts and conflicts between differently entitled categories could no longer be referred to the authorities for adjudication.

No longer protected in their limited enclaves by the state and the police, and no longer able to cocoon within the former Indian spaces and institutions, Indians had to develop a new sense of themselves. Encounters with Africans were now direct, close, and a part of everyday life—in the township, in schools, in the dreaded encounters with criminals, and also with confident and assertive Africans who were firmly dominating the world of politics.

The immediate response was heightened anxiety. At the eve of the elections in 1999, an anonymous pamphlet was distributed to thousands of Indian homes across Indian areas in the northern parts of Durban. Titled "An important message to our Indian brothers and sisters," the pamphlet stated, "we forgave you in 1994 and 1996" (when most Indians voted for the New National Party) but "on 2nd June we will not be so forgiving." The text in the pamphlet continued, "The votes will be counted where you voted. We will be watching these places closely—we will know who people in your area voted for." At the bottom it read, "We are watching you" and was signed as "WARNING from your African brothers."[54]

The incident caused panic and worry. Unsurprisingly, the turnout in the affected areas on Election Day was even lower than had been expected. Like the imagined criminals roaming the streets, Africans were now right at the doorstep, asserting their presence and rights to land

and demanding to be seen and recognized—but also keeping a watchful eye on Indian life.

What became clear during those years was that for more than a century, racialized identities in Durban and the entire province had been governed by two separate dialectics of recognition that doubly alienated Indians. On the one hand, whites and Zulus were locked in a longstanding, extremely violent, but also intimate struggle for recognition, which began with wars of conquest in the nineteenth century. This was a relationship shot through with antagonism and paternalistic love. There were many attempts at producing a form of mutual martial respect through the elaborate "museumization" of traditional Zulu culture, as was abundantly evident in the current heritage industry, the "Anglo-Zulu battlefield tours." In this relationship, Indians were intimate strangers who were fully integrated into society and economy in Natal, yet undecidable in culture, language, and disposition. The figure of the Gujarati trader remained at the heart of this stereotype and elicited strong emotions of both hatred and envy among whites and Zulus, who saw traders as an unintelligible and crafty—yet weak and effeminized—parasitical surplus. This position is akin to Zygmunt Bauman's reformulation of Simmel's description of the stranger, the figure of the Jew, in social theory: "He stands between friend and enemy, order and chaos, the inside and the outside. He stands for the treacherousness of friends, for the cunning disguise of enemies, for fallibility of order, the vulnerability of the inside" (1991, 61).

On the other hand, there was an equally long-standing dialectic between Indians and whites, albeit less reciprocal. Indian attitudes to the English-speaking whites of Natal were ambivalent: shot through with a desire for imperial recognition in Gandhi; attempts at recognition as responsible heirs to a great civilization during apartheid; but also a deep sense of betrayal and nonreciprocated affection. Among whites, Indians were seen as fundamentally strange people with self-sufficient and complex cultural practices and refinement whose adaptation to a "white modernity" and subsequent demands for recognition were seen as nothing but signs of their treacherous nature and cunning. In this skewed and nonreciprocal relationship, Africans were always categorically outside, relegated to a form of external, if natural and strong, primitivity; not strangers in Simmel's sense, but embodying an irreducible presence, as if not fully human.

The double estrangement of Indians was strangely illustrated by social psychology research on stereotypes and social distance that was conducted among thousands of students from nonwhite race groups across the country at the height of apartheid (Viljoen 1972). The underlying rationale of this research was obviously to provide scientific evidence of social distance as a naturally existing fact and the high status of whites as "natural."[55] Some of the results, largely ignored by the author, are highly revealing. Indian respondents felt closest to English-speaking whites and furthest removed from Africans as a whole, and from Jews (here placed and defined as "white" but obviously not quite). Interestingly, Zulu students evaluated English-speaking whites most positively of all groups, while they saw Indians and Afrikaans-speaking whites as the least desirable. Strikingly, in all cross-tabulations in the study, Jews and Indians were categorized by other groups in the study in almost identically negative terms.

The analogy with the position of Jews may be helpful in understanding this peculiar economy of identification, desire, and suspicion, which was written so deeply into the entire region. Economically influential sections of Jews and Indians occupied a structurally similar position in the economy as traders and middlemen who employed strong traditions of kinship network and intra-ethnic trust to integrate into South Africa's booming economy in most of the twentieth century. Both groups also enjoyed a precarious cultural position "at the edge of whiteness"—Jews as internal strangers within the white category, Indians as external to whiteness but still within the ambit of "civilization." Both groups were regarded as parasitical purveyors of the commercial culture and cosmopolitan networks that were so resented by many Afrikaner intellectuals, English planters, and missionaries. Like in the case of Jews, multiple misrecognitions surrounded the accumulated mytho-knowledge of how Indians "really are," which allowed the figure of the wily trader to stand in for the entire group. Standard German anti-Semitism insisted that inside even the most urbane and assimilated Jew were traces of the dirty and irredeemably alien and physically weak *Ostjude*, the supposed truth of any Jewish body, a deception that in turn accounted for the duplicitous nature of the Jew. Likewise, as we have seen earlier, the white stereotype in Natal was that inside even the most urbane Indian was a "dirty" and effeminate coolie—alien, clannish, and untrustworthy.

Reversely, in Russian and Eastern European anti-Semitism, even the most impoverished *Ostjude* was regarded as nothing but a degraded embodiment of a powerful, cosmopolitan Jewish conspiracy and thus a mortal and powerful enemy, even more despicable because of his lack of actual power and connection. Similarly, for conservative Zulu nationalists (and others), even the most impoverished Tamil charou was nothing but an embodiment of a network of rich, parasitical, and scheming Gujaratis who were exploiting innocent Africans. Once again, the categorical double, whose source of sustenance is an archive of mytho-knowledge, always shadows any appearance. Inside the modest appearance of a charou body sits a rich and treacherous Gujarati. This obvious lack in the charou ("he is not even a properly clever and rich Indian") makes him or her an even more obvious object of contempt.

Let me reach back to Fanon and to wider psychoanalytical discussions of race to conceptualize this deep historical archive of mytho-knowledge. Fanon stressed several times that the condition of blackness is akin to a form of castration: "the black is not a man" (1967, 8), but is reduced to pure physicality, "merely a genital" (180) that may be in possession of sexual prowess in the form of a penis, but lacks power, lacks the phallus. By comparison, as Boyarin has pointed out, "European cultures represented Jews as 'female' . . . men without penises." More precisely, circumcised Jews were seen as effeminized and truncated men, and Sander Gilman reports that the popular slang for clitoris in German-speaking parts of Europe used to be "the little Jew" (1993, 38). In a fascinating discussion of the relationship between castration and racial difference, Boyarin concludes, "The black man is a penis; the male Jew is a clitoris. Neither have the phallus" (1998, 224).

It is quite obvious that colonial rule and apartheid in Freudian terms performed two forms of metaphorical castration: violent subjugation of Zulus and the effeminization of Indians. In both cases it was the phallus, white power, presence, and gaze that regulated social practices and enabled the two groups to interact and establish a limited measure of mutual intelligibility. Leaders such as Buthelezi, or Rajbansi for the Indians, were respected by the other community mainly because they wore "white masks" and were propped up by the white government.

After 1994, the question of the phallus, or the gaze of the master, was rendered deeply divided, if not schizophrenic. The realm of politics was undoubtedly dominated by the ANC, but this fact has not yet transformed the view of Africans among Indians in a fundamental way, nor has it changed the disparaging view of Indians among the average African in and around Durban and Johannesburg. Only Africans with power, money, and the style of the new elite can inhabit the new space of mastery in South Africa, a world whose tacit rules and centers of capital remain dominated by an increasingly multiracial, English-speaking elite that now, as before, constitutes the country's most vital link to global flows of capital and technology. However, the racial common sense as embedded in prosaic life practices lives on, as ever before.

As the disillusionment with the slow pace of change continues, it is unsurprising that better-educated and enterprising strangers are singled out as the "thieves of [national] enjoyment." This is Slavoj Žižek's famous term for the peculiar logic of fascination, hatred, and desire that drives the objectification and violence against racial and ethnic others who by virtue of seemingly enjoying "it" (cohesion, culture, and community) blocks the formation of a true national community (1994). The xenophobic pogrom in Johannesburg in May 2008 targeted foreigners from across Africa, as well as impoverished immigrants from Bangladesh and Pakistan, who were decried as alien parasites that were presumably standing in for wealthy Gujaratis as well. The perceived intransigence and arrogance of Indians vis-à-vis African culture and the inability of Africans and Indians to properly "see" and recognize the individuality and humanity of each other is one of the oldest and deepest elements underpinning the current xenophobia.

Let me close by quoting excerpts from the song "AmaNdiya," which the well-known Zulu struggle poet and musician Mbongeni Ngema released in early 2002:

> Oh brothers, oh my fellow brothers.
> we need brave and strong men to confront Indians
> whites were better than Indians / . . .
> they don't vote when we vote /,
> and yet they are full in parliament / . . .
> Indians have conquered Durban . . .
> they are speaking Fanagolo,
> thega lapha duza kamina yena, sibhile [buy from me, it is
>   cheap]. . . .
> Indians keep coming from India,
> the airport is full of Indians . . . oh fellow brothers.
> (Mbongeni Ngema 2002)

The song caused a storm of protests from many sides. Although chastised by Mandela, Ngema refused to withdraw his song or even to apologize.[56] Little has changed at a more fundamental level of identification and recognition: Indians remain misrecognized as treacherous fence-sitters and undeserving parasites who hide their wealth and women. Many ordinary Indians still refuse to grant Africans any other position than that of undeserving usurpers of the place and the gaze of the master and a people excessively possessed by sexual aggression but who do not actually possess the phallus.

CHAPTER 4

Autonomy, Freedom, and Political Speech

As the rift between the Zulu-speaking majority and the Indians deepened in the 1950s, mass mobilizations of Indians subsided dramatically. By the end of the 1950s, the once-powerful Indian organizations, the Natal Indian Congress (NIC) and the Transvaal Indian Congress (TIC), were reduced to shadows.[1] The two organizations sustained themselves mainly through already-existing kin and community networks among the wealthier and well-educated Gujaratis. Left-leaning, nonracial forces had a strong standing in the Indian community in South Africa until the onslaught of apartheid. Much of it was premised on the well-organized labor movement and the presence of accomplished leaders from Yusuf Dadoo of the 1940s and '50s to Jay Naidoo, the student activist turned trade union activist who headed South Africa's strongest trade union movement, COSATU, for nine years and later became a minister in Mandela's cabinet.[2] From the 1960s onward, the critique of apartheid came mainly from the upwardly mobile and educated sections. The legacy of the trade union movement was a high capacity for organization and what I termed "recalcitrance" among working-class Indians. However, the spatial and social isolation of Indians in new townships demobilized political interest among several generations of Indians. The memories of the 1940s and '50s lingered but gradually fossilized into mythical structures rather than active networks. In their stead, a broadly defensive attitude of internal consolidation emerged. To some, this indicated nothing but a resurfacing of the old clannishness that was characteristic of Indian culture. As Jay Naidoo writes in his autobiographical account, "The clannishness of the Location—the fact that Tamils married Tamils, Calcuttias Calcuttias, Malays Malays, Koknies Koknies, Khojas Khojas . . . was absurd and regrettable. The whites set up barriers and we, in our own petty way, set up barriers as well" (1990, 127). This process of introversion coincided with the moment of intensification of the ANC's campaigns and passive resistance protests in the late 1950s, which caused incipient capital flight and precipitated a serious economic and fiscal crisis (Innes 1984). The response of the state was swift and brutal. After the infamous gunning down of dozens of people at a rally in Sharpeville in 1961, political parties were banned, leaders were arrested, and political activity among people of color was strictly monitored and violently repressed in the following decades.

The new Indian social world that was born in those decades slowly became more affluent and underpinned by basic welfare provisions. Living conditions became more equalized than earlier, albeit at a low level, within the township itself. The immersion of Indians and other people of color in new surroundings that were dominated by an emerging consumer-oriented lifestyle but devoid of political freedom seemed to work, at least for some time. As Arendt writes about prosperity under conditions of unfreedom, "The Greeks knew very well that a reasonable tyrant worked to great advantage when it came to the city's welfare . . . the arts, both material and intellectual, flourished within it. . . . Citizens were banished to their homes, and the agora, the space where interaction of equals was played out, was deserted" (2005, 119). Under tyranny, however egalitarian in its effects, both words and deeds are subsumed under the functions of mere laboring and doing. For Arendt, there can be no true freedom, and thus no true politics or transformative "action," without the freedom to meet, mingle, and speak to one's equals (120).

Apartheid did indeed abolish any possibility of a multiracial agora. Instead, consultative organs were set up to "represent" the point of view of the country's communities and race groups to the government. In the new township areas and in older areas of Indian settlement, the impact of the Group Areas Act was deep and painful. Expropriations of land, razing of older houses that had been lived in for generations, and forced removals still affected thousands of families each year. This was not a time for open protest in the conventional sense. As Lal described the period to me:

> Today it seems strange, but in those years it seemed that the whites were going to stay in power forever. We were busy making things work for us . . . all my mother cared about was to get a new vegetable garden. We wanted to go to school and get a job. You cannot imagine how things changed—new buildings shooting up everywhere, shopping malls—we never had them before; highways came and all of a sudden many people had cars . . . all the *laities* [boys] just wanted wheels.

At this point, politics seemed to no longer be about exercising a free voice in Arendt's sense but to work through the thickness of "the social" in order to incrementally improve the life of the community. Political speech itself had become social and concerned itself primarily with issues of practical governance and service provision, mainly at the local level. It seemed indeed as if the apartheid project worked. Larger issues of legitimacy, sovereignty, and political representation had been literally banished, at least for some time.

However, in apartheid's second and "mature" phase from the early 1970s, there seemed to be an emerging recognition that cultural/religious expression and a meaningful political life were irreducible, universal desires that were intrinsic to any community. The result was the policy of separate development, which emerged in different forms across the country (Norval 1996, 174–18). The doctrine developed into a cornerstone in the (self-)administration of Indian life, and to many it seemed to promise a return to the 1940s, by now a heavily mythologized era of Indian autonomy, cultural sovereignty, and dignity prior to apartheid. While the idea behind the emerging Bantustans was that they were to develop into statelike structures with armed police, armies, and a limited measure of *sovereignty*, the operative concept with regards to coloreds and Indians was that of *autonomy* in the realm of local affairs and cultural institutions. "The ultimate objective," the Ministry of Indian Affairs stated in 1966, "is to guide the Indian population on the road to self-development in order that they may be enabled to accept . . . a steadily increased say in and eventually such measure of self-government in those matters that are peculiar to them, e.g., welfare services, education, local government."[3] Both variations of this policy were informed by a Herderian, classically anthropological idea of race: the race spirit of a people articulates itself in a range of cultural (and religious) and linguistic practices around which deep and enduring emotional attachments are (re)produced. Enduring political legitimacy and sovereignty could only be assured if and when these attachments became the basis of a political community and political identity. In the wake of decolonization throughout Africa in the 1960s, apartheid ideologues superimposed the language of self-determination upon this compact. In 1976, under the impression of the crisis that was generated by the Soweto uprising and its long fallout throughout the country, the minister of Indian Affairs stated:

> We believe that the separate identities of our peoples are so important that the whole philosophy of the Western world, of international politics, is based on the concept of self-determination. The policy of this government is based on the concept of self-determination of communities. . . . We, in South Africa have to devise new, amended and adapted methods of Government, methods of democracy, in order to solve our multinational problems.[4]

In this formulation, South African society was not just multiracial but multinational, and each of the cultural-racial communities within its borders were to be regarded as proto-nations. The road to political stability was to recognize that each community was to be set on a course of ever-increasing self-government and autonomy for it to realize its natural telos as a separate nation that lived and administered its own affairs under the sovereign umbrella of benevolent white state power. The challenge for the state was to develop means and ways to let this natural spirit and aspiration of diverse peoples develop within political institutions without jeopardizing the dominant configuration of sovereignty and economic power.

One challenge in the case of Indians was their physical proximity to, and economic imbrications in, the white world; another was their seemingly irrepressible capacity to speak and contest; a third was the consistent difficulty in mobilizing broad support for the institutions that were administering "Indian autonomy." The clumsy and disingenuous attempts to foster a sense of "administration of own affairs" in Indian areas has had a long political and cultural afterlife. The realm of local politics, political speech, and political representation became imbued with an irreducible whiff of unreality, an "as if" world that is defined by doublespeak, pretense, blatant lies, and rampant corruption.[5] This world was peopled by individuals who were driven by greed and seemingly irrational desires of self-aggrandizement, a world best apprehended through the register of the comic and the ridiculous. This legacy still defines political and public life in the township of Chatsworth.

Local Affairs and the Problem of Indian Speech

In 1963, the government created the South African Indian Council. The objective was "to set up a body with which the Government could consult on matters affecting the Indian community." In a longer perspective, the council could develop into a "democratically elected body which in time would control those affairs of the local Indian community which might be delegated to it by parliament."[6]

The appointees were, without exception, men from wealthy families who owned and controlled substantial trading and industrial houses (Desai 1987, 82). Speaking one year after Idi Amin's expulsions of Asians from Uganda, an influential member from Durban, H. E. Joosub (aka Atomic Joosub after his demolition firm that carried this evocative name!) expressed a broad-based pragmatic opinion of the Indian elite when he stated that for the Indian community, "the political choice for us was a simple one—to be dominated by the Whites or the Bantu . . . we could disregard the lot of Indians in some African states—a lot far worse than our own. Apart from that we had to consider the several bloody riots in Natal in 1949 and 1959, when large numbers of Indians were killed in Bantu fury."[7] The South African Indian Council (SAIC) was an isolated affair that was bereft of a broader legitimacy or even a voice among Indians. The world of the commercial elite and that of the ordinary working-class Indian remained immensely distant from each other. The members of the SAIC were merely able to win miniscule concessions from the state, for instance, that "Indians in the Transvaal were allowed to employ Bantu domestic servants" (Desai 1987, 114).

In 1977, direct elections for the SAIC were scheduled. A mere 17 percent of the eligible voters registered on their own will. Only through imposition of substantial fines on nonregistered households did the authorities succeed in getting 70 percent of the voters registered by 1978 (Desai 1987, 141). Open defiance of the authorities was increasing in the wake of the Soweto uprising. In 1979, younger radicalized Indians led school boycotts and launched the Transvaal Anti-SAIC Committee, which denounced the SAIC as ineffective: "[only] action outside the Government created institutions have produced results."[8] The effective boycott campaign in Transvaal and widespread indifference in Natal marked the end of the SAIC as a political body.[9] This was not an Indian rejection of separate development, Desai argues, but SAIC's "inability to counteract the devastating effects of the Group Areas Act" emptied it of relevance to the majority of Indians (ibid., 189).

The new administration of Indian affairs that was set up in the 1960s also stipulated that creation of so-called Local Affairs Committees (LACs) should be "the first step in the process of development of autonomous Indian local authorities."[10] In 1971, the first LAC was set up in southern Durban in an area that included the densely populated Chatsworth township. The members were all locally elected among adult Indians, who for the first time could exercise limited franchise. In 1973, a Northern Durban LAC was set up along similar lines and comprised a number of the slightly wealthier and older Indian settlements, such as Overport, Springfield, Clare Estate, and Reservoir Hills.

The history of polling for the LACs from 1971 to the end of 1992 shows a very clear pattern of initial enthusiasm turned into decline in terms of interest in the elections. The turnout in 1971 and 1973 varied between 50 percent and even 75 percent, but ten years later, most wards showed a voter turnout well below 20 percent, and in 1988 well below 10 percent. In many cases members were returned unopposed. In the southern committee—mainly Chatsworth—most seats were fought and contested vigorously, and most of the elected members were self-made men of working-class backgrounds who had become small businessmen, teachers, or professionals. The most well known were Amichand Rajbansi, J. N. Reddy, and Pat Poovalingam, who were to play prominent roles in Indian politics for decades to come.

The LAC system embodied the structure of "as if" politics. Each committee was entitled to send one representative to the city council meeting who was allowed to speak only on matters relevant to Indians but had no vote, not even on matters pertaining to Indian areas. The number of votes polled per candidate remained more or less stable from 1971 to 1984, with very low winning margins (fifty to one hundred votes per candidate). The falling percentage was mainly connected to the rapid population growth in the electoral wards in the 1970s.[11] The interest and disinterest in this style of local politics seems to have been relatively constant in Chatsworth and other Indian areas. In each ward, it seems that no more than a few thousand voters (from 15 to 30 percent of the voters) of conservative political persuasion kept these political institutions alive. Meanwhile, the overwhelming majority was quiet, and most often, indifferent.

It is indicative of the contradictory terrain opened by the LAC system that the concept of autonomy immediately became a point of contention. The paper trail left by the Southern Durban LAC, which also included Chatsworth, makes it clear that it never behaved as the pliable body of reasonable and moderate men of SAIC. A year after their election, the LAC suggested that a new Indian LAC be created and empowered to raise taxes and run its own affairs. The proposed areas included three Indian areas that had been turned into industrial parks (Clairwood, Springfield Flats, and Mondi Paper Mills) and thus represented both "ancestral" land and a considerable future tax base.[12] The city council rejected the proposal and asserted that only a fully residential area like Chatsworth could be under full Indian local authority.[13]

This challenge to the city council may not quite have been an act of *parrhesia* (the speaking of truth to power), the classical Greek virtue of the citizen so exhorted by Foucault,[14] but it was, nonetheless, an attempt to interpret the notion of autonomy to its logical conclusion without directly challenging the doctrine of separate development. Underneath rumbled constant demands for Indians to be fully included in the structures of political representation on an equal footing with white citizens. Limiting speech and political desires to matters cultural and local was more complex than envisaged by the doctrine of separate development.

City council minutes from the period reveal considerable annoyance with the new LAC, particularly the flamboyant Rajbansi, who on several occasions was accused of showing open contempt for the town clerk. Formal complaints and attempts at getting him suspended on the grounds of alleged financial irregularities ensued. A year later, Rajbansi was indeed suspended from the LAC and banned from seeking reelection for three years.[15]

In 1979, yet another round of discussions of the status of local authorities took place in the city council. Once again the two issues of direct representation of all race groups and the sharing of infrastructural services and facilities came up. A racially mixed working committee summed up the discussions: "We believe that the ideal would be to ignore color or race in local government franchise. However, it is accepted that such a proposal, for a number of reasons is not practical, and would be unacceptable to the overwhelming majority of the white electorate who has the power to effect change." The committee stated further that "all citizens living in urban areas should be subject to the same franchise and qualifications. Domination should be avoided and unfair discrimination should be abandoned."[16] The lofty statements of avoidance of "domination" were informed by economic and demographic realities. Indians constituted more than half of the city's voting population in 1978 (51.5 percent) and whites barely 40 percent. The Indian population was young and projected to be almost double the white population a decade later (1988). In voting strength, the older white group would constitute 35 percent of the electorate, while Indians would stand at 55 percent. In addition, the colored group was growing in strength, and the number of Africans (though formally under the sovereignty of the KwaZulu homeland) was also growing rapidly.[17] Any truly representative government of the city would not favor whites. In view of this the committee recommended that "All communities should, so far as it is practicable[,] govern themselves in viable, independent local authorities, in respect of all parochial affairs and matters of a localized nature."

The crux of the matter was whether the nonwhite areas were a burden on the city's economy. The town clerk estimated the relative weight of different communities in paying rates. The figures were compiled on the basis of "ratable valuations of developed property in Durban," that is, property values (and not actual rates paid). The official figures showed a white population, a clear minority, paying almost 70 percent of the rates while Indians allegedly paid only 28 percent and colored 2.5 percent. The rhetoric of avoiding "domination" and of implementing structures of government that are "practical" reflected precisely the perception that a hardworking white population shouldered most responsibilities and bankrolled the poorer and less productive majority of color in the city. The system of LACs and other "autonomous" bodies was not merely a way of "introducing of the Indian and Coloured communities into the art and practice of responsible and worthwhile government at the municipal level" as the town clerk's report stated.[18] In practice, it provided an interpretation of autonomy that amounted to avoiding "domination" by the city's majority population, and a way of reserving the vast majority of funds that were generated in the city for the development of the white areas. It was an assertion of racial domination that was disguised as a form of differential economic citizenship.

Many activists in the Indian townships had pointed to this problem since the 1960s. In their view, the figures of the city were completely doctored and manipulated to make the Indian contributions invisible. Now retired from his job as an accountant, and an active member in a ratepayers association in Chatsworth for many years, Mr. Pillay explained to me:

> The city always overcharged the Indian areas but always hid the actual figures. Many Indian households actually ended up paying more per house than in white areas because the market for Indian land is so restricted and the prices are so artificially inflated. Indian families often paid more than the whites although their earnings were much higher than ours. The Council always claimed it only used property values as a guideline, but that was only a smaller part of the combined rates . . . in their official figures they inflated the values of white property and reduced the value of Indian houses to make it look like they paid more than us. . . . Many whites also got big reductions on their rates. We Indians always paid much more than we actually received.[19]

In the 1980s, the city council had a new crisis on its hands that was precipitated by the refusal among many civic and cultural organizations in the new Indian township of Phoenix to support a new LAC for the township. An organization called Phoenix Working Committee denounced LACs as "a body without power," and a body "that has never been able to do anything for the Indian people." The committee called for mass protests against the LACs and demanded a referendum on the issue.[20]

The respected Durban Indian Child and Family Welfare Society took an early stance against the LAC system. The organization "regards participation by its members in bodies such as the SAIC, LAC and Regional Welfare Boards as undesirable and detrimental to the long-term interests of the child welfare movement as a whole." The term "child welfare" had now come to stand as a metonym of the cause of the Indian community as such. Its reasoning was that these "racially exclusive authorities" would make the delivery of welfare services "fragmented, uncoordinated and inefficient," would cause "uncertainty among professionals," and that these institutions did not enjoy the support of a "majority of South Africans." One painful consequence was that two senior and long-standing members of the society were suspended on the grounds that they had been standing for LAC elections in 1988.[21]

In early 1988, the chairman of the Northern Durban LAC, Kamal Panday, was caught by the camera in a strip club, where he was onstage with a stripper who had undressed him and herself to a bare minimum.[22] This incident soon became a minor scandal. The authorities tried to do some damage control by holding a series of large inclusive meetings, entitled the "KwaZulu Indaba," in order to generate a new consensus on local government, but to little avail.[23] The air of unreality and bad faith surrounding these initiatives was simply too pervasive at this point. Reggie, a retired teacher with a keen interest in politics, expressed a widely shared sentiment in Chatsworth.

> Look, in the beginning some people thought we could have some influence in the LAC. Personally, I think Rajbansi did some good there when he was young. . . . He was never afraid of telling the white councilors to their face that they were lying or bluffing . . . but that was all before he became corrupt . . . none of these characters had any principles. It was clear that if you wanted a license for a liquor store, a building permit, or whatever, you should get on the LAC . . . this is what these people did, grease palms and stuff their pockets like the white councilors . . . they were clowns and they were an embarrassment to all of us. I never voted and none of my friends or colleagues ever did either.

Val Pillay, who served on the Southern LAC for a decade and is today an active supporter of the Minority Front, disagreed:

> It is true that the system was rotten. I spent years protesting the way we were treated by the Council. They overcharged us, ignored us, showed contempt for us in meetings. Still, someone had to speak up for us and at least try to do something . . . we helped Indian businesses, that is true, nobody else did that, and it benefits the community. . . . The communists hated us, I know that, but I never thought they had any idea how the average Indian thinks. He is conservative, he likes his house and he wants to be respected. Most people here [in Chatsworth] do not want to share what they built up by themselves. See where Mbeki and all his communist friends got us today [2001] . . . Some people are very rich today but I am not sure that is what Mac Maharaj and the rest of them wanted . . . there was less poverty and also more equality in the past.[24]

Meanwhile, the bureaucracy churned slowly and steadily. In 1989, the government produced incredibly detailed stipulations of the issues that "may be delegated to Coloured and Indians management and Local affairs committees." For example, the provisions were to supervise and regulate "the keeping of poultry and animals," "rules pertaining to dogs," "camping and picnicking," to put up public lighting and certain traffic signs, to create public lavatories, to grant building permits, to determine library opening hours, and to propose the renaming of streets and places to the city council.[25]

Debates on the exact meaning of autonomy continued into the early 1990s when the CODESA negotiations in Pretoria between the National Party, the ANC, and other stakeholders were about to produce an entirely new administrative and political order in the country.[26] However, the most significant event that recast the political landscape among Indians as a whole, and in Chatsworth in particular, was the short and heavily contested career of the Indian house in the Tricameral Parliament structure that came into being in the 1980s.

The House of Delhigoats

In its characteristically stubborn and inflexible style, the Botha government insisted that the language of self-determination was put in service of consolidating and incorporating Indians and colored into a governing structure as political minors. This would, in turn, consolidate the fundamental exclusion of Africans from any formal representation in the state. Drawn up in collaboration with a range of U.S.-based political scientists, among them Samuel Huntington, the strategy was one of representation without real influence. In addition to the existing House of Assembly (178 seats for whites), two additional houses were to be set up: the House of Representatives (80 seats for coloreds) and the House of Delegates (45 seats for Indians). All houses were based on universal adult franchises within the respective race groups and had the "power to legislate on affairs affecting that population group" (*Fiat Lux*, August 1984). Each of the chambers was supposed to constitute a Ministers Council, which was elected to oversee the specific affairs delegated to the House.

The real power remained firmly in the hands of the state president, who was elected by whites, and the cabinet he appointed, which was comprised of white ministers. The colored and Indian Ministers Councils had an "advisory role" to the president but no real power or influence. The new class of politicians who were jockeying for power was assured that all colored and Indian ministers were to be given status and privileges equivalent to that of the "real" ministers in the cabinet.[27]

The ideological text behind the new construction espoused a form of make-believe multiculturalism: "The South African population consists of diverse minorities," brought together by history, as President P. W. Botha put it in an address to luminaries of the Indian community in December 1983 in Durban: "There is no single majority in South Africa: we are all members of minorities of differing sizes and number."[28] The task, Botha said, was to find a way "to permanently ensure the rights of minorities within a framework on the basis of community security and joint responsibility, ensuring not only self-determination but also national purpose and a national will." Botha acknowledged that many Indians were either indifferent or hostile to the government's policies. He continued, "You had little say in the history of South Africa. You now have the chance to become joint architects of your own future and the future of South Africa."[29]

The new administration reconfigured existing departments in the Ministry of Indian Affairs and city councils across the country and comprised areas declared as "Indian." The new administration comprised all the needs of the new Indian social body: welfare, health, education, community development, and local government. The leading men of the new system were drawn mainly from Chatsworth's new layer of small businessmen and professionals who had risen though the LAC system. Two parties faced each other: the National People's Party, led by the reenergized Rajbansi, and the Solidarity Party under J. N. Reddy. The programs of the two parties were not vastly different, and both outfits were by and large personal fiefdoms of their leaders and a few trusted men. One significant difference was that Rajbansi was seen as representing North Indian interests, while Reddy was assumed to attract more Tamil votes. Another difference was one of style: Rajbansi excelled in robust populist rhetoric and posturing, while the profile of Solidarity was that of educated and suave operators in the corridors of power.

The electoral campaign and the counter campaign in 1984 proved to be an effective if short-lived rallying point for large numbers of younger and educated Indians who had been radicalized by the many protests and the general air of opposition that characterized the post-Soweto moment. In Durban, the campaign for a boycott of the elections marked an important moment where the larger nonracial platform represented by the United Democratic Front made its first real impact in the province, which was often out of sync with larger national trends. It also marked a high point in the mobilization of Indians who were critical of apartheid. A former activist who was a high school student in Chatsworth at the time told me, "Many of us wanted to do more, but we could not just join the mass protests in the black townships or the strikes. Campaigning against the House of Delegates meant that we could do something meaningful where we lived."

The campaign was supposedly coordinated and initiated by the NIC, but it soon acquired a local momentum beyond the control of the often secretive and starkly Leninist modalities of control and organization that dominated the NIC leadership at the time. Another former activist told me, "For me it was not about the NIC, it was about being with friends in political meetings, being part of a moment where we felt we made a difference. . . . We went from house to house, knocked on doors, talked to the aunties, to people our own age also. We really thought we were shaking up the system." Both sides of the campaign declared the final result in 1984 a success.

The National People's Party won the majority of seats, and Rajbansi, who at this time had developed a close working relationship with P. W. Botha, was made head of the Ministers Council with all the honors and new patronage power this entailed. For Rajbansi, this was a crowning moment in his career but also the beginning of his downfall, as we will see. The elections had not produced a new political class, however. More than half of the elected members had at some point been members of SAIC or a member of one of the LACs (Desai 1996, 69). The turnout had been very low—a mere 16.6 percent of eligible voters (20.3 percent of those registered) had bothered to vote despite a lavish and expensive election campaign. The boycott campaign saw this as evidence of ordinary Indians turning their backs on the new political system. The turnout was only a bit higher than for the LAC, and many of the newly elected members accused the progressive activists of undue manipulation and intimidation of voters. A Rajbansi supporter put it like this: "Their campaign was organized by the communists, you see . . . they told people lies and twisted their minds. Most of them were not even from Chatsworth. They were rich people who came down from Johannesburg and from Reservoir Hills. They were educated and spoke well and many of the older people may have been impressed with them." While this assessment may be paranoid, it pointed to an enduring structure of political and social attitudes among Indians in general. The educated middle class was far more critical of apartheid and its institutions than the blue-collar workers and the new class of businessmen for whom the consolidation of the relatively secure world of the township was more important than equal political representation.

An officially commissioned study found that the fault lines ran along lines of age, class, and prior political participation. Those who voted (20.3 percent) and/or supported the new tricameral system (30 percent in total) were slightly older and less educated than the average, and a significant proportion had voted in earlier elections for the LACs or SAIC. Those who were against the tricameral system (34 percent) and/or supported the antiapartheid UDF (21.4 percent) were better educated as a whole, slightly younger, and with a lower record of previous voting.[30]

Another point emerging from this survey was that the segment of Indians favoring "collaboration" with state institutions was relatively stable at around 20–30 percent, while the segment actively opposing apartheid was likely to be of equal size, if steadily growing during the 1980s. This assessment was supported by the fact that in the second round of elections for the House of Delegates in 1989, the turnout stood slightly higher (22.9 percent) without the impact of a vigorous boycott campaign (Desai 1996, 82).

The activists behind the election boycott claimed that the vast majority of Indians had rejected the institutions of apartheid. On balance, it seems more likely that the vast majority of Indians were simply uninterested in voting or in politics. In the survey, respondents were asked whether they had interest or conversations about politics. Interestingly, there was hardly any difference between those who voted and those who did not. The overwhelming majority stated that they rarely or never talked about politics (72–74 percent) and an equal number said that they were almost not, or not at all, interested in political matters (75–77 percent).[31] It seems that the effect of the boycott campaign was less to turn the majority away from voting than simply to confirm to the vast majority that matters political were dangerous, irrelevant, and best left to others (whites, Africans) or to the few individuals within the community who were interested in exercising power.

This fear of politics seems to correlate with the equally stable attitudes toward other race groups discussed earlier. Three official surveys were conducted among Indians in the early 1980s to determine their attitude to the possibility of an African majority rule. All three surveys showed that a clear majority of Indians rejected this possibility.[32] The support for Indian "autonomy" and the "self-development" promised by the apartheid ideology was consistent and decisively shaped by the memories of the 1949 riots and the Group Areas Act. The real paradox was, as Desai points out, that the "state failed to facilitate the development of an 'Indianism' . . . the fostering of some sort of 'Indian nationalism' could have been expected" (1986, 239). It seems clear that the apartheid project never really engaged in systematic ideological persuasion of subordinated people of color. The apartheid project was based on the combination of a hyperrealist body politics, an assumption of natural racial solidarity, and hyperbolic performances of state power, rhetoric, and pomp that increasingly assumed absurd and profoundly unreal dimensions.[33]

This unreality and absurdity peaked during the presidency of P. W. Botha from 1978 to 1988. This era of *Die Groot Krokodil* was the deepest crisis of legitimacy of apartheid. The House of Delegates played its distinctly ethnic part in this larger staged world of make-believe politics, which was built on crumbling foundations—a perpetual political theater disembedded from, and largely irrelevant to, the flow of ordinary life in the townships.

At the time of my initial fieldwork (1999–2000) in Durban, I asked many people about their memories of the LAC system. Younger people had no idea or recollection of the LAC system, but everybody knew about what popular wit had renamed the House of Delhigoats. Among slightly older people, a majority had vague and largely dismissive ideas about both these bodies. The most common term for this style of Indian politics was in fact that they were all "clowns" and an embarrassment to the community. The magazine *Fiat Lux* is a good example of a peculiar instrument of state propaganda, which in the 1980s became ever more shrill and pompous in its attempts to sell a particular image of the House of Delegates and the benevolence of the South African state. Its main function was to explain the various policies to the limited world of Indian bureaucrats, local politicians, and officials who were partaking in the activities described in the magazine. The structuring effects of the apartheid project were not ideological but lay in the long-term reinvention of Indian life through the deep biopolitical interventions I described in the first chapters. The air of unreality and involuntary comedy of political minors in the House of Delhigoats reached a climax in the scandal that forced Rajbansi to resign in 1988.

"Scandals Are the Foundations of the State"

The unreal, scandalous, but also fascinatingly excessive had accompanied Rajbansi's political career from the outset.[34] Rajbansi was, as we saw, already at the center of an affair in the 1970s that involved a trademark combination of assertive speech and allegations of financial irregularity. In 1986, Rajbansi made his maiden speech in the white House of Assembly in Cape Town. Ignoring attempts to interrupt him from the floor, he presented himself as a follower of "Mahatma Gandhi, the greatest pacifist of our time." Rajbansi praised the great innovator of political recalcitrance and passive resistance in the following words: "If Gandhiji was alive today this would have been his proud day because he did not believe in boycott politics. He was a negotiator who believed in adopting a tactic and a particular strategy dependent on the circumstances of the time." He then extended sincere thanks (again, seemingly without a hint of irony) to the cabinet and the state president for "75 years of tremendous understanding of one another and especially for one another's problems." In a complete contradiction of this, the rest of the speech enumerated the hurtful legislation that had affected the Indian community throughout the twentieth century. At the end of the speech, several Afrikaner MPs yelled at him than he was a *verraaier* (traitor) and that his speech was a *skandale* (scandal). Undeterred, Rajbansi closed his speech with a poem by Rabindranath Tagore.[35]

The speech summed up the impossibility and blindness at the heart of the politics of autonomy and self-determination of the late apartheid state. The tricameral construction was based on relinquishing any effective aspiration for sovereignty by formalizing a permanent minority status for coloreds and Indians. The construction presupposed that this limited autonomy was underpinned by a proud ethnic history and identity. Such community histories were, however, necessarily defined by perpetual subordination to whites, being the object of abuse, denunciated as traitors, and seen as irredeemably alien. In short, a history defined by injury and loss was to be followed by a form of representation that was defined by bad faith and doublespeak.

Among many Indians, and also white politicians and administrators, the assumption was that those participating in this political theater did so for pure material gain rather than any genuine political investment. Material gains were a priori apportioned and distributed along racial lines, and political elites were assumed to be the gatekeepers of the economic and political crumbs that had been handed out to them. The Indian commercial elite was subjected to harsh regulations and strictures that severely impaired their prosperity and enterprise at the national level.[36] However, at the local level, business deals and land transactions were often conducted across race boundaries to mutual benefit. The Gujarati traders across the small towns of Transvaal managed to keep their livelihoods and practices intact in the face of the Group Areas Act. In Durban, the cash-rich community of experienced Indian businessmen ensured that their world of local privilege continued within elite residential areas that were designated for Indians. Prominent Indian businessmen and politicians managed to buy or retain land and property that in principle was rezoned for whites, and they managed to keep white capital out of Indian areas.[37] This gave the Indian business elite monopoly status in the "internal" economy of the Indian community. Many of the members of SAIC, the LAC, and later the House of Delegates enhanced their economic status enormously in the semimonopolized crony economy that characterized late apartheid.

One such example was the state-aided creation of the New Republic Bank, which was entirely controlled by Indian businesspeople, notably J. N. Reddy, the leader of the conservative Solidarity Party.[38] Indian business practices were routinely depicted as clannish, closed, and essentially "dirty"—based on mutual help within networks of relatives and friends. Similarly, it was also expected that political alliances would form along lines of community and kin. Rajbansi was seen as an essentially North Indian politician, while Reddy was based on Tamil and Telugu votes. However, the pattern of ethnic solidarity was never clear-cut and provided a very poor guide to the dynamics of political alignment among Indians, both then and now.

Allegations of cronyism, corruption, and shady backroom deals did indeed surround Indian politics from the outset. The illegitimacy of both the LACs and the House of Delegates meant that much of the critique of these institutions from progressive and well-educated Indians easily incorporated and recycled a large number of essentialized ideas of Indian traditional clannishness and backwardness. All of these elements came together in the scandal that eventually led to the dismissal of Rajbansi as the chairman of the Ministers Council in the House of Delegates in 1988.

In the eyes of liberal, left-leaning, educated Indians, Rajbansi's performance on the Ministers Council was scandalous from the outset. He performed the part as the good and subservient Indian to perfection by feeding tasty samosas prepared by his richly adorned wife to local white political bosses and wearing the same hat as *Die Groot Krokodil* president P. W. Botha, while pursuing a ruthless patronage politics in his own constituency that involved very substantial intermixing of his political clout and his business interests. To many educated Indians, Rajbansi simply represented all the most shameful and infuriating aspects of Indianness in South Africa.

In 1987, it all came to a sudden halt as Rajbansi's murky property transactions and corrupt practices came to the attention of sections of the so-called mainstream, or white, press in Durban. Rajbansi was quickly relieved of his duties, and a commission headed by Justice Neville James was appointed to probe into the Rajbansi style of politics. The final report was a detailed examination of the political micropractices, especially in Chatsworth. It paints a bleak and sordid picture of how Rajbansi and his cronies (of all ethnicities and faiths) engaged in shady property deals, attempted to get cuts and parts of liquor licenses, and how political influence served self-enrichment. The evidence of Rajbansi's blatantly partisan style of leadership, his greed, corrupt practices, and unrelenting bullying tactics against his adversaries was indeed damning in every respect. While the report pretended to uphold the principles of fairness and the ethics of lawful action, it studiously ignored the very principles of apartheid that had enabled this hothouse of monopolistic cronyism.

Unusually, the report began with a commentary on the character and personalities of key witnesses that revealed the class and racial bias of its author. About Mr. Pillay, Rajbansi's erstwhile business partner, the judge writes that he "has a fervent desire to make money." About Rajbansi, James wrote, "he is a quick thinking man of enormous energy and determination who adopted a bold and indeed pugnacious attitude to the problems confronting him." James characterized Rajbansi as "arrogant and unscrupulous . . . a mean-minded bully . . . unwilling to concede that he was ever at fault and ready to lie boldly and without hesitation . . . an inordinately ambitious man obsessed with a desire to achieve personal power."[39] About the Crown witness, a Mr. Hunt, director of local government in the House of Delegates, the judge wrote that he was "a conscientious and fair-minded person . . . honourable and reliable." The officials (all white) who assisted in the investigation are praised by the judge for being men of "great skill and efficiency," who are able to distinguish fact from "gossip and unsupported rumour," and who exhibit "remarkable patience, courtesy and sound judgment" (87–88). The commission recommended that Rajbansi should be relieved of all duties permanently and stated famously that "he should not in the future be employed as a minister in the House of Delegates or in any official or semi-official post which calls for integrity" (87). For a short while, a deeply anti-Indian white opinion and the progressive and educated Indians could unite in condemnation and ridicule of the murky world of greed, ambition, and corruption created by the marriage of "plumb" Afrikaner politics and the avarice and untrustworthiness of Chatsworth premier charou figures.

Later that year a play, simply called *The James Commission,* was staged in Durban. It was written by the Durban lawyer and actor Charles Pillay and directed by his wife Saira Essa. The play was an almost two-hour-long one-man tour de force by Charles Pillay. He was drawing on the well-established narrative tradition of South African Indian theater but obviously also on the work and performance of Peter Dirk Uys. Uys was already an accomplished impersonator and political satirist whose parodies of leading National Party politicians made him a household name across communities in South Africa at the time. In the polarized climate of the 1980s, Uys was often accused of making politics laughable and cozy by portraying the leading figures of the state as more endearing and human than they deserved. The critique of Rajbansi was, by comparison, much more unforgiving.

Charles Pillay said at the time, "I don't know if I wrote the play. When I went through the Commission's report I knew I had a play, it was there in front of me."[40] Here, there was an echo of Dirk Uys's almost identical remarks several years earlier when he used the report of the commission investigating the TV and communication scandal in the early 1980s as material for political satire.[41] When it was announced that a play of this nature was being staged, Rajbansi offered to play himself. "I can do it much better than Charles," he said to a newspaper,[42] but Charles Pillay insisted on playing the part. "I had to turn down the offer," Pillay said, "he would not have stuck to the script."[43]

This was one of the only Indian plays that ever found mercy in the eyes of white reviewers in Durban, who generally had only praise for any Indian production that conformed to a classical and mythological genre.[44] The *Mercury* went to the extent of saying that it was a play "that no longer was Indian"[45]—presumably the highest praise imaginable. The play's appeal to white audiences was undoubtedly that it systematically confirmed white prejudices regarding "the Indian" as the proverbial "wheeler-dealer," unfit to be entrusted with serious matters such as the affairs of state.

Interestingly, this scandal did not damage the House of Delegates or Rajbansi as much as expected within the rather well-consolidated and limited circles that were driving and supporting this peculiar style of "autonomous" Indian politics. Rajbansi stepped down as leader of "his" party and was temporarily suspended from Parliament. Two months later, Rajbansi was reinstated in his party and in Parliament. The dramatic events in the country were quickly hollowing out the relevance of the tricameral institutions, and the ruling National Party began wooing the Indian members to cross the floor, luring them with the prospect of posts in the "real" cabinet that actually ruled the country. It was a blatant and transparent attempt to prop up a regime and a party whose time in power was quickly running out. The only member who insisted that he could never join a "white" party and, according to his own narrative, "stood firm in the time of crisis," was Rajbansi. In one of several interviews I conducted with Rajbansi, he took a long, retrospective view of his career: "I have always been with the people. . . . When I was in the House of Delegates, I looked after my people by working within a system we never supported. . . . Yes, there were mistakes, but I am the only one of the former members of the House of Delegates who has had the guts to face the electorate in our new democracy and ask for their verdict. We have gone from strength to strength. I can walk the streets with my shoulders high."[46] By 1993, Rajbansi was the only member of the House of Delegates who had not defected to the ruling party. This stance enabled him to find a legitimate place in the momentous CODESA talks at Kempton Park that eventually led to the dismantling of apartheid and free and fair elections in 1994.

On his home turf in Chatsworth, his reputation was damaged but not beyond repair. A few years later, Rajbansi had bounced back, now as the tough-talking and unapologetic defender of the ordinary charou. To many in Chatsworth, whether they actually ever voted for Rajbansi or not, it seemed clear that he had been framed by his enemies and that the James Commission was nothing but an attempt to shut him up. A local shopkeeper gave me the following interpretation of the affair, which I later found repeated in many other forms:

> Raj was condemned because he was Indian. . . . Other people are doing the same—also white people with much bigger money and they are not caught. Why? . . . We Indians prefer to do business with

people we know, people we can trust. So when they accused him of selling land to people in his own party, people who were also North Indians, and at a good price, they say it is corruption because he takes some of the profit himself. Well, that is how we do business most of the time. What is wrong with that? Someone had to get the land and the contracts and most people in Chatsworth thought it was good that he gave it to Indians and not to some of these white companies . . . nowadays they run everything, supermarkets, cinemas, etc. Rajbansi just tried to help the Indians. . . . Why do you think the Muslims are so rich in this country? They do business like this all the time, but no one asks questions because they never disclose anything; nothing is on paper so no judge can look at it. If Rajbansi really thought he had done something wrong, do you think he would have written it all down and have followed all these procedures? . . . No, it was a white plot.

Who Speaks for the Community? The Particular as Universalist Gesture

The Natal Indian Congress had lived an almost shadowy existence since the clampdown on open political activity in the early 1960s. In the early 1980s, the leadership sensed a possibility of renewal of its older Leninist self-perception as the apex structure of "the community"—the place where serious political strategy for the entire community could be determined. Characteristically, the response by NIC president George Sewpersad to the government's new plans for limited political autonomy for Indians and coloreds was to present nothing less than a plan for the future of the entire country.[47] The proposal basically reiterated all the basic demands enshrined in the Freedom Charter of 1955—universal franchise, repealing of apartheid laws, equality before the law. This was an attempt to rekindle the sentiments and mythos of the 1940s, according to which the NIC acted as the general strategists of the struggles of "the Indian masses."

The problem was, however, that the NIC's leadership was drawn from a limited circle of privileged families in the city. The organization had no local presence in the townships. Tensions between a youthful grassroots base and a relatively closed leadership of the NIC bedeviled progressive politics in Durban throughout the 1980s.[48] The boycott campaign against the elections for the House of Delegates in 1984 brought the NIC back as a household name. However, the discrepancies between a leadership "drawn from the educated elite who had turned to politics with their degrees and careers safely tucked under their belt" (Desai 1996, 56) and the newly educated youth from the townships were unbridgeable. The NIC opposed campaigns against exploitative Indian landlords and employers, many of whom actually supported and bankrolled the NIC (57).

The NIC was also unable to generate any meaningful response to the many signs of racial tension, fear, and prejudice that circulated, especially after the destruction of Indian homes and Gandhi's Phoenix settlement in 1985. The NIC leadership was broadly regarded as a secretive and self-interested "cabal," out of touch with ground realities. After the unbanning of the ANC, various Indian members of the ANC and Mandela himself reached out to Indian organizations and encouraged them to facilitate "Indian recruitment for the ANC." The leaders of the NIC welcomed this as recognition of the fact that "ethnic factors were crucial to the mobilization of the masses," as Farouk Meer put it in 1991.[49] However, as we will see later, the actual delivery of the "Indian vote" to the ANC in the 1990s was to be facilitated by the irrepressible and reincarnated Rajbansi.

By the late 1980s the driving force of the progressive opposition to apartheid was the organizations that sponsored broadly social causes. The most important of these was the Durban Housing Action Committee, which coordinated a rates boycott and channeled a range of local complaints into a sustained confrontation with the city council. To some, the rates boycott was a local issue that was also driven by opportunistic Indian self-interest. As Lal put it, "We should not fool ourselves. Most of the people who boycotted rates did it because they hated paying to the Council . . . were they against apartheid as we all used to say? I am not sure . . . but we all gave the Council a lot of trouble. That was what counted." Those embracing the Black Consciousness movement argued that local activism and opposition to "ethnic" Indian politics remained captive to apartheid's own categories. "There is no 'Indian struggle,'" argued Saths Cooper, a high-profile leader (of Indian origin) in the Black Consciousness movement, "if people continue to believe that they are Indian, they will have no place in a future Azania. They must begin to prepare to go back to India."[50]

There were certain junctures where the particular issues arising from the Indian townships escaped from the "ethnic self-imprisonment," as Cooper called it, and merged into larger issues. Some of the campaigns by the Mass Democratic Movement (MDM; an offshoot of the Housing Committee) in the late 1980s managed to produce such links to the larger political thrust in the country toward transforming the system itself.

Reserving Durban's famous beaches for whites (smaller sections were reserved for Indians and Africans, respectively) had for a long time been the most visible symbol of petty apartheid. In 1982, the city council proposed that a limited portion of the beachfront should be made multiracial but on the condition that nonwhites should be charged a fee. The initiative elicited mixed responses, mostly because those considering it were skeptical of the idea of payment. A Mr. Bugwandeen objected, "Why must we pay a fee—and they call it the Indian Ocean!" Others were less interested in the beach as a place for swimming than in the possibility of fishing and barbecuing on the beach.

The beaches only became a real locus of mobilization seven years later when rumors spread that the infamous Separate Amenities Act was to be repealed in 1989. In early September 1989, thousands of activists—Africans, whites, and Indians—entered the "whites only" beaches and spent a good deal of the day "netballing, toyi-toying and chanting freedom songs." The protest was a copy of a similar action in Cape Town that had been met with police officers *sjambokking* (whipping) African and colored protesters. The Durban action had been announced and prepared well in advance. It was led by a number of religious and political leaders and proceeded without violent incidents, despite concerted attempts by white racists to provoke violence.[51] NIC leaders declared an important symbolic victory and stated, "South Africa will never be the same again" (ibid.). The action was significant and is still remembered fondly. A former activist from a Muslim background told me,

> We were not sure what was going to happen. There was police everywhere, and they had already arrested some of the MDM leadership . . . but we were so many that once we were on the beach we felt that no one could do anything to us. For me this was the first time on the beach and the first time I was in a protest with many white people also . . . I am not so interested in the beach except for picnics. I don't swim and I think there should be separate areas for women also, but we made a point that day.

The significance of the beaches was divided along class lines. The working-class men I talked to about their memories would generally say that the beachfront was no good for fishing. "There are too many surfers, and we like the Bluff beach [old Indian territory] better—we can fish and *braai* [barbecue] without worries." For others, the beachfront epitomized white privilege, a closed but also attractive world of carefree leisure. A successful media personality who grew up in Chatsworth told me:

> As a child I used to look at the surfers, and I was thinking "I'd like to do that," but I knew that I could not. We could not afford all the gear, and the Indian beaches were no good for surfing. . . . But I really envied these guys and their lifestyle. Lots of us used to talk about that at the time. The funny thing is that when they opened the

beaches no charou ever went . . . they still go fishing only. . . . If we go to the beach for a picnic, where do we go? To the Blue Lagoon [a part of the beach that was set aside for Indians in the 1970s] with all the other charous!

The MDM was one of the more successful attempts to develop a form of mass politics that went beyond the confines of local and irrevocably racialized interests and concerns. However, it was still clear that the particular concerns of Indians and others required a shared enemy, the white racist state, as a general equivalence that could transform the local into a universalist gesture. Without this element, collective action remained local and Indian. The inherent contradictions of this structure of political consciousness were to show themselves in the momentous events after 1994.

THE ONLY GOOD INDIAN IS A POOR INDIAN: THE ANC AND THE INDIAN TOWNSHIPS

The period after the unbanning of the ANC saw hectic activity in Chatsworth, Phoenix, and other Indian areas. Meetings were held in which leading ANC functionaries and leading members of the NIC assured Indians that they had nothing to fear from the transition to majority rule. An audience of mainly educated Indians meeting at the Aryan Benevolent Home in Chatsworth was told to "share their resources with the historically disadvantaged communities," and Jerry Coovadia of the NIC implored the crowd to "integrate into the larger community without losing cultural identity."[52] The ANC leadership formed a task force that was charged with finding ways to attract the Indian minority. The ANC was aware that both the National Party and the conservative Inkatha Freedom Party were doing their best to capitalize on the palpable sentiments of fear among Indians in the face of majority rule. Roy Padayachee of the ANC, who headed the task force, stated that "apart from a handful of collaborators, the majority in the Indian community has always stood against injustice, racial discrimination and oppression." However, in the period of "great confusion . . . a dangerous illusion [exists] that there could be a separate future for Indians."[53] The year after, Mandela was touring the Indian townships for the first time and was received enthusiastically by thousands in mass meetings. He stated that the groundswell of opposition to the tricameral system showed that the common Indian was against apartheid. He promised nonetheless to open talks with the old members of the House of Delegates, "just like the ANC talks to leaders of homelands and others."[54]

Despite these concerted efforts, Indians turned against the ANC in a manner that even skeptics had not anticipated. In the 1994 elections, the ANC won 25 percent and the National Party won 64 percent of the votes in Chatsworth Electoral District. In the simultaneous provincial vote, the Minority Front won 19.5 percent, almost as much as the ANC's 22 percent. In spite of massive enthusiasm and another series of huge rallies, the voter turnout stood around 60 percent, a major jump compared with the 1980s elections but still one of the lowest in the country.

On the eve of the 1999 elections, I met with a small group of long-standing ANC activists in Chatsworth. They were deeply concerned about the outcome of the elections. Throughout the campaign they had felt resistance and skepticism among the poorer sections in the township. They did not think the ANC would get more than the 20 percent of the vote they had won in 1994, perhaps even less. "We have completely lost the Indian working class," one of them told me, "they are afraid of what is going on in the country . . . many of them tell us that they thought things were better under the Nats." They were dismayed by the fact that in the Indian areas, the ANC was almost exclusively a middle-class party: "We thought we had a mass base here, but people's memories are short . . . none of the candidates we fielded have a local record . . . what does it help to bring in former Indian militants like Ebrahim Ebrahim if people don't know them? What does it help when ANC leaders in Durban after the last elections stated openly that the areas that don't vote for ANC will receive fewer amenities?"[55] They felt that at the provincial level, the ANC wanted to punish the Indians for not voting for the ANC. In response, they had drafted a small discussion paper in pithy phrases that summarized the problem of the ANC, in particular, and progressive politics in Chatsworth more broadly. They blamed the problem on the NIC's attempt to capture the moment in 1990 when the ANC was unbanned. This produced "sidelining and marginalization of the established political leadership within the Indian community and allegations of 'cabalism' traversing the entire country. A climate of demoralization overcame a large number of activists."[56]

The paper conceded that Rajbansi had arisen, once again, to his older position as the primary broker between the community and the state. "Rajbansi gets swifter responses from the ANC leaders than local ANC structures," they complained. The paper offered a precise analysis of the failed mobilization of Indians: "To tell people in Chatsworth that their futures are secure under a non-racial ANC and evidence that the ANC indeed is accommodative of Indian aspirations by citing a large number of Indians in the cabinet and the upper echelons of the ANC sadly misses the point. The community in Chatsworth and Phoenix do not aspire to cabinet posts—they want jobs and security."[57] The frustration regarding the Indian vote was fully understandable in view of the considerable effort that had been expended in cajoling and attracting Indians to vote for the ANC. Mandela took a special interest in the Indian community and campaigned in the township during virtually every major campaign in the 1990s. In 1996, Mandela appeared before a large crowd, garlanded in the traditional manner, and said, "Because of the sacrifices and contributions of the Indian community, I have always regarded them as part of my own flesh and blood."[58] Two years later, Mandela went on the popular radio program *Viewpoint* and implored Indians "to leave the sidelines and join the majority."[59] Nothing indicated that these efforts changed the level of support for the ANC.

The resentment against township Indians was palpable among most progressives I met in the late 1990s, regardless of race. Several questioned my choice of field site, and implored me to work with people who were less "clannish and reactionary," as a white colleague put it; or not "racists fence-sitters" as a friend, a Zulu-speaking schoolteacher from Umlazi, told me. The gulf between the networks of progressive political leaders and activists-turned-administrators on the one hand and the ordinary charou on the other seemed to deepen. Among many people I met in the townships, the fears of African majority rule was indeed a factor, but the more immediate resentment was directed against the local "ANC Indians," local people who had climbed up the social ladder and had become lahnees, educated doctors, teachers, and professionals. Many saw them as haughty and arrogant, and said that they treated the ordinary charous as irresponsible children in need of discipline and education.

After the 1999 election, Rajbansi's Minority Front had once again appeared as the most effective local outfit in the Indian townships, and the ANC changed its tactics to one of electoral "subcontracting." Rajbansi forged informal but effective alliances with the ANC at all levels—from the city council in Durban to the provincial legislature and Parliament. This allowed the ANC to indirectly rally the support of the Indian working class, which it was unable to win over by its own rhetoric and organization.

In 2000, a new development promised to change the political configuration in Chatsworth. The well-known sociologist Fatima Meer, a personal friend of Mandela and long-standing member of the tight-knit social network that had sustained the NIC for decades, decided to take on the municipal authorities in Durban. Her group, Concerned Citizen's Group (CCG), counted many of the city's prominent Indians, "a who-is-who of our Indian political aristocracy," as a friend in the city put it. The cause was the plight of poor tenants in Chatsworth's extensive council flat areas. After 1994, the new city authorities had continued to encourage tenants to buy their own flats. This was supposed to improve responsibility and social attitudes in the community. Many of the tenants, who by the late 1990s were a mix of both Indians and Africans, were in hopeless arrears and were threatened with evictions by the authorities. Deputy Mayor Trevor Bonhomme, the erstwhile hero of the MDM's beach invasions and a long-term spokesperson for the Durban Housing Action Committee, was now in charge of housing policies in the city.

The CCG was one of the most direct attacks on the ANC from former allies, and the effect in Chatsworth was initially electrifying. In his breathless and deeply partisan account of the movement, Ashwin Desai writes that the CCG assumed that the reason "Indians did not vote for the ANC was because of their racist fear of Africans." The CCG initially thought it would be able to move them "beyond a minority false consciousness" (2002, 8). What the CCG found was staggering levels of absolute poverty, deprivation, and wholesale dependency on dwindling pensions and benefits.[60] The flat dwellers expressed their anger not at the past but at their "present oppressors"—the city council. The activists also found, in Desai's hagiographical account, that at this level of deprivation, race was not an issue, nor were questions of socialist strategy or other "older categories of political thought" of relevance (2002, 10). What mattered was to oppose neoliberal policies and to create alliances among poor people. Over time, and due to the learning experience of a common struggle, the poor would begin to overcome "curious prejudice" regarding religion and sexual lifestyle (12).

Desai's account of this movement is indeed arresting and engaging while also strangely oblivious to the longer historical memories imprinted on the township. It is indeed ironic that the CCG and its dedicated group of middle-class activists were critical of letting the township residents "remain ensconced in the ghettos to which apartheid consigned them" (98), but without suggesting an alternative path. However, to oppose the city council and to contest issues of amenities and housing was no new modality of popular politics in Chatsworth. It was, as we saw earlier, the very original form of activism and particularistic politics that was born with and upon this space itself.

The historical ironies were many but not only those Desai notes. One paradox lies in the fact that movements like the CCG—mobilizing middle-class Indians to care for impoverished Indians—repeat an even deeper modality of activism that began in the 1930s. In chapter 3 we met a forty-years-younger Fatima Meer reporting on the plight of those displaced from Cato Manor in the early 1960s. Another irony lies in the fact that the CCG had combined resentment against the city authorities with another and more complex sentiment that had existed across Chatsworth for a decade: the resentment against the ANC and its ostensible sidelining of Indians by disproportionately attending to African areas mixed with a measure of class resentment against the local "ANC Indians," who were often regarded as lahnees.

Desai's and the CCG's assertion that poverty was able to overcome—or make irrelevant—cultural and religious dispositions was undoubtedly true during brief and intense moments of confrontation. Implicitly, however, this assertion stands on the shoulders of long-standing assumptions among left-leaning activists: first, that the petty differences and prejudices of culture are burned away in the "white heat" of true class struggle; and second, that racism, intolerance, and social conservatism are less entrenched among poor sections than within a home-owning petit bourgeois status that was anxious to defend their tenuous social respectability. However, these assumptions are based on a desire for the "people" to emerge as a truly progressive force in and of itself, rather than a more complex understanding of the lives and cultural horizons of poor township dwellers. As we will see in subsequent chapters, religious identities and complex cultural identifications, however imprecise and fleeting, play just as important roles in the poorest areas of Chatsworth as they do in its relatively consolidated blue-collar areas.

"ALL THE WAY": ON THE WAYS OF THE TIGER

In 1999, the Minority Front launched a new slogan: "Minority Front— All the Way." I discussed it with local party workers. Most of them liked it. "This is how we are—we stand firm on our policy, all the way," a young businesswoman and mother of two told me. "The Tiger is like that himself, no? We should all learn from him." Another party worker, a Muslim man in his forties who spent the better part of his life in left-wing unions, told me, "It means no compromises from us—if you are with us, it is only us and no one else." He found that the idea of "absolute loyalty" was necessary but difficult too: "In the union we always said unity with other workers was more important than anything else, no personal politics was allowed . . . but it was never like that really. Some people develop ambitions and want to do their own thing, be the baas . . . with the Raj that is difficult. There can only be one top man." This was the explanation for why the party could never really grow beyond the Indian townships, another worker explained: "Raj does not want more than that, I think." These remarks reflected what I experienced when following the party on the campaign trail. Every decision had to be cleared with "the Raj," and he kept the different workers in a tight set of concentric circles—a few trusted confidantes, among them his second wife, Shameen; a second circle of dedicated workers and volunteers, many of them women who were quite personally dedicated to their leader, who in turn treated them kindly and with much affection. The men in this circle were often experienced campaigners—former LAC members, trade unionists, and so on—less subservient but never in straight opposition, merely sulking when publicly reproached by Rajbansi. The third circle was a more motley assemblage of volunteers who were drawn to the party for different reasons—gratitude to Rajbansi, opposition to the ANC, or an unfocused resentment about how the township was changing.

For these people "All the Way" meant loyalty, firmness, resolution—all the qualities that Rajbansi projected in his new populist incarnation as the Tiger of Bengal, protector and defender of the charous, the meanest and proudest beast in the jungle that is Chatsworth. However, for most township residents, "All the Way" had slightly different connotations—more akin to supporting Rajbansi "through thick and thin," or perhaps "despite myself," or even an assertive, "I'm Indian, damn it!" as someone summed up Rajbansi's attraction despite his obvious shortcomings as a political leader. "All the Way" seems to suggest an invitation to be and remain oneself, without apologies.

Rajbansi's rebirth as a populist leader of the overlooked and marginalized Indian people was an exercise in good political timing. Rajbansi never disappeared from the political scene, and he maintained his base in Chatsworth. Since winning a fifth of the vote in 1994 (more than he ever achieved in the House of Delegates system) his influence steadily grew in municipal and provincial politics. After the elections in 1999, the party and its four mandates in the province, and two at the national level, provided the crucial mandates that ensured the ANC political dominance.

Controlling the decisive vote enabled him and his party to secure influence on the vital interests of Indians—jobs, education, housing—and to protect them from the hostility they face from many Africans (and whites). At the time of this writing, Rajbansi has become the minister of Sport and Recreation in the provincial coalition government of KwaZulu-Natal. The party's website boasts an interesting renarration of Rajbansi's life as a true South African working-class hero: "a mature politician at 14," a supporter of the ANC, and a key negotiator in the talks that founded the new republic:

> From a shy young lad in the volatile area of Clairwood which was the hub of NIC activities, where an important SACTU office was situated and where the young lad of 14 met Albert Luthuli, Madiba and Moses Mabida, and where thoughts went through his mind about

the Nats resettling railway workers in Montclair and Wentworth—Amichand Rajbansi the politician and man who would dedicate his life to serving the downtrodden emerged. Later the famous cartoonist, Nanda Subban dedicated his first book to the person he described as one of the most colourful politicians. . . . Even Madiba loved him when he was young and honoured him by having lunch with him at his residence in Chatsworth where Madiba said that he came to thank him for this contribution. Only the Raj and Madiba share the secrets when at 3am they discussed breaking the deadlock at CODESA to get South Africa's first democratic constitution. . . . He tells his detractors that the system did not make him. He was a mature politician at the age of 14 and attended every ANC rally addressed by Dr. Luthuli and Moses Mabida in Durban.[61]

The website sells Rajbansi as the "Tiger of Bengal," a "comeback kid," a "political cat with nine lives," and so on. The strength of Rajbansi is, in other words, his stubbornness, persistence, and sheer staying power in a world of power that is alien and distant from his own background.

Like most ordinary Indians in the country, Rajbansi comes from a humble background, and his ancestry stretches back to northern Bengal. What is relatively unknown in South Africa is that the popular stereotype in Bengal of the Rajbhansi community, a tribal and nomadic people of Bihar and northern Bengal, is that of timid and meek people who were never deemed fit for military service by the British or the Muslim princes before them.[62] This contradicts the public image that Rajbansi has so effectively created of himself as the courageous, manly, and unrelenting protector of Indian interests in the country. What Rajbansi represented with his imperfect English pronunciation, unpolished manners, crude desire for power, and lack of style and appearance (epitomized by his notoriously ill-fitting wig) was the charou world, the world of the Indian working class: deeply immersed in their own life world, inward-looking, superstitious, and even vulgar. His attempts to garner respectability and recognition from the white political elite in the 1980s have given way to a decidedly populist style. Today he derides the former white masters for their abuse of Indians, and he accuses the many Indians who support conservative or liberal parties that are identified as "white" (NP and DP) of being "stooges," collaborators, and coconuts—ironically, the exact same charges he faced so severely two decades earlier.

In the eyes of most progressive Indians (and liberal whites), Rajbansi continues to symbolize all the faults and shortcomings of the community, yet he also continues to be the most popular leader in the townships and a relentless and energetic presence in the media, in everyday conversations, and at virtually every major social or cultural gathering that involves Indians. Everything about him is known and public, and often scandalous, as his drawn-out divorce in 1998–99. In order to understand his popularity, we need to look at his practices as a political retailer.

The power and reputation of Rajbansi is based on his effective presence in Chatsworth, where he lives in a big house in Arena Park adjacent to the main shopping center in the township—a shopping center that played a central role in the James Commission. The area is colloquially known as "at Rajbansi's house." His house is known as an accessible place, and Rajbansi is known as a highly approachable man. The stories about his readiness to help, assist, and protect local people, or anyone Indian, have almost mythical qualities. He facilitates express admissions to hospitals in the middle of the night, arranges transport of a deceased person from India to South Africa, fast-forwards applications and permits, and gets people housing. No problem is too small to merit a few well-placed phone calls to bureaucrats who are afraid of putting their job at risk, or by playing well-placed contacts in the major political parties he always worked with as a subcontractor. Rajbansi is a wealthy man, but unlike most wealthy Indians, he has not left the township for the white suburbs. He continues to live as a charou in a dense network of contacts, dependency, and mutual favors. Rajbansi styles himself as a charou and obviously feels most comfortable among the people of the township.

As I followed him and his workers on the campaign trail in 1999, it was obvious that he mastered an immediate rapport and communication with people of his own kind, but he was stiffer and more awkward in interactions with people from elite environments, regardless of race. Rajbansi has all the bearings of a charou—affable and at ease with ordinary folks and their way of talking—yet he is not just an ordinary charou with a bit of success. He is truly extraordinary for his capacity to ignore criticism, sustain a high-profile presence, be himself, and speak and behave as he does in formal as well as ordinary settings. Whether driven by vanity or a desire for power, and however cunning and consummate a player he obviously may be concerning political alignments and tactics, he comes across as a man who really believes in his own role as the Tiger of Bengal: the protector of Indians, the strongman who will stand up and take the blows if need be, and the designer of townships that have been transformed into livable and inviting places to stay. He appears as a man who is driven by his own passion for that role, as someone who really wants to be Rajbansi, the robust man who takes everything standing up. In his neighborhood, among political colleagues, workers in his party, and ordinary voters, he is understood as a force of nature—irrepressible, constantly on the move, and possessed by the desire to actually be this larger-than-life figure.

Many people find something endearing in this figure in spite of all of its flaws, which include his vengefulness against people who betray him, his greed, his love of women, and his predictable and somewhat transparent righteousness and denial in the face of criticism. Many find it easy to identify with these traits, and Rajbansi's "thick skin" enables him to live a life where details of his divorce, womanizing, financial affairs, and rows with his children are all in the public domain. He is the most widely caricatured voice on radio and by comedians in the community; everything about him has been said, explored, and ridiculed—and yet he repeats exactly the same things. This essentially travestic quality about the public representation of his life enables him to capitalize and even reverse the ridicule and turn it into endearment and political capital.

A crucial part of the success of Rajbansi is the sense that he belongs to "our culture": he is a screen upon which the weaknesses and insecurities of the charou can be projected, but he is also a charou extraordinaire in that he, unlike the stereotype of the coolie, never budges, never backs down, but claims to protect the ordinary man. Rajbansi is a man who unashamedly wields power and is not afraid of using deceit. One of his classical remarks, "I will double-cross any bridge" (which he stated after his indictment by the James Commission), combines imperfect English, a clumsy attempt at pompous rhetoric, and a ruthless nature, which sums up the man: the laughingstock of the middle classes and the defender of the charou, to whom the niceties of proper pronunciation are of little concern. Rajbansi lives as a broker between the segmented racial worlds of South Africa; worlds separated by race and culture but also by different moral regimes and repertoires. A teacher in his forties, a man with ANC leanings who would never vote for Rajbansi, expressed a very widespread view of him: "Rajbansi is like the uncle we all know. The one who is a bit too loud, boasting all the time, his tie a bit too much, bad jokes and all that. . . . But you live with him. . . . You know what he will say, same jokes and tricks, and he cannot always be trusted. But he is a part of the family and you know that the day you really need help he will be there because he has a heart, and he will help you because you are family. . . . That is how I think of Rajbansi."

FROM TRAGEDY TO COMEDY: POLITICS AS A FORM OF ENJOYMENT

In 1982, Muthal Naidoo staged the comedy *We Three Kings* about how three not too bright Indian hobos are being put up as candidates for the Indian Council to merely deliberate and do nothing. The play derided subservient Indian "sellouts" who creep for the white man and accept the apartheid order. In a hilarious scene the hobos agree with their white benefactor that, "we should protect our Indian culture . . . Hindustanis should speak Hindi, Tamils should speak Tamil . . . and for a mother tongue, everybody must learn Afrikaans." A critic described the play as "broken heart surgery—reflecting on the powerlessness of the Indian community by making fun of itself."[63]Although conventional in its set and form, *We Three Kings* inaugurated a new and powerful genre of Indian theater in the 1980s.

Ronnie Govender invigorated this genre in 1984 when he staged *Offside!*, which refers to Rajbansi's past as a football referee (that is how his infamous index finger developed so well, I was told) and a year later the sequel, *Inside*. Both plays are about the clash between two "giants," both politicians of the House of Delegates, Bun Thrasee and Tit-for-Tat Pookadidum, the so-called giants of survival and their wives (one of them with elaborate hairdos and lots of makeup—guess who?). Govender was drawing on the narrative structure of the great Indian myths, where clashes between giants is a commonly used narrative device, and he used the North Indian Muslim tradition of devotional *Qawwali* songs to great effect in order to frame the plays and their very popular songs. Govender based the satire on the public transcripts of the parliamentary debates, and a great deal of the jokes one finds in subsequent parodies on Rajbansi were actually conceived here.[64] Once again, Ronnie Govender demonstrated his artistic authority and his ability to influence and add new layers to the emerging canon of South African Indian theater.

In 1998, the Rajbansis were going through a divorce. It was alleged that Ashadevi had had an affair with a prominent MP from the Inkatha Freedom Party. In the following months the divorce proceedings, details of court orders, and interviews with the couple, their children, and their friends stoked headlines in the Indian newspapers. Soon the affair became the object of a play by Aldrin Naidoo called *Mooidevi's Muti*. The title of the play drew on three languages and cultures and brought forth the central ambiguity of the public figure of Ashadevi Rajbansi—her vanity, vulnerability, and her cunning opportunism. *Mooi* means pretty in Afrikaans, while *moo* in Tamil means lazy; *devi* refers to the name Ashadevi, but also its Hindi meaning as goddess; while *muti* (traditional medicine) signifies a dimension of African culture that is particularly riddled by popular myths and rumors. The play consisted of a number of sketches, dialogues, and songs that were woven around a simple narrative that depicted the careers of the Rajbansis and their divorce (all facts were presumed to be known by the audience). Amichand (called Tajbansi in the play) accuses Ashadevi of using *muti* against him; he claims she is possessed by a demon (*tokolosh*), and she is then taken to "Father Demon," a greedy African priest and healer who speaks with a thick West African accent. This refers to a Nigerian pastor of dubious reputation, Famudima, who had some success in posing as a Christian healer in the township of Phoenix. In July 1998 he was literally driven out of the area by a joint front of Hindu, Muslim, and Christian organizations. In the play, Father Demon pretends to exorcise the *tokolosh* from Ashadevi for a handsome remuneration, and the couple is temporarily reunited.

In the beginning of the play Ashadevi sings, "Don't cry for me, Bengal Tiger" and continues, "I know I made you balder." Then she goes on with "Annie Get Your Gun" and sings, "I can do everything better than you, except lying." Now the surprise comes. Suddenly, the real Rajbansi comes on to the stage, pointing characteristically. When I watched the play, he delivered the following few lines, in which he precisely, and crudely, portrayed an Indian (Hindu) identity space squeezed between white money and contempt, and an abyss of demonic Zuluness:

Ashadevi, are you prepared to abandon everything, children, husband, grandchildren for the sake of money? You should do like Sita [the virtuous wife of Lord Ram in the epic Ramayana] who stood by her husband in good and bad times. She never roamed around with Ravana [the black demon-god threatening to destroy Ram's just rule]. Do you know what they call you in the community? Ashazulu! Tell your financiers—all these prestigious people—that they cannot defeat me, not in a debate in parliament, not in an election. The person is not yet born in this country who can defeat the Bengal Tiger. I will forever remain the great survivor. (*exit Rajbansi, enter Tajbansi, the actor*)

The reaction of the large audience was one of exhilaration and a somewhat hesitant approval. There was a murmur flowing through the audience and spontaneous applause by some, but no negative reactions. It was as if the audience acknowledged the guts of a man who had been ridiculed so often and was now appearing before the crowd in a play that ridiculed him and his public life yet again for the following ninety minutes. His appearance at this and many of the following shows seemed to actually blunt the edge of the satire, and to signal that he was an accomplice to the satire. Had he stayed away, we would all have been able to entertain the idea that this satire actually touched him and hurt him. Instead he reaffirmed the image of "the Tiger" as a proper man, as someone who can take it, who knows that being a public person means that one is ridiculed and that is something one needs to face up to.

The play proceeds with flashbacks to how the couple met, framed as a Bollywood song/dance routine, and their drive to the top is illustrated by state president P. W. Botha visiting their house and enjoying Ashadevi's samosas while dancing a samosa dance with the couple. Then the couple starts to drift apart. He speaks to a lady friend on the phone, horny, with his tongue out of his mouth. She is called by her lawyer (Piranha) whom she tells, "Oh I am abandoned by all, my husband, my children, the media—no story in the *Post* [largest Indian weekly] this week, and even my makeup won't stick to me anymore." Referring to a much-reported quarrel over a gun in a bathroom in the Rajbansis' house, we now see the couple fighting behind a curtain in a shower, with the "gun" positioned in a rather suggestive way. She grabs it, and after some fighting it "shoots" and she screams.

> *He:* Why do you need a gun? Isn't my shotgun good enough? (*pointing to his fly*) Am I not a good Hindu husband?
> *She:* Why can't you be big, black and strong like Buthelezi?
> *He:* What? Big, black and long like Buthelezi's? Remember, I have donated my organs to public service!

Some in the audience felt embarrassed at this juncture but most had a hearty laugh. The play continued in this style, which was considered puerile by some, but it was obviously taken as good, plain entertainment by most audiences, except on a few occasions. The audience was almost exclusively Indian and stretched across generation and class.

The many references and allusions to sex and community stereotypes that ran through the play seemed to be the elements that elicited most laughter (and embarrassment). Tajbansi meets the "SAA Steamy Screamer" (a local Indian beauty queen who was caught having noisy sex with a businessman in an airplane toilet) at a relative's house and asks, "Why did you bring her here? Imagine what she can do to my reputation? Wonders! . . . I want you to blow the horns at my convention." Or when Father Demon, greedy for Ashadevi's jewelry, tells Tajbansi, "Why didn't the 'Lada' [Lord] help you? Because you give him no jewelry. . . . Take three pieces of jewelry, apply it to your Minority Front (pointing to his fly) and it will rise up and grow and grow."

The play portrayed Ashadevi as obsessed with beauty boxes, money, jewelry, and status. When the Tajbansis have a row, she mocks his low origins, calling him a "blackie" and a "chamar" (untouchable caste), and his vanity ("we came from humble beginnings. I was the one that bought him his first wig"). He mocks her figure, "look at those big roti-rolls," and her heavily accented and caricatured South African Indian English, which the audience obviously found hilarious. As a whole, Ashadevi and Rajbansi are portrayed as the quintessential Indian parvenus who are obsessed with the outer trappings of wealth. The legendary Indian obsession with expensive cars enters when Tajbansi says,

"I cannot be silenced. In the James Commission they tried to crucify me. . . . But look at them today! Look at the F.Ws. [de Klerk] and the P.Ws. [Botha], now they drive VWs." The producer, Aldrin Naidoo, told me that he himself had asked Rajbansi to come onstage, and Ashadevi as well. She was unwilling but had been present at the show on more than one occasion. "When Rajbansi went onstage and spoke to his wife onstage, he spoke to the real person sitting in the back of the hall. That created some very intense moments; it was as if there were only these two people in the hall."[65]

Rajbansi dealt with the satire of Aldrin Naidoo in ways that indicated that he knew that critique could hardly damage his political fortunes. I asked Rajbansi why he had chosen to appear onstage evening after evening at Naidoo's show. His response was evasive and yet illuminating: "You see, if you want to represent the community and be a leader you must be where people are, you must live with the community, and also laugh with them."[66]

Why did the pathos of progressive politics never take hold in Chatsworth? Why was its critique of oppression and its interpretation of Indian history in South Africa one of loss, tragedy, and injustice and never a narrative that enabled progressive politics to be fungible and effective? Why did humor and laughter take over as the dominant media through which politics could be discussed and reflected on? Why was it the ambiguous—if not ridiculous—figure of Rajbansi that came to define the charou world?

At the heart of charou humor stands "comic belief"—it is the very sincerity of belief and the lack of consciousness of self-deception that is comical, because it happens against a backdrop of a fundamental alienation from oneself, a fundamental alienation from ever hoping to become connected or identical with oneself. Rajbansi is indeed such a comic figure with his unrelenting performance of his self-styled role as a community charou hero. However, as we have seen earlier, the township is not perceived as a place where "words can be led home," in Veena Das's sense. It is a fundamentally alienated place at the edge of the bush. The homeliness of Rajbansi in this world resides in the fact that he seems to have understood that in enduring the bittersweet and ironic laugh that follows his words and gestures lies precisely the acknowledgment that he, indeed, is one of us.

CHAPTER 5

Movement, Sound, and Body
in the Postapartheid City

THE RAPID ACCUMULATION OF WEALTH IN SOUTH AFRICA MADE AUTOMOBILE and bus transport crucial elements of urban life from the 1920s. With apartheid's more comprehensive approach to urban planning and segregation, an extensive road system was laid out to service white areas across the country. Areas for people of color were connected to this grid by separate access roads, bus routes, and rail lines. It became possible for whites to commute between work and home and shopping facilities without ever passing through nonwhite areas. Whites would enjoy the freedom of individualized movement that cars afforded, while "nonwhites," not yet ready for freedom, were supposed to rely on public transport. The small African-owned taxi industry was simply disbanded in the late 1950s as townships were built. Instead, bus transport became dominant. Long-standing frictions between Indian bus owners and African customers in Durban, and the successful Alexandra bus boycott in 1957 in Johannesburg,[1] prompted the authorities to extend an urban commuter train system that was designed to transport labor from the townships to urban centers and commercial districts. The characteristic yellow and grey trains with their limited and rigid timetables, their rundown carriages, and recurrent incidents of muggings, pickpocketing, and violence soon became one of the most resented features of urban life during apartheid.[2]

The Indians played a dual role in this racial division of modes of transport in Durban. As early as the 1920s, Indian businessmen acquired cars and buses, and soon emerged as the primary providers of transport to Durban's burgeoning African workforce. Later in the 1960s, the city authorities tried to limit the operating hours and range of Indian bus companies. The city wanted to minimize the presence of buses on Durban's roads and to force more people into the suburban trains (Singh 1999, 150–53). In the 1980s a new phenomenon, the kombi taxi, emerged as a successful alternative between private cars and public transport. Small African entrepreneurs were the first to invest in this industry, and soon Indians and colored followed the trend. By 1995, kombi taxis provided

65 percent of all public transport in the country, a market that is heavily concentrated in townships and informal settlements.[3] More than any other sign, the kombi taxi marked the beginning of a new way of using urban space, a new form of automobility, movement, and also play and violence, which has come to define the postapartheid city.

After apartheid, the use of cars, taxis, and public transport emerged once again as major areas of friction and contention in the city. But let me briefly explore the place of the car and vehicular mobility in urban theory before I turn to the relationship between physical movement, the morality of exchange, and public recognition in the postapartheid city.

The Steel Cages of Modernity

Until quite recently, urban theory treated motorized transport as a negative and alienating force that disrupted the flow of pedestrian life and social interaction in the streets. Lefebvre mentions the car only as a symbol of alienation: "There are many individuals who 'realize' themselves by driving their car. They deploy qualities that lie fallow elsewhere: daring, virility, mastery of self, energy and even sexuality. . . . It is laden with ideology. And the pathetic comedy begins: conversations about the car, anecdotes, stories about accidents, etc." (2002, 212). In Jane Jacobs's classical work on American cities, along with real estate speculation, cars and the road system were key elements in the destruction of urban life (1961). De Certeau's canonical essay, "Walking in the City," never mentions cars. His only attention to transport is to rail transport, which he conceptualizes as a subspecies of the general disciplinary powers of modernity (1988).[4] Recent writings on cars and the global "system of automobility" also emphasize the destructive and atomizing effects of cars on social and physical life in cities.[5]

The car is indeed a deeply controversial and divisive topic in political life and in social analysis. The proponents of private cars see themselves as promoting the key instrument of true liberal emancipation of the full potential of human beings against what they see as the latent socialist potential of public transport. Alan Pisarski, of the so-called Automobility and Freedom Project,[6] argues that cars and the associated "democratization of mobility" and urban sprawl are cornerstones in providing women and ethnic minorities freedom to move, work, and prosper. Pisarski's deeply tendentious counterexample is that of African Americans who are more concentrated in inner cities, have lower automobile ownership than any other group, and, as a result (!), experience less social success and integration into mainstream society (1999).

However, it is clear that the car merits more reflection in urban theory. The car complicates the standard opposition between movement in space as pregnant with possibility and pushes against the strictures of the planners' fixing of people and processes in place. The freedom of the driver and the freedom of the pedestrian are of different orders and consequences. The former enjoys a significant power of movement based on huge institutional forces of planning and industry while also being encased in a machine that limits, directs, and shapes both subjectivity and possibilities (Thrift 2004). The latter is more vulnerable and limited in range yet indispensible to the very idea of the modern city as one of visual heterogeneity and anonymous density and potential. These two figures are complementary in a highly structured relationship: walking often takes place to and from a car. Both walking and driving are structured by necessity and perceptions of risk and appropriateness, and both promise a measure of individual improvisation. In most of the world the distinction between those in cars and those who are walking is one of class and entitlement—and often race. While walking represents the quintessential rhizomic kind of urban movement with all the subversive potential that de Certeau famously ascribes to it, the same is not necessarily true of the driver. The free-roaming or even reckless driver is not merely a figure of defiant freedom or insubordination but can well represent an expression and affirmation of social hierarchy. In South Africa, modes of transport were historically organized as an expression of racialized personhood. The recent local witticism "the working class has been replaced by the walking class" reflects that walking is regarded as a sign of poverty and marginality. Conversely, the emphasis on expensive cars as symbols of status and power is inordinately strong across most communities in the country.[7]

Recent anthropological work has shown that cars, like people, also function as surfaces of creative self-expression—colors, styles, makes, and sounds (see Miller 2001)—and thus recognition and communication. However, encounters on highways or in streets between people in their cars are invariably more superficial and impersonal than the face-to-face encounters in the street that Simmel described so vividly in his essay on the face and the importance of seeing (1959a, 276–82; Frisby 1997, 109–20). In traffic encounters, there is little chance of "full recognition," or even an appreciation of the totality of the face with its individual features and expressions that Simmel alludes to (281); nor is there the possibility of the "arousal of emotion" by the other's humanity (Sennett 1990). Social encounters mediated by cars are highly structured by speed, infrastructure, and traffic rules, and thus depend heavily on preformed registers of surface marks—categories such as the model, color, and size of the car; the sound of the horn; the skin color of the driver; and so on. These encounters are so many and routinized that they also become socially effective and affective—funny, disturbing, and provocative. There is indeed *flaneurie* in cars, but it is a highly structured form of seeing and being seen that is more akin to racialized metacommunication: here it is not merely the color of the face but the car—its colors, sound, style, and its driver and passengers—that function as categorical doubles that can be inhabited, played with, and reversed. Just like other categorical doubles, these surface signs often dominate and overshadow the individuality of the actual car and its driver.

Such economies of visual misrecognition are fundamental to cities that are marked by enduring social and ethnocultural segmentation of space and everyday life. Here, the street, traffic, or public transport are not the celebrated spaces of possibility at the heart of most urban theory. In the postcolonial city, space is never neutral. Particular places, including their streets, buses, and cars, are always/already coded in quasi-domestic terms as belonging to one group or another. Space is never an unmarked category, a realm of the possible and the potential. Urban space is always/already defined, owned, and coded, and rarely open for the swift and unpredictable escape or "line of flight" (Deleuze and Guattari 1980, 350–424). Physical movement beyond one's own place is a movement into an unknown, risky, and perhaps hostile environment, where one is being seen, read, interpreted, and probably acted upon whether one walks, drives, or sits in a taxi or bus. If cars are the steel cages that structure modern mobility as such, the function of cars and motorized transport in postcolonial cityscapes are multiply coded vehicles: protective containers of solipsistic social and racial privilege, expressions and transgressions of racial and social stereotypes, and individual expressions of respectability or enjoyment, to mention but a few dimensions of the complex semiosis involved in postcolonial and multicultural automobility.

Driving while Brown

The Indian-owned bus industry in Durban was one of the many points of friction between Indians and Africans from the 1940s onward. Many Africans felt mistreated and overcharged by the Indian drivers and conductors of the sprawling fleet of old, overcrowded buses that serviced the outskirts of the city. The Commission of Enquiry into Riots in Durban in 1949 devoted considerable attention to these complaints but ultimately found them baseless. The commission found it unlikely that Indian conductors would openly mistreat people who were numerically superior to them and constituted the bulk of their customers. The natives should not expect "first-class services at fourth-class fares . . . in a large measure we think this grievance is kept alive by Natives who are anxious to compete with the Indians in running bus lines" (Van den Heever 1949, 15).

Another grievance on the part of the Zulu speakers pertained to morality. The report paraphrased the complaint: "The Indians have motorcars and money; we on the other hand, are poor. With his blandishments, motor rides and offers of finery and money, they seduce our women who give birth to Indian children" (ibid., 14). This allegation was found to be true by the commission, which in turn recommended that the Immorality Act be extended to other race groups in order to curb this "evil." The Indian bus and motorcar as a site of moral corruption of African women was indeed a hotly debated topic at the time where male anxieties about a new class of educated Zulu women emerged. Sexual liaisons with African and colored girls were undoubtedly a part of the life of Indian and white males from more privileged backgrounds. The Zulu intellectual H.I.E. Dhlomo regarded the bus as a vehicle of a new era but also as a sign of impending moral decay unless controlled by Africans themselves: "In parts of the country buses are ethical questions. An Indian bus is introduced into self-contained, quiet rural or mission areas with high standards of morality. In no time, pop goes the self-sufficiency and morality and ethical codes of the place. An enterprising African ousts the Indian, and morality like the coy and slow moving maiden she is, returns slowly and diffidently through the back-door" (*Ilanga Lase Natal*, January 10, 1948; quoted from Soske 2009, 181). The marginal status of single Zulu men working in the city—barred from any access to women from other race groups—created much frustration and anger. Soske astutely shows that in these debates "the Indian became a screen on to which African intellectuals could project internal conflicts within Zulu society, thus locating the social disruptions produced by urbanization outside the process of modernization and nation building" (2009, 180).

In the following decades this friction disappeared as more or less separate transport amenities were set up for Indians and Africans. Indian areas continued to be served by a fairly extensive network of bus lines. In addition, Indian-owned buses serviced many African settlements in the city. In the 1970s and 1980s, more Indian-owned cars appeared on the city's roads. Soon, Indians assumed a dominant position in the city's vast market that catered to automobility: service stations, mechanics, sellers of spare parts, scrap yards, and much more. A genuine car culture developed among working-class men in the Indian townships. Illegal car races over the weekends on little-used strips of road and parking lots became part of an illicit and transgressive youth culture that was fueled by dramatic injuries, drugs and alcohol, and sometimes death. Predictably, this provoked outrage among respectable Indians and police officers. Working-class youths began to spend large sums of money on extensively decorating vehicles and souping-up engines; a fleet of spectacular-looking and spectacular-sounding vehicles, which were easily recognizable as distinctly charou, cruised the township and the city over the weekends.

More than any other group in the city, young Indian men have embraced, if not fetishized, automobility as a medium of self-expression. Cars are objects of emotional investments, but not merely of the individualized kind discussed by Mimi Sheller (2004). Indians were always allowed to move freely around urban space, while social mobility and political sovereignty were restricted. The car seemed to offer an irresistible thrill to young, relatively disempowered men, because it embodied a potential force that could kill but could also be controlled and tamed through skill and daring, as Michael Balint suggested in the 1950s (1959). This observation appears even truer among young men who felt emasculated and threatened by both black and white masculinities that were regarded as more violent and more powerful than their own. The souped-up and roaring car thus became a screen upon which fantasies of power and aggression could be projected and enacted on the road, rather than in face-to-face encounters with categorical others. The car thus became a mask that enabled a secret fantasy of one's own excessive desire that could not find another language. Yet, because it is part of a stereotyped, exterior, collective, and playful self, it could also be separated and even disowned as just a thing, just some wheels. What remained in place, and remains an irritant to authorities and to middle-class sensibilities to this day, was the sheer abandon with which money, cars, and lives were being expended and ritually wasted in defiant, if pointless, assertions, not of sovereign power but the sovereign force of desire and enjoyment.[8]

Today conversations and small talk about cars, engines, prices, maintenance, performance, and qualities, and watching Formula One races on television, constitute a pivot of everyday male sociality in the township. The newly painted, flashy, or overly decorated car was invariably seen by my informants as "charou wheels"; so would the run-down and overloaded car with furniture, vegetables, and groceries spilling out of it. Another sure sign was the old, tiny car with long fishing rods sticking out of it. A young man described this to me in the style of playful self-deprecation, which is so characteristic of the townships: "Charous are crazy about fishing—everybody else goes to the beach to have a good time, but only we charous go there to take some smelly fish home for dinner! You can always tell if a car has been owned by a charou—the smell of fish never goes [away]."

Among the more respectable and moneyed sections, European lux-ury cars (Mercedes, Audis, and BMWs) are as important to the display of status and success as in any other segment of South African society. The obsession with cars among wealthy Gujarati Muslims is the stuff of many jokes and lore.[9] Rehana Ebr.-Vally has provided a fascinating glimpse into how personalized number plates—which can only be pur-chased at a considerable price from the authorities—have become an important way of displaying wealth, individuality, and cultural identity on the busy highways around Johannesburg. For a range of complex and largely obscure reasons unknown to most drivers, the number 786 has emerged as an important sign of piety and something like a good-luck charm among Muslims: "786 is the short code for seven hundred and eighty six, which is the sum of all letters composing the entire verse of *Bismillaahir rahmaanir raheem*, meaning 'In the Name of Allah, the Most Kind, the Most Merciful'" (Ebr.-Vally 2001, 278). This works as an al-most secret code, known only within the community, and not necessar-ily among the officials at the Department of Transport who sell these special number plates at a high price.

To Ebr.-Vally, this is a sign of how piety and identity become increas-ingly expressed in commodified signifiers: "These number plates are in their large majority affixed to luxury cars. On a Friday afternoon, out-side the mosque in Laudium, a Pretoria former township, about 20 % of approximately 100 cars parked outside carried a 786 number plate and were luxury cars" (278). It seems that among members of this fi-nancially secure community, the road and the car remain sites of en-joyable, identity-affirming, and competitive expenditure, albeit in more subdued and discreet forms than in the townships.

(Auto)mobility in the Postapartheid City

At first sight, the major cities in South Africa do not appear to have changed much over the last decade, yet the diverse spaces of the city are today imbued with a new set of meanings related more to the senses than to economic functions. A city like Johannesburg has become the site of radical heterogeneity and proliferating desires of many kinds. Its new dynamism both reinvents the city's founding moment of creativity and moral transgression during the gold boom of the late nineteenth century and indicates its emergence as a new, creative African metropo-lis. The distinction between the erstwhile white centers of South Af-rica's cities (clean, modern, and universal in aspiration) and the racially defined townships (designed as enclosed, stable, and quasi-domestic community places) have given way to what Mbembe and Nuttall call a new "social velocity" (2004, 349) that unsettles stable patterns of life and imagination and generates new and potentially productive fissures across the urban landscape. The remainder of this chapter focuses on how the kombi taxi—the eight- to twelve-seat van—has emerged as one of the most effective and literal manifestations of such social velocity and new forms of movement and inhabitation of South Africa's urban spaces. In a social sense the kombi taxi is an interesting hybrid between the private car and the public bus—in principle open and public as a commercial vehicle and yet strongly marked as an extension and a symbol of a particular racial or ethnic community that is governed by tacit rules and norms internal to that community. In these senses, it is a perfect image of the postapartheid city.

The final stages of apartheid saw a flurry of initiatives aimed at fostering a black middle class and removing the worst excesses of the "petty apartheid." One of these measures was to liberalize the inadequate transport sector and to open the market for private transport. From the early 1980s, a growing fleet of kombi taxis began to service the townships, taking the workforce to and from the city centers and plying between the major cities, urban centers, and densely populated Bantustans. The taxi trade proved a relatively inexpensive way to start a business, and competition was stiff and violent from the outset. The trade was unregulated, and soon a number of rival taxi associations, based on existing networks of ethnic bonds or political affiliation, emerged.[10]

Rival associations clashed in shoot-outs that frequently killed and wounded innocent bystanders and passengers. The overall scarcity of jobs increased the pressure on the taxi trade, whose potential as a money-laundering device attracted powerful crime syndicates. In the province of KwaZulu-Natal, the virtual civil war between the ANC and the Inkatha movement suffused and structured the turf wars between taxi associations aligned with either political formation.

After 1994, the new government imposed regulations designed to define routes, areas, fares, and the number of taxis.[11] Many taxis remained unauthorized and broke the rules by hunting for passengers outside their own territory, overcharging, overloading, not paying attention to maintenance standards, and so forth. The regulation of the industry now made political connections essential for the major operators. Soon influential members of the taxi associations began to enjoy considerable political clout as patrons of local political figures. The so-called taxi wars were now fueled by rivalry in business, politics, and underworld activities. The violence peaked in 1996 when official police statistics reported more than three hundred deaths and six hundred wounded in taxi-related violence in South Africa. Most of this violence was perpetrated by professional hit men who were employed by taxi associations to shoot rival owners and drivers and to terrorize passengers of rival taxi associations (see Dugard 2001).

Taxis soon made their appearance in more upmarket areas and neighborhoods. Here they generated considerable anxiety, even if in the main they were meeting the transport needs of African residents in these areas—domestic workers and informal settlements. The formerly Indian area of Clare Estate in Durban saw a particularly virulent and violent set of conflicts between long-term Indian residents, operators of Indian-owned bus lines, and African-owned taxis that were servicing the large shack settlements in the area. In 1997 and 1998, several bus drivers were killed, presumably by people in the taxi industry. Indian residents saw this as an attack on Indians and Indian livelihoods. In January 1998, the killing of Sudheer Debba, a bus driver, almost resulted in a full-scale attack by Indian residents on nearby African informal settlements where the killers were supposedly hiding. The situation was only defused by the intervention of the army, which was called in when the Indian residents accused the local police of protecting the killer. Tensions lingered in this area long after this incident. According to Anand Singh's rather partisan account, one of the effects of these clashes was that several Indian bus operators scaled back their operations and ceded the streets to the taxis (1999, 157–67).[12]

In South Africa's urban landscapes and highways, the taxi industry defines its own rules. Taxis have become a metonym of the underworld, as well as a poignant symbol of postapartheid freedom. The promise of earning a fast buck in a job that does not require formal training, the cool style of the drivers, and the sheer promise of a world flush with quick cash and potential have made the industry a highly attractive place for many young men. The taxi business has been an important arena for black economic empowerment, emerging alongside but independent from more formalized transport sectors like the bus services, which had been an important source of quasi-monopolistic self-enrichment by black elites during apartheid. Taxis have been central to the gradual reconfiguration of the former sociospatial order of the apartheid city. In the kombi taxi, black people have explored the formerly white world: its beaches, parks, exclusive neighborhoods, and shopping malls. For drivers and attendants, this enjoyment of a now-formally democratized space was crucial in their experience of "freedom"—a term that came up in virtually every conversation I had with informants in the taxi business. The experience of freedom, however illusory it may be considering the economic imperatives that govern the lives of drivers, emerges from the everyday phenomenology of taxi driving: the open road, the unpredictability of the wishes or directions of your next customer, the inchoate promise in flirting with nameless women, and, not least, the experience of being a hunter, with its associated possibilities of "luck" on the road (making lots of money) or of "making a mess" (fatal accidents). This precarious experience of freedom and autonomy qua incessant movement and unpredictable fortune undoubtedly characterizes taxi driving across the world, but it acquired a particularly powerful symbolic force in the postapartheid generation.

This sense of freedom, autonomy, and enjoyment was often compounded by claims of being legally untouchable. Many drivers claimed that they never paid speeding tickets, thanks to the legal protection of their politically well-connected bosses. While such claims are impossible to verify, there is little doubt that the very large taxi industry enjoys a very substantial de facto autonomy in terms of regulation and police intervention. Police stations, government officials, and all the affiliated sectors—spare parts, sound systems, and garages—are today involved in a vast network of deals and financial flows that remain almost impenetrable to law enforcers and anticorruption squads.

VEHICULAR VERNACULAR: VISUAL AND SONIC

Taxis have become poignant, fine-tuned sensors of trends in the youth culture of the townships. The style of the taxis, the make of cars (Toyotas being common, Volkswagens the solid and expensive choice), their decoration, and the size and quality of their sound systems are all key parameters of style. Loud music, dominated by a deep and thumping bass, has become the trademark of the coolest taxis—those catering to young and highly fashion-conscious teenagers. The sound of the bass has, in fact, become the quintessential signature of the taxis—one can hear them and even feel the vibration of the bass before they come around the corner. The sound signals many things—sensuality, the infinite play of desire and pleasure in the city, assertive masculinity—but it also signals the township itself; that is, a space of blackness that is plebeian, no-nonsense, defiant, and potentially violent. While the thumping bass signifies a certain youthful insubordination within the black township itself—the sound of undisciplined gangsters—it also signifies an assertive and defiant black identity when moving in the formerly white areas or, as we will see, the Indian townships. South African cities are not immediately walkable spaces for the flaneur or the jaywalker. In their stead, the speed and sound-space of the taxis embody the ever-present and enticing element of strangeness that remains an irreducible mark of the urban.

There is a clear hierarchy among taxi owners in terms of their influence and economic power. The richer owners flash their status through new, well-painted cars with big sound systems. Their drivers and attendants (those who solicit customers, charge the fees, and crack jokes with passengers and drivers) often reflect that status in their own behavior by being loud and cheeky in their dealings with passengers and colleagues. This elite league of taxis is preferred by young people and often elaborates a certain daredevil masculine aura that is underlined by recurrent racing contests in which the drivers compete to get from the city center to specific townships in the shortest possible time. Those lower in the hierarchy have older cars, less flashy drivers, lower prices, and are placed in less conspicuous locations in the taxi ranks.

Let me turn to the musical styles that are so central to taxis, young people, and, more broadly, the various youth cultures that have emerged after apartheid. Life in South Africa's townships has always been defined and expressed in a rich variety of musical forms, from the predominantly Zulu *isicathamiya* tradition to the rhythmic *maskhandi*,[13] which spread through small clubs and shebeens in African townships in the 1940s. By 2000 one musical form, kwaito, dominated the African townships, airwaves, and cities. Kwaito is South African pop music that combines the beat and style of rap, house, and hip-hop music with older South African musical forms, for instance, the so-called bubble-gum pop music of the 1980s of which Brenda Fassie was the most famous exponent. Official and semiofficial websites link kwaito to a celebration of freedom, to the democratic transformation in the country, and to the huge commercial success of black music in South Africa after 1994. More commercially minded websites, addressing a young audience, explain kwaito as a South African version of American house and hip-hop; thus, as black music that is intrinsically urban, irreverent, youthful, and provocative. Other websites describe the music as expressing "power to the party people," therefore playfully opposing those who like to party and those who are in the party. A widespread story goes that kwaito began when some DJs started to play 45 rpm American house singles at 33 rpm to allow South Africans more space to dance and move. The next step in its evolution was the introduction of rap (again, more slowly than in the United States), often with several singers doing the chorus.

The result was a unique sound that is now spreading from its creative core in Johannesburg back into the "Black Atlantic." As Gilroy demonstrates, black musical forms have circulated across the Atlantic world (in both directions) for more than a century, with New York, London, Kingston, New Orleans, Johannesburg, and more recently Lagos, Dakar, and Kinshasa as major nodes. These musical forms have established connections with other black people and have also balanced awkwardly between essentialist notions of black identity and more open, antiracist attempts to undermine the very idea of race and thus blackness itself (see Gilroy 1993, 72–110). Kwaito clearly positions itself as black music and draws heavily on African American notions of the ghetto, masculinity, and of being streetwise—all translated into a celebration of the township, the erstwhile key symbol of apartheid's oppression, and as the quintessential space of black life, black sexuality, and black expressiveness in postapartheid South Africa.

The normative reversal, or recoding, of the township is expressed in the term "kwaito" itself. Many expressions in township slang, known as *isicamtho* (which derives from *tsotsitaal* or "gangster slang"), are derived from Afrikaans. *Kwai* comes from the term "*kwaai*," which has a rich and suggestive set of meanings and connotations—bad, miserable, poor, nasty, angry, even stupid. In contemporary colloquial Afrikaans, *kwaai* is often used to describe things that are enticing, morally ambiguous, and attractive, that is, things that are both hot (e.g., girls, food, and spices) and cool (e.g., men, style, and music). As with the origin of the music itself, nationalist voices claim that the word "kwaito" originates in African languages. Yet it is obvious that urban popular cultures in South Africa all depend on demotically modified Afrikaans, the lingua franca of most urban South Africans.

Kwaito is seen as black music by its performers and main audiences; it is popular among the young generation, and its lyrics are daring, racy, provocative, and suffused with sexual connotations and innuendo. Many kwaito lyrics have clearly incorporated the hypermasculinist, if not misogynist, pose of many American rappers. Reformulating Stuart Hall's remark that race is the modality in which class is lived, Gilroy argues that "gender is the modality in which race is lived. An amplified and exaggerated masculinity has become the boastful centerpiece of a culture of compensation that self-consciously salves the misery of the dis-empowered and subordinated" (1993, 85).

This observation resonates not only with the public poses of kwaito performers but with a hypermasculinist township culture that is characterized by one of the highest levels of rape in the world, extensive domestic violence, and widespread abuse of minors. Some of the lyrics are overtly political and tackle issues of racist abuse, crime, unemployment, corruption, and the sense of disappointment and hopelessness that defines the mood among many young people a decade and a half after the fall of apartheid. Yet most of the best-selling artists, like Mdu, Ismael, Skeem, Skizo, and the very popular Mandoza, sing about everyday life in the streets, the impossibilities of true love, sudden death, the hope of a glitzy life, and other such things.[14]

Taxis play many types of music, but it is the core market of the young, the highly mobile, and the style-conscious who define their cultural profile. The compact of sound, music, and movement constitutes a dynamic field upon which notions of ethnicity, sexuality, and racial anxiety are formed and contested.

Taxis, Charou-Style

Taxis became a dominant part of Chatsworth's street life in the mid-1990s. A taxi owner, nicknamed "Mandela" for his active role during the antiapartheid campaigns in the area, pioneered the organization of taxis into proper ranks in fixed places in the township and designated areas of operation, but soon lost his influence and status. He told me, "Now the gangsters control the whole thing . . . before we all owned our own vehicle, but now the big drug lords buy taxis to become legit . . . they threw me out of the taxi association and they charge new members fifteen to twenty-thousand rand."

Mandela and others have formed their own association, which mainly services the less profitable routes within the poorer areas of the township. The main taxi ranks that service the profitable route between the city center and the township are controlled by big owners with fifteen to twenty taxis each. With job losses and the informalization of the economy, the number of private cars has declined and the demand for transport has grown rapidly, not least among young people and teenagers who go to Durban for shopping and entertainment. Many former industrial workers have spent the package they received upon their dismissal on buying a taxi or setting up small car-related businesses (such as selling cars, tires, or spare parts), which today are dominated by Indians across the Durban region. The competition is stiff and the profit margins are often thin among the township's three hundred taxis. Violence is common in the Indian taxi industry in Chatsworth, but it is less politicized and lethal than in the African taxi ranks, and often related to personal rivalries between taxi owners.

In a bid to attract the burgeoning market of style-conscious teenagers in Chatsworth—keen consumers of white, African American, and the globally circulating South Asian forms of fashion and music—taxis began to compete on style and sound. By the late 1990s the so-called swanking taxis, or swankers,[15] appeared—painted in bright colors and sporting striking and dramatic motifs, seats in matching colors, and huge sound systems. The motifs range from dragons and huge weapons to half-naked blondes in leather outfits. The names range from Bad Boyz, Bone Crusher, or Spiderman to distinctly unsubtle ones, such as Ladykiller and Big Willie. Other taxis take their names from the local soccer heroes, the Manning Rangers (also known as the Mighty Maulers), and some taxis flaunt the Muslim identity of their owners with

Figure 8. A SWANKER IN CHATSWORTH

green colors and inscriptions such as *Allah-hu-Akbar* (Allah is great). To-day, almost half of the taxis are swanking, and each time a new taxi, or a redecorated one, hits the street with new, fresh colors and a huge sound system, it becomes the object of rumors and much interest. The swanking taxis charge twice the regular price but remain the most pop-ular. Today many African-owned and operated taxis are also painted in fresh colors and carry names like 100% Zulu Boy or Psalm 91. Many teenagers have their favorite taxis, and their constantly changing prefer-ences drive the competition and the production of ever more fanciful motifs and extreme equipment. Customers are discerning; both young boys and girls will dismiss taxis without "white walls"—the wide and white-walled tires that have become de rigueur—and most would never consider using a taxi without a sound system. The styles of the driver and the conductor (who solicits customers)—their clothes, jokes, and reputations—are also important to the success of a swanking taxi.

The life span of a swanker before redecoration or renovation is about one year or less, and the initial investment of up to two hundred thou-sand rand (nearly $30,000 in U.S. dollars, a large sum of money in the local economy) must be recovered in that time. Many of these taxis are hijacked and stripped of assets—sound systems, tires, headlights, and even engines. To drive a swanking taxi is therefore more risky, but also more rewarding, than working a more anonymous vehicle. The earnings are much better, the visibility is higher, and a certain romantic aura of being "wild at heart" has developed around the drivers and conductors of these vehicles. Many drivers and conductors see themselves as mavericks and freebooters, and they enjoy the rush of traffic, intensity, quick money, and the attention of women. Conductors and drivers of swanking taxis like to see themselves as "sexy beasts"—men well versed in the law of the street and the world of gangsters, the ubiquitous hijackings of cars, and other such things.

The swanking taxis and their decorations are distinctly Indian interpretations of the world of taxis. For taxis in the African townships, style is marked by the style of drivers and conductors and the style of music rather than by visual decoration. The style of decoration and equipment in the Indian townships reflect the wider obsession with cars—the single most important staple of everyday male conversation—and the technical competence that abounds in Chatsworth. However, it also reflects the difference in emphasis that historically has been placed on the visual as compared to the sonic. The sonic (singing, toyi-toying, drumming, loud music) has always been central to the black township, while the visual (the use of color, clothing, and adornment) has traditionally been central to the marking of "Indianness," and possibly to South Asian cultural forms more generally. As we will see later, this distinction is becoming increasingly blurred. The emergence of new forms of Indian pop and fusion music, as well as kwaito, have indeed afforded Indian taxis a new and powerful sonic medium.[16]

The style of decoration on taxis reflects an ironic play on stereotypes about Indians—the loud and colorful style, the over-the-top quality of the Bollywood style and aesthetic—as well as a more assertive Indian identity in the postapartheid context. The official denunciation of racial categories has in fact produced a growing urge to visibly mark racial and ethnic identities in an increasingly mixed, plural, and also permissive society. As we will see below, the half-embarrassed play on the charou enjoyment of oriental excess is also central to the style of music played in the taxis.[17]

Let us return to Unit 2 in Chatsworth. The center of this area is a slightly run-down shopping complex on the road that separates the row houses and bungalows on one side from the large council housing estate, the sprawling Zanzibari community, and the informal African settlements on the other side. The shopping complex has a gas station, some small supermarkets, a butcher, a hardware store, and two bars, while fruit sellers and other small vendors are set up in the shopping

Figure 9. ANOTHER SWANKER, FROM THE REAR

complex's chaotic parking lot, where there is a constant bustle of taxis incessantly using their horns, while the conductors hang out of windows soliciting customers, making comments on women, and showering one another with lighthearted abuse. Because of the presence of the Zanzibari community and the large informal African settlement, many taxis are "black" taxis, that is, taxis with a black driver and conductor. Some of the Indian taxi owners have hired black drivers and conductors in a bid to keep out the competition from taxis based in the neighboring township of Umlazi. These black taxis are the hip (*kwaai*) ones preferred by the younger black people when going to or from the clubs and popular shopping malls in the city center.

Among Indian customers, the black taxis are regarded as both exciting and potentially dangerous. Young Indian men use them frequently. Here, they encounter what they see as a cooler African interpretation of Afro-American music, hairstyles, and dress codes rather than any traditional black South African culture. Similarly, kwaito has gradually become popular among young Indians (and many young whites as well) because some lyrics are in English, and because the style is seen as a rough Johannesburg interpretation of American rap styles. Many

Figure 10. SHOPPING CENTER IN UNIT 2, CHATSWORTH

young Indian men told me that they liked the aggressive beat, the sexualized lyrics, and the masculinist poses that are so associated with both kwaito and black township culture more generally.

There is undoubtedly an intimate nexus between music, ethnicity, and notions of race. Music relates directly to sensual and bodily registers and allows an often pleasurable fusion with one's social corporeality and the stereotypes and collective ideas of how "our bodies" feel and enjoy. Music is enjoyed with and in the body, and this is particularly true of styles like house, kwaito, and *bhangra* (Punjabi folk music mixed with drums and bass). There may be tunes or styles you do not particularly like, but your foot will start to move as the music gets "inside your head" or "inside your body," as my informants put it, referring to the transient feeling of one's body being more in oneself than one's reflexive, cognitive self. Music is at the visceral heart of ethnicity, not merely as ethnic music, but as an emotional anchor for feelings of attachment that may relate to childhood or to banal pleasures of community life. As Charles Keil and Steven Feld have noted, listening to music involves the invocation and remembrance of locations, recognition and categorization of styles, and the enabling of a range of emotionally powerful associations—images and sensations (1994, 83).

In this light we may understand the embarrassed admissions by young Indians that they like Hindi films and their songs, which were so distinctly uncool until quite recently. Kiru Naidoo, an astute political commentator who grew up in Chatsworth, recently coined the term "bhangra nationalism" for the process whereby conservative Indian politicians at big, free "bhangra bashes" consolidate and recreate an emotionally strong Indian identity in the face of the country's momentous change. This effect resonates with Mark Mattern's notion of "musical action . . . [when] music express[es] meanings that give listeners direct access to emotions and ideas" (1998, 17). Indeed, the bhangra bash has become the standard populist technique that is used to attract and gather Indians across generation and class; it is deployed by radio stations, political parties, and commercial advertisers, and it is even mobilized to accompany public celebrations like the Hindu festival of Diwali.[18] The flip side of this emotive-cohesive force of music and dance is the anxiety generated by the compact of unfamiliar African music and bodily movement, such as those deployed in toyi-toying.

While bhangra in its traditional Punjabi forms has been around for many years, it was only when it was combined with heavy bass and linked to contemporary dance tunes that it became available as a consolidating factor in contemporary Asian identity in Britain (Huq 1996). Since the 1940s in South Africa, the music of the Hindi films had been a dominant source of entertainment in the Indian working class (see Veeran 1999). In the 1970s, Western pop music began to dominate this music scene, and by the early 1990s, the interest in Bollywood among younger people was almost nonexistent. The arrival of bhangra, and later the more dance-oriented music by artists such as Bally Sagoo, Apache Indian, Asian Dub Foundation, Punjabi MC, and many others, made a sound available that seemed both modern and Indian, that sounded Western, Afro-American, and oriental, in a mix that was accessible and in tune with the new and increasingly assertive Indian youth culture. Bhangra and its successors, not least the increasingly popular Indy pop and Indy rock coming from Mumbai, London, and North America, offer an experience of authenticity that rests on the possibility of racial identification with other so-called brown folks across the oceans. Not unlike the African diaspora's discomfort with the actual Africa, as opposed to its idealization by the intellectuals of the Black Atlantic, the theorizers and producers of what one could call an emerging "Brown Atlantic" (its nodes being London, Birmingham, Toronto, New York, Trinidad, Mumbai, and Delhi) are also wary of any direct identification with the supposed cultural "motherland" of India (Sharma 1996).

The authenticity sought by this music is not the one of blood and origins that is pursued by Hindu nationalism, but one that thematizes the shared predicaments of nonrecognition and misrecognition as minorities. It is a music that seeks to enjoy and interiorize South Asian sounds while recognizing the fundamental embeddedness of diasporic Indians in a modern, urban, and decidedly non-Indian environment.

The arrival in South Africa of these new sounds—both Western and Asian—coincided with the reinvention and rethinking of Indian identity after apartheid. As the official racial definition lost legitimacy but retained its existence as common sense, a new culturalized definition of "Indianness" began to emerge. The music provided a signifier of an identity that had enormous visceral energy and reach by virtue of its own hybridized and low-brow character, which was nonetheless distinctly Asian. The range of references invoked by the music is vague and eclectic, and thus it is in almost perfect tune with the geographical-historical vagueness that marks the cultural self-identification of most charous. The new Asian dance music and aesthetic evolved internationally and won recognition among some whites and a few educated blacks in South Africa (though far less so than in the UK or North America), where it became an important symbol of "our thing" and the "Indianness" that otherwise remained so vaguely defined. The new music constituted a repertoire by which the space of the township could be sonically marked and asserted, and at decibel levels matching those of the black township culture. In both the bustling streets of Chatsworth and the big taxi ranks in the city, music is a key marker of identity and presence along racial lines—sometimes in friendly and teasing "matches" of subwoofers while on other occasions in more aggressive sonic wars involving horns, shouting, and verbal abuse. This stands in sharp contrast to Michael Bull's notion of cars as "sonic envelopes" that turn the music inward for the solipsistic enjoyment of the driver, who is alienated from her urban environment, which "float[s] by as some kind of filmic embodiment" (2004, 248). The music in taxis is meant for consumption inside the taxi, but it also creates a public sonic signifier, transmitting particular styles, an aura of the township, or simply an ethnoracial identity. Yet music like kwaito appears as a significant leveling force because it is a genre distributed across racial lines and across subcultures.

The power of loud music with a heavy bass is not merely cultural or political. It is also locally interpreted as suggestive, sensual, and seductive. In South Africa, Afro-American R & B has become universally accepted as dating music among all racial and cultural communities. The appeal of its lyrics of pure and devoted love and its celebration of romance must be understood against a reality, in black American culture and even more so in South Africa, of feeble family structures and the agonistic relationships between men and women, which Gilroy sees as one of the deepest and almost irreparable damages of slavery and emasculation. The association of black music with sexuality and licentiousness does indeed have deep historical roots both in North America and the Caribbean. Calypso music and its associated dancing were for decades seen as deeply immoral among Indians in Trinidad. Much like the impact of bhangra on Indian dancing in South Africa, it was only the emergence of the upbeat and popular Indian Chutney music in Trinidad in the 1990s that made dancing more respectable among Indians (Manuel 2000).[19]

The actual and lived realities of Indian family life (such as the high number of female-headed households, the many divorces, and the pattern of sexual liaisons in Chatsworth's charou culture) are indeed much closer to familial patterns in the African townships than to any received idealization of the Indian family. The change in youth culture in Chatsworth and the overt sexualization of body, dress, conduct, and soundscape in the erstwhile purely Indian spaces probably constitutes one of the most significant and visible transformations since 1994. To most of my informants, this is squarely linked to the presence of Africans. The taxis, with loud music and young, loud teenagers, are regarded by many adults as moving signifiers of blackness—that is, sexuality, danger, and aggression—regardless of the fact that most passengers are Indians. A woman from Unit 2 expressed her reactions to this new street culture in the following way:

> These taxis make me a little nervous. Some of the drivers look like gangsters and their loud music is very aggressive. Even when you walk the streets the conductor will shout things like, "Come on mummy, come with me, I give the best rides in town." They laugh all the time, but I don't like it, and I never go with them. Many of our Indian taxis have also started to do the same thing, but I will not go with them . . . I prefer the taxis without music, or the ones with nice Indian music like in the films.

Local newspapers regularly carry articles condemning the loud music and, in letters to the editor, readers complain that the taxis' culture of music and flirting makes them into "rolling nightclubs." Worried parents, teachers, and religious leaders see the taxis and the permissive youth culture they represent as responsible for the growing rate of teenage pregnancies, prostitution, drug use, and crime. Drivers and conductors are routinely described as school dropouts and as antisocial elements. For girls, riding alone in taxis, especially black taxis, can be enough to cast doubt on their moral habitus. The simple proximity to younger African men, however superficial and economic such a relation may be, is seen as a moral problem. Yet it is clear that Chatsworth is far from being dominated by Africans, but rather is dominated by a new, louder, and more conspicuous charou culture that has incorporated taxis, kwaito, bhangra, and ever-growing drug use within the last decade or more.

As so many others in the township, Ramesh had coined an English nickname for himself, but somehow the name "Rocky" did not sit too comfortably with his skinny body and slight appearance. Ramesh was twenty-two years old and had been a conductor in a taxi owned by his brother for two years. It was painted bright red, called the Mighty Mauler, after the local soccer club, and had the logo of the club painted all over its sides. Following current fashion, Ramesh's head was shaved, and he displayed golden earrings, one gold front tooth, and three other front teeth with gold rimming. He dressed in black jeans, big boots, a shiny golden shirt, and Ray-Ban sunglasses. The driver, who was a bit older, also wore black and gold and a leather jacket in the heat of the midday sun. Ramesh said,

> This is our style. You get customers with your style, you know, how you dress, your music, and the way your car is done. We play bhangra in the daytime, not so loud in the mornings, but then in the afternoon when many of the kids leave school we shift to R & B and then mostly kwaito in the evening. . . . Many of the kids like it to be loud and some of them will wait for us outside their school, because they know us and like us.

Ramesh admitted that a part of the attraction of the job was that he got to know a lot of people and that chatting, joking, and flirting was part of the job. Sometimes he had been in trouble with the boyfriends of the girls he knows, but as he said, "It depends on which taxi you *graf* [work]. If you work in one of my brother's taxis you are safe . . . everybody knows his reputation and no one messes with him."

Ramesh did not mind black customers; they were better than the charous, he insisted, because they never tried to run off without paying. His ideas of Africans were strongly gendered, however, and he asserted that he prefers black women as customers because "some of them are very shy and sweet, not like these charou chicks, they have such loud mouths." Too many black men in the taxi at a time was clearly a threat, he thought. "I will rather go [*sic*] half empty than with a load of these guys—they are arrogant when they are in a group."

Ramesh had been held up and robbed more often than he could remember. It was a part of the job, he said, and so they never kept much money in their car. He had a gun himself, which his brother gave to him, but wouldn't use it out of fear that he might get shot. He was very practical about the muggings: "You give them [a] hundred rand [about

Movement, Sound, and Body • 197

Figure 11. WAITING FOR CUSTOMERS

fifteen U.S. dollars] and they run off—my life is worth more than that," he said, and claimed that he had never been threatened or mugged by Indian men because they did not dare do it out of fear of being found and punished. "Besides," he said, "we Indians stick together in this taxi business. If we don't, the darkies will take everything from us." Ramesh's fortunate experience was undoubtedly conditioned by his brother's reputation. In contrast, many other drivers and conductors readily admitted that most of the crime and muggings in Chatsworth were indeed committed by local charous.

CONCLUSION: "INDIANNESS," AFRICAN-STYLE

Although denied by most people of Chatsworth, it seems that there is a convergence of patterns of life, movement, and cultural enjoyment among the younger generation in Indian and African townships. The taxis are vehicles of the "party culture" that has been the primary refuge for an emancipated but also bewildered postapartheid generation.

The taxi industry itself has produced many forms of convergence between Indian and African worlds. It has introduced new forms of criminality and has allowed drug lords and other operators in the informal economy to develop a highly conspicuous and profitable legal business. This has earned them unprecedented levels of visibility and respectability as the spokesmen and public faces of both local communities and their taxi associations. Such a nexus between criminality, the taxi business, and political eminence has long been a feature of local politics in African townships. While criminal networks previously played a role in the Indian townships during apartheid, they are now acquiring a new level of everyday visibility.

Another convergent form is the style of masculinity and, more broadly, of gender relations among ordinary charous. While the emerging youth culture in Chatsworth has provided more personal freedom for young women in terms of appearance, mobility, and choice of partners, the level of sexual and domestic violence against women is also growing. The African township culture, especially the more violent forms associated with the taxi industry and gangsters, articulate codes of masculinity that are widely copied among young Indian men. These include black hairstyles, baggy pants, colorful caps, and an emphasis on muscular bodies, plentiful cash, and a certain ruthless and misogynist attitude toward women. Many of these styles are vernacularized interpretations of commercialized elements in black American culture. It is perhaps predictable that as kwaito has gained popularity across racial boundaries, it is no longer seen as properly black by many young Africans. In its stead, another American genre called "house music" has gained tremendous popularity among restless and assertive unemployed youth in the African townships. The taxi industry is regarded by many young men as a perfect place for raising quick cash and for gaining access to what colloquially is known as "charou chix," or supposedly easy Indian women. The kwaito music and its lyrics fit quite seamlessly into this masculinized street culture.

Yet none of this is actually recognized as elements of "black" culture by people in Chatsworth. Such forms are seen as Indian because racially Indian bodies are performing these forms of masculinity, because the music often has Asian tunes in it, and because the lingo is South African Indian English rather than Zulu or *isicamtho*. What in reality amounts to a gradual "Africanization" of the culture in the formerly Indian townships is interpreted by most middle-class Indians as the dominance of a morally inferior charou way of life. In this way, the fundamental misrecognition of markers of race and class seem to continue, albeit in a different form.

If apartheid was built around a system that institutionalized racial oppression and segregation as the lived form of class subordination, it seems that the reverse is true among non-African communities in postapartheid South Africa. Here, the reality of increased influence of

Figure 12. Council housing flats in Unit 2, Chatsworth

black and African culture in everyday life is attributed to differences in class. The supposed moral decay of the charous and their pollution by African (and Afro-American) culture after the fall of apartheid has prompted multiple Indian organizations in South Africa to attempt to purify religious practices among the charous and to forge links with the wider Indian diaspora. The local sense of "Indianness" is now challenged by a proliferating range of global and translocal identifications, as well as a new and unmistakably Africanized way of inhabiting the city through the senses.

In view of this wider South African context, the taxi, its colors, and its deafening kwaito signify much more than a demotic celebration of postapartheid freedom. It also signifies a new inhabitation of urban space and a new morally ambiguous cultural genre—"Afro-Indian"—that cannot recognize itself as an identity. Not yet.

CHAPTER 6

The Unwieldy Fetish

DESI FANTASIES, ROOTS TOURISM, AND DIASPORIC DESIRES

THE STANDARD NARRATIVE OF INDIAN IDENTITY IN SOUTH AFRICA WAS PRESENTED in a fully formed and explicit fashion in a series of articles in the *Post* in 2010 that commemorated the 150th anniversary of Indian indenture in the country. The key themes were loss and recovery: indenture was a traumatic migratory experience forced by abject poverty and colonial despotism. Despite internal differences Indians were united by a natural urge to retain core values—family life and kin relations, religious cosmologies, food and aesthetics—in the face of a hostile and indifferent colonial society. The ties with India were severed and Indians were left at the mercy of the apartheid state. The postapartheid society has inflicted a new set of losses—of jobs and personal safety—but also offered new connections with a global Indian diaspora.

The fundamental assumption in this narrative is that attachments to India are natural and fundamental. This requires some qualification: First, the diverse communities that left the Indian subcontinent between 1860 and the 1890s left one colonial territory for another one, and the identification with "India" was not yet there. The imagination of a unified Indian nation only gained popular momentum from the 1930s onward. Second, those leaving South Asia did so for diverse reasons. A substantial number of those who settled in South Africa were indentured for the second time—that is, had returned to India only to sign up for a second round of indenture.[1] For those who came as passengers, the trip to South Africa was integral to the commercial enterprise of mainly Gujarati trading communities who followed British colonial expansion through eastern and southern Africa. Third, India only emerged as an important point of reference in the 1930s and '40s. Yusuf Dadoo was like many others across the world inspired by the strength of India's nationalist movement, and he called India "a resting place of the imagination," by which he meant a place that demonstrated the dignity of self-government (Raman 2003). During the same period, the

Urdu language emerged as the preeminent symbol of a unified Muslim nationalism in South Asia and also in South Africa.

Fourth, many of the Indian institutions in South Africa were a result of apartheid's project of separate development, including the promotion of "Eastern values," language, and religions at schools and cultural and educational institutions designed for Indians. Fifth, there were many and diverse contacts between South Africa and India during the decades of apartheid. Durban newspapers of the 1960s, '70s, and '80s abound with articles on Indian religious groups, films, and popular music troupes that circulated with only minimal hindrances. These visits were important occasions for both the South African state and local Indian politicians to demonstrate their cultural credentials. From the point of view of the Indian government, the cultural boycott was only applied with diligence to performances of high culture.

India as an Unwieldy Fetish

For all these qualifications, India features prominently in South African Indian life—through Bollywood films and associated music, fashion, and gossip; a rapidly growing tourism and pilgrimage industry; and Hindu and Muslim religious organizations with roots in the subcontinent.

How can one understand the relationship between South African Indians, India, and "Indianness" in a dynamic fashion that avoids reified notions of Indian culture and Indian religious practice? All major works on the postindenture world struggle with this question.[2] My proposition is that the attachment to things and phenomena that are "Indian" are best thought of as fetishistic. In a subtle study of Tamils in Malaysia, Willford argues that the dominant Malay modernist ideology has transformed the "ethnic past" of the nation's discrete elements to an "uncanny double" (2006, 5). This "backward" and disavowed attachment to Hindu rituals and identity emerges in full force around ritual events and other manifestations of folk "Indianness" (117). Such events manifest disturbing echoes of the Indic past throughout Southeast Asia that need to be expunged in order to create pure and strong Malay Muslims.

In South Africa, the fetishization of Indianness is structured by the fact that Indians have historically been seen as completely alien to the land. India was a site of authenticity, "our motherland," but also a site of non-African loyalties. The coolie past was indeed seen as a shameful and imperfect past, not because it was Indian but because it was not Indian enough, or rather, it was Indian in the wrong way. The attachment to things regarded as properly Indian promises to purify and solidify a cultural identity that is always haunted by its contested legitimacy in South Africa, and whose own authenticity and purity were always in question among ordinary charous. Attachment to things Indian has thus had a fetishistic character because these things are discontinuous with everyday life and are ambivalent—objects of desire and disavowal at the same time.

A fetish is normally understood as an object that is unusual, awe-inspiring, uncanny, or highly desirable because of the qualities and powers it represents and condenses.[3] In a more psychoanalytical perspective, a fetish can be said to constitute a "lie that works," an object in which hidden or more opaque powers are invested so that it seems as if this object itself indeed *is* and embodies those powers. This does not preclude the fact that those who use and "believe" in a fetish, mask, image, or thing very well know that there is no direct identity between the mask and the ancestral power it is said to represent (Krips 1999, 57–70). The fetish does the complicated work of maintaining the aura of something while also accepting its unreality. Freud writes, "The fetish remains a token of triumph over the threat of castration [loss] and a protection against it" (2000, 353). Or as Pierre Fedida argues, the power of the relic is that it not only provides a mediating force between the world of the living and the world of the dead but it also enables and protects the living by providing an object of mourning. The fetish, on the other hand, re-presents an active and at times menacing power of that which is lost, made invisible, or even denied but still active as a force that is intimate and yet unknowable, an unchosen shadow companion one cannot get rid of (Fedida 2003).

The fetish represents a relationship to experience that is not "real" in a conventional sense but fundamentally phantasmic—shot through and propped up by fantasy, hope, fear, and imagination. Like any signifier, a fetish can stand in two different relationships to its referent: either a metaphorical relationship where a thing, or phenomenon, becomes a condensation of what it stands for, its true essence; or a metonymical relationship where the fetish is a fragment, or plain object, that gains its significance by referring to something else that is bigger or more important.

Can one apply this logic to a referent as unwieldy as a country or a subcontinental civilization? The labor of compression and simplification that makes India into something like an object has already been performed by geographical and historical distance and by scholarship and political discourse, as well as by the flow of images, artifacts, and symbols in popular culture that attempt to capture India.[4] It can be so as its spirit, or character, in a metaphorical form (spirituality, tolerance, complexity of kin and family, Hinduism) or in a metonymical form, as spices, saris, the Bollywood film song, biryani, and/or ornaments. Although India can never be contained by single images or signs, South Africa's racialized regime of recognition imputed to the "fact of brownness" of certain people a relationship to things Indian. Thus, both desires and disavowals of India or various ideas and experiences of Indianness always needed to perform a sustained labor of abstraction, erasure, and simplification to make themselves possible and plausible.

In the following, I will explore the attachments to India, and its supposed power to authenticate cultural identities and practices, in narratives of roots tourism in contemporary India that have been related to me by individual South African Indians. I will also explore the changing relationship with India through the medium of Bollywood films from the late 1990s onward.

THE SPIRITUAL HOMELAND

There has been a surge of interest in travel to India among Hindus since 1994, both as roots tourism and as religious pilgrimage. Today there are multiple tour operators in South Africa who organize trips to India, typically as guided and planned tours. Some travelers try to retrace family roots and ancestral villages, but most travel agents I talked to confirmed that the overwhelming interest is in sightseeing and shopping.

Several tour operators specialize in Hindu pilgrimage tours to the major sacred sites in North India. Some even try to retrace and follow the peregrinations of Lord Ram in the epic Ramayana—a text that today is promoted by many religious organizations as a sacred scripture-cum-historical narrative. These India tours, whether religious or not, cater to a middle-class audience. The interest in purified Hinduism, India, and cultural authenticity has become central to the performance of respectability within the middle class among South African Indians.[5]

To many of the roots tourists, the encounter with India becomes an encounter with themselves and their romantic imaginings of an exotic and "oriental" India. The narratives of encounters with the actual physical India also elicit interesting reflections on modernity as an attitude—to be confident, self-reliant, individualistic—and modernity as mastery of organization, hygiene, and rationality.

SEEKING ANCESTRAL ROOTS

I met Mr. and Mrs. Pillay the first time in October 1998 in the Durban Archives, where they had come to check the nineteenth-century ship registers in the hope of locating the village from which Mr. Pillay's great grandfather had come.[6] Mr. Pillay was a secondary schoolteacher and Mrs. Pillay had a part-time clerical job in a municipal extension office. Their two children were studying in secondary school and at an engineering college. Their story was typical of the social mobility of many Indians since the 1960s. Mrs. Pillay shared, "We think that going to India will be a good educational experience for our children. We are Indians, and now that we can afford it, we thought that the first place to go abroad should be India. We are Tamil speakers, but as you know, very few people speak Tamil anymore, so we hope that we can find someone to help us there."

The Pillays spent several hours in the archives going through many lists of laborers who had arrived on ships from Madras in 1881 when the grandfather was said to have come. The problem was that hundreds carried the name Pillay,[7] and the first name Muruga was very common as well. After some hours, the clerk advised the couple to check the list of those passengers who had paid for their journey themselves, and soon after the Pillays found a name and village that almost precisely matched their information. But they were mildly puzzled. It turned out that the ship this Pillay had arrived on had set out from Mauritius and not India. As so many other Indians in Durban, the family history they had grown up with fit the standard story of indenture. Mr. Pillay told me:

> We were always told that my great-grandfather left for South Africa because of poverty and drought in his village, and that going to South Africa was the last possibility he had. When he came here he worked hard for many years, managed to buy himself a patch of land in Springfield, and made a living as a gardener. In fact, gardening was our profession in my family until my generation where we Indians began to get a chance to get some education. I remember my father going to the market every morning with his vegetables, together with some of his laborers. . . .
>
> But now it turns out that my ancestor paid for his trip here, from Mauritius, so somehow he must have stayed there for a while and managed to get hold of some money. I am sure the agents promised these people that South Africa was a land of milk and honey.[8]

For the Pillays the fact that they found the great grandfather's name under paying passengers was the first of several experiences that did not fit with the knowledge they had received about their own past and the cultural "motherland." As Mr. Pillay said to console himself, "Maybe it is a mistake that his name was placed there . . . we will know when we come to India."

I met the Pillays again several months later, after they had returned from India. They seemed pleased but also slightly troubled by their experiences in India. Mrs. Pillay thought it had been a wonderful trip, in spite of the fact that their children had been less than thrilled. Mr. Pillay had many questions he wanted to ask me about India. He shared their experience with me:

> Our travel agent had arranged that a young man, a college graduate, would meet us at our hotel and go with us to the village to translate and help us. I remember that I asked him if we could look up the village in the telephone directory to check whether there were any Pillays there. . . . He just smiled and said, "I think this is your first visit to India, sir." . . .
>
> It took many hours before we reached the village. It was poorer than anything I had seen in South Africa ever in my life; you know, this smell of cow dung all over, animals walking around, and the children running almost naked and quite dirty. . . .
>
> It turned out that there were several Pillays in the village—like in Durban! We walked around and asked many Pillay families if they had relatives in South Africa. Nobody knew about that. Then we asked if any of them had relatives who had gone overseas. Again no one knew so many generations back. We ended up talking to a very old lady who remembered talk about this distant uncle called Muruga, like my ancestor, who had left the village many years before she arrived in the village as a young bride.
>
> The next day we spent all day with this family who we thought could be our distant relatives, but we were not sure. We could not really talk to them. They are farmers and not very educated, and they had no idea about where our country was and how we lived. . . . We showed them some pictures of our house in Chatsworth, and this old lady just said, "America" all the time and smiled.

Mr. Pillay showed me a picture of himself standing outside the house in the village. Standing next to the two elderly men in the family, Pillay—with his white Polo shirt, smart sunglasses, and his paunch—looked every bit a prosperous NRI (Non-resident Indian) who had returned to his village to flaunt his wealth. But he was not. He was, in fact, a complete stranger who had to rely on the young man they had hired as an interpreter. The Pillays shared with me their different perspectives on their visit to India:

> Mr. Pillay: To this day I feel strange about what happened in that village. How can we be sure that they were relatives? They were very happy with the things we had brought from South Africa. But we also realized that they were not as poor as it seemed at first sight, at least if we compared [their situation] with other houses in the village. They had a son who was studying in

Bangalore and they also had a TV. But it was difficult to communicate with them.

Mrs. Pillay: Well, I liked it there. It was poor and not very clean, perhaps, but inside it was very nice. We stayed only one night, but it was so quiet, peaceful, and beautiful. There was a little pond next to the old temple, and it was like a dream when the sun set on that. We have nothing like that in South Africa, this peace of mind and nothing to worry about, no hassles, and no crime . . . we have all the modern things in life and a big house. But are we more happy than these people? I don't think so . . . but to be honest with you, my children did not like India much, the food was different, they did not like the smells, going to the bathroom, the noise, and all those things. I grew up in a poor household, so I don't mind so much if there are no modern comforts, but they say that we should have gone to Australia or Mauritius.

After they had told their story, Mr. Pillay, who is a science teacher and a rational man, began to ask me all kinds of questions about India, about the public administration, relations between Hindus and Muslims, and what he called "work culture."

I don't understand the attitude to work over there. There are so many people just sitting, doing nothing . . . I mean grown-up men who could work. They just sit there, and there is so much to be done; they could clean the place or maintain the houses. But nothing happens. They don't have this idea of doing things on their own. . . . But it is their own country, nobody is keeping them down like here in this country, especially with the black man in the past. Do you think it is because of poverty? Or maybe the caste system?

Mr. Pillay was not convinced by my explanations (which were too complex, he felt), but he seemed to accept that corruption was an important factor, and that "culture" in and of itself could not account for what he had seen.

No, it is not because people there [in India] are Hindus or Tamils. See all my neighbors here, they are all Hindus, and look at our nice houses, see how hard we all work. . . . The thing with us Indians is that we always fight among ourselves. But you know that. I can see it all over. Ten years ago we had one Tamil organization here in Chatsworth, now there are three or four. . . .

I know it sounds [a] little strange, but in some ways apartheid was a blessing in disguise. It made us Indians unite and work together and forget all our little differences. But now it is every man for himself, all the communities fight each other . . . Hindus, Tamils, Muslims, Christians. We are becoming like these fellows in India!

For the Pillays, as so many other South African Indians, the encounter with India was an encounter with something disturbingly unknown, a place that made them feel very alien, very South African, and very modern. It made them realize just how different they were in their "work culture" and their habits, and how inauthentic their own embodied sense of Indianness was. Yet to Mr. Pillay, the encounter with India was also an encounter with elements in his own community and everyday life in Durban, which he detested as negative marks of, or residues of, something essentially "Indian": internecine strife, petty politics, and narrow-mindedness, as opposed to what he saw as the inherently rational approach of "whites." This was a disturbing encounter with a sense of cultural essence he denounced but could not ward off completely.

Mrs. Pillay experienced India within a truly orientalist framework: as authentic, a place imbued with a certain inner beauty and harmony, and a place that exuded history and timelessness. These features not only outweighed or neutralized the lack of modern amenities, but the lack of rational modern organization of life was also one of the very preconditions for maintaining the orientalist idealization of India. This elevation of India's physical deficiencies to symbols of an ineffable spiritual depth is even more pronounced in the next story.

FINDING SPIRITUAL TRUTH

Rashni's family decided some years back to become proper modern Hindus. Her father told me:

> Like so many Indians, we took to the white lifestyle—drinks, parties, *braai*, outdoor life. I remember when I was a young man I would watch the surfers at the beachfront—only for whites then—and I was so envious. I wanted to be like them . . . but some years back some friends took us to the Sai Baba ashram here in Durban and that changed our lives. We are Indians, we were brought up like Indians, and we should not deny that. We will never be accepted by the whites. That is one thing I have learned.

More than ten years back the family had moved from their apartment in the large, sprawling Indian township of Phoenix—a place known to be more working-class and rough than other Indian areas—to a house in the prestigious Reservoir Hills, which was designed as an elite area for Indians in the 1970s. As the family turned toward the Sai movement seven years ago, they became vegetarians and abstained from alcohol and smoking. They also decided to send their daughters to extra classes in Tamil and classical dance (Bharatanatyam), which were offered by local organizations. Both of the parents had grown up with Tamil being spoken by the elder generation in their homes, but both of them had lost the language and could barely follow the dialogue when they sometimes rented a Tamil film from the video shop nearby.

RASHNI'S FATHER: Last year we decided to go to India to visit the ashram outside Bangalore. We traveled with other Sai devotees, and everything—accommodation, visas, and all—was taken care of by the people both here and in India. We were picked up in the airport and taken to a sort of hostel outside the ashram. It was very simple and basic, but absolutely clean and well organized, not like the city of Bangalore we went through—such noise and pollution, I have never seen anything like it in my life. How can that be the Silicon Valley of India? I don't understand that. But the week we spent in the ashram was a beautiful time.

RASHNI'S MOTHER: The ashram is very big and like a garden, full of flowering trees and very neat everywhere, and only people dressed in the robes you get there. Nobody will shout, or be rude, and many people simply take the vow not to speak while they are there—just to relax and get away from the usual life. We all felt so good, so clean, and so much at ease with ourselves. We were all the same in there—people from all over the world, but what difference does it make? In there we were all devotees, and nobody asked how much money you made or how many sons you have. It was a beautiful time.

RASHNI'S FATHER: After this week, we had a week to travel around a bit. We went to Mysore and then to Bombay, where we spent four days . . . I think Bombay is like Johannesburg, a big place with so many different people, and all they care about is making money. They are also rude like in Jo'burg. But there is no crime—it is a wonder. I walked out at night in the city; I haven't done that since I was a young man in Durban. But one thing I don't understand is why can't they clean the streets? It is awful, garbage and flies all over. People just accept it. You can say many things about the white man, but he knows how to run a place. You can see how Bombay must have been beautiful in the past, in colonial times. Now it is a mess. Again it makes me think of Jo'burg. Have you seen what has happened to it now? Homeless people all over, bonfires in the streets, and these young black guys behaving as if they owned the place.

Compared to that, I surely prefer Bombay. At least nobody will shoot you there.

RASHNI: To me it was a bit of a shock to be in Bombay, I must admit, especially after being in the ashram, which was so nice and beautiful. They seem to have lost something in a big city like that. There are no manners, people are rude. . . . You know that people always say here that Indian traders cheat their customers. It is true that some traders are dishonest, especially with Africans, and it is shameful for our community. What made me angry over there [in Bombay] was how these men in the market behaved. You could not trust them at all. I don't understand why they do that, there is no need.

This narrative resembled the type of narratives one might hear from most Western travelers in India. There was nothing particularly diasporic about the idealization of the type of purified and sublimated Indianness and spiritual community that was manufactured through elaborate rules and discipline in the ashram outside Bangalore, and replicated in Sai ashrams elsewhere in the world. In this and other neo-Hindu movements, the spiritual and the mythical is presented in a generalized, vague form, as Hinduism elevated to a new universality through its encounter with the West. Many upwardly mobile families have been attracted to these movements and their apolitical assertion of Indian spirituality that is disentangled from what many Indians see as "backward" and ethnic features of traditional and ritualized worship of earlier generations.

As in the former narrative of the Pillays, similar misgivings were shared about the encounters with what is seen as an excessive representation of the stigmatized marks of backward Indian ethnicity: disorder, chaos, and dirt. To Rashni's father, Bombay represented the abyss of "third-worlding," which South Africa would also slide into without the managerial skills of the "white man." To Rashni, the encounter with the actual India was a disheartening encounter with the stereotype of greed and the fetishization of money, which is still attributed to the Gujarati trader in South Africa.

CATALYSTS OF MODERNITY

Anil grew up in Tongaat, a prosperous town located in the sugar district north of Durban. The city is almost entirely Indian, but as all urban areas in South Africa, it has a number of densely populated African townships located outside the city proper. Tongaat has a strong Hindi-speaking community that takes pride in originating from some of the first indentured laborers and traders who came via Calcutta to Natal from the Bhojpuri region more than six generations back. Many Hindi speakers in Tongaat speak Bhojpuri Hindi in their homes. Anil grew up with a strong sense of Hindu identity, the great Hindu epics, Hindi films and film music, and with many relatives who were engaged in North Indian cultural organizations.

Anil had a keen sense of the political and economic realities of the postapartheid situation. Indians had become very vulnerable under "black majority rule," as he called it. Anil supported the ANC "because there is no alternative for a minority like us." But he despised what he called the "ANC Indians" who, according to Anil, are mostly rich Gujaratis and "communists who discard their own background." The new South Africa required one "to know oneself and one's background . . . ask a Zulu who he is and he will take pride in his culture and language. We Indians must do the same," Anil said.

Some years back Anil began to devote more time to activism in the Hindi Shiksha Sangh (HSS), the primary association for promotion of Hindi and North Indian culture in South Africa. In connection with this work, he got the opportunity to visit India for the first time:

> The first time I went to Delhi with some of the people from HSS, it was so nice to be in a place where everybody could speak Hindi, but I must admit that sometimes they would speak it in dialects I had never heard before. So I asked them to slow down. Many educated people received us very well and many times they wanted me to speak about what had happened to Gandhiji's ashram in Phoenix. I had to tell them the sad story [of its destruction in 1985] but I also realized that Gandhi is not so important anymore in India. . . . We spent most of our time with people who work in education, mostly Arya Samajis and people from the BJP [Bharatiya Janata Party] and the RSS [Rashtriya Swayamsevak Sangh]. I admire the work they do in education and their selfless attitude. . . . We surely need more people with that attitude and that sense of history and pride in their own culture. . . . We must overcome that sense of inferiority that the whites have given us here. I think Mbeki is right when he says that colonialism and apartheid have wounded all of us . . . Indians in this country are a bit ashamed of their own culture because so many still believe that "white is right." That is the attitude we must change.

Anil found many things in India surprisingly old-fashioned:

> Like the way they speak about women . . . that women should be in separate organizations and so on. It will never work in South Africa. You have seen how young Indian women are here. They are educated

and want careers . . . so that is something we should not bring here. . . . Another thing I did not like was all this hatred for the Muslims and for Pakistan. That is not something we need here. We have enough problems, and why should we not work with our Muslim compatriots? I know that some people have started RSS here where they do physical training and all that. But who is it they want to fight? I think that is dangerous. It can make sense in India, perhaps, but do we have a chance if the Zulus turn against us? . . . I saw all that when I was in Bombay with my boss. We visited two different companies manufacturing machine parts. They were very suspicious of the financial arrangements we suggested and wanted to check everything. Nobody would make any decisions without consulting the owner . . . finally we signed a contract and went back. We have received some pumps from them but they were not up to the mark. Somehow I find this very embarrassing, because I'm Indian. The system there is so stiff, there is no professionalism and no pride in one's job.

Like many well-educated, successful, and culturally conservative Indians, Anil has a desire to purge Indianness and Indian culture of what he sees as a backlog of conservatism and parochialism. Indians must assert themselves, and the only way to do that is by adopting modern forms of knowledge, modern work ethics, and a more self-confident attitude to the challenges of modern urban culture without discarding Hinduism or language. These stories were all from people who had been to India in the 1990s. Recent accounts are slightly different, but most visitors still notice a stark discrepancy between the talk of India's modernity and what they actually encounter.

In spite of many reservations, virtually every informant I met who had been to India was quite defensive about the place and would often take any critique of the country—and Hinduism—very personally. Once back in South Africa, the question of India became one of seeing the homeland as a fetish that condensed the greatness of the civilization and the "spirit of India," as it was often put to me. The experience of the actual India in all its contradictions was disavowed in order to maintain a strong attachment to a phantasmic and fetishized India that is understood as a world civilization.

GLOBAL DESI DREAMSCAPES: THE REVIVAL OF BOLLYWOOD IN SOUTH AFRICA

The Hindi film *Kuch Kuch Hota Hai* (*Something or Other Is Happening*; hereafter referred to as *KKHH*), riding on the back of its huge success in India and across the world, was released in South Africa in late 1998. The rumors of its success among "mixed audiences" in Britain and North

America convinced the manager of a large cinema complex in Durban's Musgrave shopping center, the heart of upper-middle-class whiteness in the city, that it would be feasible to screen the film in one of the smaller halls. A few months later in December, the manager, Shaffie Mohammed, received what he called "a request from one of our white patrons to acquire a subtitled copy of the film." He succeeded in getting one via Mauritius, which for decades had been an important supplier of cultural products from the Indian subcontinent. For the next six months the cinema hall was continually sold out.

Meanwhile, other copies without subtitles ran in the Indian townships for half-empty halls. Here the screening was stopped after a few months, which was considered very good for a Hindi film. But in Musgrave, the craze continued well into June 1999. This was the first Bollywood production ever to be shown in a formerly white area in the city, and also the first Bollywood film ever to be shown with English subtitles. Although the overwhelming majority of spectators were of Indian origin, quite a few whites had their first encounter with Bollywood. Very few Africans ever saw the film. Unlike many other African countries where the Hindi cinema has drawn mass audiences for decades, Indian films and other cultural products from the subcontinent have been "racialized" and confined to Indian areas and audiences in South Africa. The film became a cultural phenomenon that revived and redefined an otherwise declining interest in Indian films among South African Indians. Many filmgoers saw the film three, five, even eight times, and its success was intensely covered and discussed by the local Indian press. Local journalists repeated the fact that the film ran longer than and was seen by more people in Durban than *Titanic*. At the same time, local Indian papers and radio programs ran features where psychologists warned against the damaging effects of repeated viewing and obsession with film stars on young and tender minds. Why did this particular film evoke a huge and emotional response at this juncture? Why did it become such an object of fetishistic desire and identification?

"WHAT DOES THIS FILM MAKE OF ME?"

Christian Metz argues that reception and viewing of films is an experience that is suspended between two viewer positions: the "inscribed" viewer who is constructed by the film's style of address, its story line, and its register of references; and the "actual" viewer, that is, those who actually sit in front of the screen. Unlike in theater, the performance and the reception do not presuppose each other in the cinema hall, and the actual viewers of films have the freedom to attend or not attend to the film, or to move in and out of various dimensions of the inscribed viewer position (Metz 1986). Metz's argument is that the viewer does not identify with the people on the screen, who obviously are fictive, but with herself as someone inhabiting this inscribed position that is created by the address of the film. What is judged and negotiated in the process of viewing is, as Ashish Rajadhyaksha argues, what the film makes of the viewer, and whether that is seen as an acceptable, enjoyable, or insulting position (2000).

The culture of film viewing in India is quite far removed from the serious atmosphere of total attention and identification with the screen, which is the ideal in modern art cinema. Hindi films are constructed around a set of easily recognizable conventions, particularly song and dance sequences, often predictable plots, and almost stereotypical characters. There is, in other words, a strong ritualistic element in the viewing of Indian films, a lighthearted, tongue-in-cheek, mimetic relationship to all kinds of styles and genres, and a certain disarmingly over-the-top quality to dialogue and the style of acting. Knowledge of these genre conventions and the ability to appreciate films in this relaxed, repetitive, and intensely social form is crucial to the larger "reading competence" that characterizes the average, often extremely film-literate spectator in India. By reading competence I mean a visceral familiarity with styles, songs, and the legacy of older films that may be alluded to, rather than any formal knowledge. Hindi films such as *KKHH* are obviously judged on the basis of how they speak to these discerning sensibilities of such ordinary Indian film literati.

Some have suggested that this culture of film viewing is derived from *darshan*, the Hindu practice of viewing an idol or image of a deity for long periods of time (e.g., Mishra 1985), while others, such as Tejaswini Niranjana (1997), have suggested that the "Indian spectator" over the last decades has become a global phenomenon, a form of relationship between film and viewing that are integral to the cinematic culture in countries with populations of Indian origin, such as, for example, in South Africa. Based on the evidence below, I will suggest, however, that the *KKHH* phenomenon in South Africa may be understood, at least in part, as a consequence of *the relative absence* of this "Indian spectator" in contemporary Durban.

Bollywood productions and the film music played a central role in the production of urban Indian communities in the Durban region. The music constituted the core of the experience of community through film viewing. Orchestras such as the Ranjeni Orchestra were heroes in the community for decades and copied Hindi film songs from the cinema hall and performed them at functions and weddings in the ubiquitous community halls. Repeated viewing of the same revered films produced an "insider culture," though far from as intense as in India, and made

Durban's Indian cinema halls important meeting places where young people and families indulged in the intense experience of the sound and the music.

In some ways the film songs became the true secret of the community, something that required a command over colloquialisms and insider perspectives—unlike the classical taste culture, which was open to the white gaze and ears. The film music marked a zone of the truly ethnic-popular, a zone of enjoyment and indulgence in ethnic pleasures that was always more associated with the working class but also shared by the Indian elite and middle class.

The interest in Indian films declined since the 1970s, along with the decline of Indian vernaculars as home languages. The decline in the viewing of Indian films was squarely linked to generations, as most of those who viewed Indian films and enjoyed the music were middle-aged or older.[9] Previously, the Indian part of the city center had four large cinemas, but the last one, Isfahan, closed in 1999. It was only with *KKHH* that this long-standing trend was dramatically reversed.

Roopanands, the manager of the leading retailer of Hindi video-tapes and other Indian cultural goods in South Africa, informed me that by the late 1990s, even huge Hindi blockbusters only sold a mere five hundred videotapes all over the country. By contrast *KKHH* sold five thousand in a few weeks. As the owner said, "It was truly extraordinary, something we hope is the beginning of a trend that can reverse the decline, but we are not sure."

Let us turn to the film itself to see how it addresses its audience, what it makes of its spectators, or how it inscribes them as spectators.

PLOT SUMMARY

The film is a love triangle between the hero Rahul (played by teenage idol Shah Rukh Khan), his friend, the tomboy Anjali (played by Kajol), and their common friend Tina (Rani Mukherji), a sophisticated NRI girl who enters the prestigious college, St. Xavier's, directly from Oxford and "cannot even speak proper Hindustani," as Rahul initially remarks. He is enticed by her amply displayed body and beauty, and the friends drift apart as he decides to marry Tina while leaving an unhappy and devastated Anjali behind. Tina dies of complications after having given birth to their daughter, who she, as a last wish, wants to call Anjali, in memory of their lost friend. The film's story line is with the child Anjali, who is living with her father, Rahul, and her grandmother. One of the high sentimental points occurs when little Anjali, who is at a talent contest at her elite school, is supposed to give a little speech over the theme "Mother" but is lost for words.

The remainder of the plot unfolds at a summer camp where the lost friend Anjali, the tomboy-turned-woman, is one of the instructors and where little Anjali is attending. Here, Rahul meets Anjali again in her new and more desirable feminine incarnation, and their love is renewed. Anjali is going to get married to another man, played by Akshay Kumar, but he decides in the last minute at the wedding to give her up and let her be reunited with Rahul, her true love.

The address in the film is clearly middle-class and aspiring to be both cosmopolitan and diasporic, and displays a range of a strangely delocalized series of styles, dress, almost exclusively airbrushed modern interiors, and a style of dialogue and interaction that draws heavily on Hollywood teenage movies. Settings are completely Westernized in clothing, body culture, sports, rock music, beach volleyball, and basketball—a fantasy West implanted onto India, minus the squalor, dirt, and the lower classes.

The film is also about disciplining women, or rather their self-disciplining. The cultivation of the true femininity in Anjali makes her a desirable object—no longer wearing jeans and T-shirts, as in the first part of the film, but dressed in a sari as a proper Indian woman. There is a total absence of any paternal authority, as well as the absence of jealousy and conflict between lovers. The film clearly depicts its main characters as unfettered individuals whose actions are guided by their own feelings and impulses, their conscience and inner goodness. Nowhere are conventions, culture, or moral injunctions presented as restraining or intervening except as benign principles of goodness and moral principle—as in the highly improbable respect of pure and true love. The film's celebration of romantic love and of "clean" relationships between individuals—no sex, no pressure, no violence—was one of the points that many viewers in Durban cited as its greatest feature. A twenty-year-old girl put it to me this way: "the beauty of this film is that it leaves you with a sense of being clean."

At the most immediate level, KKHH inscribed its viewers as modern, middle-class consumers, cosmopolitan and equally at home in the East and the West. It also represented an attractive and airbrushed modern India. Consider this letter from a retired school principal to the editor of the Post regarding KKHH: "For the enjoyment of non-Indians who have already developed a palate for Indian cuisine and have begun to notice the beauty of Indian belles, Kuch Kuch Hota Hai ought to be televised. It would help to modify the negative perceptions some people have of Indians" (January 20–23, 1999). A part of the thrill of KKHH was that it presented images of an Indian form of modernity that many South African Indians felt comfortable with, and it displayed female beauty and elegance of designs and sets—essentially commodities marketed as India's contribution to the global cultural economy. In the debates unfolding around the phenomenon, an exuberant reader of the *Post* referred to *KKHH* as, "a thousand times better than most of what passes as entertainment in mainstream cinemas—no sex, no copulation, violence—only pure love and true emotions." Some defended the simplicity, if not banality, of the plot by pointing out that "even Shakespeare used simple stories," while others stressed the important emotional appeal such films have to Indians living abroad. As another letter to the editor said, "It gave me goose bumps and made me feel proud to be an Indian. It is of particular significance to an ex-patriot [*sic!*] Indian such as us who live out of the motherland and sometimes lose touch with values that should be dear to all true Indians" (*Post*, March 17–20, 1999).

Another part of the exhilaration had to do with the occupation of formerly white spaces. Kings Park Stadium was hired for a show with the four stars of the film, who were marketed as the Awesome Foursome and performed the dance routines and playback songs. An excited journalist wrote, "usually Kings Park is full of biltong-munching and beer-drinking rugby fans [whites], but soon it will be the scene of a colorful and exotic world-class show." The space normally occupied by unsophisticated, white, working-class men would now give way to the Indian middle class enjoying a "world-class show." Indians flocked to Musgrave Center to watch the movie in formerly "white" elite space, often along with whites, despite the fact that it was difficult to get tickets. Throughout its run the film was screened in a small hall, which explains in part why it was sold out most of the time—the rumor of which again had the self-perpetuating effect of attracting even more viewers.

The address of *KKHH* was part of a wave of Indian music and film that successfully catered to communities of migrant Indians and larger audiences around the world. Bollywood, in this tailor-made and utopian fashion, provides a space wherein images of the modern city, Westernized habits, and bodily gestures can be reconciled with romantic notions of India, and thus domesticated as acceptable ways of being Indian. The film was welcomed by so many, in Durban and elsewhere, because it served to make the Indian community visible and recognized on the basis of its distinct cultural heritage, suitably de-ethnicized and packaged to suit the tastes of so-called cosmopolitan audiences.

The success of *KKHH* was quickly picked up by cultural organizations and business operators, and soon the music from the film appeared at a host of shows, musical performances, and fund-raising events. When the Hindi Shiksha Sangh celebrated its fiftieth anniversary in 1999, the highlight of the show was a copy band playing the *KKHH* songs. Many others took it up, including political parties around the general elections in 1999. Ela Gandhi, an MP for ANC, recorded an election song on the *KKHH* song called "Kuch Kuch ANC." Ela Gandhi, who sang the tune with a somewhat thin voice, stated, "There are a lot of freedom songs in African languages but nothing really in English or for the Indian community. . . . The movie did so well, people identify with it and it conveys important themes of sacrifice, love and non-violence. It also brought out the colonial mentality that some people suffer from which makes them think that only the white man can do things" (*Post*, May 23,1999).

WHO ARE WE INDIANS, AFTER ALL?

In the debates unfolding around the film, the older rift between a "classicized" taste culture and the popular enjoyment of film songs was reconfigured along gendered and generational lines. On one side stood elderly or middle-aged men who criticized the depletion of true Indian values by the film, or denounced it for being too silly, banal, and displaying the worst sides of Indian culture. On the other side were younger women, and some men, who had strong feelings and attachments to the fantasy space that *KKHH* offered them. They reacted strongly against criticism of *KKHH* on talk shows on the phenomenon. "Don't criticize our heroes just because they are not yours . . . you don't understand our world," a young girl said angrily to a university intellectual who criticized what he saw as an unbearable lightness in the film's story line. "It touched our hearts, brought tears to our eyes . . . that is enough for me," said a middle-aged housewife. And another woman said, "I'm glad I saw it . . . it brought me a happiness and warmth I hadn't experienced for years."

Even one of the feistier hosts at the popular talk show *Viewpoint* at Radio Lotus had to give in after he saw the film. He started a debate on air by saying, "I felt the warmth of this story, it made you believe in real values again, that there indeed is true love and friendship to be found out there." Then the floodgates opened. Masses of people called in, mostly women but some men as well. Some were critical of "the mass hysteria," as one said, while others defended the right of women to be sentimental about such things. "I went with my mum and sister," a young man said, "I thought the film was well made, as good as any American film, but I did not cry like them. But they were happy afterward, so what is wrong in that?" he asked. The debate revolved unmistakably around the painful negotiation of the nuclear family and its ideal foundation in enduring romance between two unattached individuals. The heavily mythologized institution of the Indian family—joint, comprising several generations, tight-knit, controlled but warm—was all a myth in the townships. However, ideals of the submissive Indian woman still persist in the face of the rapidly changing gender relationships. The result is high levels of domestic violence and also frequent cases of "love murders."

Another part of the debate was about whether the film was typically Indian or not. For some, *KKHH* was a typical Indian film and thus represented a long-overlooked genre with universal messages, comparable to Shakespeare, as several participants in the debate claimed. To critics it was exactly the fact that it was typical, with its unbearable ethnicity and connotations of gossiping aunties and Indian "backwardness," that was its main problem and limitation. A male schoolteacher told me, "I find this film tasteless and crude. Don't you think that Indians can do better than that? We have been telling our kids for years that they are as good as any white kid . . . then people praise this film, which shows Indians as amateur clowns, if you ask me."

Others welcomed the film because they thought it was atypical. Now, at last, there was an Indian film one could relate to and enjoy because of its Western framing. Yet, for others of a more conservative persuasion, this was precisely the problem of *KKHH,* what commentator Yogin Devan called its cheap aping of a Western form: "While the pastel-coloured saris and blouses worn by Tina were beautiful to admire, the fuddy-duddy in me would not easily accept the clothes worn by the students at Xavier College. Who in Mumbai goes to college in a silver lamé miniskirt or tight disco hot pants . . . the actresses resorted to cheap clingy western clothes. I quickly blamed it all on India's recently adopted open economic policy and free trading" (*Tribune Herald*, January 24, 1999).

The core audience of the film, those who saw it several times, consisted mainly of younger people who were generally disinterested in politics and who had rather vague ideas about what Indian culture was supposed to mean. For them the main novelty was that because of the subtitles, they could for the first time understand and follow the dialogue of a Hindi film. A young man said to me, "Now we understand a little better the gibberish of the aunties." Riashney, a student from a Tamil background, told me, "We grew up with both Hindi and Tamil films, but I rarely watched them. They were on the video when the family was together; my mother and aunts would sing some of the old songs and talk about their youth, but it meant nothing to me. To be honest, I always found the old films terribly silly. I never understood their humor." Many younger people enjoyed this new sense of understanding a medium they had experienced throughout their life as series of images, music, and words—mostly unintelligible—as a part of the family home, family gatherings, and so on: a sphere of Indianness, whether Hindi or

Tamil, belonging to an older generation. But with *KKHH*, this Indian-ness was no longer a sign of a backward, working-class, and excessively ethnic and alien culture. It was, in the words of a fifteen-year-old girl, "a film I could invite my white classmates to see with me. They liked it, especially to look at Shah Rukh Khan."

Another interesting thing was the relative lack of interest in the actual content of the film. The story line and the characters were much less im-portant than the atmosphere, the state of mind, the sentimentality, and visceral register that was evoked as such by the film, not least the music and the songs. The reliance on viscerality rather than plot, and on music and songs rather than characters, is a well-known facet of the "culture of viewing" in India. In South Africa, however, this "reading competence" was not in existence among the younger audiences. Besides, the senti-ments evoked by *KKHH* related to other and more specifically local dimensions: first, the desire to inhabit the white gaze, or perhaps global gaze, in a favorable way. Second, *KKHH* was an enticing sign because it spoke to a fantasy of India that is widely held among Indians in South Africa: an India devoid of squalor, dirt, and chaos. Paradoxically, this fantasy seemed to actually be nurtured by South African Indians' con-frontations with the real India through travel and roots tourism. To inhabit the fantasy space of *KKHH*, or the two-week, air-conditioned, whirlwind tour of India, seemed at least to elicit surprisingly parallel commentaries and emotions for some.

Consider the affinity between these two statements about India as an experience: Neena, who had been to India many times as a devotee of Sai Baba, told me, "For me everything in India is wonderful, the pace of life, the landscape, the way people go about life—there is some-thing spiritual about it, as if people are at peace with themselves. After some days in India I also get this feeling of being calm and relaxed and happy. This is the spirituality we lack in this country, and in our community people have nothing but petty envy and jealousy to put instead." And the following statement is from Uma, a college student, about why she had seen the film nine times: "I have seen this film nine times, and I know every detail in it. But I would not hesitate to go a tenth time because it brings me such a good feeling of hope, of good-ness, a feeling of being at ease with myself—something that lasts for days after I have seen the movie."

I am not suggesting that the film functions as an illusory dream es-cape from the hardships of everyday life. The inherent discrepancy be-tween the "inscribed viewer" position of the easygoing modern Indian and the actual viewers of young and anxious South African Indians in the townships gave a glimpse of the possibility of being both modern and South African Indian at the same time. The success and approval of the film from non-Indians produced a hope that some distinctly non-autochthonous cultural practices, if suitably modern in presentation, perhaps could win a measure of public recognition.

Diaspora and the Unwieldy Fetish

The phenomenon of *KKHH* raises the question, once again, of what "diasporic" actually means. Tejaswini Niranjana employs the term "diasporic" for situations where groups are actively involved in interactions and the exchange of goods, signs, and symbols with what they see as their ancestral home, which is a workable definition of a diasporic relationship (1997). Many of the creative artists and musicians in Trinidad that Niranjana has worked with are indeed involved in reworking, localizing, and expanding the possible meaning of what can be seen as "Indian" (2006). Yet for many of those belonging to what Niranjana calls the "subaltern diaspora," and that would include the majority of South African Indians, India itself remains immensely distant, and at best a part of a vague family history. The effective signs of ethnicity lie in local religious practices and institutions, in the pressure for arranged marriages, food habits, and the cultural preferences of their parents and older people—including Hindi or Tamil films. While many Indians have tried to de-ethnicize themselves in the last decades by adopting white lifestyles, the immense insecurity and new possibilities opened in the last decade in South Africa have also brought about a quest for re-marking of bodies, territory, and social practices in cultural terms. Yet India is nowhere in the picture as an object of full identification but remains a destination for sentimentalized roots tourism, shopping, or visits and pilgrimages to ashrams and sacred sites. In these senses, India is always a fetishized and hyperrealistic location. The relationship with this India arrives in the form of obligation, an imputed "call of culture" that all brown people in South Africa are expected to respond to in one way or the other. This call, or interpellation, comes from the state, community leaders, religious discourse, and the increasingly assertive official discourse of a global Indian family that emanates from the Indian state.

KKHH portrayed a dreamy, global Indian diasporic space that is imagined to be more hospitable and generous than South Africa, yet distinctly Indian and modern. The fascination of *KKHH* thus correlates closely to the fact that the many young Indians who leave South Africa each year do not merely follow "white" emigration, but rather head for the big centers of diasporic Indian culture—Melbourne, Toronto, London, and New York. The virtual, floating, and rather abstract sense of being Indian that is articulated through sensuous and visceral signifiers such as film, music, or religious devotion appear much more attractive and noncontroversial than conventional notions of lineage, blood, or political loyalty.

Subsequent developments in Durban have corroborated the significance of the transformation *KKHH* ushered in regarding the reception and circulation of Indian films in South Africa. Both of the large cinema corporations that dominate the distribution of films in the country now screen subtitled Indian films in the large mainstream cinema complexes in Durban, Johannesburg, Pietermaritzburg, and so on. Global blockbusters such as *Lagaan* and *Asoka* attracted massive audiences—white and Indian—in 2001, and a large newly opened cinema multiplex in Durban's northern suburbs depends heavily on the four to five Indian films it constantly screens. The Hindi cinema has become an integrated part of Durban's urban culture, much of which today is effectively shared by Indians and whites. Yet the deep-running racialization of cultural practices in the country means that unlike the popularity of Indian film in much of Africa, there are no signs of the Indian cinema becoming a medium of entertainment and visceral engagement between the city's Indian and African worlds.

Let me finally reflect on how diaspora is perceived and conceptually deployed. Since the late 1980s, the term "diaspora" has been proliferating as a descriptive term for the entire range of activities that involves contacts and ties—emotional or material—between a society and "its" expatriate population, or between these expatriate populations.[10] The term has become something of a companion to globalization, a symptom of the interconnectedness of the world, and not uncommonly celebrated as popular responses and strategies in a globalizing world—strategies that seek to preserve cultural diversity and identity in the face of Western cultural hegemony.

However, the latent heroic connotations of diaspora have become more pronounced and crude as the term has become a key word in political strategies deployed by governments, businessmen, and cultural entrepreneurs. The rhetoric of a global Indian family promises a symbolic inclusion and recognition of the descendants of indentured laborers within a larger and global community of modern Indian (Hindu) civilization. While these initiatives have been greeted with some enthusiasm among people of Indian origin across the postindenture world,[11] they also generate doubts about the usefulness of diaspora as a noun, a "total identity." Diaspora can at best be used as an adjective (diasporic) or as a verb (diasporization) to describe an aspiration, a fleeting, contested—at times important—form of imagination that may, or may not, succeed in providing an effective identity.[12] There are diasporic sentiments and attempts at diasporizations that, as in our case, may aim at turning various groups of "brown folks" into a more consolidated Indian diaspora. The latter may be an effect of such diasporic strategies, never their starting point. This "diaspora effect" concerning the creation of India as a political project emerged in the middle of the twentieth century, and it reemerges now in the attempt to create a global Hindu culture.

Yet, as we will see in the following chapters, the category "Indian" appears evermore obsolete in South Africa. Muslims increasingly see themselves as linked to the Middle East; some South African Tamils see themselves as linked to a global Tamil diaspora whose central point of reference is Jaffna in Sri Lanka;[13] and many South African Hindus convert to Pentecostal churches, making Jerusalem, Kentucky, and Tennessee more meaningful references than the subcontinent.

CHAPTER 7

Global Hindus and Pure Muslims

UNIVERSALIST ASPIRATIONS
AND TERRITORIALIZED LIVES

IT WAS A SUNNY AND QUIET AFTERNOON IN 2007. I WAS VISITING THE SHRI Vaithianatha Easvarar Alayam (Umgeni Road Temple) complex in Durban, the oldest and most venerated Hindu temple in South Africa (built in 1883) and said to be the largest Hindu temple in the Southern Hemisphere. We were soon in conversation with the senior pujari, who enjoyed practicing his native Tamil with my partner. He was gently shaking his head as he narrated to her how he had found Durban when he had arrived more than a decade earlier from Sri Lanka. "I was a bit shocked by how little people here knew of our tradition," he said. "People do not really speak Tamil here anymore, and they are quite ignorant of even the basics of Hinduism. When I came here with my family, we were quite alone. It was as if there was no real society . . . but now it is better, and people are keen to learn more. We try to educate and help." The pujari was called to the gate of the sprawling complex to consult with a young couple. They had come straight from the showroom in a new Golf GTI and wanted the car to be blessed. The pujari went through a complex ritual, applying lime juice and vermillion to the tires and the front of the car. Finally, he garlanded the front grill of the car, and the young couple paid a handsome donation to the temple.

"We have to adapt to the times," the pujari told us with a half smile. "People here are discovering more spiritual sides of life, but they also love their cars and other possessions and they want them blessed . . . so we do this and many weddings too, for all the communities, not just the Tamils, although this is more of a Tamil temple."

Maharaj, the young and dynamic chairman of the modern Shri Luxmi Narayan Temple in southern Chatsworth had studied Hindi and Hinduism at the famous Benares Hindu University and is today a lecturer in religious studies at a local university. He has launched a range of initiatives that explain modern Hinduism to a younger generation. Among these is a website that lays out the basic tenets of Hinduism, the meaning of essential rituals, and the meaning of colors and symbols, such as AUM, which the website calls "the essential brand of Hinduism." Despite his own undisputed learning, the pressure to get an Indian pujari has nonetheless been "unrelenting," as he put it.

> For many of our people it has become a prestige thing to have an Indian pujari at weddings. It is a little sad to admit that despite our efforts at conveying the basic values of our ancient tradition, the question of having a pujari in the temple is one of money. . . . In the last ten years we have had three pujaris from India and they have all left us. We have taken them in, helped them, and paid them as we could afford it. One went to a much richer temple in Johannesburg; another went freelance and is now a real showman and businessman doing many weddings every week, and the third one is now about to go freelance. . . . People want that Indian accent and the idea that it is an authentic Brahman, and we cannot compete with that.

There has indeed been a growing market for religious services among Indians in Durban, and there has been a steady flow of pujaris coming from the subcontinent since the early 1990s. Sri Lankan priests are particularly popular because of their flexibility and willingness to adapt to new circumstances. Even Maharaj admits that "they are really good showmen, very entertaining and good at explaining our tradition, even though they come out of the Tamil tradition."

For Maharaj and others around the temple, this presented a challenge. While they encouraged the study of Hindi, travels to India, and a real ethical engagement with what they called "modernizing our Hindu values," they found that the attraction of the authentic pujari was driven by competitive prestations among the devotees. He says, "Some of the people of the older generation and some of our pujaris are very hostile to my idea that the temple must engage ethical questions—AIDS, family values, violence, and interracial harmony. They want the pujari to come to their son's wedding as if to tell their neighbors, 'I am a better Indian than you.' Most pujaris go along with this for the sake of the money . . . well, many come here, I suspect, because of the money." Money and the use of donations and payments given for services, such as weddings, remains a serious and contentious issue, however. Another recurrent issue is the appropriateness of rituals: are they authentic or inappropriate banalization of the Hindu tradition? In South Africa the sense of having been isolated and peripheral has exacerbated these feelings.

Many local people in Chatsworth still recalled the embarrassment caused by the "false pujari," another Sri Lankan who served in a local temple for about a year. Not long after his arrival, one of the trustees of the temple proudly took me to meet the new pujari. The priest was living with his young family in a small house within the temple compound, and he was eager to show me the temple and to perform a puja for me. He seemed a bit halting and nervous, and he was not at ease with the situation. He found South Africa difficult. He had limited English, he had no driver's license, and his wife was frightened of the rampant crime rate at the time. The trustee explained that they were taking care of the family, shopping for them, and paying them well. He was confident that the pujari would soon adapt to the local circumstances. "But we don't want him to pick up any of the charou habits," he said and laughed loudly. The pujari also laughed politely, but did not catch the joke.

When I returned a year later, I was told that the pujari and his family had been sent back to Sri Lanka. It turned out that he had no training from Sri Lanka, that he in fact was a car mechanic, and that the chants he was performing in the temple were mostly made up. The incident was embarrassing for the trustees but also at the center of many local jokes about the gibberish and greed of the local pujaris. In the wider world of Hindu organizations across the city, the incident seemed once again to confirm the long-standing idea of the charous as deracinated and inauthentic Hindus.

In this chapter, I will return to the theme of cultural self-doubt and the pervasive anxieties about the authenticity of quotidian charou practices and dispositions that surrounded the idea of "the Indian family." The other major pillar, which in most people's minds undergirds Indianness in South Africa, is a persistent devotion to Hinduism and Islam but also to a range of neo-Hindu outfits and many branches of Christianity. The bulk of this chapter explores the contemporary replay of the historical tension between the "low" popular forms of worship and the purifying strategies deployed by religious organizations, both Hindu and Muslim. Increasingly, an older spatialized notion of religious authenticity as being rooted in the subcontinent has given way to ideas of religious purity as an index of social and cultural aspiration. Today, the main distinction is one of commitment and aspiration to be part of a proper, global, and universalized tradition within Hinduism or Islam, and those whose attachments to a religious tradition are mainly territorialized and ancestral. The quest for universal, deterritorialized, and purified religious identities has become the most prominent route to escape the stigma of charoudom and the historical territorialization of Indianness in South Africa.

The entry to the township of Chatsworth is marked by the large white Temple of Understanding that was inaugurated by the International Society for Krishna Consciousness (ISKCON) in 1986. For years Rajbansi had been supporting ISKCON's project and had successfully rallied support among local Hindu organizations. Rumors of shady backroom deals were rife, as in the case of Rajbansi's other projects, but the inauguration was a major event that was attended by a crowd of 125,000 people, and included guests of honor such as Chief Buthelezi. The temple was hailed as a testimony to the strength of Hinduism, despite the "siege like Christian efforts to convert Hindus," as a conservative Hindu publication put it at the time.[1]

During my first months in Chatsworth, I was taken to the Temple of Understanding and its vegetarian restaurant many times. Some of my new friends and contacts felt that this was the most appropriate way to introduce me to the Indian culture of the townships. On other occasions, I was taken there on the assumption that a deep if not yet realized spiritual quest indeed was the underlying reason for my interest in things Indian. It was discreetly pointed out to me that here I could meet other people like me, white people "who are also interested in understanding our Indian culture." I did indeed encounter more white people in this temple than at any other site in Durban's Indian worlds. They came as regular visitors but also worked as attendants and volunteers in the Temple of Understanding. The presence of foreign ISKCON volunteers in the township was seen as a recognition of Durban's Hindus as proper Hindus, which counted for something in the larger world.

Later on, when informants praised the vegetarian food in the temple, I would praise the local home cooking in Chatsworth because it was spicier and more wholesome. This always produced smiles and knowing chuckling, because my opinion of the rather bland food in the temple was widely shared. "But this type of food is really good for you," my friends would say with some deference. Their own diet was much meatier and spicier, "real Indian chow." They'd also tell me that the ISKCON was not very local and definitely not charou. "Most of them are *witous* [whites]," and some informants joked about the local Indian devotees at the temple as socially ambitious lahnees who were hanging around this neo-Hindu organization in the hope of becoming white.

Figure 13. Shri Radhanath Temple of Understanding, Unit 5, Chatsworth

None of this was ever said publicly, and the ISKCON was always included in the list of bona fide Hindu organizations and institutions in the city and the country. The status of the Temple of Understanding as a highly visible, pure, and modern front piece that was only superficially connected with the township behind it was a very accurate metaphor of the relationship between modern Hinduism and the heterogeneous and irreverent forms of religious life of the charou world. It is precisely these forms of ancestral tradition—described below—that many educated Indians see as embarrassing and "primitive." Neo-Hindu organizations of many kinds, such as the Ramakrishna Mission, Sai Baba, ISKCON, and Divine Life Society, have substantial and growing followings among local middle-class Indians in Durban. Most of these organizations have plush and well-funded ashrams and branches. ISKCON's annual Ratha Yatra, which celebrates the life of Lord Krishna and culminates in a procession to the sea, began humbly in 1989 as one of the first multiracial events allowed on the Durban beachfront—although most of the devotees in the early years were indeed white. Since then it has grown into a regular event that conspicuously displays symbols of Hinduism, and thus Indianness by association, in the heart of the city.

The Temple of Understanding had indeed emerged as a key element of what Shryock calls "Identity 1," the front stage public display of "our culture," conveniently purged of virtually every element of the actual ancestral practices that Hindu organizations had sought to weed out for more than a century. A newlywed couple of Tamil background, both educated professionals, explained why at the end of the day they found neo-Hindu traditions more attractive than the tradition they grew up with. Vivek explained to me:

> We both grew up in Chatsworth. We did all the things people do— some fasting days, pujas at my uncle's big house, some festivals where families came to visit and there was lots of food, weddings with even more food (and booze), some outings to the temple on Umgeni Road now and then . . . no one ever explained why we did it. I found that strange when I started thinking about it. So when we got married we both thought that we should find some good place to go . . . you know, we are Indians and religion is important to our culture; we can't just not have anything like some of my white colleagues. How do you bring up a child if you don't have a religion?

Vivek and Kavita had "shopped around" for a while, as they put it. In the end they found that the Sai Baba ashrams and events were the most welcoming and easy to understand. "The teaching there is about how you live your life here and now. We liked that better than all the long stories about gods and sages in the past that you find in other places." They also liked that Sai Baba was everywhere, with multiple branches in the city and with a mixed group of devotees. "There were many white people too . . . it felt more like the people I work with in my job; it was comfortable and open, more cosmopolitan in a way," Kavita emphasized.

Religious Practices, Hindu Missionaries, and Cultural Purification

The indentured laborers brought with them a wide range of popular, ritualistic religious practices, both Muslim and Hindu, the latter often with Tantric components (such as the still-popular Kavady festival of Tamil origin), and widespread use of animal sacrifice. Well into the twentieth century, religious life revolved mostly around homes and informal shrines. More organized forms of worship developed along the linguistic lines, which remained the primary loci of identification and of social and religious practices for people from the subcontinent well into the 1960s.

As in India, the invention of Hinduism as an organized religion owed a great deal to the many reform movements that sprang up in the later half of the nineteenth century. Arya Samaj especially had a very distinct proselytizing agenda, and the defense against conversions of lower-caste Hindus to Islam or Christianity was central to its larger project of organizing, purifying, and homogenizing the Hindu community.[2] Arya Samaj was active among indentured communities from around 1900, when it found a dire need for organizing and consolidating Hindu practices among people who, according to more orthodox views, had already been polluted by the passage across the *kala pani* (black water). Popular Hindu practices were often decidedly heterodox, and many Hindus partook in the Shia Muharram festival, known in colonial Natal as the "Coolie Christmas" (Vahed 2001a, 80). According to the movement's own chroniclers, Arya Samaj missionaries who arrived in 1905 were "alarmed at the spiritual and religious degeneration of their Hindu brethren in this country."[3] The religious ritualization was "devoid of meaning" and "grotesque," and "within Hinduism they exacerbate a form of religious degeneration with sometimes quite alarming results" (Naidoo 1992, 56).

The arrival of Swami Shankarananda, "the first Hindu monk ever to visit South Africa" (Naidoo 1992, 63), led to the formalization of the South African Hindu Maha Sabha in 1912, Arya Yuvak Sabha in 1915, and later to the formation of the Arya Pratinidhi Sabha in 1925. The Aryas targeted the Hindi-speaking segment of the Indian community where the organization succeeded in establishing a very commanding position. Local and popular forms of worship gradually gave way to more Sanskritized religious teaching and rituals. Arya Pratinidhi Sabha sponsored the education of young men of South African birth in India and soon began to establish a presence in every town and neighborhood in South Africa where there was a substantial Hindi-speaking or Gujarati population.

The Aryas also pioneered vernacular education in South Africa by sponsoring community-based schools in Durban, Johannesburg, and smaller cities from 1912 onward. Initially these schools were mainly run as sites of religious instruction where children were told stories and religious parables, and taught the Arya Samaj mode of worship and philosophy. Later the schools were more formalized and the emphasis shifted to teaching Hindi and maintaining Indian culture in the face of the spread of English and the adoption of Westernized lifestyles, which accompanied the transformation of Indians into an urban community in the 1920s and 1930s. The Aryas were in the forefront in all these domains. They opened schools for girls and promoted various social institutions, notably the Aryan Benevolent Home, now located in Chatsworth.

The reactions to the Arya activism among adherents of more orthodox and ritualistic forms of worship soon emerged in what appeared as a belated replay of the protracted conflict in northern India between the orthodox *sanatanis* and the reformist Arya Samajis. The rift between Aryas and other forces widened regarding styles of worship and the Arya Samaj critique of caste and openness to lower-caste communities. In 1941, Orthodox forces formed the Shree Sanatan Dharma Sabha of South Africa. Although *sanatanists* in public debates in the 1920s and '30s had tried to defend the virtues of Brahmanical Hinduism and the legitimacy of caste, the relative fluidity of the caste order in South Africa militated against this line of argument. Instead, the major disagreement revolved around the legitimacy and use of *murtis* and idols generally; that is, whether the divine could be appreciated in the more abstract form advocated by Arya Samaj or could only be fully understood when taking the concrete form of an idol (Naidoo 1992, 80–82).

Vernacular languages remained the most important vehicles of Indian identity. For generations, most Indians lived in a bifurcated world: the home and the neighborhood were marked by vernacular languages, Indian cooking, and religious rituals, while the larger world was dealt with in English (or Fanagalo), and governed by the etiquette and submission expected when working as waiters, drivers, and workers. In his sociolinguistic study of the transformation of the Bhojpuri dialect of Hindi, Mesthrie argues that the process of "koineization" produced a new lingo, which he terms "Natal Bhojpuri." This became a marker of community among the Hindi speakers but equally important as a marker of ethnoreligious identity (Mesthrie 1996).

As we saw, the desire to replace the vernacular parole of Bhojpuri with the langue of Sanskritized Hindi grew stronger in the following decades.[4] The Hindi Shiksha Sangh was set up in 1948 to promote the teaching of Hindi and the preservation of (North) Indian culture in South Africa. Arya Pratinidhi Sabha also promoted Suddhi Samskara (lit., purification/upliftment rite), the (re)conversion rite of Hindus who had left the faith but wanted to return to the Hindu community. For many years, the organization worked on a low-profile basis, mainly within the Hindi-speaking community. As Indian languages and religion began to receive official attention from the 1970s onward, the agenda of preserving Indian languages and defining the Hindu community as a whole became more manifest.

The early 1980s saw an official promotion of the study of Indian philosophy. According to a staff writer at *Fiat Lux*, it "shares with the

Western tradition the ability of rationally articulating eternal human problems—such as the ultimate meaning of existence, man's means of knowing his world." The study of Indian philosophy in South Africa should, however, strive to establish a "causal linking of cultural habits and locally active organizations . . . to relevant traditions of Indian thought."[5] The study of Islam and Hinduism was also introduced as part of divinity studies, and the study of Indian languages and Arabic was promoted at the same institution. Islam was treated with distinct respect and grace in official publications. In an article praising the habits and piousness of Muslims, Paul Kruger, one of the "Urvaters" of Afrikaner nationalism, was quoted as saying, "Have respect for the Muslims, for they are people of the Book."[6] As a religion, Hinduism was treated less respectfully, and an article from the same period argued in classically modernist terms that Hindus should present the "rational core" of Hinduism because "in a multicultural situation such as that of South Africa, no individual culture will succeed in keeping itself alive if it by withdrawing to a merely internal ritualized self-understanding fails to communicate itself to the public outside its own realm of faithfulness."[7]

A Nervous Relationship: Contemporary Hindu Practices in the Townships

In contemporary South Africa, virtually every cultural and religious organization among Indians agrees that a general "Westernization" constitutes the most serious threat to Indian identity and culture in the country. The postapartheid scenario and the opening of South Africa to various global trends have only strengthened the Christian denominations, especially those linked to economically powerful churches in the United States.

Another effect of the fall of apartheid was that the question of who is entitled to represent Hindus, Muslims, or even Indians as such have become more fractious than before. After 1994, the public representation of religion and cultural identity of groups and communities was rendered in limbo between an older and partly illegitimate discourse of ethnicity (as Indians) and a more legitimate discourse of faith, particular denomination, or sect, whether Christian, Muslim, or Hindu. Among Hindus, the quest for representation has given rise to numerous new organizations, temple trusts, and ashrams that promote particular traditions, yet emphasize the importance of Hindu unity.

Compared to such efforts at classicization and purification, the lifestyle, language, and practices of the ordinary charous in the township inevitably appear less than perfect if not morally deficient. Over the past decades, something akin to a "nervous condition" has emerged regarding the meaning and forms of Hindu rituals in the township. Many feel torn between the comfort and intimacy of routinized rituals that have been followed for generations, often differing from family to family, and the injunctions by local cultural organizations to refine and purify religious practices, which leaves them with the sense that their practices are inadequate. In response to this, some Hindu families apply various routines of self-purification, from shorter periods of fasting (i.e., abstaining from meat and alcohol), contributions to the ongoing construction or renovation of smaller local temples, or somewhat irregular attendance of vernacular language classes, listening to Indian classical music, and so on. This emulation of the more "correct Indian lifestyle," as it was often called, was never uncontested. Some saw this as a betrayal of ancestral traditions, or more commonly, as social ambition dressed up as piety. Bobby, a local builder in Chatsworth, told me rather bluntly that he preferred the charou way: "What is wrong with following what our ancestors did? They did not have much, but they liked to eat well and enjoy whatever life had to offer when there was a wedding or a festival . . . now these clever people with money tell us that is wrong and not the thing that Hindus should do . . . but maybe we like it that way. If you ask me to stop being a charou and become like some *ou* from Reservoir Hills, well then, I will stay right here with the charous." Bobby referred to the protracted and recurrent debates on how weddings were to be performed and celebrated, and how the consumption of alcohol and meat on these occasions had become a major concern. The length, ritual, music, and permissiveness at weddings had emerged as a matter of constant dispute between those adhering to a more ornamentalist *puranic* (lit., "old") tendency, and those promoting more purist and strict Vedic rituals. The latter tendency was inspired by the Arya Samaj idea of the primacy of the *havan*, the fire and the simple fire ritual that the movement had promoted for many decades.

For Pavan, who headed his own small prayer group in Chatsworth, embracing the Arya rituals was not about social ambition but about self-discipline. He had been a truck driver all his life, and when he got older he turned to a deeper understanding of Hinduism: "From our scriptures, we learn that there are four stages in life and that in the third stage when one gets closer to retirement one begins to withdraw a little from the world and take interest in getting closer to *jnana* [knowledge] as we call it. . . . In the old days in India people would wander off and become sadhus, but that is not practical here. So I studied Sanskrit and our scriptures and started our group where we meet for the *havan* ceremony and singing of *bhajans*." For Pavan, the vestiges of a proper Hindu life had to be retrieved from the corrupting influence of consumer society. For him, embracing his tradition was not really about "blaming the West . . . that is rubbish . . . look at all these corrupt people in India, I mean morally corrupt." Hinduism was not really about faith in the conventional sense. To Pavan, being a proper Hindu was an ethical position: to live and behave with dignity and to take responsibility for oneself and one's community. The problem in today's world was, said Pavan, "that we don't have to grow up or take responsibility—life is like a party and having fun is all that people want." Pavan detested the way especially weddings and other ceremonies had become so "cheap . . . there is no seriousness or attention to the meaning of what we do . . . and yet, ours is the oldest tradition in the world."

Pavan performed pujas at home and with his prayer group, and he also officiated at weddings if people asked him. There were only two conditions, he emphasized: "no alcohol and no dancing. . . . If people want they can do it the rest of the year but not when we call upon our deity to be present." For Pavan, the key element in becoming a good Hindu was indeed *shuddhi*—literally, purification/uplift/improvement of oneself but also in the sense of conversion from other religions or practices back to Hinduism.[8] Pavan explained,

> In those days, people resisted British missionaries luring people away from their tradition . . . today our task is to make people return to their culture, to who they are. . . . I don't blame the people here in Chatsworth who are going to churches. At least they are taking life seriously . . . they are looking for something. We Hindus only have ourselves to blame. We let our young people forget their roots, their language, and their culture.

This sentiment was echoed by some of the activists who had recently renovated and revived the Shri Vishnu Temple in Chatsworth. The chairman of the temple trust, L. M. Maharaj, was emphatic in his rejection of any "call to arms for the Hindu cause," as he said.

> We have to make ourselves relevant to people around here. This temple was falling into a state of disrepair, nobody cared much and nothing happened. Why do we blame the single mother, or the lonely old person who is forgotten by her children, for going to a church where people help and care for them? Are they bad Hindus . . . ? Nobody gives up their culture, everything they grew up with, except if they are disappointed. The Christians in Chatsworth are neglected Hindus, and we must show them that our tradition and our language [Hindi] has values and a beauty that you will not find elsewhere. Every family has members who have left the tradition, and we have to meet the challenge.

The response of the temple volunteers was to promote the study of Hindi—"good, *shuddh* Hindi not Bhojpuri," as Maharaj put it—and the study of the Hindu epics and tales for children, the singing of *bhajans*, and the collection of funds for charitable work. However, the volunteers were unequivocal that this was not a question of repeating what their ancestors did. "We try to bring modern Hinduism to our people—we have good and strong speakers from India, people who have the knowledge but also have the skill to address young people." In 2010–11 this attempt at improved visibility resulted in the building of a monumental forty-foot brightly colored statue of Hanuman that dwarfed the temple.

Popular Hindu rituals were, however, well and alive, not least among people of Tamil background, where the various purification movements never gained much ground. Here, worries about "the proper" were less centered on expunging alien elements from Hinduism than on questions of codification and public performances of rituals. The non-Brahman movement in South India had challenged the ritual hegemony of Brahmans in the twentieth century and had promoted a range of popular practices and festivals. In South Africa, public figures such as the well-known actor Kessie Govender and other left-leaning intellectuals took strong stands in favor of retaining non-Brahman practices among Tamils. The popular Pongal (harvest) and fertility festival was always of greater significance in rural and cultivating communities than among the higher-caste communities. In Durban, it has receded from its earlier position as one of the premier Tamil festivals in the beginning of the twentieth century.[9] Instead, the Kavady festival devoted to Lord Murugan—denounced by the colonial authorities in India, Malaysia, and elsewhere as a barbaric custom of "hook swinging"—has emerged as the most popular of the Tamil festivals and attracts thousands of devotees and visitors to the old temples in Durban's industrial areas.

The austere and righteous Murugan, a deity of lower-caste origin, has since the 1950s been promoted by the non-Brahman movement as a key symbol of Tamil identity. In Durban, men prepare for months in advance for the demanding task of carrying or pulling images of the deity by hooks pierced through their skin. Today the festival is widely advertised and promoted by the Durban City Council and the official KwaZulu-Natal Board of Tourism as a display of the diversity of the province's popular culture.[10] Fire walking has assumed a similar position as evidence and display of popular religious and cultural disciplines that require concentration, devotion, or even a trance to be carried out successfully. Fire walking signifies devotion to Draupadi, the princess in the Mahabharata who is humiliated and (almost) disrobed but retains her strength by devotion to Krishna. The fire walking is a metaphorical repetition of the ordeal of Draupadi and was histori-

Figure 14. FORTY-FOOT STATUE OF HANUMAN AT THE SHRI VISHNU TEMPLE IN CHATSWORTH

cally most popular among lower-caste communities in South India as a form of worship of the mother goddess Mariamman. Today, both fire walking and the Kavady festival remain more significant cultural events among Tamils in South Africa, Malaysia, and Fiji than in India itself.[11]

Anand used to participate actively in the Kavady festival. He took pride in being able to carry dozens of limes in small hooks hanging from all over his body while pulling a chariot with an image of Lord Murugan. He stopped in 2001 because he thought it was no longer "a community thing":

> We were a whole group of friends who did all the things one needs to do for the festival. It is not just a question of enduring pain, although that is also there. The main thing is to eat the right things months before, to rest, fast, and to prepare yourself mentally. You have to tell yourself, *I am going to do this better than last time . . .* I am proud of being Tamil and I am still a devotee of Murugan, no doubt. But I felt that the whole festival is too much of a show nowadays. Last time I did it there were more tourists with cameras than there were Tamils! . . . It made me ask myself, *Why do I do this? For whom?* Some of my colleagues at work joked that I must have found another hobby, but this was not a hobby for me . . . I wanted to keep our culture alive.

Like many others, Anand is disappointed in how Tamil culture is becoming a public performance. He was missing more "commitment," more "pride," as he said. In the mid-1990s the search for pride and strength began to be addressed very directly by the right-wing Hindu nationalist movement, which for decades has built strong support across what is increasingly referred to as the "Hindu diaspora."

THE CALL OF GLOBAL HINDUISM

Vishwa Hindu Parishad (VHP), the powerful Hindu nationalist organization that acts as a fund-raiser abroad, and a deadly front organization in communal clashes in India,[12] had no presence in South Africa until 1995. That year, Krish Gokool, a wealthy businessman, opened a branch in Durban. The subsequent attempts of Gokool and others to establish VHP as a new global umbrella for Hindu organizations faced stiff opposition from the South African Hindu Maha Sabha, which had represented Hindu organizations for decades. The organization promotes itself as strictly cultural and has maintained cordial relations with the authorities, both during and after the era of apartheid. As the dismantling of apartheid began, the question of representation of the "Hindu community" vis-à-vis the government gained new actuality. At the time, the vice president of Hindu Maha Sabha denounced the underlying political agenda of VHP: "We don't need the political and religious conflicts of India to come to South Africa . . . it could even be dangerous in our present situation."[13]

In a similar vein, Dr. Hemraj, the leader of the Hindi Shiksha Sangh, a broadly conservative organization promoting Hindi and North Indian culture, asserted that culture and politics should not be mixed:

"Man needs to know his roots, I believe, and only when you know your-self and your culture can you appreciate others, or even criticize your own culture . . . we don't want to convert anyone or push a certain po-litical agenda as it happens in India."[14] The resistance to VHP was con-ditioned by anxieties regarding the style in which links to India could be forged and publicly represented. Gokool recognized the need to be cautious: "I would like to see India become a Hindu state, but not in that way. . . . We Indians are a minority here and we need to be careful and prudent in politics . . . just like the Muslims sought protection of their rights and religion within Congress, we need to do the same with ANC here."[15] The Hindu nationalist agenda appeared in South Africa in the 1990s as a discourse of a modern, globalized, portable version of Hinduism as a shared civilizational identity competing with Islam and Christianity. The Global Organization of People of Indian Origin (GOPIO) promotes Indianness as attachment to modern Hinduism and to India as the motherland of all Hindus. GOPIO was formed in 1989 in New York at the initiative of Indian businessmen in the United States, Canada, and the Caribbean who felt that Indians abroad should be organized along the lines of other diasporas, such as the Jewish, the Anglo-Saxon, and the Chinese. The official home page reads:

> An unofficial estimate of the total number of people of Indian origin living outside India is about 22 million people. Whether they come from Africa, Asia, the Americas, Australia, the Caribbean or Europe, they are Indians in body and spirit. Almost all of them maintain their Indian cultural traditions and values. They seem to have meaning-fully integrated in their countries without losing their ethnic identi-ty. . . . A new global community of Indian origin has been developed. Most of the people of Indian origin have become highly successful in business and the profession. If their professional expertise and financial resources are to be pooled together, it will benefit not only people of Indian origin but also their countries and India. In addi-tion, people of Indian origin could assume a new role in providing help in case of crisis . . . to project a good image of India and the countries they live in. (http://www.gopio.net/pio.htm)

GOPIO's objective is to provide networks for businesspeople, educa-tional facilities for children and students of Indian origin around the world, and fora that can strengthen and maintain the cultural identity of Indians abroad. Gokool managed to host the annual GOPIO con-ference in Durban in 1998, and its activities expanded rapidly. The con-ferences, with its six hundred delegates, attracted considerable interest from Indian cultural activists who were keen on undoing the isolation that apartheid had forced upon Indians in South Africa.

GOPIO's general narrative of Indian perseverance and industry in the face of intolerance and obstacles resonated with the dominant story line of Indianness in South Africa. GOPIO president in South Africa, Haseem Seedat, the only Muslim in the organization in South Africa, wanted to retrieve the richness and linguistic treasures of Indian culture: "We must unite the people of Indian origin to make them realize the strength of their diversity. We must undo the 'scrambled eggs' that [were] created here as the colonizers suppressed our languages and customs."[16]

Other members of GOPIO differed. Gokool found the conventional linking of language, religion, and Indian identity altogether outdated and detrimental to the Hindu community in South Africa: "The language issue is outdated. Do you really have to be able to read Sanskrit to be a good Hindu? That is rubbish. Let us translate scriptures into English and make our religion accessible to young people. They simply don't want to learn such a difficult language. . . . What is wrong with English? Isn't it in fact our mother tongue here?" Today, GOPIO is campaigning for permanent representation in the Indian Parliament; for the appointment of People of Indian Origin (PIO) for the Rajya Sabha (Council of States), the upper house in the Indian Parliament; and for voting rights for Indian expatriates. In early 1999, the government of India began to issue so-called PIO cards, which gave the holder quasi-citizenship rights in India: multiple entry for ten years, right to do business, right to transfer foreign currency, right to own land and property, right to get admission to educational institutions on par with Indian citizens, and so on. In this move, the Indian state has in practice adopted a jus sanguinis principle for recognition of citizenship rights in the country. In turn, this raised the issue of racial determination of who was of Indian origin.[17]

So far the card has mainly been a success among Indians in Europe and the United States, and GOPIO is now pressing for extending eligibility six generations back in order to include the descendants of indentured laborers. An official from the Indian Ministry of External Affairs told GOPIO members: "We view the overseas community as more than just investors. . . . The Government expects them to play a role of unofficial ambassadors acquainting the people of the host countries with life and culture of the motherland, its potential, problems and needs."[18] Like in Malaysia and Fiji where the position of Indians is also contested, opinion in the Indian community in South Africa was divided. Some interpreted the card as a sign from the Indian government that it looks at them as quasi-citizens in whose favor it would intervene if need be. Others found such a scheme potentially risky. A businessman in

Durban put it this way to me: "It would leave the back door open and people from the majority here could say, 'Look, India is only waiting for you; pack up and go home.' . . . Let us face it, nobody wants to live in India. It is a very difficult life there, and I know that when people return from India they say, 'Thank God we are back again.' That also happened during apartheid."

South African Indians do not figure very prominently in the government of India's schemes for attracting overseas investment nor in constructing a "Global Indian Family," the slogan launched at the ambitious Pravasi Bharatiya Divas, a conference for NRIs/PIOs held in New Delhi every year since 2003. Dual citizenship was announced in 2003, but the list of countries did not include South Africa. For the South Africans attending the conference, it was clear that the global Indian family was distinctly Hindu and had a first- and a second-class compartment. "The descendants of coolies still belong to a category of second-class Indians," as a disappointed delegate told me on the flight from Mumbai to Johannesburg a week after the conference.

It was clear to leading people of GOPIO in South Africa that the celebration of cultural origins in South Africa must remain firmly nested within the larger narrative of the predicament of colonialism and the autochthony of the African majority. A legitimate Indian myth of origin could only start at Addington Beach in 1860, where indentured laborers first disembarked from the SS *Truro* to enter into a brutal indenture system. India itself must remain an abstract, historical, and nonpolitical entity, a cultural fetish rather than a sovereign and powerful state. The current emergence of India as a significant economic and technological power may well make GOPIO more relevant among professionals and entrepreneurs, but it may also relaunch the older issue of cultural and political loyalties.

GLOBALIZED ISLAM AND THE IMPURITIES OF THE PAST

A few months into the U.S.-led invasion into Afghanistan in 2001,[19] I got into a long conversation with a shopkeeper in the Indian township of Lenasia southwest of Johannesburg. He was selling tapes with sermons by famous Islamic preachers and books on Islam and piety. He found the label "Indian" objectionable. He explained: "We are Muslims, first and foremost, and just because our forefathers came from Gujarat, it does not make us Indians as we were told by the government for so many years." He lamented the fact that many still do marriages and ceremonies in the old Gujarati way. "It has nothing to do with Islam; it is all cultural influence from Hindus . . . we should get rid of that," he said, and continued explaining that the heart of the matter was that many of his own people, Surtees (Muslims from Surat), believed that they were converts from Hinduism.

> Some will even say that our fair skin and light eyes are because we were Brahmans . . . but all that is not true. We were never Hindus; our forefathers were Arabs who came as traders and soldiers to Gujarat more than a thousand years ago. They took local women as their wives and that is why there are many Muslims in Gujarat. In Islam it is the blood of [the] father that determines what you are, so even if the women and mothers were born Hindus, it can never make us Hindu. We are Arabs from Gujarat.

He felt that correct Muslim living was the only way to cope with the impact of Westernization and the chaos that the postapartheid situation had brought about in South Africa.

> I give financial support to the da'wah [conversion/preaching] work our brothers are carrying out on the other side [in Soweto]. Our black brothers need guidance, and they come to Islam in growing numbers. But first our own house has to be brought in order. How can we spread the teachings of Islam if our own people still believe in superstition that uneducated people brought over here from India? Or if Western living destroys our families?

The first part of the shopkeeper's narrative, which is far from unique among Gujarati Muslims in South Africa, departs sharply from virtually every other position on "Indian" identity in the country. The second part, however, shares a striking number of similarities with the positions of both conservative and reformist Hindu organizations on the need for moral and religious reform in order to save the country and its people from moral implosion. As we will see, the debates among Muslims in South Africa regarding identity, morality, class, and the predicaments of being a minority are molded by the same fundamental social contradictions that, despite our shopkeeper's protest, generally affect and fragment Indian life and identity in the postapartheid republic.

Muslim Durban

The majority of Muslims of Indian origin arrived from Surat in Gujarat and from Kutcch and Kathiawad. The other substantial group of Muslims was the Urdu-speaking indentured laborers known as Hyderabadis. Many came from Andhra Pradesh, Tamil Nadu, Bengal, and Bihar, and were generally of lower-caste origin, often physically different from the Gujaratis (in complexion, build, and comportment), and never allowed into the networks built by the Gujarati Muslims. Much of the welfare work done by wealthy and successful Gujarati Muslims throughout the twentieth century had this group of Urdu-speaking Muslims as their primary beneficiaries.

The social distance between these two groups was vast. A large number of the indentured Muslims followed traditional Sufi-inspired forms of Islam, which in turn found a local form in Badshah Pir, an indentured laborer who became the spiritual head and leader of a large number of poor Muslims in and around Durban from the 1860s (Vahed 2000, 57). In 1895, Muhammad Soofie Siddiqi was sent from India by the Chishti Sufi order to South Africa in order to consolidate the hold of Islam among ordinary Muslims in the country. Upon arrival Siddiqi, who later took the name Soofie Saheb, encountered a situation of close proximity and mixing between Muslims and the large majority of Hindu laborers—a nonantagonistic relationship that is still the norm in the Indian townships of Durban. Muslims participated widely in Hindu rituals and festivals, and to counter this syncretism Soofie Saheb encouraged the use of South Asian Muslim folk rituals among the Urdu-speaking Muslims. One of these was the celebration of the birthday of the Prophet (*Milad al-Nabi* or *Mawlid al-Nabi*); another was the large-scale celebration of the Shia Muharram festival in the streets of Durban, where the *tazziyah*, the procession carrying an effigy of the tomb of Ali (the Prophet's grandson) to the Umgeni River, was until recently one of the major religious spectacles in the city.[20]

Soofie Saheb established relationships with powerful trading families, especially among the Memons, which allowed him to start construction of almost a dozen large mosques in Durban, Pietermaritzburg, Johannesburg, and Cape Town. His tomb at the old Indian area at Riverside in Durban is today the center for a large, mainly working-class following that is led by his descendants, the Soofie family, who are spiritual heads of congregations stretching from Durban to Johannesburg to Namibia.[21]

The Gujarati traders provided political and cultural leadership for the Muslim community for many decades.[22] Wealthy businessmen sponsored educational institutions, religious sites, and cultural events, and were instrumental in maintaining links between South Africa and India through trade, family relations, and cultural exchanges.[23] The primacy of community and class distinctions was particularly evident in how mosques were constructed by mosque committees (*jamaats*) that often consisted of businessmen from one particular community. All the older mosques and their associated madrassas in Durban were dominated by particular communities, just as da'wah (conversion) and *zakat* (welfare)

Figure 15. DARGAH (TOMB) OF HAZRAT SOOFIE SAHEB IN RIVERSIDE, DURBAN

work was often divided along sectarian lines. The West Street mosque in Durban was built by Surtees, the large Grey Street mosque by the Memons, and so on. Newer mosques, built in the apartheid townships after 1960, were constructed with support from jamaats that had their base either among Memons, Surtees, or the Soofie family.

The most significant countertendency against this segmentation along community lines was the rhetoric and symbols of pan-Islamic brotherhood and solidarity, which developed across the subcontinent from 1900 onward. The passenger Indians effectively used their status as imperial subjects to secure land and permission to build mosques, sometimes under vehement protest from local white residents and sometimes with tacit support from Afrikaner communities or local authorities (Tayob 1999, 78–85). The emergence of Muslim nationalism, and later the Pakistan movement, affected the style in which Muslim identity was expressed in South Africa. During the Khilafat movement in India (1918–20), Turkish flags were hoisted in South Africa, the fez became widely used, and the Urdu language acquired a symbolic importance it did not have before, not least among the dominant Gujarati Muslims. The instruction in the madrassas was in Urdu, sermons in the

Figure 16. PLAQUE AT THE HAZRAT SOOFIE SAHEB DARGAH IN RIVERSIDE, DURBAN

mosques were in Urdu, and books and texts on Islam were all drawn from the strong Urdu tradition of the subcontinent. The public use of Gujarati now became strongly associated with Hindus, yet Urdu never carried any prestige as a home language, where it remained a sign of an indentured past.

With this new emphasis on the mosque as a symbol of community and Muslim identity, the quality and education of ulema (Muslim scholars) acquired crucial importance. For decades the individual *alim* (scholar) had come from India on the invitation of the jamaat and depended on the whims and wishes of the community. With the new ideological thrust of Islam as a collective identity, the status of the ulema began to grow and with it a new emphasis on purity, correctness, and uniformity of rituals and practices. Ulema began to organize in *Jamiatul* (committees of religious scholars) and began to form a pole of authority that clearly challenged the erstwhile dominance of the jamaats. Young men were sent to India for religious education at the prestigious Deobandi madrassa, as well as the rival Barelvi madrassa, both situated in North India. They brought back the notion of the alim as not merely a moral authority but also a jurist whose knowledge of the Koran and the hadith (stories and commentaries on the sayings and life of the Prophet) enabled him to determine the correctness of various practices and phenomena.

They also brought with them the influence of the Tablighi Jamaat, which established itself in 1962 in South Africa.[24] Muslims were increasingly being lumped together in areas designated for Indians. Being reduced to mere Indians along with the descendants of the indentured laborers of Tamil and Bihari origin generated unease. The Tablighi project of internal conversion of Muslims to a new and reawakened sense of sincere purpose and intention (*niyyah*) fit into a long-standing discomfort with the ritualistic folk Islam presided over by the Soofie family.

The critique of Sufi practices was inspired by long-standing theological disputes across the subcontinent, but in South Africa they were animated by anxieties concerning cultural pollution and accretions that derived from Hindu practices. For many young and well-educated Gujarati Muslims, Tablighi Jamaat also provided an alternative to the internal politics of the Gujarati community, which was seen as backward, clannish, and myopic. Instead, Tablighi Jamaat offered a broader and more developed commitment to Islam as a form of life based on a true understanding of texts and injunctions.

The Tablighi method of preaching is still organized around *gasht*, or frequent walk-arounds by small parties of men in neighborhoods and cities who invite people to the local mosque. The objective is to cultivate men who are willing to set aside time each year—preferably forty days (known as *chilla*)—to do these rounds and to convince local people through their example that the life of the Prophet is the ideal that if followed can solve all problems. The emphasis in the movement is therefore heavily on hadith, on an ethics of sincerity of purpose (*niyyah*), on living in the spirit and remembrance of Allah (*dhikr*), and on showing respect and care for other Muslims.

Many intellectuals have dismissed the movement as an introverted, quietist movement that withdraws into the community of believers and away from political life. However, Tablighis are indeed political insofar as they seek to produce ethical attachment to the *ummah* (community of believers) and not humanity as such or a nation-state. The improvement of society at large goes through purifying the souls and practices of Muslims. To be a Tablighi is thus a worldly project insofar as one's practice serves a higher purpose—the consolidation of *din* (faith).

Curiously, this movement of lay preachers, which in South Asia was so clearly pitched against the dominance of the ulema, became identified entirely with the Deobandi ulema in South Africa. This was by and large an alignment structured by class and community: the Tablighi message found good resonance among the scattered but highly successful and very affluent Muslim communities that were historically under strong Deobandi influence. Their success and affluence in a society dominated by a consumer culture and hedonistic lifestyle posed new challenges for the maintenance of a Muslim identity. Many younger professionals were drawn to the powerful liberal and secular tendencies of the 1960s and '70s, while others were impressed by the message of the Tablighis.

The impact of the Tablighis and the Deobandi teachings was less pronounced among the wealthy Memon community. More than most other groups the Memon community was based on endogamous marriages, often within the transnational networks of Memons throughout the world, wherein notions of blood, the ancestral villages and districts, and the language continue to play a central role.[25]

In the 1970s the rift between Deobandis and Barelvis, which has a long history on the Indian subcontinent, resulted in a split of the ulema in Natal. The Barelvis, who in South Asia represent the Sunni mainstream (Sanyal 1995), founded the Sunni Jamiyat-e-Ulama, S.A., which consists of the ulema who favored the preservation of a range of folk practices of South Asian origin. The organization set up a madrassa in Chatsworth, and from here and elsewhere in the city they defended established ritual practices against the Tablighi promotion of austerity, interiority, and minimalism, and the condemnation of folk practices as *bi'dah*, innovations, and cultural accretions contrary to the life and ethos of the Prophet.[26]

One of these conflicts concerned the control of the Grey Street mosque, the symbolic center of Islam in Natal, if not the country. The jamaat has historically been the locus of considerable envy and rivalry, although it was always firmly controlled by the Memon community.[27] In the 1990s the senior imam at the mosque came under fire from the Barelvis, who claimed that he gave preference to Deobandi scholars and ulema to lead the Friday prayer. Heated arguments and fistfights broke out between Deobandis and Barelvis—not least of which included members of the more militant breakaway group in the so-called Raza Academy in Durban. In 1995 the rivalries and enmities led to a clash after Friday prayer that involved knives and swords and left several people wounded. This led to the dismissal of the imam who, disgruntled, joined the campaign for holding elections for the jamaat, which had been on hold for more than ten years. The trust deed outlines a fixed distribution of the nine seats: five Memons, two Surtees, one Kokani, and one "colonial born"; that is, those who can trace their ancestry to people who lived in the colony of Natal prior to its merging into the South African Union in 1910—in other words, Urdu-speaking descendants of indentured laborers. According to the deed, the rules of the

Figure 17. GREY STREET MOSQUE, DURBAN

elections are fixed so that only Memons can vote for Memon candidates, Surtees for Surtee candidates, and so on. A commentator called this "a perfected model of apartheid style politics" (Desai 1999, 110).

As elections were called in 1997, strong opinion among the "colonial born" was building up that the trust deed should be revised and that it should reflect the actual composition of worshippers—Urduspeaking and Africans in the clear majority—rather than reflecting the long-standing class divide among Muslims. The trust deed was never amended, but after its contested election, the new jamaat has taken more care to balance the composition of speakers, and to encourage Muslims from the townships and the African areas to attend Friday prayer.

In South Africa, the Tablighi Jamaat notion of lay preaching seamlessly merged with the Deobandi emphasis on textuality and the preeminence of the ulema because it was governed by class and race structures internal to the Muslim community. In Durban, the assertion of piety and the purification of practices and religious performances crucially mark and police the boundaries of smaller communities of wealth and respectability.

DECULTURATION AND THE INVENTION OF THE PURE MUSLIM

The Overport and Sparks Road area in Durban condenses many of the rifts and contradictions within the Muslim community in the city. An affluent area laid out by the apartheid planners as an Indian middle-class location, the area has a mix of dense high-rise buildings with relatively spacious flats and independent bungalows, many of them large and extended to accommodate the joint families that still dominate among Gujarati Muslim families. The area is a center for retailing vegetables, Indian food, and building materials; a center of drug trade in the city; and for decades a hunting ground for late-night revelers (whites and Indians) in search of food, drugs, and entertainment. Today the area is also the hub of religious activities. Many of the Tablighi or Deobandi institutions are located here, several new Muslim schools have opened, and the area is also home to Radio Al-Ansar, a Muslim radio station that mainly broadcasts programs on religious and moral issues. The manager of this small station explained how the area has changed.

> Previously many of our people were given to empty pleasures of drugs and crime . . . there is no point in denying that drugs are a big problem . . . it is a Muslim thing. In school we were taught about Christianity and that the white man was right. Although we had strong leaders in the community and were better off than our Hindu brothers, the dignity of being Muslim was not there. . . . But everything has changed the last 10–15 years and our scholars from the Tablighi Jamaat should be thanked for this. They have shown us the dignity of knowing Islam and to be a Muslim. Much of what we thought was right to do was just culture and superstitions that our forefathers brought with them from India.

Within these dense networks of Tablighis, adherence to a new and purer lifestyle has emerged as a moral anchor in the stormy waters of the new South Africa. This lifestyle implies a stronger separation of the sexes at home and in schools, an emphasis on madrassa education, the reintroduction of the veil and headscarves among women, strictures on women's physical movements, evening classes in Arabic, and the simplification of rituals, ceremonies, and weddings into more austere forms.[28]

One day in early 1999, I was invited to meet a group of Tablighis who had come to Durban to carry out conversion work. From the outside, the house looked like any of the houses in the prosperous neighborhood. Inside, there was one large room, white, without decorations. Here, the fifteen men prayed, slept, and rested. They were all from Johannesburg and from small towns in the northern province, and most of them were well-to-do professionals or businessmen. Each devoted a month every year to worship, concentration on the scriptures, and discussions on faith, morality, and conduct with their fellow travelers. The main content was long days of walking from house to house with only a prayer mat while dressed in white clothes and the headgear of either traditional Pakistani/Indian or Arab style. One of them explained the significance of doing the da'wah work:

> The idea of tabligh is different. We want to show our Muslim brothers the true path; we want to show them that they are Muslims, first and foremost. We know that in the teachings of the Prophet and the word of God lies the answer to even the most difficult question we are facing. We are not simple people; he is a dentist, I am a computer technician, Rafi is an engineer, and so on. We are not against science; we use it every day and we also know that it gives no definite answers, only the Koran can do that. . . . We don't want any disturbances; we want to concentrate on this only and on the fellowship we have. Imagine what would happen if there was a woman here with us.

I followed this group of men for some time and saw how they were mostly received with respect and hospitality. The Tablighis were treated as men who by their temporary transformation into Muslim ascetics, and in their performance of restraint and modesty, embodied a collective conscience of the community.

Within the households the atmosphere, tone of language, and performance of gendered roles changed as the Tablighis entered. Women would retire to the kitchen and cover their heads, while men would sometimes excuse themselves and come back into the living room after having washed and changed from shirt and trousers into kurta pajamas. Some Muslim homes have a "Western" section with a settee, coffee table, and so on and another "traditional" section of the living room with rugs, pillows, and mattresses on the floor. The Tablighi preachers would be invited to sit in the latter section while I was often served a cup of tea at the table. The conversation would slip into Gujarati once in a while when they referred to family members or domestic matters, but for these men, who were mostly in their thirties and forties, English was the preferred language, except for the recital of long verses from the Koran in Arabic, a part of the performance that seemed to particularly impress many of the men and boys who we visited. While these ritualized encounters gave the Tablighis a sense of spiritual power and respect by reiterating the Prophet as an ideal of piety and purity, they also reminded the families in the visited homes of their less than perfect lifestyle.

Later in 1999, local Tablighis had organized an *ijtama* for its follow-ers from all over Africa. Thirty thousand men lived in tents on a sports ground, prepared meals, and listened to discourses on a range of topics that were delivered by scholars from Pakistan, Sudan, Egypt, Nigeria, and South Africa. The place was well organized and quiet. Most lived in tents and quarters according to country and languages. As a result the interaction between Africans and people of Indian descent was much more limited than it seemed at first glance. Outside the gates, hundreds of car guards were watching over a conspicuous fleet of hundreds of large Mercedes-Benz, BMWs, Audis, and other luxury cars, many of them with personalized number plates. Inside the gates the men were all dressed in white. Expensive wristwatches, chains, and rings were hid-den, and it was only language and bodily comportment that betrayed class and status. Most of the men I talked to were successful business-men or professionals for whom this was "almost as Haj" as one of them told me, "it is the same feeling of brotherhood and being together as Muslims only, and only with the single purpose of improving oneself and becom[ing] more humble before Allah, blessed be his name." An-other man told me that he was there with a cousin and some friends, and that he enjoyed "the peace of this time—you are away from home, from commitments and family and can concentrate on your faith—it is hard sometimes when you live a hectic and modern life. This is like a pause; it is like purifying your mind." He also added that he kept on bumping into people he knew from Johannesburg, business associates or colleagues whom he would never have expected to meet.

The Deobandi ulema has built its authority on reiterating an almost impossible ideal of piety, a complex set of rulings, fatwas, and prohi-bitions supposedly derived from the consummate life of the Prophet. The result has been that many Muslims feel a permanent sense of lack, guilt, and incompleteness in their religious and moral lives. Instead, many have developed more practical ways to display their commitment to the purified and de-ethnicized Muslim identity. One example is the increasing popularity of Arab-sounding names, a trend also observed in parts of the Indian subcontinent. Names like Riaz, Ebrahim, Omar—even Osama—are popular among boys, while girls are given names like Fatima or Zahra more often than was the case earlier.

Girls are now enrolled in private Muslim schools. Most parents see the new multiracial character of public schools as being responsible for disciplinary problems and strains on resources. Enrolling daughters in a Muslim school adds religious prestige and signals commitment to con-servative family values and the modesty of the girl. Between 1995 and 2001, the enrollment in private schools almost doubled and the number of private institutions went from 90 in the province of KwaZulu-Natal in 1995 to almost 180 in 2001.[29] A significant number of these are Muslim schools. A group of educators and businesspeople, who are connected with the Al-Ansar radio station, is now openly discussing the possibility of creating a private Muslim university in South Africa that would provide both religious and secular training and education.

This trend toward thinking of oneself as part of a global Muslim community also manifests itself in a gradual language shift among Muslims of South Asian descent in South Africa. Indian vernaculars are disappearing from homes and domestic spaces as well, and the public language among Muslims—including sermons in mosques—is increasingly English interspersed with Arabic.

One of the most colorful and flamboyant Muslim figures in Durban was Ahmed Deedat. His Islamic Propagation Center International (IPCI) was a vital force in the "Arabization," global orientation, and religious purification of the more affluent layers of the Muslim community in Durban. Deedat, the story among his followers goes, started as a seller of sandwiches and cold drinks outside one of the prestigious white schools in Durban. Deedat, who had little formal education, was teased and humiliated by the rich white kids who quizzed him about Islam and laughed at him when he could not give proper answers. He got so incensed that he decided to memorize both the Bible and the Koran. Over the years he became capable of providing trenchant critiques of inconsistencies and logical breaks in the Bible, which he then compared with the ostensibly impeccable and consistent logic of the Koran.[30]

Rumors of this extraordinarily gifted man and charismatic speaker soon spread and he set up his organization in Grey Street. He expanded his organization and led da'wah initiatives against a perceived threat of conversions of Urdu-speaking Muslims in the townships to Christianity. He organized welfare initiatives, raised large amounts of money, and spread out to Transvaal and Cape Town as well. His target was always mainly Christianity. In South Africa in the early 1970s, this inevitably acquired both a racial and political tinge. His most famous line was, "I have nothing against the Bible, but it is unfinished, just a step toward the final truth as revealed in the Koran." Similarly, he would argue that Christians were not quite as developed or as rational and consistent in their thinking as Muslims. In the local context, this kind of cheeky challenge—delivered with wit and inexhaustible oratory and verbatim quotes from the scriptures—proved to be quite a sensation. Many younger Indians, both Muslims and Hindus, admired Deedat for his guts and his undisguised contempt for condescending white theologians and pastors. Deedat's interpretation of Islam was strictly scriptural and orthodox, but none of the major Muslim organizations ever managed to control this unusual maverick.

In the mid-1970s, Deedat was discovered by prominent businesspeople and religious entrepreneurs in the Middle East. Substantial donations from Saudi Arabia made his organization into a smooth, almost corporate outfit by the 1980s. The IPCI acquired a high-rise building in Grey Street just next to the mosque, and from the top five floors, Deedat's empire was efficiently managed in an exclusive environment of wooden panels, thick rugs, elaborate security checks, CCTV, beautiful secretaries, and a small army of young, well-groomed "men in black"—young men in black business suits who had neatly trimmed beards, wore white skullcaps, and who had impeccable manners and accents. Deedat was now traveling the world and meeting famous American TV preachers, such as Jimmy Swaggart. In the long debates on words and quotations, Deedat's tremendous energy and humor often made him appear as a winner in terms of performance and stage presence. He discovered the potential of the video revolution, and soon all his discourses, debates, and lectures were turned out as videotapes that were available via mail order and distributed throughout the world. By the1990s, Deedat was much more famous in the Middle East and Pakistan than in South Africa, and videotapes with his debates or his discourses on Islam and science have now become classics among the conservative parts of the ulema and students in many parts of the Muslim world. As Larkin points out, Deedat's popularity in Nigeria derives force from the way he adapts Islam to an already well-known and dominant format of modern evangelism (2008).

In Durban, moderate Muslims and liberals were getting increasingly disturbed by the extremely literalist interpretation of the Koran that Deedat made popular. In the mid-1980s Deedat began attacking Hinduism as well and made statements and videotapes where he ridiculed Hindu practices and Hindu deities with characteristic arrogance and acerbic commentary. For the next decade or so, Indian newspapers and radio programs were routinely reporting yet another "outrageous" statement from Deedat.

More than any other figure, Deedat provoked a clear, public articulation of religious identity in Durban, first among Muslims and, through his attacks, among many Hindus. An official of the Hindu Maha Sabha of South Africa said, "I don't know if Deedat has done anything good among Muslims, but he has done more for Hindu unity in a few years than we could have achieved in a lifetime." The last chapter in the Deedat saga was written after Ahmed Deedat was paralyzed by a stroke in 1996. A few years later, the trustees of the IPCI forced his son Yusuf Deedat to leave the organization after a drawn-out court case. Yusuf

Deedat, who tried to outdo his father in creating controversy, has been described as "a car without brakes and steering wheel." At the UN conference on racism in Durban in 2001, he appeared in one of the several demonstrations against Israel's policies on the West Bank, which was staged by the (very strained) alliance of leftist forces and conservative Tablighi Muslims. Yusuf Deedat was seen marching alongside Fatima Meer, a long-standing friend of Mandela, and carrying a placard with a picture of Hitler on it. The text said, "He knew the problem but had the wrong solutions." Ahmed Deedat died in 2005.

"Oh Lord, Won't You Buy Me a Mercedes-Benz?"

I had visited the shrine of Soofie Saheb at Riverside and heard about the famous family, but it was only when Osman, my friend from Chatsworth, insisted that I go with him to see Soofie Saheb that I met him personally. Osman was in his thirties and had a clerical job in a small company. Like many other Muslims in Chatsworth, he had grown up with the Soofies as an integral part of his life. As a child, he had been taken to the *dargah* many times to attend functions, celebrations, and the mosques, and especially to listen to one of the Soofie brothers, Abdul Rauf, whose discourses were very popular for their good-humored style. He still went to the big Soofie Darbar for functions and Qawwali music, and he bemoaned the fact that Muharram no longer was celebrated as it was in his childhood. In spite of this emotional attachment to the Soofies, he had developed doubts about how the family conducted its business. He was also slightly embarrassed that elderly people believed in spirits and demons.

> I respect Soofie Saheb, but I can't help feeling that he is tricking some of all these naive people who come to him with problems and ailments. Then he tells them to read so many *du'a* [pronouncing verses from the Koran] at certain times, even when they go to the bathroom, and then they will be cured. I just can't believe in things like that. If you are ill you go to the doctor, not your imam. That is how I think. When people are cured they give Soofie Saheb so much money . . . and I don't know, it is all in the family. There are no trustees, no rules or anything. Have you seen their cars? Even his young son who is a student has a big Bimmer.

As we arrived at Soofie Saheb's big house, we were seated and served tea. In the next room, just separated by a curtain, Soofie Saheb received the people seeking his advice. We could overhear everything. I felt a bit uneasy, but Osman seemed thrilled by this unexpected peep into the private lives and troubles of people who, fortunately, would remain anonymous to us.

In the next hour or so we were given a glimpse into which problems were presented to Soofie Saheb and how he counseled his followers. One woman had come all the way from Namibia to get advice on her wayward son who had dropped out of school, kept bad company, and possibly was involved in drugs. Another woman complained about her husband, who was drinking and stayed away from home. She was in financial trouble and feared that he might have another woman or wanted to divorce her. A young couple could not conceive and had problems with the husband's parents, especially the mother-in-law, who abused her daughter-in-law, called her names, and said that she was barren and not right for her son.

Soofie Saheb's responses were soothing; he told them that the trouble was inflicted by evil forces but would pass if they had faith and observed certain rituals. He recommended certain *du'a* (supplication/petitionary prayers) to read in the morning or evening a certain number of times; he scribbled *du'a* in Arabic on pieces of paper and recommended that they be put under beds or pillows, or even on the barren woman's stomach during the night. Some of the devotees had brought containers of water and Soofie Saheb told them to come back the day after when he had performed his evening prayers over the water. He instructed them on how to use the water, where to sprinkle it, when to drink some of it, and so on. He instructed the woman with the errant husband to talk to one of his assistants regarding financial support.

Finally, the session was over and Soofie Saheb entered our room. He was a smiling and kind man who exuded calmness. We talked for a while, and soon the long-standing conflict with the Tablighis came up. Soofie Saheb said quietly:

> These people think they have the right to decide who is a good Muslim. They come up with these fatwas saying that we are grave worshippers and that everything we do is *bid'ah* [an innovation]. But who is a better Muslim? The rich man who reads the Koran for himself or the poor man who follows simple rules and comes to us for guidance and wants to live a decent life? We have many families who have followed our *pir* [spiritual leader] as long as they can remember. They come to the *dargah* [Sufi shrine] with their sorrows and joys, and are as sincere in their faith as any Tablighi. Our forefathers came from India, we are Indian Muslims, our *pir* belonged to the Chishti Naqshbandi [Sufi order], but there are Chishtis all over the world. Does it make us less Muslim if we are not Wahhabis?

On our way back to the township we talked about the encounter with Soofie Saheb. Osman understood that he helped a lot of people, but he still felt that something was lacking. He said, "I feel all this is more for the aunties and the older people. You will hear when we go for the *Milad* how they all speak in Urdu. It is like a family gathering. But show me a young man with some education who will sprinkle himself with water and read *du'a* in the evening, say, to succeed in an exam? It is all bogus." Osman was drawn toward the stricter and intellectualist Tablighi notion of Islam as inner conviction and a lifestyle consistent with "pure" Islam. To him the ornamental rituals of the Soofie family were merely entertainment. He enjoyed the warmth and comfort of it but did not "believe in it," he told me.

A few weeks later we arrived at the *Milad*, which was held at the large Soofie Darbar, a mosque now mainly used as a meeting hall and madrassa. The program was supposed to start late, at 11:00 PM, and Qawwali groups would then continue until the break of dawn. Several thousand people had gathered inside and outside the compound. All the women and girls (who were not allowed to enter the mosque) were dressed in Indian clothes, while most men and boys wore shirts and trousers. Outside the gate there was a brisk trade in cold drinks, snacks, and the smell of grilled beef boerewors—strictly halal of course—was all over. Men stood in small groups smoking and talking, but beyond the gate of the compound no food, cans, or cigarettes were allowed. The fleet of cars betrayed an audience that was very different from the *ijtama* I had attended. It was a medley of run-down family cars or smartly beefed-up *bakkies* (pickup trucks) or older sports cars. As in the township, cars constituted an important topic of conversations and jokes among the men outside the gate.

Finally, the Soofies arrived. Four big silvery Mercedes cars drove slowly into their designated parking lots. All of them had personalized number plates. Soofie Saheb had "SOOFIE 1," his brother Rauf had "SOOFIE 2," and the younger brothers had numbers 3 and 4. Osman, duly impressed and yet ambivalent, told me that he had heard there was supposed to be a number 5 as well, but that he was in Johannesburg. The brothers stepped out of their cars, formed a procession, and moved slowly forward, with Soofie Saheb in front, walking under a purple palanquin carried by four young boys. We all lowered our heads as they were passing, slowly, while Soofie Saheb smiled gently to the crowd. Soofie was given a small golden bowl with grains of rice, which he threw toward the north, south, east, and west while reciting verses from the Koran. The procession dissolved and Rauf took to the stage and offered a short prayer. He welcomed all in Urdu and English, and said that the *Milad* should be a joyous occasion, a time to praise the

Figure 18. THE SOOFIE DARBAR MOSQUE IN SPRINGFIELD, DURBAN

Prophet, and that there was no better way than to enjoy the Qawwali the rest of the evening.

The musical program carried on until 4:30 in the morning, with five different groups—one Indian and four local groups—who all offered explanations of the different songs in both Urdu and English. The occasion was peaceful, informal, and had exactly the sense of a family gathering that Osman had talked about. People walked around, men and women were sitting in mixed family groups, and the young children slept or moved around and enjoyed the festive atmosphere.

This was the heart of the popular Islam the Tablighis so resented. It was ornamental, ritualistic, and decidedly South Asian in terms of practices and language, but the acceptance of the hereditary charisma of the Soofie brothers and the fundamental inequality in the congregation all appeared "feudal," as a local critic put it to me. The Soofies allowed an almost carnivalesque atmosphere to prevail outside the gate, with a relaxed mixing of genders and families in a gesture of acceptance of the lifestyle of their predominantly township following.

Let's return to John Bowen's observation that discourse, performance, and "the word"—written and enunciated—are as crucial to Muslim identity as the exact form of performance is contested. It is clear that the difference between Tablighis and the followers of the Soofie family can be boiled down to the style in which "the word" is performed. Tablighis are indeed literalists in that the words and deeds of the Prophet are formats of ideal conduct that one should strive toward. Through this striving and concentration, which should be interiorized, quiet, and sincere, one moves closer to understanding the revealed truth, and faith-as-belief emerges as the effect of the seriousness of concentration. As a result, many Tablighis see science as a major challenge to be dealt with, to be discussed, and to be somehow incorporated, as it potentially disturbs or undermines the Koran's status as a final truth. The Tablighis also aim at producing a lifestyle that is suffused with this truth so that it, in the form of a coherent system of belief and conviction, may inform and give meaning to even the most everyday and banal acts, adornments, or accessories.

To the Soofie followers, by contrast, "the word" is neither prescriptive nor denotative. *Du'a* and verses from the Koran are magical and sacred, and do not belong to the same order of knowledge or reference as the words of the mundane world. The emphasis is on the performative efficacy of "the word"—as a means to heal sick bodies, to stave off the onslaught of evil forces, and to create a mood and sensory state of mind through which one can receive and glimpse the greatness of God. The essence of many Sufi practices, and indeed Qawwali song, is that the emotionally intense repetition of those special words and praise of God in song and prayer produces a state of mind and body that can open the heart and cleanse the soul. In this view, Islam is less comprehensive as minute, practical regulation of everyday life, and thus more flexible and able to accommodate and recognize human fallibility.[31]

DA'WAH IN THE TOWNSHIP

As we have seen, there is a long tradition of patronage of both Urdu-speaking and African Muslims by the wealthy Muslims in Durban. Tablighis consistently present their view as those of a refined and rational Islam that is attuned to the modern world. The theology of the Sunni ulema is less aggressive than that of the Tablighi and is generally reactive and defensive of older practices. The former have consistently been at the forefront of representing "Muslim points of view" to the government and enjoy higher status and visibility than the Sunnis. However, the townships are far from Tablighi territory.

I followed the work of some Tablighi preachers in Unit 2, which has the biggest concentration of Muslims in Chatsworth. Standing in front of the run-down shopping center, they looked rather alien to the environment. Tall and well-groomed in their white kurtas, with big beards and white turbans, they stuck out from the physically smaller people in the area. At first they tried to engage people at the parking lot in discussions, but many tried to avoid them. Many were evasive and apologetic: "I'm not really a good Muslim," "I am not educated" were frequent excuses. Only some groups of young, cheeky boys found the conversation interesting but did not take it very seriously, although they were never openly disrespectful to the preachers. Instinctively shunning the housing estates, the preachers decided to try the row houses nearby. As they were leaving, the boys started making jokes, aping their Johannesburg accent, shouting things like, "Oh, they are trying to find their Bimmers now, but they are gone, man, the charous have taken them."

In the nearby row houses the preachers had slightly more luck and managed to get invited inside some houses where they were asking people how often they went to mosque, if they sent their children to the madrassa, and so on. While there was respect for these obviously wealthy men, and an acknowledgment of the purity of the Islam they represented, several of the families found it uncomfortable to have them in their houses. A man told me, "They were polite and all that, but I know that I don't live the life that I should. We are struggling, I work all the time, and my wife is sewing at home to make ends meet. We should send our children to madrassa, but they like to play. I like to send them for extra tuition if I could. Maybe I am not a good Muslim all the time, but it is easy for them to do the right thing all the time. If you have money you can do anything." I heard similarly ambivalent reactions from others in the area: a measure of respect based on class, accent, and comportment but also slight irritation, a feeling of being patronized but also exposed, an embarrassment about showing their modest homes to such "big people," and embarrassment about not living up to the ideal life of a righteous Muslim.

The preachers themselves were quite happy with their day and found that people had been nice and receptive, and they were confident that their visit would have an impact. Their condescension was unmistakable, however. "We need to remind such people that they are Muslims. It is easy to forget when you live in a place like that," one of them said.

As an interesting contrast, Maulana Khan from the Jamiatul Natal had opened a permanent office in the shopping center in Unit 2. Khan was an Urdu-speaking Muslim himself and grew up in Chatsworth. He was only too aware of the social distance between the township and the predominantly Gujarati ulema who run most of the organizations in Durban. He had made his office into a sort of multipurpose extension office for both the Jamiat, as well as welfare organizations with a Tablighi orientation. Khan's office was open almost round the clock and manned by local boys who have been trained by Khan. It has become an important point of contact for local Muslims who are seeking financial aid for funerals, free meals, widow pensions, rent, and electricity arrears. Khan also offered marriage counseling, spoke in the mosques in Chatsworth, and provided printed material, fatwas, and new material for the local madrassas. In mid-October 2001, one could find pamphlets with a lecture entitled "The Need of the Hour," by a Pakistani scholar who was addressing the war in Afghanistan, in all the madrassas in the township. Khan was enthusiastic about how the war would galvanize the Muslim community: "Before when we tried to collect money for Bosnia or Palestine, people were very reluctant here. They don't have much and they are not interested in Muslims abroad. But now it is different, I feel. Everybody talks about the war and what happened in New York and everybody feels that we need to stand together against the American bullies attacking our brothers in Afghanistan. I am sure that even the people here in Unit 2 will come closer to Islam because of this." What the long-term effects would be was uncertain, but when I met Khan again a few months later he was less enthusiastic. He had tried to mobilize local people to attend a big antiwar rally in Durban that had been organized by left-wing groups and a range of conservative Tablighi-oriented organizations, but only a handful showed up to fill the bus he had organized. Khan put it down to the political character of the rally and the traditional apathy—if not outright resistance—to participate in politics in the Indian townships. "Had it been a rally to defend Islam, they would have come," he asserted.

The everyday reality of deep cleavages along lines of community, class, and, indeed, also race makes the rhetoric of Muslim brotherhood largely fictitious. The advances made by the Tablighis in South Africa and elsewhere testify to the global strength and the attractiveness of their brand of Islamic universalism to upwardly mobile communities that are anxious to preserve and harness their status and identity. The embracing of anything Arab or Arabic as a sign of a modern, pure, and de-ethnicized identity, and the accompanying cocooning behind what amounts to "culturally gated communities," can be observed from South Africa, across South Asia, to Malaysia. The self-cocooning within institutions and community spaces by wealthy Gujaratis is not looked at with much understanding from other groups in South Africa.

At the heart of it lies a completely unresolved question of race and racial attitudes to Africans in general, and African Muslims in particular. Hardly any welfare work is carried out by Muslims in the African townships; African Muslims are barely tolerated in larger congregations in Durban, and the preference seems to be that Africans should remain in their own separate congregations and mosques. Even if one accepts the unstated premise that Africans only become worthy of attention insofar as they convert to Islam (a point of view that elicits little understanding among most non-Muslims), it is still striking that so little attention is given to conversion in the vast African townships—and that is almost exclusively delegated to Muslims from various parts of Africa.[32] While the world of Islam in South Africa and elsewhere is indeed a universe of debate and contention, the question of how Muslims will fit into a future South Africa has barely been addressed.

REACHING FOR THE UNIVERSAL

Among Indians in South Africa, the postapartheid scenario has produced a stark paradox. On the one hand, educated Hindus and Muslims identify ever more strongly with universalized and global forms of Islam and Hinduism. This amounts to an orientation toward purified and classicized forms of devotion; highly codified and portable packages of ritual practices and ethical discourse, often communicated in English in print and in the blogosphere. This is premised on a disavowal of older and primitive forms of devotion associated with a colonial and subdued past. This aspiration correlates locally with a deep and enduring set of sociocultural cleavages along the lines of class and locality. The township Indians are overwhelmingly seen as hopelessly stuck in the past—stuck in strongly territorialized communities that are still defined by the history of indenture and by low, popular, and untranslatable forms of religious practice.

To the wider South African public, on the other hand, these attempts at reaching for the global Ummah, or a global Indian family, appear to affirm the exact opposite: assertion of a particularist racial and ethnic identity. These global aspirations seek to escape the weight of local history and culture by reaching for other universals—the legacy of Arabic in the Muslim world, for instance, or India's mythological past. In so doing they appear to bypass, if not neglect, another universal aspiration: the creation of what Mbembe calls "the first non-racial society on the planet" (2008). That latter aspiration is heavily, if not always explicitly, premised on efforts at working through the colonial and apartheid past without amnesia, or in the terms that frame this book: any real sublation of the historical contradictions between and within racialized communities requires a deep acceptance of their embedded and embodied reality. Only by "going through the trauma" and actually facing one's neighbor can one produce a real recognition of the racial and cultural others one encounters in everyday practice.

The embrace of modern and globalized Islam and Hinduism promises ethical guidelines and a moral compass, and, in turn, a measure of equivalence with the Christian languages of redemption, dignity, and forgiveness that suffuse South African public culture. However, in practice, the sight of well-off Indians celebrating their culture as both global and universal also perpetuates deep-seated prejudices against Indians as a whole. As we have seen, the caricatured image of the aloof and inward-looking Gujarati "fence-sitter" is still routinely made to stand in for the entire category "Indian." The sheer weight of such suspicions, and the dominance of a Christianized mainstream culture in South Africa, shape the milieu of the townships in which evangelical Christianity seems to provide another and perhaps easier route to inclusion into both a national horizon of belonging as well as a larger globalized culture.

CHAPTER 8

The Saved and the Backsliders

THE CHAROU SOUL AND THE INSTABILITY OF BELIEF

THERE HAS ALWAYS BEEN A SMALL PROPORTION OF CHRISTIANS AMONG INDIANS in South Africa. Some arrived from India as Christians and others were converted by missionary societies that were active among the indentured laborers.[1] Preference for Indians with anglicized names in public sector jobs, and the strong patronage by established churches in Natal, increased the number of Christians during the colonial and the apartheid eras (Brain 1983). One of the most controversial developments in Chatsworth over the last decades has been the rapid growth of Pentecostal churches in the poorer sections of the township. An official survey put the percentage of Christians in Chatsworth at 12.5 percent in 1980.[2] In 2002, several schools in the poorer units—2, 3, and 5—reported that almost half of the students were Christians. All the large cinema halls and several big industrial halls in the township, some holding two thousand people at a time, have been converted into churches. In open grass areas one finds a variety of tent missions that are often conducted by Pentecostal splinter groups. Some of the big churches have many branches all over Durban, congregations that in most cases are racially separate and have distinct styles according to which area they work in. A pastor in the large Full Gospel Church in Chatsworth explained:

> It is what people feel more comfortable with and we Indians probably prefer to be with each other. We also have some whites coming, but they also have this idea of a certain restraint, singing, listening, praying in concentration, and sometimes silence. With our Zulu people it is different—they like to sing in Zulu, very loud, and to move, shout, and dance when they worship. Our people don't like that. They are maybe more conservative, you can say, but we can't force a new style on them all of a sudden. . . . This is why we have separate services in Zulu and in English.

The Full Gospel Church has a unique history of transnational connections and aspirations among Indians in Durban. The church was founded in Durban in 1925 and was led and developed by J. F. Rowlands, a legendary banjo and ukulele-playing lay preacher from Bristol. Rowlands spent time in India, learned Tamil, and decided to start a Pentecostal church among the very Tamils he encountered in and around the bustling port of Durban in the 1930s. The subsequent success and growth of the church led Rowlands to affiliate himself with various other church bodies in the country and in the United States.

Rowlands and other missionaries believed firmly in what he called the "purity of nations," and he warned against interracial mixing and interracial marriages. If the Lord had created different nations in the world, it was not for man to change this without potentially dangerous effects, the argument went. Rowlands tried to keep his congregation as Indian as possible. He encouraged the wearing of traditional dresses, especially for women, the covering of heads, the use of simple musical instruments, and the singing of hymns and giving of testimonies in Indian vernaculars. Rowlands never opposed apartheid but protested the displacement and removal of Indian homes in the 1960s and vowed to protect the community the best he could. Although he discouraged divorces in the church, Rowlands did not oppose divorces if a union had been performed according to Hindu rites, or if the marriage was arranged. None of these practices were deemed legitimate or valid as compared to anything blessed in a church. Rowlands also opposed the celebration of weddings in the traditional, lavish Hindu way, with saffron-colored rice, Sanskrit symbols, and popular Indian music.

Most of the critiques of Hindu practices and the outright demonization of the Hindu pantheon by Pentecostal pastors have been borrowed directly from missionary discourse in India. Here, ever harder and more racialized critiques of Hinduism as a primitive and barbaric religion emerged in the course of the nineteenth century (Kaplan 1997; van der Veer 2002; Viswanathan 1998). Although Rowlands was known for his caution and moderation in criticizing Indian religion and customs, paternalism and penchant for firm governance of the fragile souls of the converted informed his "moral guidance." His main worry was the genuineness of belief among Indians and whether that could be translated into a capacity for moral self-governance that could prepare members of the congregation for more responsible tasks, such as the Christian ministry.

> I know them well—very well—and I love them! . . . Many have proved their genuineness to the core. Some have disappointed; a few have grieved; but this happens in every community. . . . The Lord Jesus was let down badly by his own disciples . . . the Indian heart is fertile soil for the planting of seeds of kindness and trust! . . . If you sow distrust, enmity, bitterness, and hatred you will reap a mixed harvest

of similar evils! . . . There are nearly half a million "gardens" where seeds are being daily sown! Let us sow what we would reap! . . . some of the kindest, truest, most lovable and genuine people I have ever met are Indian.[3]

When Rowlands passed away in the late 1970s, a major succession battle ensued as some of the white custodians of the church opposed Indian pastors being leaders of the church. The arguments recast earlier suspicions regarding the sincerity of the belief of Indians. Did the Indian pastors have consciences and convictions that could match those of whites? Would Indians, when left without a paternalist gaze, slide back into Indian culture and customs? The succession crisis was ultimately resolved, and from the early 1980s the Full Gospel Church emerged as a completely Indian church from bottom to top.

The Full Gospel Church has always targeted South Indians, who it regarded as more approachable than the more assertive and organized North Indian Hindus. The church's main Bethesda Temple is located in an old cinema hall in an area in Chatsworth nicknamed Bangladesh because of its concentration of poor residents and its large and low-priced market. At the main entrance, one meets a large world map covering an entire wall. Across it are painted circles of red, which indicate the concentration of people in need of salvation and the "work of God." The biggest circle is drawn around India, but the accompanying text indicates that the focus is indeed on South India, where Christianity has a long history. Other circles indicate groups of Indians elsewhere in the world, as well as concentrations of Buddhists in Southeast Asia. There are no circles around any area dominated by Islam. The Full Gospel Church is but a minor player in the bewildering array of churches and movements working in South India today, but its particular ethnoracial focus has until recently been a vital component in the attempt to embed the church in the Indian community in South Africa. Money is collected in Durban for missionary work in India, pastors go there on a frequent basis, and links are forged with local Pentecostal movements that have been active in India for decades.

One of the older pastors explained to me, "We Indians can do this work better because we know the demons that people live with [Hindu gods] . . . we grew up with them, we lived with them under the same roof . . . as Rowlands said, if you give the word of God to the Tamil, he should also live like a Tamil Christian." Although Indian culture is systematically disavowed in the Pentecostal communities, as we will see, the attachment to India is retained in some respects—not as a cultural desire but as a preferential mission field, a place where the embodied experience of "brownness" and living with but overcoming the "demons

Figure 19. UNIT 3 IN CHATSWORTH

of Hinduism" can be an irreplaceable asset. If nothing else, this effort at embracing a fully Indian and vernacular Christianity has been crucial in transcending the deep-rooted sense among Indian South Africans of Christianity as the religion of whites, and of conversion as submission to colonialism and the apartheid state.

In addition to the big churches and the tents, every Sunday most schools in Chatsworth host smaller congregations (from thirty to a hundred people) who gather in a classroom for prayer, song, and healing. The motives for converting to Pentecostalism are multiple, predominantly emotional and existential but rarely explored in public debates. Many Indian intellectuals and political leaders in Durban simply see the conversions as indicative of the continuing social crisis and deprivation of the township charous. A community activist and ANC member correlated conversion with economic crisis and the weakness of community spirit: "These conversions have to do with poverty and desperation. The last big wave of conversions was in the 1960s when thousands of families had come here and felt uprooted and alone . . . when we were fighting in the 1980s, few people had time for the pastors, but now again they are fishing among our people, the poor, the widows, and so on."

The conversion issue was conceptualized as a "social problem" from the outset and thus an area of academic knowledge and multiple studies. Some, like those of the prolific Dr. Oosthuizen (himself an ordained minister in the Gereformeerde Kerk), saw the conversions as a symptom of Westernization and disenchantment among Indians. Unmoored from earlier traditions, and amid rapid change, Pentecostal churches "save the adherents from considering their lives to be futile and meaningless . . . one finds withdrawal from the social order rather than attacking it . . . amidst confusion it comes with a sense of direction."[4] In a trenchant critique of Oosthuizen's tendentious academic studies of Pentecostal "penetration" into the Indian community published in 1974, the Tamil Trust, which is based in Johannesburg, questioned the authenticity of conversions. The language betrayed the fundamental class bias that has marked the debate ever since: "We do not object to conversions if it is the choice of any one individual person . . . but the kind of conversion that compels an alcoholic Tamil in metropolitan Durban to change his name from Soobramoney or Ramsamy to John or James and pose as a pseudo-white man in search of pride and prestige, we treat with the contempt it deserves."[5]

After a systematic analysis of converted working-class families in Phoenix, an anthropology thesis from 1987 concluded that conversions are caused by negligence on the part of the Hindu elite. Echoing the broader sentiments of purification and the need for codification of Hinduism, the author concluded:

> The average Hindu living in Phoenix and Chatsworth cannot be solely responsible for his ignorance of Hinduism. . . . The Hindu educated elite have not made a concerted effort to educate these ignorant Hindu masses . . . the gap between the philosophical approach of the small minority of the educated elite and the ritual approach by the uneducated majority must be closed in order to curb conversion. Hinduism must be institutionalized. (Valodia 1987, 41–42)

The suspicion of a fundamental incommensurability between Indian culture and Christianity remains active in the milieus opposed to missionizing. The House of Delegates excluded the mention of Jesus in prayers because it was regarded as offensive by most Hindu and Muslim delegates.[6]

Among local intellectuals the same correlation between lack of education and anxiety has been invoked to explain the mass conversion of poorer Indians to Christianity. The older class stereotype of charous as steeped in an anachronistic universe of magic and superstition that disables them from making qualified individual choices has been repeated in almost identical terms over the past three decades. In 1979, a pastor named Alfred wished to build a Christian orphanage in Chatsworth to prevent them from falling prey to Hindu "devil and idol worship," as he indelicately stated. Rajbansi seized the opportunity to defend "the community" and its children:

> It seems that Mr. Alfred is taking advantage of the fact that the Hindu community has been very passive when people like him have been using devious tactics such as poverty, poor housing and unemployment and illness to mislead people ... if Mr. Alfred wants to take Hindu children who are not able to decide for themselves I will be prepared to lead a crusade against him and his un-Christian actions.[7]

Secular and left-leaning Indians, and conservative and purist defenders of Hindu practices, are equally critical of these types of pastors, who are accused of financially exploiting gullible charous. The sentimental style of sermons, the emphasis on healing and miracles, and the donation of tithes to the churches all seem to testify to the shallowness and inauthenticity of this type of Christianity. The result is a double alienation: "neither properly Indian, no knowledge of their own culture, and not even properly Christian either," as a schoolteacher described these (not so) new "halfway-men." This critique of the Indian churches clearly reproduces the older middle-class worries about the fallen and deracinated Indians and a suspicion of the lack of sincerity and depth in charous, as well as the paternalist assumptions about the charou self as inherently fragile and unstable. The life of the charous is constantly in need of herding and supplement by the community spirit and the proper Indianness hovering over the township as an echo of a more wholesome past.

THE FRAGILITY OF THE CHAROU SOUL

The modern ideal of firm and individual convictions began as a Judeo-Christian ideal of faith, which in turn morphed into a broader modern ideal of introspection and reflexive interiority. In a seminal essay, Talal Asad has shown how the formation of the idea of an autonomous and authentic self was premised on medieval monastic disciplines that were designed to purify the soul through bodily pain and thus convert profane desires into true and sublime religious attachments (1993). In the early modern period, this ideal of convictions, and the capacity to "have interiority," left the monasteries and became generalized, now premised on the ability to exercise restraint and self-control; that is, to be fully in control of one's emotions so that the inner self was never too exposed to uncontrollable excitement and passion, and thus could stay true to its own unique character (Trilling 1972; Hirschman 1977; Taylor 1992; Hansen 2009).

The central problem faced by conversion and missionary work was the enduring suspicion that many new converts lacked a fully developed interior wherein true belief could be anchored and secured. Conversion to Christianity was assumed to be a conversion to the dominant cultural ideals of modernity and individualized personhood (van der Veer 1996). This problem assumed new proportions in the encounter with colonized populations for whom the notion of an interior core of the individual person as a battlefield of moral injunctions, drives, and will seemed to be utterly alien. New converts were seen as shallow believers without true convictions and only capable of mechanically performing rituals and prayers without these being nurtured by a deep inner, individual life. Similar charges had for centuries been leveled against popular, ritualistic Catholicism by Protestants and by elites against the lower classes.

Jean and John Comaroff's work demonstrates how the Nonconformist Protestant missionaries grappled very concretely with this problem. Their solution was to build the new native soul from without—by moral clothing and adornment, new bodily regimes, and new and structured domestic arrangements. They aimed at reforming the native soul by establishing a new relationship with objects. Things should be mastered, domesticated, and made into a means of expression of a modern self.[8] The global career of Christianity demonstrates, however, that the production of modern, individualized selves was neither a precondition for, nor a corollary of, successful proselytization. What is somehow unbelievably ignored in most discussions of Christianity and modernity is that the majority of the actual practices of the two largest Christian denominations in the world—Catholicism and Pentecostal churches—corresponds very poorly with the standard academic matrix of (Protestant) Christianity as constituted by individual belief, guilt, interiority, and conscience. While Catholicism retains a highly ritualized and stylized set of practices and spatially immovable institutions and liturgies, Pentecostalism is in fact fundamentally premised upon a permanent instability of belief in the individual and an understanding of the interior of the believer as extremely porous and vulnerable to an omnipresent evil; hence, the all-important imperative of constant invocation of the power and omnipresence of the Spirit (and Jesus) to keep the Christian soul full and stable, and to constantly heal the body and protect it from omnipresent afflictions, which are always seen as a symptom of demonic forces.

Pentecostalism has significant Protestant elements: the emphasis on the lay preacher; the lack of formal institutions and hierarchies; the congregation as a site of human warmth, social support, and the appearance of the divine; and, finally, the totalizing and exclusive character of the faith and commitment of the born-again. However, few of the born-again Christians I met in South Africa ever claimed that they were driven by a deep inner conviction that determined and disciplined all their actions in the world. Few, except some pastors, would claim that they in any way were engaged in a constant, interior battle with their own innate sinfulness, akin to Asad's monks seeking the pleasures of purity through painful disciplines. The born-again instead claimed to have renounced her agency and exteriorized the source of evil. The disciplining and protection of individual practices and bodies in order to maintain the new Christian self was a constant, collective work of mutual surveillance in the congregation, which was presided over by the pastor, an imperfect object of envy, misgivings, and surveillance while also a true, if limited, agent in the world.[9]

The process of mass conversions of township charous to Pentecostalism shows that in these proliferating church communities, the individual soul is actually seen as empty. It is akin to a vessel or container that in principle is open to both good and bad influences—both to the devil and to God, or rather to Jesus, who in the rather thin and populist Pentecostal theology comes across as a powerful warrior and protector. Unless vigilant in one's practices and prayer, omnipresent evil forces will fill the soul and contaminate the body. The sincerity of inner belief or the autonomy of one's interiority are less important than the ability to open oneself and let the Holy Spirit flow through and cleanse body and soul. There are two obstacles to this process, which is essentially giving oneself up to God: first, personal pride and the arrogance of knowledge; and second, objects or practices that can attract and channel the vile demonic forces, almost like magnetic fields, back into the vulnerable new convert. Given that most of the people in this story are former Hindus who still live in a world suffused with Hindu imagery, objects, clothing, and food that connect to the ancestral culture, the risk of such forms of "backsliding" is seen as particularly grave among people of Indian origin.

Three reasons for "coming to the Lord" recurred in most accounts I gathered over the years: (1) the warmth and mutual support of the community around the church, big or small; (2) the pleasure of the live gospel and soul music of black American origin and the praying and singing in a language one understands (English); and most important (3) the ability of prayer to heal and to keep the evil forces at bay.

The purging of the vices of charou culture—drinking, smoking, unstable family patterns, and superstition—and creating a sense of respectability are central to the ethos of most congregations. However, the Pentecostal churches remain charou in one decisive respect: they take seriously the universe of demons, black magic, evil spells, evil eyes, and possession, which is an important dimension of life for many people in the township. This is a universe that is dismissed by mainline churches and by most Muslim and Hindu religious authorities as pure superstition. Explicitly dealing with this universe and claiming that they can keep the evil at bay earns these churches tremendous support.

SIGNS OF THE SPIRIT

In response to a question about why Christianity has become so popular in Chatsworth, a pastor in the Full Gospel Church explained that the image of Christ is simple and accessible:

> Most of our Indians are simple people who work with their hands. Jesus the carpenter is easier to understand than some holy man sitting in a cave somewhere, right? They could see that he was walking in the Spirit, and they too wanted to be filled with that extraordinary power. This is what our church is doing . . . letting them be filled by the spirit to cleanse their lives. This is the meaning of being born again. . . . Give me one hundred people, let me talk to them and I will be able to tell you who is born again. Maybe you cannot see it, but if you live in the spirit you can always recognize a brother or a sister.

No one I met in the course of my work would claim that a true Christian could be identified by one distinguishing mark. There were many: the manner of speaking, the way people dressed, the way they carried themselves, what they were eating, and so on. "You can see it in people's faces. If the spirit is in them, it will show on their faces," a recent and enthusiastic convert told me. This unfathomable and yet pervasive mark of the saved, the X marking the true Christian, was neither a mark of belief nor of conviction but rather of a new mental and bodily disposition. The true Christian was someone who had given up her pride, self-regard, and arrogance and instead had given herself over to God. A truly saved person was someone who was able to open her soul and her mind to be filled by the Holy Spirit, the crucial X that provides agency and morality of conduct.

I use the feminine here on purpose because conversion almost invariably started with women, who are regarded by pastors as more "emotional" and open, more attuned to the world through their senses than through their minds. The highly eroticized language of conversion—openness, giving oneself up, penetration—is also no coincidence. It refers both to what we may call the "primal scenes of the Pentecost" as well as to everyday practices of conversion and surveillance of the saved within the congregations.

The theology of Pentecost has two important references to miraculous events. The first is the opening of the grave and the resurrection of Jesus by the intervention of "an angel sent by the Lord" (Matthew 28:1) that shows itself and allows the few people present at the grave, all women, to witness the resurrection, to be stricken by fear, but also to witness the greatness of God. They had wanted to anoint the body of Jesus, and they may have believed that something miraculous could happen. Their minds (and bodies) were indeed ready to be redefined by the spirit. The second reference is the event taking place fifty days after Passover, when many pilgrims had gathered in Jerusalem to celebrate Pentecost. The room is suddenly filled with the spirit "like the rush of a mighty wind" (Acts of the Apostles, 2:1–4), and this enables the congregation to understand each other regardless of their natural languages.

Death and miraculous rebirth are the central themes here. The near social and physical death and resurrection and social rebirth of a man, aided by a woman, was the myth of origin of virtually every Pentecostal church community I came across. It is the foundational narrative of the born-again movement: the (almost) social death, extended period of spiritual death, and familiarity with the forces of evil makes it possible for men to be reborn as exceptionally powerful administrators and guides of the spirit. This is not a rebirth as a calling that is realized through long periods of rumination and interior reflection, as in the classical missionary tale, but as a pure miracle, a complete reversal of a man possessed by evil to become a powerful instrument of the good. Pentecostal practices are, in fact, a form of antibelief—conviction premised upon constant ritual performances of limited efficacy and duration rather than confidence in the stability of beliefs lodged in the interior life of the saved.

Reconfiguring Patriarchy and Gendered Surveillance

Biweekly prayer meetings in the homes of the faithful, or those who aspire to be saved, are one of the mainstays of the Pentecostal congregations. For several months, I followed prayer groups that met in various homes—mostly the homes of women who were widowed or single mothers. One prayer group had ten to twelve members, among them only three to four men. The women were the most consistent in attending, as was one man, Sam, an intense and large man in his forties who had been entrusted by the pastor with the task of being the spiritual guide of the group. Most meetings would last two hours and always started with singing a hymn or two. Sam would typically open the evening with a small speech based on a quote from the Bible. The themes would vary: envy, selfishness, dealing with mistrust and condemnation by others, protecting children from evil influences. Sam was not an educated man with a polished language, but he put his points across with clarity and in everyday language: the world of the township was suffused with danger, immorality, and evil, and only the vigilant observance of good Christian practices, prayer, and total honesty in the face of God and the congregation would keep one's mind and house clean.

Then the testimonials began. Each one in the group would recount events over the past week, or worries about money, a child's health, an upcoming exam for a child or a relative, and so on. In one of the sessions a woman, a single mother in her thirties, who had only been in the church for a few months, said:

> This has been a difficult time for me. My older sister is scolding me all the time and calling me names. She does not understand that I have found the Lord. She tells me to save my money and not give to our church. She tells me I am a bad mother and that I am selfish, that I only think of myself and forget to feed my children properly. What can I tell her? How can I make her respect me? Maybe she is possessed by the demons in our community. She has a sharp tongue and I think she is envious of me. The other day I felt all the anger in me very strongly. I felt as if demons were entering me and I had evil thoughts of hurting her. . . . I was very sad and upset. I called some of the sisters and they came in the evening. [She looked around and smiled at some of the women in the room.] Together we prayed for a long time and we became filled by the spirit . . . slowly I could feel that my anger disappeared as the demons had to leave me. But I still feel the anger and I am still afraid that my sister wants to hurt me or my children.

Sam thanked her and asked everybody to pray. He led the prayer: "Oh Lord, please help this good woman. Please help her to overcome what has been planted in her by evil forces. Please let us be filled with your spirit, that mighty force that is our only protection against the darkness in our community, the darkness that can fill our hearts."

The praying went on for some time; another man led the prayer and tried, albeit haltingly, to emulate Sam's booming voice and the easy flow of his enunciations. Some of the older women also led the prayer briefly before Sam took over and led the small group in singing a hymn. On another occasion, an elderly woman wanted to join the group, and she had invited the entire group to her modest house. She was a widow with big, sorrowful eyes. Her husband had died recently and she felt alone. Her two daughters lived several hours away and she was clearly devastated by her husband's illness and premature death. She nervously welcomed everybody and served tea and biscuits. Sam took it upon himself to welcome "our new sister" and asked the group to follow him in prayer that would bless the house and make it into "another home for our Savior, another house of the spirit." He then asked the woman to tell about her family and her worries. She told about her husband's death and illness. She also told about her youngest daughter who was soon to take an exam. The daughter was nervous and shattered by her father's death, and the mother feared that she might not pass the test and not get the job she was training for as a dental assistant.

Sam made a little speech, lamenting that the couple had not turned to the church for help. The husband had clearly been made ill by the demons lurking in our community, Sam said, and had he found the Lord, he would have been with us today. The woman started to cry. She sobbed quietly while Sam led the group in a hymn and called upon the spirit to "chase the evil out of this house" and to fill it with joy and good fortune that would also help the woman's daughter find a job and recognize that as a sign of the power of God to reach out and bless even those who were not yet saved.

According to Sam and most other men I met in this and other congregations, one of the main objectives of the church was to restore the natural order of the family. Women should be protected because they were the naturally weaker and more emotional beings. Only men of self-discipline and devotion could protect them properly, but only when their minds, bodies, and lives were suffused with the spirit. However, women should also be revered because they were almost instinctual believers. Like the primal scene of the Pentecost, men could only be saved through the grace and love of a woman, the only force that can make them overcome pride and arrogance within themselves.

The reformed men could only be properly trusted as long as they spent enough time with, and within, the congregation. The relationship of authority and submission to the saved men was also those of the weak but virtuous women putting the men under permanent surveillance. Their beliefs and character notwithstanding, they had to stay near the pastor, his assistants, and near the devoted women of his family. The evil forces lurked out there, and even a strong and trusted pillar of the church like Sam could not be trusted entirely. One of the reasons for this permanent suspicion was that the township was suffused with symbols, artifacts, and substances that were connected with a recent Hindu past. The task of remaining among the saved did, in other words, involve a constant struggle against "backsliding." In this constant struggle, the figure of the pastor occupied an important, if ambivalent, position.

ON SUITS AND SERMONS

The emphasis on performance of the words of God, on the style of sermon, and the enunciation and agility with which perfectly memorized fragments of the scripture can be recited and presented makes the pastor the absolute key figure in the Pentecostal movement. It is neither his learning nor knowledge of the text and context of the Bible, and even less the fact of his status as ordained or officially recognized by a church hierarchy, that makes his authority. The pastor is a man who can become a true leader of his flock—which must be created and maintained by protecting it from other pastors and churches—by building up a reputation and fame for himself and his church. There are basically two routes to this position: the flamboyant star or the elder brother.

The flamboyant star was the gifted orator and performer whose reputation was built through the power and quality of preaching, the quality of the shows, and the music, all of which reflected the size and financial power of the church. The more successful pastors of this category ran their churches like business empires: they had branches and subsidiaries and a range of trusted men who ran the finances, public relations, and took care of much of the healing sessions, the counseling, and administering mutual help within the congregation. The power and performance of the pastor remained at the heart of these churches. It inspired younger men in the congregation to "apprentice" themselves or simply to adopt and mimic a style that in turn would enable them to start their own church.

One of the most successful churches in the area was run by Pastor B, a highly energetic man in his early forties. He had been part of the Full Gospel Church, the parent church of most Pentecostal churches in Chatsworth. He decided in the mid-1990s to start his own ministry in the township. His main church was in another of the old cinema halls that held fifteen hundred people, as well as a number of smaller churches in both formerly Indian and colored areas. He was a very energetic speaker who was singing, shouting, and walking around on the stage with his cordless microphone. His style was "Southern": his accent had an American twang and his hairstyle and dress imitated the legendary style of the Southern Baptist preacher—sharp suits in light cream colors, white shirt, strongly colored tie, and, of course, a minor fleet of expensive cars. The church was known for its good band and singers who warmed up the congregation before the pastor entered the stage to a hushed whisper of anticipation in the audience.

Figure 20. One of Chatsworth's large churches

The pastor belonged to the colored community, and his success among Indians was based on a powerful reversal of the conventional prejudice against coloreds as somehow impure, immoral, and oversexed—and also violent. The very light-skinned colored can be a desirable and acceptable figure, as the whiteness supposedly predominates in body and soul, whereas the dark-complexioned coloreds were seen as dangerous and unpredictable. Pastor B was dark-skinned and had unmistakably African features and hair. His integration and acceptance in the community was in no small measure based on the fact that he had an Indian wife and five children. "He looks colored, well, he *is* colored, but he lives here in Chatsworth and he is just like our Indian people," someone told me. "He loves curries and he speaks just like us when you hear him outside church" were some of the answers I got when I asked about the pastor's background.

The pastor himself used the story of his marriage to great effect. From the stage, he deployed all the stereotypes and signifiers of "alien" but domesticated blackness in order to produce a local version of the parable of the stranger king who is domesticated through his marriage to a woman of the people (Sahlins 1985, 73–80). Pastor B fell in love with the girl who came from a conservative Hindu family. The family was outraged and forbade the girl from seeing or meeting him. However, young love could not be stopped, and before long she had eloped with him (a much-loved component of the older Bollywood love story). She renounced her Hindu past and they got married in a small church in Johannesburg, where they stayed for a while until tempers had cooled in Durban. The family had gone to an old Tamil woman who was known for her knowledge of magic and curses. She put a curse on her, and she was told by her family that she would never be able to conceive. Some time passed and she indeed did not conceive, but after prayer and much concentration she became pregnant. "The spirit opened what had been closed by those demonic forces," as the pastor put it. "They said she would be a barren woman, but look at her! What more fertile woman can [one] imagine—five children and she could bear many more."

I heard this story a number of times, and each time there was a sense of titillation involved as the pastor quite frankly referred to his very active and fertile marital life: on the face of it, another story of the triumph of Jesus and the spirit over the demonic forces of a Hindu past; on another level, an inversion, if not sublimation, of the proverbial sexual prowess of colored and African men into a story of infinite fertility produced by the intervention of the spirit—in the form of the pastor's phallus.

There were at least a dozen smaller churches in the area that had adopted similar styles of preaching and similar styles of positioning the pastor and his wife as an exemplary "senior couple" at the heart of the church. They were the exemplary family and also the example of social success in material plenty, which had been provided by the grace of God—a plenty that everybody also knew was made possible by the quite substantial financial contributions and tithes made by the congregation.[10] The pastor was for many the symbolic heart of the church—what we really are (but what I never can become myself) and a symbol of hope and prosperity, as much as a self-made star, a charou who has made it good. Yet this was, in a very literal Durkheimian sense, a collective product, a glamour production made possible and financed by thousands of small contributions, some collected during the service, others as individual contributions discreetly arranged by assistants who never would disclose the actual amounts donated. This financial area of darkness was at the heart of the proliferation of churches and at the heart of the almost constitutive doubt about the sincerity and authenticity of the pastors.

Many of the smaller splinter churches were started by men who used to be close to a big church and a well-known pastor but fell out with him because they realized that "something was not right"—there was embezzlement and financial problems. Selfishness, vanity, and greed had entered the pastor and made him vulnerable to the omnipresent forces of evil, which in turn was corrupting the church. I never heard anyone accusing the glamour pastors of being evil people or ill-intentioned as such. The explanation was that one invariably became much more vulnerable to the demonic when in possession of money and material objects.

Most often the decision to become a pastor was narrated as a revelation. Pastor J, a heavyset man who worked as a boilermaker for many years, related his decision to become a pastor and create his own flock as a dream vision where "God intervened directly" in cinematic style. He told me:

> I was resting on my couch one day after work, talking to my wife about our future. I fell into a deep sleep for a few minutes and dreamt that I was in a wide open wheat field, full of ripe axes. Then I saw the sky open, light came through, and I heard a voice, alien and powerful, command me to take up the ministry and serve God. I woke up, with sweat on my brow, but full of resolve to take on this new life that would involve sacrifices for me, my wife, and our three children.

The pastors of the smaller congregations thus set out to create their own and purer version of the church, almost invariably modeled on the idea of a large family network in which the pastor was the father and his own nuclear family a highly visible, regulative ideal. Many of these classroom churches had eighty to one hundred or fewer in their flock, and the language of kinship was only used indirectly. The men were "brothers" and the women were all addressed as "sisters." The family was more like a band of brothers with the pastor as the elder brother and his wife as the elder sister. The language of parenting, of the flock as children, had been used by Rowlands. Most of the younger pastors—and the average age would be early forties—studiously avoided paternalist language and any invocation of generational authority. This was in part to avoid overt references to the joint family, which is still believed to be the true vessel of Hindu tradition and practices; and partly to assert that having "come to the Lord" as an Indian must involve a discarding of the authority of tradition and traditional habits. The two nodes for these smaller churches of the "elder brother" type were run partly in classrooms at municipal schools and partly in the homes of the pastors and a few trusted men.

Breaking with a past denounced as demonic and barbaric is a central part of the strategy of the Pentecostal movement in much of Africa (Meyer 1998). In Chatsworth the imperative of performance of faith and obedience had turned into a constant and pervasive exorcism of everything seen as Indian, and thus capable of attracting demonic forces.

In this case the problem of backsliding focused on objects and things that were assumed to carry residues and echoes of Hinduness.

LOOKING LIKE KENTUCKY . . .

Rowlands and other white missionaries had never set out to destroy the joint family as a form but they did encourage the formation of nuclear families among their closest and exemplary followers. The joint family became a target of a more sustained critique as the churches became fully Indianized by the 1970s. The Indian pastors understood that Hinduism should not be opposed as a religious belief to be combated at the level of doctrine but as a way of organizing domestic life. Authenticity and cultural distinction could never rely on the color of the skin, as most other things in the country. A more thorough transformation of everyday life was required to secure this grounding of belief. As an elderly pastor explained to me:

> In this country Hindu religion was never guarded by learned Brahmans like it always happened in India. There we have always faced many obstacles, even today. In this country Hinduism is more or less customs in people's homes and most people cannot even explain to you why they are doing certain things. All they can say is that this is what we always did in my home; that their grandmother always did this or that.

The battle for the Indian souls thus had to move from the church and the tent into the homes. The objective was to encourage nuclear families and purge the homes of Hindu aesthetics and objects but also to project a clean and unmarked style of decoration, diet, and domestic consumption. The homes of the pastors and of the pillars of the church thus became showcases of this striving for a form of "determined blandness"—an ideal of domestic life that was closely modeled on a local interpretation of the average American middle-class home. Here it was less a question of imprinting proper domestic disciplines and rather a proper appreciation of things as a moldable means of self-presentation. That work had already been done by the apartheid state and the invention of the new Indian social world in the township.

The presentation of the Christian house as "neutral" signified an embrace of a universally modern and non-Indian style: an unmarked space in which the spirit could dwell, undisturbed by any metonymic reference to the cultural past of the people of the house. As Lehmann points out in his study of Pentecostal churches in Brazil, the style of architecture, music, and decoration chosen by the Pentecostal congregations demonstrate that, "the Pentecostals' resolute indifference to both the

Figure 21. Double houses from 1960s, Unit 7 in Chatsworth

exigencies of sophisticated modern taste and to the taste for [local] au-thenticity, which is itself a sub-product of that taste. It projects popular culture onto itself and itself onto popular culture" (1996, 188). These neutral interiors were understood and discussed in dramatic ways as sites of an ongoing battle against the staying power of the Hindu gods, conceptualized as Fallen Angels turned into demons in the service of Satan himself. As in the case of prayer and the social life of the congre-gation, homes and domestic habits needed to be carefully calibrated so that all habits, in minute detail, help to keep the ubiquitous evil at bay.

The most immediate sign of being Christian was the style of dressing and adornment, especially among women. Few *shalwar kameez* (North Indian female dress) were to be seen, saris were only displayed at wed-dings, and the style of jewelry was decidedly neutral and discrete. The changed adornment of the female body has often been held forth as an example of the cultural colonization effected by Christianity, and the debate goes on. During yet another row over conversions, a recent convert to Christianity wrote in a local weekly in Chatsworth that wear-ing the *bindi* (vermillion dot on the forehead) is part of Indian culture, just like the sari. She defended the use of it because "we are not of the west but of oriental character." She emphasized, "I no longer wear the vermillion dot, which is a part of Hinduism, but a stick-on, cardboard one."[11] Here, as in subsequent examples, it is clear that although the Christian fear of backsliding concerns itself with surface displays of fidelity, it revolves around a fear of substances (such as vermillion) that are believed to contain and transmit the demonic power of the Hindu spirits.

Traditional ideas of modesty and appropriate covering of the body no longer applied strictly. The morality of proper dress had not only been key in civilizing the savage by covering but also by producing separated and moral bodies, which reflects what the Comaroffs call "the Protestant ideal, a self 'discreet' because 'discrete'" (1997, 225). For many of the younger women in the congregations, one of the attractions was indeed that dress was no longer a moral issue, that they could dress "as they wanted," "like when we go out," or "like when we go to work." Dress and clothes could thus escape the long-established moral injunctions of being properly ethnic or being a sign of "our culture," and instead merge with an imagined, universal standard fashion. Many of the late services over the weekends saw young couples dressed up to go to parties or even nightclubs after church, although this was discouraged by the churches. While there was a general emphasis on dressing in a culturally neutral way, the display of money—from expensive suits and dresses to expensive cars—was seen as less problematic. The older churches, notably the Full Gospel Church, regarded ostentatious display of wealth, as in the case of Pastor B, as a sign of lacking sincerity, as a gospel of wealth that betrayed the work of the devil rather than the blessing of the spirit. For many younger people, ostentatious display of financial success was seen as a sign of that which became possible when one became filled by the spirit.

Another major feature of life in the new Christian home was the removal of all objects that could be connected to Hindu gods or Hindu customs. Objects that were seen as ritually pure, such as brass, gold, and silver—whether lamps, figurines, plates, and even bracelets and bangles—were to be removed. In most households, posters or embroideries with letters in Devanagari script—such as AUM—were removed. In some cases the households had absolutely no aesthetic objects that indicated the cultural background of the family living there. Such homes were called "clean" and the explanation offered for why these objects had to be removed was that they, like magnetic fields, attract the demons—that is, Hindu gods and spirits—to the household.

Several of the churches have special teams of trusted men who go to the homes of new converts to "clean them up," as Matthew put it. He was a staunch member of his church and headed such a cleaning team:

Many homes here in Chatsworth are very chaotic, and people live in ways that are not healthy. The first thing we do is to get rid of all the things that are Hindu, especially the brass objects, which attract the demons. We also take away the garlands people keep around pictures of their late relatives. We don't mind that people revere their parents; that is a good thing in Hinduism, but not in this Hindu way . . . the last thing we do is to wash all the doorposts with Dettol to remove all the lime juice and turmeric people smear around their doors to keep out evil spirits. That is, of course, all rubbish to believe in, and we think that only prayers can keep the spirits at bay.

It was striking that Matthew and other "cleaners" I met emphasized the cleaning of doorways with Dettol—the most widely used disinfectant across the late-colonial and Commonwealth world. Various native substances (and superstitions) had to be removed by a chemical agent that is also a popular metonym of an extreme act of cleansing, so that "the spirit of God could enter through the front door," as one of Matthew's aides put it in a half-joking manner.

In a strikingly Hindu way, beliefs in the character and composition of food as substances that could transmit and transfer qualities were very important in the reproduction of the cleanliness and stability of the bodies in the Christian household. At times I found myself in an almost uncanny replay of the famous reversal skit in the British Asian comedy series *Goodness, Gracious Me*: a South Asian party goes to an English restaurant to have "an English"—something really exotic, something "Really, really bland," while the women in the party flirt with the anemic-looking, ginger-haired English waiter who is "so cute and pale." The meals I was served were often bland, unspiced, and typically "white food," as people said locally—stews, roasts, baked and boiled vegetables, and so on. The eating of both copious amounts of beef (non-Hindu) and pork (non-Muslim) was of course crucial to this production of new and carnivorous Christian bodies and souls. Like many of their family members, I would speculate about whether the meals I was served were performances and whether "normal" spicy food would be consumed when the Christian identity was not on public display.

The explanation given for this dietary regime was, again, that excessive use of spices would attract the spirits and demons to the kitchen and that they would enter the food, and thus the bodies of the newly converted, in the process weakening them, polluting them, and making them liable to backsliding into their old and well-worn habits. In his work on the increasingly staged Afro-Brazilian heritage culture of Salvador's historic Pelourinho District, Collins notes a not dissimilar projection of a "devilish past" into food: one of the city's iconic popular dishes, *caruru*, is often denounced as "devil's food" by local working-class women who have turned to Pentecostal churches. This food is now associated with Afro-Brazilian Candomblé practices, which are increasingly embraced by the local elite as signifiers of a popular authenticity, while denounced by local people as elements of their own undesirable past, which is associated with slavery and exploitation (Collins 2004). This act of cultural disavowal is as much of an embarrassment to the local elite in Bahia as the charou denouncing of Indian food habits is to the respectable middle-class Hindus in Durban.

Many families have been deeply divided by the conversion of one branch, or some members, to the Pentecostal churches. Pastors and church elders encouraged the believers to refrain from any contact or commensality with their Hindu families during the time of Hindu festivals where the demons, aka Hindu gods, were seen as being particularly active and strong. Many families encountered problems around weddings and funerals, where Christian family members either stayed away or excused themselves and left the room when the pandit was chanting Sanskrit verses and incense was burned. Reversely, the stauncher Hindus in many families would also have apprehensions about eating in Christian households, about the cleanliness of their kitchens, and so on—attitudes that were actively promoted by many of the new and modern Hindu preachers and their organizations. The notion of Christians as unclean was, of course, laced with class and caste prejudices that were actively mobilized in the ongoing conflicts both within families and between religious formations.

The love marriage of Joseph and Anjali demonstrated these tensions and the idea of the new Christian family in multiple ways. Anjali was from a middle-class Maharaj family who are traditionally regarded as powerful and respectable custodians of Hindu tradition, while Joseph came from a lower-class Telugu family that was troubled by domestic violence and alcoholism. To his sister and mother, his marriage to Anjali was an act of class betrayal, of disavowing his "own people" in favor of his fair-skinned and prosperous in-laws. To Anjali's family it was also a form of class betrayal, albeit downward. They have now grudgingly accepted the union and their grandchild, but when Joseph was around, they would eat separately and pray over their food. "Only when I go there by myself, I eat with the rest of the family," Anjali told me. The experience has turned Joseph into a staunch believer in the modern nuclear household as a way of recuperating the self-respect of Indian men as fathers and householders:

> We need to show them that they must take responsibility for themselves so they can be good fathers and husbands. . . . In our Indian

culture there are many conflicts in homes, and the wife and the mother rarely get on. In most cases the sons don't stand up to their mothers, and the wife always becomes the victim and the outsider to blame . . . I think that the Bible says that one must leave one's home and set up a new home with one's wife, and that is the right thing to do. Or else, the man will never grow up. We encourage that among the people in our church.[12]

It was explained to me by many that precautions around food, commensality, and family arrangements were only necessary for those who felt vulnerable, but the longer-term goal was, of course, to bring about a more systematic separation of life worlds, networks, and families. The house was no longer the site of commensality and tradition but now a site of display of the nuclear family, and new, clean, and unmarked modern ways of life and reproduction. It was the congregation that had become the site of new extensive socialities and forms of social disciplines and surveillance.

RACE, GENDER, BODY

A collective "nervous state" has indeed gripped the township since 1994. This has made the existing ontologies of evil develop into more dramatic forms among the new Christians. These were expressed in highly stylized, often repetitive narratives of experiences of evil and illness and the subsequent healing. The narratives were performed in the church communities, in prayer groups, within the family, in front of my tape recorder, and as testimonies to the rebirth of the person as a new transformed body and soul. But the healing, and the narrative thereof, was portrayed as essentially belonging to this new person, a foundational and transformational act, always talked about in the singular as "his" or "her" healing.

Most men narrated structurally similar stories about how their selfish life with alcohol, smoking, dance, and women suddenly turned around when a female in their family—wife, mother, or sister—suddenly fell seriously ill or became mentally disturbed and seemed beyond medical cure. Driven by a sense of familial duty, the men tried every option and healing method available. In the end they resorted to a pastor who was known for his healing powers. Through prayer he would heal the woman, who would immediately convert, while he, only gradually, would be drawn into the church by his now healed and purified wife, sister, or mother. Narratives of healing and illnesses were strongly gendered, and the birth of the new strong paternal figure, and the new Christian family, very rarely happened through the bodily weakness or afflictions of the man but almost invariably through the women he was supposed to protect. Men's narratives revolved around near-death experiences due to excessive drinking, road accidents, or drugs. These events humbled him and made him aware of the fragility of life and the weakness of his own self. One man told me, after a session where he had narrated his story of a life of sin, "You cannot live your life alone. No one has the strength to resist the force of the devil. Only if you walk with Jesus can you get through this life."

If a woman's behavior changed and she appeared rude, aggressive, uncaring, and unwilling to observe personal hygiene (which made her unclean and undesirable), she was often considered to be possessed by the devil. In these circumstances, she would be brought to a pastor who healed her by driving the demonic force out of her body or neutralizing the spell that was cast on her. This was often a protracted and dramatic process where the demon would resist and sometimes identify itself by speaking through the woman with a deep, unrecognizable voice. The demon could be a Hindu deity and respond to names like Kali, Durga, or other Hindu goddesses, but in the harder and dramatic cases, the demon was of African origin and would make the woman speak Zulu or another African language. Eventually, the demon was overpowered by the presence of Jesus, and the woman was cleansed of evil and restored to an almost original purity; a mother, daughter, or wife was purged of her evil charou ways and emerged as a more respectable and desirable woman.

The milder "Indian" and thus more domesticated or *heimlich* forms of possession referred to malevolent spirits and forces that have a long history in the community. The notion of the *peey*—the malevolent spirits that are ghosts of those who died prematurely (especially young, unmarried women) or committed crimes in their lifetime—has a long history in South India and was well and alive in Chatsworth. The stronger and more bloodthirsty forms of *peey*, Lionel Kaplan reported from urban Chennai in the 1980s, are uncanny (*unheimliche*) spirits living in the outskirts, in the bushes, and on the railway tracks—like the outcasts and the tribal communities (1987, 110–27). In Chatsworth, the place of the strong, autochthonous, and alien spirits was occupied by African spirits, who were seen to be close to nature and the soil. Like in Indian popular etiologies, these spirits preyed on women, especially menstruating or pregnant women, who were in great danger of pollution and possession.[13]

The more extreme cases were invariably those involving African spirits. In most cases they were caused by the possession of a woman by a *tokolosh*, the type of demon that can be found in popular cosmologies among the Nguni peoples of southern Africa (Zulu, Xhosa, Ndebele, and many others). The *tokolosh* was rumored to be a small, black, hairy two-feet-tall being with a foul smell and often equipped with a large penis. It entered houses and women's beds, where it had sex with them while they slept and sometimes entered the body through the vagina. Once inside, either permanently or intermittently, it transformed the woman by making her rude, lewd, lazy, and lascivious. She would begin hating other women, cast spells on them, and try to seduce their men and spread evil around her. The cause of the predicament could be many but typically involved contact with Africans, sleeping in a bed where an African woman has slept, eating food that was polluted or mixed with *muti* of magical powers—or even worse, and rarely spelled out in detail—sexual or other physical contact with an African. This contact with African bodies would make the body of the Indian woman—seen as particularly delicate, soft, and open, and thus in need of constant protection—vulnerable to invasions of the ubiquitous *tokolosh*, which was always looking for suitable places to dwell.

In most of the testimonies I heard, the woman was taken to Zanzibari healers who supposedly could brew the *muti* and perform the rituals, including animal sacrifice and the piercing of the body with various animal objects at the river at midnight, which was all performed in the presence of the woman's male relatives. Much of this was recounted in excruciating detail and with some glee and pleasure in the extreme character of the rituals, and pleasure in narrating them after the fact, after having reached a higher stage of consciousness. The Zanzibari community had developed a thriving business as African healers in Chatsworth. They were seen as domesticated Africans with a reputation for being able to exorcise African demons and spirits. Although a long-standing practice, this had only surfaced as a more respectable and common trade in the last decade or so. Several of the Zanzibari healers had regular clinics and ads in the weekly newspapers wherein they promised to cure most diseases and also claimed to have remedies that provided "natural potency, stronger than Viagra," as a sign in Unit 2 read.[14] Like in the case of the racial anxieties, women's bodies constituted the terrain upon which these illnesses and possessions manifested themselves. Female bodies could turn into extreme manifestations of evil when the woman was possessed by the hypersexualized *tokolosh* and turned into a repulsive and dangerous half human in need of the strongest antidote available to restore her purity and femininity.

In this respect, the Pentecostal congregations were indeed adapting themselves and existing ontologies of evils of Indian origin to an African world in which the significance and importance of witchcraft, spells, and magic have grown dramatically since the fall of apartheid. The modern township, Adam Ashforth has argued in his book on witchcraft in Soweto, is a site of displacement and alienation, devoid of ancestral spirits, unclean, and a site of immoral living and mixing of lives and spirit. Even when rituals are performed there, they can never be "proper," because they are displaced from ancestral homes (Ashforth 2005, 20–111). In the African townships, the ancestors were under attack by Pentecostal churches that effectively employed the language and method of exorcism and healing to cut the ties with the past and the rural. In Chatsworth the Hindu gods and their demonic apparitions were under attack, but the goal was the same—the erasure of the past.

The most powerful resource at the disposal of the Pentecostal churches was in fact their flexible incorporation and epistemological reduction of multiple forms of evil into one form—the devil as a ubiquitous, amorphous, and always dynamic presence as the default form of the universe, an opaque mass of darkness that will always creep in and fill every available space and every self that does not constantly keep vigil.

While the discursive reduction of all evil into one was carried out by the pastors, the dirty work of confronting evil and administering the antidote were always carried out by men who had lived full and often sinful lives. In Pastor B's church, Mr. Pillay, a rugged, muscular man in his sixties, and his younger assistant, who was an accomplished singer and guitarist, were leading the very popular "Hour of Power" healing session. Pastor B would enter the church and "warm up" the crowd with a brief, stirring sermon peppered with lots of rhetorical questions that elicited shouts of "YESSSS" or "NOOOO" from the crowd. Then the assistant would take the stage and lead the crowd through a series of hymns at the maximum volume of the PA system. Microphones were directed at the crowd, who would then hear their own song amplified. About half of the congregation would then line up in a long row, and Pillay would take off his jacket and begin to pray in a booming and deep voice. People, mostly women, would come up one after another, and he placed his hand on their shoulders or heads and asked them to pray with him. The whole atmosphere became more charged; the room was hot and humid, and the sound of singing and music was so loud that one could barely hear any voice except Pillay's powerful baritone.

Some would fall down, fainting; others would start shaking their bodies, their mouths frothing, while others painstakingly tried to keep their cool. After about forty loud, sweaty, and heady minutes, the music would change and the volume was lowered. The assistant would begin to sing slow, soothing hymns, and many of those who had been healed would lie down on the floor to be tended to by their friends and relatives. Pillay would walk around, speaking softly to the women, asking them how they felt, calming them. A feeling of release and relaxation would spread though the room. Many of the participants told me that they had to go home and take a long rest after such sessions. They felt completely emptied and tired because all the evil thoughts and energies that had been pent up in them had suddenly disappeared. Pillay told me that he could only do this twice a week, and even that was almost too much for him. Like any diviner and healer, he, who knew evil intimately (a former seaman, nightclub bouncer, and—rumor had it—something of a hard man with dirty hands in the past), could take it into himself, process it, and get rid of it through the strength of his body and the robustness of his mind. He did this work for B, he said, because he wanted to help and protect the pastor, who otherwise "would be eaten up by this work . . . Pastor B has much to look after, and he has to remain close to Jesus. My job is to help people get rid of the evil. I shall do it as long as I can find the strength."

Pillay saw this work as paying for his past sins, as a way of cleansing himself and others of the wages of sin and ignorance in their past. It was but one of the many elements of the discursive and emotional universe of great drama and intensity that Pentecostal theology generated, wherein even mundane objects and gestures in everyday life assumed moral if not universal significance. The attractions of such an interpretive frame that directly addressed an everyday existence troubled by political, cultural, and economic marginalization should be obvious. In her slightly hyperbolic attempt to escape reductionism, Ruth Marshall calls the born-again movement in Nigeria an "event" that introduces a new "discursive regime," new styles of conduct, and new truths, or even a Deleuzian "line of flight" (2009, 35–37). The Pentecostal movement does indeed provide its followers with powerful, new, and universal horizons for self-making, but those horizons never encompass or hegemonize the larger sociopolitical world of the township. The nimble and portable Pentecostal practices are adaptable to many historical situations, also in South Africa, but hardly transformative. The political-cultural marginality of the average township charou is ably interpreted by the Pentecostal churches, yet the only transformative promise they hold out is a form of collective disavowal of their own past and cultural markers, against the promise of being fully included in a universal community of empty vessels.

BETWEEN VESSEL AND SUBSTANCE: ON THE EXTERIORITY OF THE SOUL

It should be clear from the preceding analysis that there is a remarkable continuity in the worries regarding the dangerous emptiness and instability of the coolie and the charou soul. A concomitant worry is that of the radical incompleteness and porosity of the charou home and domestic life, which are always in danger of contamination by omnipresent evil. In the case of Chatsworth, "the African" is seen as the ultimate source of pollution, of a radical and exterior evil represented by African bodies that are unrestrained by the stronger cultural and intellectual resources of "civilized people." This is as true in these tales of possession and healing as it was in the case of schools, taxis, and public spaces. What is equally remarkable testimony to the effects of a century of racial separation in South Africa is that social mixing with Africans remains very limited and socially unacceptable. Instead, the ongoing import of music styles from church gospel to kwaito, youth cultures, and universes of evil and healing practices are widely interpreted as taking place within a parallel moral and social universe of the charou: the emasculated and feminized underbelly of the Indian community, which is particularly susceptible to contamination and unable to control the moral decay and depletion of Indian cultural values.

In all these senses, the Pentecostal churches in Chatsworth work decidedly from within a charou universe and from within the dominant assumption of the constitutive incompleteness of the charou, the impossibility of producing a self-reliant interiority. The questions of belief and the inner life of the congregations were projected onto a variety of objects and things, to what we may call the exteriorities of conviction. The central problem for the pastors was not that things and objects were imbued with significance and meanings. That has been a matter of course among Christian missionaries for more than a century in this part of the world and elsewhere. The question was more precisely how objects and things could be transformed and manipulated, and to what extent objects and substances had agency, or inherent properties, that resisted conceptual recalibration.

In the current flurry of writings on materiality that herald a "decentering" of anthropology by approaching things and objects as agentive (see, e.g., Miller 2005), the fact that most contemporary things and objects are entirely commodified and designed have largely evaporated as a relevant concern. Yet the "original" provenance of things, the spirit (*hau*) and aura embedded in them by strategy and design, plays an important role in how they are used and valorized by most people.[15] It was precisely the commodified nature of modern objects that made them morally appropriate for Christian missionaries. Needless to say, objects were at times put to other uses than intended because the interpretive frame of the native world was stronger than that embedded in the thing. Things are believed to have certain properties because they are made (by people or corporations) in particular ways and with particular intentions. They enter everyday life and intimate spaces with those powers and designs intact, a form of accumulated "auratic essence," which in turn enables them to appear as agentive, nonhuman powers acting "as if" they were agents. These auratic properties can indeed be changed and recoded but not infinitely, and never without taking their historicity into account through incorporation, reversal, or disavowal.

In his essay on the public life of things, Latour argues that we should move from a concern with objects as artifacts (he uses the German term *Gegenstand*) to "Things," by which he means material objects, concepts, or images whose meanings are publicly contested and debated (2005). Latour strangely ignores what time, design, and historicity of objects do to objects and their significance. The word *Gegenstand* has an echo of something that resists, that stands against (*gegen*)—something that resists free manipulation or inscription of meaning. A *Gegenstand* has something in itself—a core or a trace—and something that cannot be fully controlled. For Freud, *das Ding* was a highly charged object: that which was so overfilled with meanings, so haunted and pregnant that it could not assume any literal form, but only a highly condensed and always ambiguous form as uncanny.[16]

Transforming objects into public things always has to reckon with older inscriptions into the object that do not go away and continue to haunt and follow the object as a shadowy presence. Even as the thing becomes incorporated and domesticated within certain worlds of signification, say a religious universe or a certain order of memory, it still carries traces of earlier inscriptions and the possibilities they open. As much as any object has the potential of becoming a public Thing in Latour's sense, it can also become a fetish—another form of public object whose sharing and public status is somewhat more complex.

The power of a fetishized object essentially depends on not being known and equally shared by everyone, of having both a visible life and hidden powers that are only accessible or perceptible by those in the know. The power of a fetish flows from an ambivalent libidinal investment and projection of qualities and innate powers onto objects, sites, or features that as a result appear both deeply attractive and repulsive.

I find it more promising to look at the charou house as *das Ding* in the Freudian sense, a place that is perpetually haunted by its past, into which histories and lives are condensed and only changed and edited with great difficulty. The objects of the past, the Hindu objects, dress, food, and even signs of the Hindu word are obviously *Gegenstände*—objects that contain their past so much so that they have to be physically removed and discarded, preferably in water. They have the power, like magnetic objects or signs, to attract the ubiquitous demons that are hovering over the household and its people. To the charou pastors, the myth of the Hindu past and its spiritual order, and its extended families and cultural disciplines, hover over the township, but are now recoded as malignant and evil forces. The pastors thus engage in a serious fetish-ist discourse where any object that is of Hindu or discernible "Indian" origin is believed to have transcendental, transferable, and contagious powers.[17]

The practices I describe above amount to a reversal of Bataille's idea of sacrifice as a form of incorporation into the sacred (1992). They are acts of ex-corporation, expunging objects and turning them away from the world of sacred immanence and reducing them to a world of things—but never completely. These objects remain so powerful and contain such power qua their past immersion in the heathen world of the charou that they have to be physically destroyed or permanently removed, only to be replaced by objects that are supposedly "neutral," industrial, nonaffective designs.

The careful management of the Christian homes of Chatsworth is based on the basic recognition that interiority and belief can only be (re)produced if supported by a comprehensive material regime of cleanliness, of things constantly purified and/or consecrated. Current academic arguments that "belief" is but an effect of ritual and material practices (e.g., Bell 1993), or that affective-sensory regimes are the real bedrocks of belief and conviction (e.g., Hirschkind 2006; Bennett 2001) seem to overlook what was well known to the Nonconformist mission-ary at the colonial frontier as to the most humble charou preacher: effec-tive belief relies on constant incorporation of material objects and their spirits into the life of the soul.

Postscript

MELANCHOLIA IN THE TIME
OF THE "AFRICAN PERSONALITY"

IN EARLY APRIL 2010 TWO SEEMINGLY UNRELATED EVENTS ONCE AGAIN CONJURED up the old specter of an all-out race war in South Africa. The extremist leader of the Afrikaner Weerstandsbeweging (AWB) Eugene Terre'Blanche was murdered by two of his farmworkers, apparently due to a long-standing pay dispute. In the same week, a heated debate flared up as the controversial firebrand leader of the ANC's youth wing, Julius Malema, was allowed to sing the antiapartheid battle song "Aye-saba Amagwala" (The Cowards are Scared) in which the phrase "kill the Boer" occurs. Many newspapers and commentators immediately connected the two events and suggested that Terre'Blanche was killed because Malema's song had reignited deep antiwhite sentiments among ordinary Africans. None of the prima facie evidence of the killing suggested that it was any different from the hundreds of attacks, robberies, and murders—fueled by complex and mostly localized conflicts over land, pay, and dignity—that have taken place in the South African countryside in the last two decades.[1] Like Zuma's use of the song "Umshini Wami" in 2008–9, Julius Malema's use of a struggle song quickly acquired a life of its own. The ANC initially defended the singing of the song because it constituted a part of the nation's cultural memory. Gwede Mantashe, the ANC's secretary general, stated that the song was only a means of ensuring South African history was remembered and not meant as an incitement to violence against whites.[2]

The two events, and the nervous reactions they produced on all sides, indicated that the past remains an infuriating and often uncanny shadow for most South Africans. Nothing is forgotten, a few things are forgiven, but in the main, history's deep frustrations are well and alive under the normalized surface of a steeply unequal and intensely commercialized society. During the debates in April 2010, commentators argued that ANC should assuage the fears of the country's minorities, which were constantly unnerved by the prospect of a new and violent majoritarian political climate. Under the panicky statement of these few weeks rumbled the fear of the new style of populist and distinctly

Africanist politics of the Zuma era, where the memories of the struggle are recruited successfully among the large number of disaffected, disappointed, and unemployed South Africans. The appeal to the specificity of "Africanness" as distinct rules, experiences, and cultural codes has discarded Mbeki's lofty rhetoric of an African renaissance and has hit the streets and quotidian political practice as never before. Zuma's supporters praise his forceful "African personality," and the president himself is an active promoter of traditional patriarchal values, including polygamy. "This is not America, this is Africa and you must follow our rules," screamed Malema at a BBC reporter who questioned Malema's denigration of the Zimbabwean opposition.[3] Or as a young Zulu-speaking driver of a kombi taxi in Durban bluntly told me in 2008 when I asked him about his view of Zuma and the charges of rape and corruption pending against him at the time, "He is our leader, an African leader . . . no white judge has a right to decide if he has done anything wrong . . . that is just the white man's law, and it has always been used against Africans."[4]

In the Indian townships, the ascendency of Zuma has been regarded with apprehension but also cautious hope. Some of my informants hoped that the new government would deliver better services to all the poor in the country, while others fear that new policies would be directed more exclusively at Africans than before. Some were afraid of the new Africanist tenor of public life. They took some comfort in the fact that whites, too, have become a minority like Indians, and potentially a powerful ally represented by the Democratic Party, which pulls the majority of Indian votes. Many of those paying close attention were encouraged by the fact that the political elite of Durban and KwaZulu-Natal now controlled the country. Zuma's first cabinet included almost as many Indians as did Mandela's first cabinet, most of them hailing from Durban.[5] As a long-standing friend in Chatsworth put it to me, "For Mbeki and his people, we Indians were some strange people down in humid Durban—they never understood us. You cannot say that about Zuma and his people. They are from Durban so they know that you cannot run things around here without the Indian . . . they say all these things about Indians to look tough and all, but when they need money or some connection, they know where to go." For my friend, and the many Indians spread across the small towns in the province, seeking protection through an alliance with a strong Zulu leader seemed neither strange nor incomprehensible. For them, Zuma's enlisting of the financial expertise of local Indians, such as the infamous Shaik brothers and the Gupta family,[6] was but a continuation of the local Zulu *nkosi* who relied on loans and credit from the Indian businessmen within his realm. As his presidential predecessors, Zuma has performed ritualized gestures toward the Indian community, praising them for "their role in the struggle,"[7] and his interest in the celebration of the 150th anniversary of Indian presence in the country was seen by some Indians as evidence of his cultural roots in the province.[8]

As we have seen throughout this book, however, overwhelming power and popular legitimacy (as in Zuma) and/or moral authority (as in Mandela) reduces the importance of race, or makes it into a question of representation of a community (as in Rajbansi). More complicated and antagonistic racial encounters take place between ordinary people and their phantasmic and categorical shadows in everyday life. The colonial scheme of racialized corporeality still imposes itself and overdetermines most everyday encounters and the ways in which South Africans feel and live in their bodies. The fears conjured up by Malema's song, or his aggressive outbursts, inadvertently map themselves onto the small remainders, doubts, and sensations of unknowability, or strangeness, that emerge from encounters in streets, workplaces, and shopping malls among people who have historically been physically separated and culturally alienated from one another. These ubiquitous remainders are always/already available for interpretation, and they are anticipated and often scripted prior to even the smallest and most insignificant exchange or transaction. This is a legacy that can only change very slowly, and most South Africans acknowledge that "it will take generations," as a common phrase goes. The significance of the racialized gaze of the other, of always living with a categorical double or shadow that insists on reducing subjectivities to what Merleau-Ponty called "the flesh of the other," the exterior schema of corporeality, shows no sign of disappearing, either on the side of the African majority or on the side of the country's minorities.

The past cannot be discarded. It is ever present and hammered out in infrastructure, architecture, and racial separations that continue to fundamentally shape the habitus of the people and communities living within these structures. South Africa's urban spaces are like huge machines that are built and designed to uphold and reproduce separate worlds and life aspirations. If apartheid used spatial distance and cultural walls as separators of populations, the postapartheid city is increasingly defined by actual physical walls. The meaning of the house and its walls changed from being a part of an Indian community that was defined by the outer, natural, and cultural borders of the apartheid township to being a closed physical container of cultural virtue. House owners and tenants began to build walls around their properties that resembled those in the formerly white neighborhoods, including having watchdogs and hiring private security companies. The walls of the house are no longer indicative of the Indian social world that was defiantly developed in the township, however unfree this had been in the first place. Today the walls are protective of racially marked bodies that feel threatened by the intrusion of, or mere proximity to, African bodies. The primary function of the walls has now moved from defining that which was enclosed and enabled inside the house to what was excluded and kept out. The Indian family today is less defined by what happens inside the house than by the mere fact that it is separated from the bush by secure walls.

As in other parts of the country, there has been a general securitization of social life in Chatsworth. That which had earlier been regarded as inappropriate or undesirable may now be seen as plainly dangerous. Doors are increasingly closed and social contacts mediated by cell phones and cars. New social distinctions, based on the level of security and the height of walls, have emerged. Earlier, the township experienced a certain mingling between the respectable lower middle class, skilled blue-collar families, and those regarded as deracinated Indians from nonrespectable backgrounds. Today, this interaction is greatly diminished on security grounds. The home without walls and burglar bars is often regarded as less respectable. These houses are in fact nothing but the more permeable houses that dominated a few decades ago. Today their permeability is seen as a moral problem and the residents as morally suspect because of the assumed openness to the street—a space that today represents Africans and the supposed immorality of African culture. This openness connotes physical proximity, sexual promiscuity, and a personhood devoid of interiority and discipline. Securitization of houses and life has, in other words, greatly simplified social relations by flattening and homogenizing the outside as one of potential threat.

In a strange sense, South Africa has come full circle from the anxious European settler who was overwhelmed by nature and seeking to construct domestic order and personhood for himself and the colonized subjects through houses and walls. Today the building and meanings of walls have been further democratized as a means to create the proper inside of a house and a family, where property and propriety meet in an anxious embrace. Walls tend to actually produce their own ostensible cause, fear, and separation, as well as a sense of loss of the innocence and carefree life that preceded them. Today the melancholia of freedom in the townships sits in the walls, which are commonly seen as sadly necessary and also as manifestations of a lost form of social life. Many of South Africa's walls are indeed melancholic walls.[9]

The preceding story of the making of an alienating township space, its gradual domestication and inhabitation, its cultural coding as "our space," an Indian space where property and cultural virtue could flourish, speaks to the force and efficacy of apartheid's biopolitical mode

of domination but also to its limitations. What made apartheid policies seem productive in the Indian townships was neither the often in-
ept and underfunded interventions by the city council nor the feeble
and corrupt practices of the formal institutions of self-government that
were set up by the regime. It was the multiple forms of public activism
among a younger generation in the townships—and the ingenuity and
ability to make the most of limited resources in hundreds of thousands
of homes—that made the townships into habitable and hospitable
places. All these efforts created a new Indian world that was wealthier
and more modern in habits and family structures, but that was also
deeply alienated—culturally, socially, and morally. This happened because the dominant horizon for political action and political imagination among Indians moved from the wider world of the city and the
nation, where it had been so prominent in the first half of the twentieth
century, to the community itself.

Political action in Arendt's sense of a striving for social transformation was greatly diminished and marginalized across the country. When
political action was reignited by the momentous events in Soweto in
1976, the vast majority of Indians had embraced the notion that the
community was indeed their actual horizon for any political action.
An earlier striving for freedom had been replaced by a striving for
autonomy—for a freedom without sovereign rights to decide on one's
individual and collective body. Autonomy means recognition of difference, even recognition of distinct abilities, a form of freedom but
without sovereignty as a central aspiration.

A combination of cautious hope, cynicism, and nostalgic fantasies of
an authentic, wholesome, or meaningful past—whether in the heat of
the struggle or in the everyday lives in ethnoracial enclaves—seems to
define South Africa in 2011. The key question is whether—and how—a
new, inclusive, but also less heroic form of public culture may develop
that can address the many glaring inequalities in the country.

Freedom arrived in South Africa as a set of formal rights that respected individual rights and freedoms regardless of race and culture.
However, the new dynamic public culture was structured by a powerful
majoritarian agenda and moral sentiment: based on numbers, the numerous crimes of minority rule, and a rhetoric of autochthony. Its present form is an ideologically vague Africanist populism that is a force to
be reckoned with. This has made freedom and the new society appear
threatening to its minorities, and especially to the impoverished and socially marginalized sections of Indians and coloreds living in townships
across the country. Real freedom and sovereignty within the new nation
have here been experienced as a partial loss, not of unfreedom but of its
predominant experiential form: cultural autonomy. The many attempts

to retain or at least reestablish older forms of sociality or comfort do not necessarily signify a simple denunciation of freedom and majority rule. They signify the embrace of autonomy as the most meaningful, and least risky, political horizon for groups that seem to be permanently "minoritized" on multiple dimensions. This is also true for minorities in most of the world for whom freedom and sovereignty are neither natural nor necessary companions.

Notes

INTRODUCTION

1. The discussion of the gaze in Merleau-Ponty is explicitly indebted to Lacan's notion of the mirror stage as constitutive of the ego. For Merleau-Ponty, both the "mirror" (= gaze of the other) and the ego remain strongly social and embedded in embodied convention, while Sartre, in his discussion of "The Look," interprets the gaze as coming from an imagined onlooker who comes to stand in for both the inscrutable other and an already interiorized split notion between an ideal self and an actual self (1965, 188–208).

2. See Merleau-Ponty 1995, 273, for this formulation, and Sjöholm 2001 for a good discussion of Merleau-Ponty's view of corporeality as an exterior life of the body.

3. See Simmel 1959a, 276–82 and Frisby 1994, 132–42.

4. Crossley argues that Foucault's attribution of social efficacy to the panoptic gaze presupposes the existence of a subject that can inhabit this "anxious awareness." He argues that one must go to Merleau-Ponty's reflections on the effects of the gaze on the embodied self to properly fathom and limit this assumed efficacy (Crossley 1993).

5. This equation is at the heart of contemporary liberal Hegelianism, such as Charles Taylor's assertion of a continuity of self-expression from Rousseau's celebration of the free will to current desires for recognition by cultural and social minorities (1994), or Axel Honneth's linkage of the possibility of proper ethical and social life to the socialization and recognition of individuals (1995).

6. When truly free, Kant writes at the end of the *Critique of Practical Reason*, "The heart is, after all, freed and relieved of a burden which always secretly weighs upon it—when in pure moral decisions . . . there is uncovered to the human being an inner ability not quite familiar otherwise even to him, the inner freedom to detach himself from the vehement obtrusiveness of their inclinations to such an extent that none at all, not even the one that we care about most, shall have an influence on a decision for which we are now to employ our reason" (2002, 201).

7. Authors as different as Lionel Trilling (1972), Michel Foucault (esp. 1984), Charles Taylor (1989 and 1992), and Lynn Hunt (2007) all explore the historical construction of interiority and the education of the senses that went into making modern selves. I have recently explored dimensions of this problem in some detail (Hansen 2009).

8. Complicity thus became a complicated issue in a system where white intellectuals were free to criticize and ridicule power both in Parliament and beyond, and free to travel abroad and to read a wide variety of literature that was ideologically opposed to apartheid. None of this mattered as long as one refrained from acting in an effective manner on one's convictions and as long as one at least officially observed the strictures on sociality and sexuality across the color bar. Complicity was actively encouraged by the state in its micro-operations of censorship and selective policing (Sanders 2002).

9. The literature on the structure of apartheid and the apartheid state is considerable. Some of the best overviews and syntheses can be found in Posel 1991 and Norval 1996. For the cultural dimensions of how apartheid was publicly constructed and enacted, see Witz 2003.

10. This stance on race is expressed most succinctly in the Freedom Charter adopted by ANC in 1955, and throughout the antiapartheid struggle it was retained as a fundamental statement on a vision of a future inclusive and color-blind South Africa.

11. The power of these diverse energies have come together in a song, which became the signature of Zuma's significant following and was performed at mass meetings and by Zuma himself onstage. The style of the song, and Zuma's slow dance movements along with it, are in the style of traditional Zulu war songs and dances. The words, however, refer to the militancy of the 1980s, particularly the chorus "awuleth umshini wami" (bring me my machine gun) (Gunner 2008).

12. The importance of the young Hegel to generations of thinkers and strategists of liberation from DuBois to Fanon and Cabral is well known. The imprint of Hegelian thought in anthropology and social sciences has largely been indirect and mostly mediated through Marx, Bataille, Sartre, and Merleau-Ponty. The clearest and most sustained engagement with Hegelian models of thought in scholarship on postcolonial situations has been coming out of South Asia, notably Homi Bhabha (1982), Ranajit Guha (2002), the entire Subaltern Studies collective, Partha Chatterjee, and, most directly, Kaviraj (1995). More recently, Andrew Willford has analyzed Tamil identity in Malaysia through a somewhat similar framework (2006).

13. It is hard to imagine the force of C.L.R. James's writings without Hegelian Marxism, a Fanon, Senghor, Castro, and many more recent revolutionaries without Hegelian figures of thought and aspiration informing their striving. For a thoughtful discussion of anticolonialism and modern aspirations through the lens of C.L.R. James's work and life, see Scott 2004. For exceptional work on the revolution in Haiti, see Dayan 1995, Dubois 2004, and Sala-Molins 1987.

14. For a suggestive analysis of the place of the extraordinary in democratic politics, see Kalyvas 2008.

15. As an instructive example of rhetoric of the miracle of the mid-1990s, see Patti Waldmeir's *Anatomy of a Miracle* (1997) and, less than a decade later, veteran journalist Allister Sparks's *Beyond the Miracle* (2003).

16. The new Constitutional Court is strikingly constructed at the highest point in Johannesburg, on top of an old colonial prison that has been turned into a museum.

17. For an exploration of multiple forms of disappointment and disaffection after apartheid, see the collection *After the Thrill Is Gone* (Farred and Barnard 2004).

18. Arendt's distinction between freedom as transformation and a property of a creative realm of politics, and "autonomy" as located within the everyday life and the social, is much closer to everyday ideas of politics in South Africa than, for instance, Nikolas Rose's Foucauldian approach to freedom. In the latter, freedom becomes a technique of power and merely identical with "'autonomy" as a technical and ethical striving (1999).

19. Freud later revised his view of melancholia by depathologizing it and instating the yearning for lost objects that cannot be known and named as a fundamental mechanism in the formation of the ego (Freud [1923] 1960). For the purposes of this book, I will retain the meanings of the original essay, written during World War 1, which usefully refers to lost objects of many forms, including ideals, such as the nation, or belief in institutions.

20. In her stimulating work on nostalgia, Boym discusses two types of nostalgia: restorative (nationalist) nostalgia and reflective nostalgia, which is more playful, eclectic, and individual (2001). Both forms of nostalgia presuppose, however, that the past is available as a legitimate object of yearning. That is evidently not the case among Indians in Durban.

21. For an overview, see Hassim et al. 2008.

22. This position is particularly clear in Ashwin Desai's *The Poors of Chatsworth* (2000), which explores and hails a series of political mobilizations against evictions among impoverished communities in the township.

23. This is the definition used by Lefebvre in his *Critique of Everyday Life* (1947; 2001, 29–51)—a world that is also the site of fundamental alienation, the work of ideology, "unhappiness," and new, incipient solidarities (52–99). Even de Certeau's much more heroic celebration of the unruliness of practice remains firmly within the orbit of the structures of alienated social life of capitalist modernity (1984).

24. See, for instance, Nancy Riess 2002.

25. Stanley Cavell, *Must We Mean What We Say?* (2002, 238–66). The proximity between this position and the broader and now secularized Protestant injunction to embrace the neighbor almost as a generalized kinsman (*Nebenmensch*) is hard to miss.

26. Cf. Partha Chatterjee's influential argument that anticolonial nationalism constructs a deep and effective divide between an "outer" and colonized realm of pragmatic adaptation and engagement, and an "inner" and pure form of the unadulterated nation, the site of true culture, the household, and the nation's women (1993).

Chapter 1: Ethnicity by Fiat: The Remaking of Indian Life in South Africa

1. For an incisive analysis of this rhetoric and its context, see Daniel Herwitz's essay, "Afro-Medici: Thabo Mbeki's African Renaissance," in Daniel Herwitz 2003.

2. On the increasing emphasis on autochthony in South Africa, see Jean and John Comaroff 2005. For a broader argument pertaining to Africa (and Europe), see Geschiere 2009.

3. For a detailed account of Gandhi's career in South Africa, see also Judith Brown 1989 and 1996.

4. Report of the Asiatic Inquiry Commission, Union Government, Cape Town, 4, 1921, para. 108, p. 30.

5. Documents Relating to the New Asiatic Bill, 13–14. Quoted from Palmer 1957, 94.

6. This was to replace an older system that encouraged repatriation, which was created in 1895 when the government taxed laborers who did not return to India. In 1914, the Indian's Relief Act encouraged a scheme of voluntary repatriation that was supervised by the Protector of Indian Immigrants in Natal, an office created in the 1860s to supervise the administration of indentured labor. The scheme had had a certain effect. Several thousand Indians returned in the following years (Palmer reports a figure of 3,199 in 1920 and 2,699 in 1921 [1957, 78]), but the birth rate among Indians was so high that it had little effect on the overall size of the Indian population in South Africa. According to Brij Lal, the annual increase in the Indian population was approximately 3 percent per year up to 1911. Between 1911 and 1921, it was reduced to 0.73 percent in spite of constant and high birth rates. Between 1921 and 1936, it increased up to 1.9 percent and stabilized in the following decades around 2.8 to 3 percent (1989, 28). See also Henning 1993.

7. The Indian Penetration Commission, Union Government of South Africa, 1941, 76.

8. *Bombay Chronicle*, March 4, 1946.

9. Speech in Pretoria, December 20, 1946. Quoted from Pachai 1971, 214.

10. The most exhaustive study of how the "Asiatic question" conditions of indentured labor, repatriation, and residential patterns were internationalized already from the nineteenth century onward can be found in Pachai 1971.

11. See ibid., 197–274, for a summary of the debates and the views of both Indian and white politicians in South Africa.

12. *Fiat Lux*, May 1966, 21.

13. See Maharaj 1992 and Maasdorp and Pillay 1977. A similar pattern applied to coloreds in Cape Town who were also settled across the city and hence disproportionally affected by the forced removals (Western 1981). In Johannesburg the removals affected the large number of urbanized Africans who had settled in Sophiatown and many other locations across the city.

14. See, for instance, Freund 1995, 64–76 and Subramony 1993, 77–90. The complaints about houses and high rents were compounded by the fact that a section of houses were offered for sale and at prices that were much higher than the often fully paid-up houses they had been forced out of without receiving proper compensation.

15. *Natal Mercury*, July 25, 1964. The governing rationale of the new urban planning was what Bozzoli has called "racial modernism," the desire to modernize both domestic and social life among people of color in the country (2004).

16. In March and April 1999, I was privileged to get access to the city's archives, in particular the archive of the Department of Health and Welfare, which was charged with the special responsibility of monitoring and restructuring Indian neighborhoods and their political and social institutions.

17. The film is mentioned consistently in the annual Mayor's Minutes from 1978 to 1986. Film and files accessed and viewed at the Durban Municipal Archives, March 1999. The film was produced in English, Afrikaans, and isiZulu versions.

18. Mayor's Minutes, 1982–83, 28.

19. Ibid., 29.

20. Mayor's Minutes, 1979–80, 13.

21. Ibid., 14.

22. Mayor's Minutes, 1981–82, 15.

23. Mayor's Minutes, 1985–86, 28.

24. Ibid., 29.

25. Mayor's Minutes, 1983–84, 83.

26. See the detailed figures in ibid., 84–85.

27. The fact that modern ideas of self-governance, autonomy, responsibility, and community care were promoted as much by idealist volunteers as by government employees is well explored within the Foucault-inspired body of work on governmentality. On the production of autonomy and community as a form of government, see Rose 1999, Burchell et al. 1991, and Cruikshank 1999.

28. *Socio-economic Conditions and Household Subsistence Levels in Four Durban Communities: Chatsworth, Newlands East, Phoenix and Wentworth*, Community Research Unit, Durban, 1986, 10.

29. L. N. Naidoo, a former municipal employee who became a full-time community organizer in the 1960s, asserted in an interview in 1992 that many of the fourteen local branches of the Chatsworth Child and Family Welfare Society each handled an annual caseload of more than five hundred, exceeding that of social work departments of many small towns (Subramony 1993, 132).

30. See, for instance, the recent social and political history of Alexandra (Bonner and Nieftagodien 2008) and Lee's recent studies of African women in Guguletu in Cape Town (2009), as well as Leslie Bank's superb study of African communities in East London (2011).

31. Di Scott's PhD dissertation, *Communal Space Construction: The Rise and Fall of Clairwood and District*, Department of Geography, University of Natal, 1995, remains the most exhaustive study of the thriving community of Clairwood and its destruction in the 1960s.

32. See the history page at http://www.luxminarayantemple.org/.

33. See, for instance, Bozzoli 2004. For an excellent account of how the townships were governed by parallel senses of "law" and justice not resembling those of the state laws, see Buur 2005.

34. Reported crime also increased steadily throughout the 1980s (see, for instance, Brewer 1994, 325). On the mis- and underreporting of crime and the manipulation of crime statistics by the police force, see Louw and Schönteich 2001, 41–49.

35. *Argus*, August 6, 1977. The official Code of Honor of the South African Police Force stated that it served a nation with a "Christian National Foundation," and the police journal, *Servamus*, exhorted police officers to see themselves as Christian soldiers stopping the evil work of Satan and "Godless Communism." For a good account of the police culture in apartheid South Africa, see Brogden and Shearing 1993, 41–89.

36. In the mid-1980s two new African police forces were created—the so-called police assistants (*kitskonstabel*), hastily trained police constables who proved highly unpopular and ineffective in the townships, and the municipal police, which was created to protect local black councillors and municipal property in the townships. These forces were all local, worked under many local jurisdictions, lived in the townships, and soon became targets of popular reprisals that involved very high casualty rates (Cawthra 1993, 61–63).

37. This particular regime of "included exclusion" of African bodies was most highly developed in the mining compounds, where the contracted labor force was subjected to a minutely controlled and supervised total regime that recorded and regimented intimate details of bodies, health, diet, and so on.

38. For a rare discussion of policing in the African townships during apartheid, see Steinberg 2009, 43–82.

39. For a very instructive comparison that illustrates this point, as well as ideas of the necessity of using "excessive force" in the colonies, see Raj Chandavarkar's work on colonial policing in Bombay (1998). On late colonialism and policing in Asia and Africa, see Anderson 1992.

40. See also Jensen 2008. Similar practices have existed for a very long time in India and elsewhere. For fresh and insightful work on policing in India, see Eckert 2002 and 2005, and Jauregui 2009.

41. *Fiat Lux*, October 1974, 4.

42. "Indiers en militere opleiding: 'N meningsopname onder Indier-Suid-Afrikaners," *Instituut vir Sosiologisiese, Demografisie en Kriminologiese Navorsing* (Pretoria 1978).

43. *Fiat Lux*, April 1980, 12.

44. "National Service Volunteers Leave for the Border," *Fiat Lux*, February 1985, 18–20.

45. The number of Indian policemen was proportionately small but more than doubled between 1960 and 1976 (Brewer 1994, 236).

46. *Fiat Lux*, August 1985, 8.

47. Minutes from the Rate Payers Association of Clare Estate make it clear that crime, both "Indian crime" and increasingly "African crime," was a recurrent issue under discussion, which caused these associations to file formal complaints to the city council and the police about the behavior of "Bantus" in their neighborhoods. Anand Singh's work in the same area (2005) has documented that informal settlements of mainly rural Zulu speakers in and around Indian areas became a large-scale and contested issue already in the 1980s. Unfortunately, Singh uncritically accepts and perpetuates the standard perception of crime as a purely "African" problem and Indians as law-abiding victims.

48. Memorandum presented to the Divisional Commissioner of Police, Port Natal, by the Southern Durban Local Affairs Committee on Thursday, September 17, at the City Hall in Durban.

49. Memorandum, 1987, ibid., p. 2 and *Sunday Times Extra*, Special Crime Report, July 8, 2007.

50. An example is the systematic extermination of criminal suspects in Bombay through so-called encounter killings in the 1990s (Hansen 2001b, 216–26; Eckert 2005), to the elimination of "ghostly criminal types" in Jakarta in the 1980s (Siegel 1998), to the cleaning-up activities (*limpieza*) by paramilitaries in Colombia (Taussig 2003), or the war on youth gangs in Los Angeles (Davis 1990, 265–320).

51. For such logics in Brazil, see Caldeira (2000, 105–210), in Britain (Garland 2001), but also in societies like China (Dutton 1992, 323–46; 1998, 112–60) and India (Eckert 2002).

52. *Post*, August 25, 2000.

53. See *Post*, March 22, 2000, and *Post*, March 4, 2000. In July 2000, the entire police station was overhauled and new management was installed. Complaints were reduced, but the structural deficiencies—lack of staff, low morale, lack of vehicles and equipment, corrupt practices on the beat, and so on—remained. See also Hansen 2006a.

54. For an overview of the role of vigilante groups in South Africa's recent history, see Jensen and Buur 2004. For a more synthetic analysis of vigilantism as such, see Abrahams 1998.

55. The critical reassessment of the Community Policing Forums as nonrepresentative, and the broader attempt to professionalize security services, was affirmed in a report entitled *Not Everybody's Business* (Pelser et al. 2002).

56. The use of private security firms paid for by property owners has a long history in white neighborhoods. The industry was largely unregulated and unaccountable until an act of 1987 brought it under a measure of governmental oversight (Cawthra 1993, 69–70).

57. John Comaroff and Jean Comaroff, "Criminal Obsessions after Foucault: Postcoloniality, Policing and the Metaphysics of Disorder," *Critical Inquiry* 30 (Summer 2004): 800–824.

58. In a letter to the local newspaper, a resident in Unit 2 complained, "The security companies do not deal with crimes being committed by residents of the area. Their focus is only on preventing outsiders from stealing cars and breaking into houses . . . the government should sort out this mess" (*Post*, March 16, 2002).

Chapter 2: Domesticity and Cultural Intimacy

1. *Post*, June 30, 1999.

2. The classic study of this problem and the answers sought in nationalism and religious purification is John Kelly's study of the politics of religious mobilization among ex-indentured Indians in Fiji (1991).

3. This culminated in the Indian Marriages Act of 1907, which made it mandatory to register marriages in Natal and South Africa. This new legislation created legibility and also encouraged "proper" marriages within religious communities and status groups. See Desai and Vahed 2007, 190–213, and Meer 1980.

4. For a comprehensive overview of debates and reforms pertaining to women's status in India since the nineteenth century, see Sarkar and Sarkar (eds.) 2008.

5. Desai and Vahed 2007, 211.

6. This reflected a much wider trend in contemporary social analysis in South Africa. Among Africans, the generational rupture and anomaly was assumed to be greatly accentuated by the transition from rural tradition to an urban modernity that was assumed to be fundamentally alien to the African. For Johannesburg, see Glaser 2000; for East London, see Bank 2011, 37–59.

7. The modern nuclear family only became a widespread reality in the early twentieth century in Europe and North America and was based on a long and gradual normalization of what essentially was a middle-class ideal in late nineteenth-century Britain, France, and Germany. This was an ideal of the proper and disciplined family life as the bedrock of the modern social order as such, which was explicitly posed against aristocratic depravity and working-class excess. See Mary Jo Maynes 2002, Kertzer and Barbagli 2002, and for an explicitly Foucauldian perspective on the invention of the modern family, see Donzelot 1997. For an incisive analysis of the "dialectic of domesticity," the simultaneous reform of bodies and souls on the colonial frontier, and in Europe's working-class tenements, see Comaroff and Comaroff 1997, 310–22.

8. Ramphal reports that by the early 1970s, more than 80 percent of Indian couples claimed to have chosen their own marriage partner (1989, 86).

9. *Fiat Lux*, February 1974, 18. There are clear parallels between these efforts at creating modern families with adequate emotional economies of individuality and unambiguous patterns of attachments and love, and similar efforts at creating modern families in the mining towns in the Copperbelt in the same decades. See Ferguson 1999, 166–206. The emphasis on creating new domestic arrangements was important to the colonial enterprise in many parts of Africa. For the intimate nexus between Christianity and new domestic orders, see Comaroff and Comaroff 1992, 265–95 and 1997, 274–322; for the Congo, see Hunt 1990; and for Zambia, see Tranberg-Hansen 1989. I will return to the link between domesticity and Christianity in more detail in chapter 8 of this book.

10. These are readily available in the thesis section of the library at the University of Durban-Westville and read as surprisingly consistent, if somewhat narrow, sociological diagnoses of Indian township life.

11. *Fiat Lux*, September 1975, 23. The idea that the transition to modern families produces immoral behavior stands in striking contrast to the studies of urbanizing Africans and the large number of "urban matriarchs" and female-headed households in African locations and townships (Hunter 1936; Pauw 1973). In the 1960s and 1970s, the modern township house was seen as an essential instrument in creating stable nuclear domesticity that was centered on the male breadwinner among urban Africans (Bank 2011, 163–81).

12. In this age-group Meer reports 57.6 suicides per 100,000 while the corresponding figures for coloreds was 33.3, 13.3 for Africans, and only 2.9 for whites; Fatima Meer, *Race and Suicide in South Africa* (London: Routledge and Kegan Paul, 1976).

13. Similar considerations applied to the making of the colonial bungalow in India. Here it was less reform of the native dwelling that detained the colonizers than it was methods to keep an overwhelming and largely opaque native world of peculiar cunning out of European lives. Many of the worries centered on how to maintain separation between domestic servants and European women and children. See Glover 2008, 159–83. For the classical exploration of colonial domesticity, see Stoler 2002.

14. For instance, Bourdieu's classical text on the Kabyle house (1990), or the many writings inspired by Lévi-Strauss's ideas of "house societies" (e.g., Carsten and Hugh-Jones 1995).

15. This was admittedly always more true of larger and more affluent households than in poor working-class milieus. See Bahloul's beautiful study of such dynamics of memory in colonial Algeria (1992).

16. The immediate example that springs to mind is the deep interventions into ownership, gender roles, and family life in Chinese villages during the Great Leap Forward and the Cultural Revolution, as explored in incisive detail by Mueggler (2001). Despite drastic measures and subversions of older structures of patriarchal control, the ancestral houses, their memories, and most of their physical layouts and functions remained intact (ibid., 51–95 and 250–84).

17. "First and foremost the Bechuana were portrayed as people governed by the primal sovereignty of their custom (*mekgwa*) . . . by their very nature they followed their tradition with little question . . . the primal force that bound these people together was inherently and self-evidently conservative, communal and anti-modern" (Comaroff and Comaroff 1997, 389–90).

18. On Fiji, see Brennan and Lal 1998; Lal 1983 and 2004. On Trinidad, see Khan 2004; Mishra 2007; and Mohapatra 1995.

19. Desai and Vahed 2007, 167–90.

20. "Eastern Languages in the School Curriculum," *Fiat Lux*, September 1979, 16–17.

21. In colloquial South African Indian English "suleman fella" means Muslim, "porridge fella" means Tamil, and "bushman fella" means a Cape colored.

22. The self-therapeutic use of this form of humor was brought home to me a few months earlier in 1999 when Ali and Khan, in one of their occasional engagements with serious productions, staged the twenty-year-old American play *The Indian Wants the Bronx*. Here Essop Khan played a gentleman from India who only speaks Hindi and lands up in a deserted street at night in the Bronx in New York, where he is humiliated and beaten by two young white toughs. The humiliation is relentless and almost unbearably credible. The reactions from the mainly Indian audience (including many Muslims) ranged from anger ("hey, fight back, man," some shouted to Khan; others left the hall cursing and slammed the door) to shock and disgust ("I should never have taken my wife tonight"; "this is not what I understand as entertainment, it was torture, man"), while others laughed nervously.

23. One set of explanations attribute it to the mixture of Afrikaans slang and English, which is prevalent in white, colored, and Indian working-class milieus. One explanation is the amalgamation of English burnt (*char*) man (*ou*), or a compounding of tea (*chai* in Hindi) and man (*ou*). Another possible etymology originates in the North Indian term "*achar*," which is the condiment of pickles that accompany a meal. *Char-ou* would then refer to men who are "small," "on the side," "aides," and so on. Another possible origin is the Hindi word *charra*, which means small or "small shot" and can also refer to ganja or weed. Phonetically the term "charou" also refers to the Hindi word *charu* (hard/stubborn/courageous), but these connotations are rarely used.

24. The term is used widely across working-class cultures in South Africa, often spelled *laanie* in Afrikaans (meaning "fancy"), or *larney* in English. Some claim that it may derive from the French *l'ornee* (fancy/ornate), others that it has a popular root in old Indian Ocean Swahili where *laanie* means "to condemn." In South African Indian English, the term first appears in writing in Ronnie Govender's canonical play *Lahnee's Pleasure* from 1972 (see chapter 3).

25. I am indebted to Steffen Jensen's description of how *gam* (disorder and criminality) and the figure of the gang member and criminal, the *skollie*, functions within the colored communities on the Cape Flats in Cape Town (2008, 54–57; 70–99).

26. This robbery and its aftermath have recently been the object of a racy and fast-paced crime novel, *31 Million Reasons* (2007), by Naresh Veeran, the former station manager of Radio Lotus and a Chatsworth boy. Veeran captures the style and the local tongue with great precision.

27. There were exceptions, such as a number of Indian families in Durban who bore the name Hansen. I realized that the families had been converted three generations ago by a Norwegian pastor named Hansen who had encouraged them to adopt his very unexceptional Scandinavian surname!

28. See Warner 2002, 66–77. In his attempt to widen the scope of how one can think of publics, Warner is very attentive to sexual difference but conspicuously inattentive to dynamics of power, race, plural language practices, and the political economy of media. This makes his reflections on "publics" strangely ineffective outside a rather small world of producers and consumers of art and culture in Euro-America.

29. A series of portraits of community leaders was broadcast in the 1990s on the weekly South African Broadcasting Corporation TV slot for Indian culture, *Eastern Mosaic*, which reiterated a standard heroic rags-to-riches style that completely obliterates deep and enduring class divisions. The controversial writer and public intellectual Ashwin Desai is a notable exception. He has consistently reminded the Indian public in South Africa of the deep and constitutive class divisions running through "the community," the reality of widespread collaboration with the apartheid regime, and so on. See Desai 1996, 1999, and 2000.

30. A similar dynamic is at work regarding the popular radio drama on the isiZulu station UkhoziFM, which is described by Liz Gunner. Here the fictional form of the drama allows controversial problems to be discussed in general terms that protect individuals and families from direct implication (2000).

31. For recent collections of short stories by colored writers, see, for instance, *Keerpunt: Stories vir'n nuwe Suid-Afrika*, ed. Jakes Gerwel and Linda Rode (1998).

32. In 2006, a local businessman launched a website for the township called www.chatsworthlive.co.za. This soon became a hugely popular site for the exchange of information and advertising. The largest section by far is the one where jokes are posted; followed by a section where cars are sold and discussed; followed by "letters," which are mostly complaints about lack of government services and declining civility, greed, and crime.

33. This absurd and bittersweet element of contemporary South African humor is very starkly expressed in the so-called *Bitterkomix*, comic strips produced by young Afrikaners in an attempt to process the many absurdities and painful truths about the Afrikaner community in an excessive and at times grotesque style of both drawing and dialogue. See Barnard 2004.

34. A more recent addition is the Charou Chick's Blog (http://charouchick. wordpress.com/), a blog concerned with current affairs as well as more local and Chatsworth-centered discussions of identity, consumption, and South Africa's future.

Chapter 3: Charous and Ravans: A Story of Mutual Nonrecognition

1. This term, as well as more general colonial classifications of Indians as higher on the scale of civilization, did undoubtedly circulate along the pathways of indenture. In her book on identity and religion among Indo-Trinidadians, Aisha Khan also finds that the descendants of African slaves were indeed termed as "Rawan" by the indentured Indians arriving in the mid-nineteenth century. She finds that the historiographical record of Trinidad speaks to evidence that Indians felt racially and culturally superior and generally apprehensive, if not contemptuous, of Africans, who they saw as "hopelessly polluted," according to Brereton 1979. See Khan 2004, 57–59.

2. Desai and Vahed 2007, 167–90.

3. Quoted from ibid., 178.

4. I owe this insight to Dilip Menon.

5. The literature on colonial Natal, the Zulu kingdom and military history, and the colonial fascination with Zulu culture is vast and varied. Recent well-informed and critical studies are Guy 1994, 2002, and 2007, and Hamilton 1998. For a critical assessment of Zulu culture in contemporary politics, see Mare 1992.

6. For an interesting exploration of Dube's career and relationship with Washington, see Marks 1975.

7. For an overview of some aspects of Gandhi's career in South Africa, see Brown and Prozesky 1996. For a critical account, see James D. Hunt 2005, who is referenced on ANC's official website.

8. My source for the James D. Hunt quotations concerning Gandhi was from a link on the ANC's website (http://www.anc.org.za) that has since been discontinued.

9. I thank Isabel Hofmeyr and Dilip Menon for pointing this out to me.

10. The incipient collaboration between ANC and Indian political organizations, the Natal Indian Congress (NIC) and the Transvaal Indian Congress (TIC), both initiated by Gandhi, was formalized in the so-called Doctors' Pact on March 9, 1947. The three leaders of these organizations, Dr. A. B. Xuma (ANC), the moderate Dr. G. M. Naicker (NIC), and the charismatic and radical Dr. Y. M. Dadoo (TIC) signed this agreement, which marked the beginning of a series of concerted campaigns of passive resistance against the new and strict racial laws that were being implemented at the time. This also marked a decisive moment where the unity of "non-European people" was strongly invoked, and where Gandhian political tactics of nonviolence were recalibrated within a generalized anticolonial horizon, which was energized by the impending Indian independence later in the same year.

11. In his careful analysis of Zulu political and intellectual discourse at the time, Soske notes that after Gandhi's assassination, the initial enthusiasm for the power of independent India changed into fears of Indian expansionism in Africa with the local Indians as its agents (2009, 113–15).

12. Soske shows that the illustrious ANC leader A.W.G. Champion claimed to have had a hand in organizing the rioters (ibid., 117).

13. *Sunday Tribune,* January 16, 1949.

14. *Daily News*, January 16, 1949.

15. *Daily News*, January 17, 1949.

16. *Daily News*, January 18, 1949.

17. *Sunday Tribune*, January 19, 1949.

18. *Sunday Post*, January 16, 1949.

19. *Daily News*, January 18, 1949.

20. Debates of the House of Assembly, Union of South Africa, 1950, col. 7442 (quoted from Kirk 1983, 134).

21. A month after the riots, the *Highway Mail* reported, "Natives Avoid Indian Shops" and suggested that the immediate beneficiaries were the European dealers in the city center (February 18, 1949).

22. The beer halls had been a long-standing bone of contention between small traders, "shebeen queens," and the authorities since the 1920s. The systematic attempt to encourage and institutionalize chiefly power and Zulu tradition during the same period only added to the apprehensions among white authorities and the Zulu elite alike vis-à-vis the alleged runaway modernity among the urban Zulu population (Marks 1995, 91–117).

23. It is characteristic of the sharp bifurcation of memories that there are no clear figures regarding the relative number of Africans and Indians removed. Indians often claim that all the inhabitants were Indians, and African leaders never mention the presence of Indians. It seems clear though that the large majority of residents by 1960 had been Africans who were occupying thousands of shacks, while most of the regular houses were occupied by Indians. More than a decade later, the well-known Durban intellectual and activist Fatima Meer gave very precise figures of what had been lost in Cato Manor: "more than 10,000 acres of land, 3,300 homes, 16 temples, churches and mosques, 11 schools, 15 factories and 115 businesses, all built and nurtured by the people." African presence or ownership figured in none of these lists of losses. She added

that home ownership among Indians had declined from 60 percent in 1960 to less than 10 percent a decade later. In the new township of Chatsworth, "The poor Indians were deprived of leadership and hurled into a relatively homogenous ghetto" (*Graphic*, April 10, 1970).

24. Iain Edwards, "Cato Manor, June 1959: Men, Women, Crowds, Violence, Politics and History," in *The People's City: African Life in Twentieth Century Durban*, ed. Iain Edwards and Paul Maylam, 102–43. Pietermaritzburg: University of Natal Press, 1996.

25. http://www.mantramedia.us/sites/cmt/history.

26. Many former residents dismissed the plans for rehousing as pure propaganda "designed to win over the Indian opinion" (*The Leader*, February 23, 1979).

27. Govender in *The Leader*, October 31, 1980.

28. The structure of externalization of violent events and riots, and the attribution of agency to anonymous outsiders, which had become akin to natural forces, not only avoids the personal narrative, it also creates a new community of shared victimization, however illusory. For an incisive analysis of this phenomenon in the case of riots in Mumbai in 1992, see Mehta and Chatterji 2001.

29. The Indian *Daily Graphic* reported in sarcastic terms that Buthelezi had been giving "advice" to Indian "brothers" by saying, "While I personally condemn Amin in the strongest terms, I would like my Indian brothers not to lose their balance" (October 6, 1972). In 1977 a major public row, followed by demonstrations and protests, ensued when Buthelezi, in a public address at University of Durban-Westville, accused Gandhi of being a "sellout" to the British colonial authorities (*The Leader*, September 30, 1977).

30. *The Leader*, August 16, 1985.

31. Ibid. The Indian vigilante groups in Phoenix are also discussed in Nicholas Haysom's review of right-wing vigilante groups that operated throughout the country with the open or tacit encouragement of the state during the last phase of apartheid (1986).

32. This version of events is supported by the documentary evidence collected by Fatima Meer immediately after the events (1985). Hughes dismisses this evidence as too partisan and looks at it "as a source book rather than a sustained analysis" (1987, 332).

33. In his seminal essay "Racism as Universalism," Étienne Balibar demonstrates that far from being an excessive aberration, race thinking is rather like its cousin nationalism, which is built on a whole formation of universalist thought and a universalist anthropology (1994).

34. This is akin to David Schneider's seminal distinction between a rhetoric of "blood" (nature) and notions of "conduct" (the order of the law) pertaining to kinship (1968).

35. Most migrants to South Africa encounter this fact in rather stark terms also today: the mere fact of being a so-called mixed race does not give one access to being "colored," which is a specific South African way of speaking, being, and acting in the world. Similarly, migrants from Africa and India soon realize that local categories of race are all indeed local and carry cultural meanings—and never just based on physical traits alone. Let us not forget that

whiteness itself in South Africa was always the most uncertain category. Jews officially became white in the 1920s; Greeks and Portuguese only in the 1960s. We still await studies of the performative economy of South African whiteness, which is partially relieved of the burden of "never to appear frightened in front of the natives" and partially relieved of the fear of "always being laughed at," as Orwell so wonderfully depicts the conundrum of colonial whiteness (1953).

36. For a discussion on the meaning of skin color in the context of matrimony in India, see Vaid 2009.

37. There is a vast amount of literature on both caste and the status of tribal outsiders in India (Skaria 2001, Guha 1999, Fuller 1996, and Dumont 1981). The question of race and racial classification has been explored in the history of colonial rule in India (see Robb 1995), while the tension between physical appearance and bodily disposition and essence has been little explored by scholars. Cinema and popular culture in the subcontinent abounds with stories of desire and prohibition across boundaries of caste, religion, and color.

38. Helene Basu 2001 and John McLeod and Kenneth Robbins 2006.

39. Aisha Khan has pointed out that color and race constitute two separate scales in Trinidad: one set of evaluation of skin tone among Creoles and another among people of South Asian origin. As in South Africa, the two scales are separated by categorical/racial difference (2009).

40. In an article entitled "Woman Tells of Ordeals of Mixed Marriage," an Indian woman narrates the difficulties she and her British partner experienced in South Africa among Indians and whites, and also in neighboring countries (*The Leader*, October 12, 1984).

41. This is based on everyday lore and everyday chat, whereby the inherent lack of morality that is generally attached to colored bodies is turned into an erotic attraction when tamed and made respectable by the strict adherence to Muslim performative codes among many Cape Malays.

42. Letter to the editor, *The Leader*, January 23, 1970.

43. Letter to the editor, *The Leader*, January 30, 1970.

44. The report by Fatima Meer and Zubeida Seedat was summarized in *The Leader* on February 27, 1970, and two years after Seedat produced a thorough study of the Zanzibaris and their history (1973). In her classical ethnography of South African Indians, Hilda Kuper notes that one of the arguments against the integration of Zanzibaris into the Indian community in the 1950s was the belief that Zanzibaris practiced "black magic" and thus were dangerous and also impure Muslims (1960, 29).

45. *The Leader*, January 21, 1996, reported that there had been several violent clashes between gangs of Indian and African pupils in the township of Phoenix. Ramon Singh of the Department of Education caused much anger among Indian parents by blaming the problems on racial prejudice among Indian teachers and students.

46. *Tribune Herald*, May 30, 1999.

47. *Daily News*, April 22, 1999.

48. *Post*, May 19, 1999.

49. *Sunday Times,* July 7, 2007. This incident had several antecedents in Durban in earlier decades where colored girls had entered and won Indian beauty pageants. In one case in 1971, the committee complained that not enough Indian girls had entered and that it was happy to accommodate four colored girls. A violent row erupted, and the argument was not the beauty of the girls or their ability to wear saris but the simple fact that they were not racially Indian (*Graphic*, April 30, 1971).

50. *Post,* October 8, 1997.

51. *Post,* March 25, 1998.

52. There was extensive reporting of this in *The Leader* on March 27, 1998.

53. A high-ranking ANC member, Dumisane Makhaye, intervened in the debate and asserted that "Indians were not just victims of apartheid. The majority of them also rose in struggle together with their African and Coloured brothers and sisters." Makhaye then enumerated Indian participation in many activities and reiterated that this fully redeems the Indians as a community (*The Leader*, March 29, 1998).

54. See *The Leader*, April 6, 1999.

55. Respondents were all asked to select and rank ninety-six defined stereotypes, from the most positive (e.g., sophisticated, honest) to the most negative (e.g., money-grabbing, dirty) with respect to their own and other racially defined groups. These were then tabulated and turned into an index of *social afstand* (social distance) ranging from 1 (would like them to be part of my immediate and family circle) to 6 (to ban them from my country).

56. *Daily News,* May 29, 2002. As Mbongeni Ngema fought a court case against the ban on his song, he was backed up by hundreds of singing and toyi-toying supporters outside the Durban High Court. Ngema asserted that his song was merely a "comment on Indian exploitation of black people."

CHAPTER 4: AUTONOMY, FREEDOM, AND POLITICAL SPEECH

1. For a clear-eyed and critical analysis of the political scene in Natal in the late 1950s, see Soske 2009, 195–262.

2. The labor movement in Durban has been explored by many scholars. The Indian side of it is summarized very ably by Bill Freund (1995). Also see the interesting work in Raman 2003.

3. *Fiat Lux*, May 1966, 24.

4. *Fiat Lux*, November 1976.

5. See Wedeen 1999 for a compelling analysis of "as if" politics in contemporary Syria.

6. *Fiat Lux*, May 1966, 12–13.

7. Essop Jassat, quoted from Pachai and Bhana (eds.) 1984, 281.

8. H. E. Joosub, "The Future of the Indian Community," in *South African Dialogue*, ed. N. Rhoodie (Johannesburg: McGraw-Hill, 1972), 424–25. The most detailed analysis and documentation of the workings and stages of the SAIC is to be found in Desai 1987.

9. In one of the constituencies in Johannesburg, only two votes were cast in total (Desai 1987, 185).

10. *Fiat Lux*, May 1966, 26.

11. I draw here on a set of handwritten compilations I obtained in the archive of the Durban City Council. The compilations were prepared by the town clerk's office in 1988 in connection with long-standing deliberations regarding an overhaul of the system. The city council was worried about the lack of political legitimacy of the system.

12. The proposal and its implications are described and summarized in a memo from the town clerk to the city council in 1979 (Town Clerk's Memorandum for Council-in-Committee, February 22, 1979, 10–23), appendix to council minutes, March 6, 1979 (Durban City Council [document 17/1/1/1]).

13. Ibid., 13.

14. See the lectures on "Discourse and Truth: The Problematization of Parrhesia," which Foucault gave at Berkeley in October-November 1983. Posted at http://foucault.info/documents/parrhesia.

15. Letter to Rajbansi from the provincial secretary, September 14, 1977 (Natalia, document 13/12/2/15).

16. Report and Recommendations of Natal Local Government Committee, Durban, February 5, 1979. Signed by ten members drawn from the Durban City Council (3), the SAIC (3), the Coloured Regional Council (1), the Indian and Coloured LACs (3), and the regional government (1).

17. Town Clerk's Memorandum for Council-in-Committee, February 22, 1979, 11–13, appendix to council minutes, March 6, 1979 (Durban City Council [document 17/1/1/1]).

18. Town Clerk's Memorandum, ibid., 14.

19. Interview, Unit 11, Chatsworth, April 1999.

20. *PWC News: A Newsletter for the Phoenix Working Committee*, December 1987. This was echoed by the Rainham Civic Association of Phoenix, which stated that it had "no confidence in the LAC system." Letter to the Town Clerk, January 11, 1988 (Durban City Council [document 17/1/1/1]).

21. "Position Statement on member's participation in LAC's and other state created institutions," Durban Indian Child and Family Welfare Society, August 10, 1989.

22. "The Night the Head Let His Hair Down," *Sunday Tribune Herald*, February 5, 1988.

23. Constitutional Proposals and Memoranda submitted to the Minister of Constitutional Development and Planning, January 13, 1987 (Town Clerk's Department, Durban) (document 17/1/1/1–vol. 14, 2–78).

24. Maharaj is a high-profile Indian member of the ANC who was imprisoned with Mandela on Robben Island, and a member of the first cabinet.

25. The town clerk developed a key for the calculation of Indian and colored sets on the council based on their relative share of the total valuation of property in the city. By this calculation, Indians would obtain the right to 1.7 seats in the all-important Management Committee of the City Council and 7 seats on the council, while colored would be granted 0.1 and 0.6 seats, respectively.

Department of Development Planning, Constitutional Development Services, "Delegation of Powers to Coloured and Indian Management and Local Affairs Committees by Local Authorities," Notice 317 of 1988, Pretoria (printed in *Local Affairs Circular*, no. 50, May 18, 1988).

26. Among them even Mr. Rajbansi, who represented the Indian community and his new political outfit, the Minority Front.

27. The new structure of governance and representation was explained in great detail in *Fiat Lux* and in local newspapers throughout 1984 and 1985, especially March 1984, August 1984, and June/July 1985. A fuller account of the prehistory of this construction is to be found in Desai 1987. A critical analysis of the workings and performance of the House of Delegates can be found in Desai 1996.

28. The standard idea at the time was that there were eleven nations in the country: nine black nations (Zulu, Xhosa, Tswana, Venda, Pedi, Sotho, Swazi, Tsonga, and Khoisan), whites, coloreds, and Indians (see, e.g., the article by P. J. Koornhof, Minister of Cooperation and Development, *Fiat Lux*, April 1980).

29. P. W. Botha's speech to the Indian community, quoted in full in *Fiat Lux*, December/January 1983/84, 12–14.

30. N. J. Rhoodie, C. de Kock, and M. Couper, *Indian Perceptions of the First Election for the House of Delegates: Findings of a Sample Survey Undertaken in June 1985* (Pretoria: Human Sciences Research Council, 1985).

31. Ibid., 13.

32. The surveys were conducted in 1980 and 1981, and the findings are summarized in Desai 1987, 242.

33. For a good analysis of the more spectacular elements of apartheid's state performances, see Witz 2003.

34. The heading for this section is a line from the play *The Death of an Anarchist* (Dario Fo 1970).

35. The speech—and the furor it caused—was reported approvingly in the liberal Cape Town paper the *Argus*, and in the conservative Durban newspaper, the *Natal Mercury*, April 29 and 30, 1986.

36. This shows, as Desai points out, that the apartheid state was rather far removed from the rational machine that optimizing capital accumulation conjured up in Marxist state theory in the 1970s and after (1987). The liberal critique of apartheid, which was represented by people like Alan Paton's Liberal Party, Helen Suzman's Progressive Party, and many other voices, was essentially that the state was ineffective in utilizing the human potential in the country and neglectful of the human spirit and enterprise found among other race groups. Today this stance is represented by the Democratic Party. For an account of Indian economic history in South Africa, see Hart and Padayachee (2000).

37. Some years ago, I visited a large and spacious house in a formerly white suburb. The owner, an Indian businessman, told me that J. N. Reddy had this house built in the late 1970s and that he had bought it from Reddy's family in the early 1990s. Reddy had lived there for many years amid white affluent neighbors. When I asked the owner how that could happen, he smiled and said, "You have to understand that the rules never really applied to anyone with enough money . . . the whites here in Durban always operated like that."

38. See Hart and Padayachee 2000, 693–94. Many Indian businessmen were also encouraged to invest in the new "border industries" that were set up along the borders of the Bantustans in an effort to recruit cheap and docile—mainly female—labor and thus avoid dependence on the more organized and recalcitrant labor force of the Indian townships.

39. Report of the Commission of Inquiry into the Allegations Concerning Any Member in the Ministers Council of the House of Delegates, Judge Neville James, Durban, January 25, 1989, 4–6.

40. *Daily News*, August 23, 1989.

41. I owe this point to participants at a seminar at the Department of English at the University of Natal, Pietermaritzburg in 2000, who drew my attention to the significance of Uys's work for satire in South Africa as such, and to the danger of interpreting Indian theater only within its own canonical tradition or an exclusively Indian frame.

42. *Daily News*, March 12, 1989.

43. *Daily News*, March 23, 1989.

44. I develop this point in some detail in Hansen 2000.

45. *Mercury*, March 30, 1989.

46. Interview in Durban, June 29, 1999.

47. The proposal was published in *The Leader*, a newspaper historically close to the older style of progressive politics, under the heading "NIC Plan for a New South Africa," *The Leader*, October 26, 1979.

48. The question of the NIC's role intensely occupied many young progressives and academics. The period saw a flurry of publications and pamphlets that discussed the issue of the "correct" line of the NIC.

49. See reports and interviews with Farouk Meer of the NIC and ANC's Ebrahim Ebrahim in the *Post*, October 2–5, 1991.

50. Interview in the *Post*, August 1–5, 1984.

51. *The Leader*, September 8, 1989.

52. *Post*, March 15–17, 1990.

53. Interview with Roy Padayachee, *The Leader,* April 10, 1991.

54. *Post*, June 17–20, 1992.

55. The resentment against Indians among ANC members was strong after 1994. After the Municipal Elections in 2000, where ANC once again did badly in Indian areas, S'bu Ndebele, the ANC premier in the province, stated that municipal services should be calibrated according to which districts supported the ANC (see the *Post,* December 13–16, 2000).

56. *Mobilising in the Indian Sector*, discussion paper, ANC, Chatsworth, March 1999.

57. Ibid., 3.

58. *The Leader*, June 19, 1996.

59. *Post*, November 4–7, 1998.

60. These living conditions and the disgruntlement they produced had been addressed for some time in the press. See, for example, *The Leader*, June 28, 1996, and the evocative piece entitled "Anguish, Despair . . . and Darkness," on the plight of flat dwellers at the edge of the township who were living without electricity. *Post*, September 1–4, 1999.

61. http://www.mf.org.za/site/MF/Leader.

62. I owe this insight to my dear friend, the late Dr. Anjan Ghosh of the Center for the Study in Social Sciences, Calcutta.

63. *Daily News*, October 16, 1982.

64. The (white) reviewer from the *Daily News* found that "if you know the personalities involved, if you are a regular reader of . . . [Indian] newspapers and if you are of a particular political persuasion, it can be very funny indeed . . . However, it is an ephemeral work, pertinent only to its time, unlikely to have much relevance" (*Daily News*, August 17, 1984).

65. Interview, Greyville, Durban, October 19, 1998.

66. Interview, Chatsworth, December 12, 1998.

CHAPTER 5: MOVEMENT, SOUND, AND BODY IN THE POSTAPARTHEID CITY

1. The 1957 Alexandra bus boycott was launched as a protest against fare hikes. It lasted from January to June 1957, during which tens of thousands of residents of Alexandra quietly walked back and forth between the township and central Johannesburg each day. The boycott was coordinated by the ANC and is widely regarded as one of the most successful mass campaigns against apartheid's reordering of urban life. The campaign did most probably take inspiration from the famous Montgomery bus boycott of 1955 in Alabama, which was one of the landmarks of the civil rights struggle.

2. The commuter train was the scene of a violent crime in the widely acclaimed South African movie *Tsotsi* (Gavin Hood, 2005).

3. The townships and informal settlements constitute almost 80 percent of the total market for public transport. The car ownership remains very low in African townships, while almost half of Indian townships own or have access to a private vehicle. See estimates and projections from the Ministry of Transport, based on 1995 figures at http://www.gtkp.com/assets/uploads/20091129-160020-1344-Urban%20NMT%20South%20Africa.pdf.

4. Baudrillard's writings on America espouse a similar binary relationship between "life" and mechanized movement, albeit reversely. In deep America, life only appears to exist insofar as one moves through space. In and of itself, outside the car, there is neither autonomous social life nor beauty or excitement, only "deserts forever" (Baudrillard 1989, 121).

5. See, for instance, John Urry 2004 and Bull 2004 for relatively dystopian approaches to the atomizing impact of car cultures.

6. This project is sponsored by the Ayn Rand–inspired organization the Objectivism Center, or the Atlas Society, undoubtedly generously supported by automobile industry-related foundations. See http://www.objectivistcenter.org.

7. The primary sign of the tsotsi or the *amagents* (gangsters) was historically flashy cars, as represented, for instance, in the film *Mapantsula* (Oliver Schmitz 1988) on crooks and gangsters in Johannesburg in the 1950s and 1960s. Car theft is probably one of the most important sources of income in the realm of organized crime, and the successful gangster and drug dealer remains known by his flashy car. Underworld lore has it that expensive BMWs are burned on top of the graves of famous gangsters.

8. It is indicative that one of the first (and only) clips to emerge on YouTube under "Chatsworth, Durban" is a small film describing dangerous drag racing in Durban's streets by young Indian men. The clip is from a short series of portraits of youth subcultures in South Africa, probably produced by people related to the team behind the SABC1 series Mzansi (the South).

9. This is how Shaun, a young man of Tamil background, described the popular topic of how "Gujus" keep their cars: "When Mohammad turns eighteen, a BMW suddenly appears in his driveway. It grows bigger the older he gets and one day, when he takes over his father's shop, it suddenly becomes a silver Mercedes. How else can he get to the mosque without being made the laughingstock?" Here, Shaun referred to the often conspicuous collection of silver Mercedes outside Durban's mosques on Fridays.

10. For a fuller history of the emergence of the African-owned taxi industry, see Khosa 1992.

11. A report on the taxi industry in the province of KwaZulu-Natal reported that almost twenty thousand taxis were organized in 287 registered associations. The report estimated that there were at least thirteen thousand illegal taxis in operation in the province (Profile KwaZulu-Natal 2001).

12. The racial and ethnic segmentation of the taxi industry, and ensuing turf wars that mix commercial and ethnic motifs, are well known from other parts of the world. Parts of the tension between Pathans and other ethnic groups in Karachi were configured around alleged harassment by and in taxis (see Tambiah 1996, 163–210). The taxi industry in many large American and European cities are similarly segmented along lines of ethnicity, which occasionally gives rise to tensions.

13. The *isicathamiya* tradition, the male a cappella singing that was made world-famous when the group Ladysmith Black Mambazo appeared on Paul Simon's famous album *Graceland* (1986), dates back to the early twentieth-century mining hostels in Johannesburg and Durban. The tradition, style of singing, and lyrics are decidedly Zulu. The style of singing and the slow dancing that accompanies it (*isicathamiya* means "like a cat") developed as a reaction to the ban on drumming and dancing—both seen as having the potential to excite workers—by the mining authorities. For an outstanding ethnography and analysis of this musical form, see Erlmann 1996. *Maskhandi* is a rhythmic music that is played on European instruments and has a very characteristic guitar sound, as well as lyrics that are sometimes spoken words (*izibongo*) rather than song. It was developed in the 1940s by Zulu musicians who tried "to teach their instruments [to] speak in isiZulu," as one of the eminent performers, Phuze Khemisi, put it in a recent broadcast on South African television (2004).

14. This self-conscious depoliticization of mainstream kwaito and its celebration of black masculinity and "predatory sex" is the cause of much concern among church leaders and social activists. Among liberals, this culture and the everyday violence it entails and condones are sources of great worry and incomprehension. For an informative but also revealing analysis of kwaito and African youth culture along such lines, see Stephens 1999, 256–73. For an exploration of the *amagents* (gangsters), their networks, their time spent hanging out

(*blom*), the ethics of never stealing "at home" (i.e., among other black people), and the "dizziness of deviance," see Segal, Pelo, and Pule 2001.

15. This term may also refer to the phenomena of urban Zulu "Swenkas" in Durban and Johannesburg. Swenkas are extremely well-dressed Zulu men who use their expensive clothes to reverse or ameliorate the marginality and deprivation of migrant labor life in the city. Swenkas "act as the curtain-raiser for Isicathamiya performances by Zulu *a capella* choirs. . . . Dignity, cleanliness and the rejection of criminality are its guiding principles which define the kind of men Swenkas aspire to be" (Isaacs 2010).

16. The distinction between the sonic and the visual in the South African context stands in interesting contrast to Miller's example from Trinidad. Afro-Trinidadian cars are marked by paint and outward decoration, whereas Indo-Trinidadian vehicles excel in elaborate upholstery and interior decoration. Miller interprets this as a reflection of different ideologies of masculinity, performed in the street and within the home, respectively, within the two communities (1994, 2001).

17. Artwork on buses and trucks is, of course, well known across many parts of the world, where they function as oblique and ironic commentaries on everything from traffic rules, the follies of life, and forms of admonishing or boasting, as is also the case with the visually impoverished culture of car streamers in Euro-America. For the famous Pakistani trucks, see Kazi 2002; for trucks in Nigeria, see Pritchett 1979; for decorations of rickshaws in Bangladesh, see Lasnier 2002; for buses in Calcutta, see Chattopadhyay 2009; and for jeeps/kombis in Manila, see Meñez 1988.

18. Diwali, also known as the festival of lights, is one of the biggest festivals in the Hindu calendar and is celebrated by Hindus across the world. It celebrates the return of Lord Ram to Ayodhya after having defeated the demon king Ravana.

19. Peter Wade also demonstrates how rhythmic music and dancing became one of the central features associated with the historically marginalized black culture on the Colombian coast. In Africa, similar connections and strong moral condemnation of dancing and drinking have remained a foundational element in the work of many missions and missionary institutions (Wade 1993, 267–94).

CHAPTER 6: THE UNWIELDY FETISH: DESI FANTASIES, ROOTS TOURISM, AND DIASPORIC DESIRES

1. Desai and Vahed 2007, 399–416.

2. Some major recent works in anthropology and cultural studies are Willford 2006 on Malaysia; Kelly 1991 on Fiji; Khan 2004 and Niranjana 2006 on Trinidad; and Eisenlohr 2007 on Mauritius.

3. See William Pietz's authoritative genealogy of the place of the fetish in the modern imagination (1985, 1987, 1988). See also the contributions in Spyer 1998.

4. The framing and condensation of "Indianness" has for long been labored over by marketing and advertising professionals in India (see Mazzarella 2003).

A recent high-profile example is the global marketing of "Incredible India" as a tourist destination. In her recent book on postcolonial literature, Cooppan mobilizes a similar idea of condensation through Derrida's idea of the nation as *ontopology*; that is, the equation of territory with forms of being (2009, 17).

5. Aisha Khan reports that a very similar phenomenon began in Trinidad in 1983 when travel agencies began advertising *Pukhon ke Desh ki Yatra* (a journey to roots). This became a popular trend and was often cast in strongly religious terms and further legitimized when then prime minister of Trinidad, Basdeo Panday, went to visit his ancestral village in Uttar Pradesh in 1997 (Khan 2004, 127–29). Questions of roots, culture, and loyalty are more controversial in South Africa than in the Caribbean, and most tour operators advertise India in more conventionally exotic and spiritual terms.

6. Today, the actual shipping lists are housed and organized at the South African Indian Archives in Pietermaritzburg. They were originally not freely available to the public, but a research project into Christian Indians (led by Professor Joy Brain) developed into a major heritage effort led by academics at the University of Durban–Westville, the historically Indian university. The project was finalized in 2003. Today the lists of the more than 150,000 people are systematically ordered and collected in 91 volumes, which are available to members of the public who would like to research their ancestors. Experts have tried to update, interpret, and transliterate place-names and personal names to make the information more user-friendly. Websites such as http://www.ancestry24.com give plenty of information and advice on the shipping lists.

7. Upon arrival in Durban every laborer was asked to give his name. Traditionally, many lower-caste people in South India only had one name, a practice that did not satisfy the officials. Many gave the name of their employer or landlord as their second name; hence the preponderance of Naidoos and Pillays in Durban.

8. The theme of the poor and gullible Indian, lured onto the ship and into the hardships of indenture by sweet-talking agents, resonates through many family narratives, not just in South Africa but also in the Caribbean. Aisha Khan calls this the "diaspora of betrayal" (2004, 125).

9. Tejaswini Niranjana reports a very similar development in Trinidad where as many as twelve cinema theaters ran Hindi films in Trinidad's capital city in 1970. The video revolution and a general shift toward American films were also partially reversed in Trinidad by the same films, which addressed an Indian diaspora. Niranjana argues that "the promise of equality on new terms is being extended to subaltern diasporic people who live in the West . . . contemporary Hindi films also hold out this promise, with the west no longer vilified but, instead, becoming the location in which a pure Indian nationalism, unsullied by the irritations of daily life in the Third world, can de practiced" (2006, 181–82).

10. For some of most influential statements on diaspora, see Clifford 1997 and Appadurai 1996.

11. VHP secretary Ashok Singhal generated quite a lot of enthusiasm when he visited Trinidad. For some observers this seemed to confirm the gullibility of the lower-caste "East Indian," Niranjana suggests, while for Indian popula-

tions in the Caribbean and elsewhere, the caste arrogance of the VHP and the violence it has visited on Muslims were largely unknown (2006, 50–52).

12. Such a dynamic relationship between local aspirations toward "dia-sporization," respectability, and "pure" and Sanskritized Hindi on the one hand, and the simultaneous embeddedness of Mauritians in a local creolized culture on the other, is at the heart of Patrick Eisenlohr's excellent study of language and belonging in Mauritius (2007).

13. A host of Tamil organizations had been raising money for the LTTE in South Africa, and many progressive Tamils saw a natural affinity between the LTTE and the ANC as two liberation movements (see *Frontline*, 15, no. 25 [December 5–18]: 1998). Mandela was cautious and maintained good rela-tions with the Sri Lankan government, which prompted Kiru Naidoo to write, "South Africa appears unwilling to accord the liberation movement the support it deserves" (*The Star*, December 14, 1998).

CHAPTER 7: GLOBAL HINDUS AND PURE MUSLIMS: UNIVERSALIST ASPIRATIONS AND TERRITORIALIZED LIVES

1. *Hinduism Today*, January 1986.

2. The Arya Samaj movement was born in the intensely competitive and conflict-ridden climate of the Punjab. The lower-caste and poorer groups were generally seen as more vulnerable to conversion, and much effort was expended on defining ritual and cultural boundaries. See, for instance, Fox 1985 and Ghai 1990. For a standard history of the movement, see Jones 1976 (repr. 1997). For a general argument about the construction of modern religious communities in India, see van der Veer 1994b.

3. N. Vedalankar, *Religious Awakening in South Africa* (Durban: Arya Pratinidhi Sabha, 1950), 15.

4. Eisenlohr reports a similar discrepancy in perceptions of the celebrated ancestral culture in Mauritius. His local informants identify themselves and their neighbors as properly Indian by their use of Bhojpuri, while the general thrust in the public sphere and the organizations promoting Indian ancestral culture takes place in Sanskritized Hindi (2007, 74–109).

5. "Indian Philosophy and Academic Art," *Fiat Lux*, February 1981, 10–11.

6. "Islam in South Africa," *Fiat Lux*, March 1980, 12–15.

7. "Hinduism in the South African Context," *Fiat Lux*, April 1982, 12–13.

8. For an account of the Arya Samaj movement in India, see Jones 1997.

9. Vahed 2001b, 108.

10. For a discussion of the relationship between caste, class, and Kavady in Tamil Nadu, see Kapadia 1996. For an analysis of Kavady and its significance in Malaysia, see Collins 1997.

11. Draupadi, and by extension fire walking, has assumed significance as a representation of female predicaments and female strength and empowerment (see Diesel 1998).

12. There is now a burgeoning literature on the Hindu nationalist movement and its various branches. See Basu et al. 1993, van der Veer 1994, Jaffrelot 1996, Hansen 1999, and Bhatt 2001, to mention a few.

13. Interview with Reggie Kallideen, vice president of Hindu Maha Sabha of South Africa, in Durban, October 23, 1998.

14. Interview with Dr. Hemraj, former president of Hindi Shiksha Sangh, in Chatsworth, November 10, 1998.

15. Interview with Krish Gokool, April 23, 1999, in Durban. Politics of the Indian subcontinent transfer to South Africa in various forms. On January 19, 1993, a bomb destroyed a Hindu temple in Lenasia in Johannesburg, probably in retaliation of the demolition of Babri Masjid in North India on December 6, 1992. Hindu and Muslim organizations unanimously condemned the act (*Post*, January 20–23, 1993).

16. Interview in Durban, October 21, 1998.

17. In practice the government set a limit of proving origins in India up to four generations, while the possibility of mixed parentage so far has not been addressed. Spouses of Indian citizens, regardless of race or nationality, are also routinely granted eligibility.

18. http://www.gopio.net/jcs_speech.htm, p. 2.

19. I began a long stint of fieldwork in Durban a few days after 9/11. Despite close and cordial relationships with many Muslims from earlier fieldwork in 1998–99, contacts and conversations with most Muslim organizations became markedly strained after 9/11 and were marked by suspicion and apprehension.

20. The festival, nicknamed Coolie Christmas, was tolerated but was widely seen as a time of catharsis and excessive smoking of dagga, drinking, and violence. Vahed documents many cases of conflict between processions and instances where the festivities produced a carnivalesque suspension of normal rules of conduct (2001a).

21. For an interesting discussion of the career of Soofie Saheb, see Green 2008.

22. One of the few exceptions to the separation between high- and lower-caste Muslims was the life and career of M. L. Sultan, originally a Hindu and indentured laborer from Tamil Nadu. After being freed of his contract, he had casual jobs in Durban and soon got into real estate and construction, where he proved to be nothing less than a genius. He converted to Islam—presumably to "fit" in with respectable society in Grey Street—and within a decade he emerged as the richest Indian in the country. He later donated his money to charities and founded what was to become Durban's largest and most significant nonwhite educational institution, the M. L. Sultan Technikon.

23. For a detailed examination of the business strategies of Gujarati merchants and multiple and complex ties between Gujarat and colonial Natal, see Vahed 2005.

24. The Tablighi Jamaat was established in India in 1928 and has since grown to become one of the most widespread and powerful global Islamic lay organizations. Emerging from the wider trend of scripturally oriented modernist Islam, its objective is to reform Islam from within, that is, to convert Muslims to a purer and more authentic Islamic practice. Its modus operandi is to use the power of networks and exemplary behavior to produce Muslims who have a strong and interiorized faith and who are capable of living in modern societies. For a brief history of the movement, see Metcalf 1993a; and 1993b on the

everyday ethics of the Tablighi movement; Ahmad 1991 for a comparison with Jamaat-e-Islami. See also the contributions in Masud 2000 for accounts of the history of the movement, its ideological dynamic, and its impact in various parts of the world.

25. See www.memon.com.

26. As demonstrated by Bowen in his seminal study of Islam in Indonesia, Muslims constitute themselves through discourse and performance, expressed most powerfully in congregational prayer, while recognizing what Bowen calls, "the optative view of scriptural prescription: that God, through the Prophet Muhammad, sometimes provided the Islamic community with two or more equally legitimate ways of carrying out a particular religious duty" (1993, 300). Bowen explores disputes between modernists and traditionalists on issues of how to pronounce one's intent to worship (*usalli*, in Arabic). Similar debates on prayer and styles and languages of sermons have recently been explored by Tayob in mosques in both Transvaal and Cape Town (1999). For an overview of the conflicts among Indian Muslims in the 1970s and 1980s, see Vahed 2003.

27. As shown recently by Goolam Vahed (2006), the mosque has been the locus of protracted litigation, rivalry, and dissension from its very inception in 1880.

28. The turn to piety may be nothing but a temporary shelter in times of great uncertainty, Vahed suggests (2000). The use and study of Arabic was already promoted from the 1950s in an attempt to break the parochialism of the Gujarati community (see Jeppie 2007).

29. *The Leader*, October 18, 2001.

30. At the time of writing, I was given access to a few chapters of a biography of Deedat that is being written by Goolam Vahed, University of KwaZulu-Natal. In this forthcoming work, *Sheikh Ahmed Deedat: Muslim Polemicist par excellence*, the more precise details of Deedat's life—already the stuff of popular legend—are recorded and documented. See also Westerlund 2003 and Sadouni 1998.

31. On saints in South Africa, see also Dangor 1995. Sufi practices are vividly described by Ewing 1997.

32. For an early analysis of this in the context of Malawian Muslims in Durban, see Vawda 1994. More recent material suggests that Muslims from different parts of Africa, like other communities, are exposed to the xenophobic tendencies across the country. This severely limits any potential of proselytization. On Senegalese Muslims in Cape Town, see Molins Lliteras 2009; on Somalis in Johannesburg, see Sadouni 2009.

CHAPTER 8: THE SAVED AND THE BACKSLIDERS: THE CHAROU SOUL AND THE INSTABLITY OF BELIEF

1. Desai and Vahed 2007, 249–69.

2. In their survey of Chatsworth in 1980, two sociologists found that the percentage of Christians had doubled between 1951 and 1980 (Oosthuizen and Hofmeyr 1981, 3). Conversions take place predominantly in working-class neighborhoods with 20 percent Christians, whereas the figure was less than 5 percent in the Indian elite area of Reservoir Hills (ibid., 7–8).

3. Rowlands, in his journal, *Moving Waters,* vol. 20, no. 239 (November 1959), 159.

4. G. C. Oosthuizen, *The Meaning of Religious Commitments in an Unstable Society,* unpublished working note, no date, 15–16. See also the detailed studies in Oosthuizen 1975 and Oosthuizen and Hofmeyr 1981. For a view of Pentecostal churches as a potentially progressive force in a multiracial society, see Reddy 1992. Other studies commissioned by the established churches concluded that poverty, ignorance, and lack of education and care by the Indian elite—regardless of faith—have contributed to the situation. See, for instance, Morran and Schlemmer 1984.

5. *Graphic*, September 13, 1974.

6. *The Leader*, September 18, 1987. It is striking that in its decades-long life span as an official publication of the South African Indian Council and the Department of Indian Affairs under apartheid, the magazine *Fiat Lux* never mentions Christianity even once.

7. *Post*, January 24–28, 1979.

8. Comaroff and Comaroff 1997, 218–320.

9. Here there are parallels with Csordas's notion of a "sacred self" that is constituted by a complex of prayer, ritual, and healing among Catholic Charismatics in the United States. Csordas draws creatively on Merleau-Ponty's idea of the self and the body co-constituted by social conventions and practices, but the colonial idea of the absence of—or inability to—have proper selves among people of color never presents itself in his material (1994).

10. The injunction to tithe was very direct and sometimes accompanied by veiled threats of being ostracized. On several occasions, I heard Pastor B liken those who do not tithe to the raven, "that greedy and selfish bird of prey."

11. *The Rising Sun*, March 9–13, 1999.

12. The emphasis on very patriarchal family values in this particular case has to do with the specific history of producing the ideal "Indian family" as a cultural artifact, a phantasmic supplement of social discipline and moral order that needs to be imposed on the actually existing chaotic family arrangements among the township charous. The Pentecostal movement as such has many examples of female empowerment and female pastors, but in Durban these are invariably women who are under the guidance and tutelage of senior men. For a different perspective from Latin America, see Martin 2002, 98–105.

13. A similar logic, if cast in a reverse geographical order of things, seems to be the case in Ghana, where Birgit Meyer found that the strongest and most stubborn spirits were of Indian origin, either transported there through the medium of film or residing in a range of imported objects (1999, 197–98).

14. The larger issue of the efficacy of African medicines entered the public debate in Durban when a minister of health in the provincial government wanted to change her office because she believed it to be bewitched. This occasioned some debate and a slew of vox-pops in the Indian press under the heading "Evil Spirits . . . Facts or Just Pure Hokum?" (*Post*, October 25–28, 2000), and another one a year later, "Do Healers Have the Power to Cure?" (*Post,* November 23–26, 2001). Many of the interviewees would initially deny the existence

of evil spirits and then proceed to narrate incidents that could not be explained, mysterious deaths, and also unexplained healings through prayer or miracles.

15. This point is shown most clearly in the introduction and in several superb essays in Appadurai 1986.

16. In his famous essay on the *Unheimlich*, Freud singles out the fears, dreams, and fantasies of inanimate objects (*Dingen*) coming to life at night or at odd moments (for instance, the Sandman in Hoffmann's tale) as a recurrent structure of the uncanny as radically "unhomely" (2003).

17. See Keane's argument that fetishism essentially is a missionary discourse (2006, 223–54).

POSTSCRIPT: MELANCHOLIA IN THE TIME OF THE "AFRICAN PERSONALITY"

1. The most compelling and complex description of these complexities remains Johnny Steinberg's book *Midlands* (2002).

2. *Guardian*, April 2, 2010.

3. *Mail and Guardian*, April 9, 2010.

4. In a recent analysis of the rape trial against Zuma, Shireen Hassim argues that conservative gender values never were confronted during the struggle years and now return in full force in the African elites and elsewhere (2009). In a highly interesting paper, Hylton White argues that Zuma's popularity is based on his profile as a modern Zulu who embraced his Zulu culture as a personal and individualized choice, not as a deferential gesture toward the entire Zulu tradition represented by Inkatha. In these sentiments among young Zuma supporters, White identifies a "post-Fordist structure of feeling," and in their support for Zuma, a fantasy of direct connection with a powerful central state (2011).

5. These are Pravin Gordhan (Finance), former trade union leader Ebrahim Patel (Economic Affairs), former militant and Robben Island prisoner Ebrahim Ismail Ebrahim (deputy minister of International Relations); Roy Padayachee (Public Services and Administration), Enver Surtee (Basic Education); and Yunus Carrim (Cooperative Governance and Affairs).

6. Schabir Shaik and his brother "Chippy" are two ANC-affiliated activists and businessmen who worked closely with Zuma for years as his financial aides. Schabir Shaik was convicted in 2004 of multi-million-dollar fraud in connection with the ANC government's infamous and controversial arms deal in the 1990s. In 2010–11 the Gupta family, a powerful business clan from India with a strong presence in South Africa, has extended generous hospitality and help to the ANC to a point that has caused public controversy, including strong and racially tinged criticism from Malema. http://www.timeslive.co.za/Politics/article937958.ece/Zuma-faces-ANC-revolt-over-Guptas.

7. See, for instance, Zuma's address to the Indian Christian Community of Phoenix on April 14, 2009.

8. This anniversary was mentioned at length in Zuma's 2010 State of the Nation address: http://www.polity.org.za/article/sa-zuma-state-of-the-nation-address-by-the-south-african-president-parliament-11022010-2010-02-11.

9. I owe this precise formulation to Wendy Brown, who suggested this to me as a way of summing up the transformation of township life in the past decades.

References

Abrahams, Ray. 1998. *Vigilant Citizens: Vigilantism and the State*. Cambridge: Polity Press.

African National Congress (ANC). 1993. *Policing in the New South Africa*. Marshall-town: ANC Department of Information and Publicity.

Agamben, Giorgio. 1998. *Homo Sacer: Sovereign Power and Bare Life*. Stanford, CA: Stanford University Press.

———. 2000. *Means without Ends: Notes on Politics*. Minneapolis: University of Minnesota Press.

Ahmad, Mumtaz. 1991. Islamic Fundamentalisms in South Asia: The Jamaat-I-Islami and Tablighi Jamaat. In *Fundamentalism Observed*, ed. R. Scott Appleby and Martin E. Marty, 457–530. Chicago: University of Chicago Press.

Anderson, Benedict. 1998. *The Specter of Comparisons: Nationalism, South East Asia and the World*. London: Verso.

Anderson, David, ed. 1992. *Policing and Decolonisation: Politics, Nationalism and the Police, 1917-65*. Manchester: Manchester University Press.

Appadurai, Arjun, ed. 1986. *The Social Life of Things: Commodities in Cultural Perspective*. Cambridge: Cambridge University Press.

———. 1996. *Modernity at Large: Cultural Dimensions of Globalization*. Minneapolis: University of Minnesota Press.

Arendt, Hannah. 2000. What Is Freedom? In *The Portable Hannah Arendt*, ed. Peter Baehr, 438–61. London: Penguin Classics.

———. 2005. *The Promise of Politics*. New York: Schocken Books.

Asad, Talal. 1993. *Genealogies of Religion: Discipline and Reasons of Power in Christianity and Islam*. Baltimore: Johns Hopkins University Press.

Ashforth, Adam. 2005. *Witchcraft, Violence, and Democracy in South Africa*. Chicago: University of Chicago Press.

Bahloul, Joelle. 1996. *The Architecture of Memory: A Jewish-Muslim Household in Colonial Algeria, 1937-1962*. Cambridge: Cambridge University Press.

Balibar, Étienne. 1994. Racism as Universalism. In *Masses, Classes and Ideas*, 191–205. London: Blackwell.

Balint, Michael. 1959. *Thrills and Regression*. London: International Universities Press.

Bank, Leslie. 2011. *Home Spaces, Street Styles: Contesting Power and Identity in a South African City*. London: Pluto Press.

Barnard, Rita. Fall 2004. *Bitterkomix*: Notes from the Post-Apartheid Underground. In *After the Thrill Is Gone: A Decade of Post-Apartheid South Africa*. Special issue of *South Atlantic Quarterly* 103 (4): 719–54.

Basu, Helene. 2001. Slave, Soldier, Trader, Fakir: Fragments of African Histories in Gujarat. In *The African Diaspora in the Indian Ocean*, ed. Richard Pankhurst. Trenton, NJ: Red Sea Press.

Basu, Tapan, Pradip Datta, Sumit Sarkar, Tanika Sarkar, and Sambuddha Sen. 1993. *Khaki Shorts and Saffron Flags*. Hyderabad: Orient Longman.

Bataille, Georges. 1992. *Theory of Religion*. New York: Zone Books.

Bates, Crispin, ed. 2000. *Community, Empire and Migration: South Asians in Diaspora*. London: Palgrave.

Baudrillard, Jean. 1989. *America*. London: Verso.

Bell, Catherine. 1993. *Ritual Theory, Ritual Practice*. New York: Oxford University Press.

Benjamin, Walter. 1978. *Reflections: Essays, Aphorisms and Autobiographical Writings*. New York: Schocken Books.

Bennett, Jane. 2001. *The Enchantment of Modern Life: Attachments, Crossings and Ethics*. Princeton: Princeton University Press.

Bergson, Henri. 2007. *Laughter: An Essay on the Meaning of the Comic*. New York: Jungle Books.

Beyers, Christiaan. 2009. Identity and Forced Displacement: Community and Colouredness in District Six. In *Burdened by Race: Coloured Identities in Southern Africa,* ed. Mohamed Adhikari. South Africa: University of Cape Town Press.

Bhana, Surendra. 1991. *Indentured Indian Emigrants to Natal, 1860-1902: A Study Based on Ships' Lists*. New Delhi: Promilla & Co.

———. 1997. *Gandhi's Legacy: The Natal Indian Congress, 1894-1994*. Pietermaritzburg: University of Natal Press.

Bhatt, Chetan. 2001. *Hindu Nationalism: Origins, Ideologies and Modern Myths*. Oxford: Berg.

Billig, Michael. 2001. Humour and Embarrassment: Limits of "Nice-Guy" Theories of Social Life. *Theory, Culture and Society* 18 (5): 23-43.

Bodin, Jean. 1992. *On Sovereignty: Four Chapters from the Six Books on Commonwealth*. Cambridge: Cambridge University Press.

Bonner, Philip, and Noor Nieftagodien. 2008. *Alexandra: A History*. Johannesburg: Wits University Press.

Bourdieu, Pierre. (1970) 1990. The Kabyle House, or The World Reversed. In *The Logic of Practice*. Cambridge: Polity Press.

Bowen, John. 1993. *Muslims through Discourse*. Princeton: Princeton University Press.

Boyarin, Daniel. 1998. What Does a Jew Want? or The Political Meaning of the Phallus. In *The Psychoanalysis of Race*, ed. Christopher Lane, 211-40. New York: Columbia University Press.

Boym, Svetlana. 2001. *The Future of Nostalgia*. New York: Basic Books.

Bozzoli, Belinda. 2004. The Taming of the Illicit: Bounded Rebellion in South Africa, 1986. *Comparative Studies in Society and History* 46 (2): 326-54.

Brain, J. B. 1983. *Christian Indians in Natal*. Cape Town: Oxford University Press.

Brennan, Lance, and Brij Lal. 1998. Across the Kala Pani: An Introduction. *South Asia: Journal of South Asian Studies*, special issue, 21: 1-18.

Brereton, Bridget. 1979. *Race Relations in Colonial Trinidad*. Cambridge: Cambridge University Press.

Brewer, John. 1994. *Black and Blue: Policing in South Africa*. Oxford: Clarendon Press.

Brijlal, P. 1989. Demographic Profile. In *The Indian South Africans*, ed. A. J. Arkin, K. P. Maygar, and G. J. Pillay, 23–40. Pinetown, South Africa: Owen Burgess.

Brogden, Mike, and Clifford Shearing. 1993. *Policing for a New South Africa*. London: Routledge.

Brown, Judith. 1989. *Gandhi: Prisoner of Hope*. New Haven: Yale University Press.

Brown, Judith, and Martin Prozesky. 1996. *Gandhi and South Africa: Principles and Politics*. London: Palgrave Macmillan.

Buck-Morss, Susan. 2009. *Hegel, Haiti and Universal History*. Pittsburgh: University of Pittsburgh Press.

Bull, Michael. 2004. Automobility and the Power of Sound. *Theory, Culture and Society* 21 (4/5): 243–60.

Burchell, Graham, Colin Gordon, and Peter Miller, eds. 1991. *The Foucault Effect: Studies in Governmentality*. Chicago: University of Chicago Press.

Butler, Judith. 1993. *Bodies that Matter: On the Discursive Limits of "Sex."* London and New York: Routledge.

———. 1997. *The Psychic Life of Power: Theories in Subjection*. Stanford, CA: Stanford University Press.

Buur, Lars. 2005. The Sovereign Outsourced: Local Justice and Violence in Port Elizabeth. In *Sovereign Bodies: Citizens, Migrants, and States in the Postcolonial World*, ed. Thomas Blom Hansen and Finn Stepputat, 192–217. Princeton: Princeton University Press.

Caldeira, Teresa. 2000. *City of Walls: Crime, Segregation and Citizenship in São Paulo*. Berkeley: University of California Press.

Calpin, G. H. 1949. *Indians in South Africa*. Pietermaritzburg: Shuter and Sooter.

Carsten, Janet, and Stephen Hugh-Jones, eds. 1995. *About the House: Lévi-Strauss and Beyond*. Cambridge: Cambridge University Press.

Cavell, Stanley. 1969. *Must We Mean What We Say?* Cambridge: Cambridge University Press.

Cawthra, Gavin. 1993. *Policing South Africa: The South African Police and the Transition from Apartheid*. London: Zed Books.

Chandavarkar, Raj. 1998. *Imperial Power and Popular Politics*. Cambridge: Cambridge University Press.

Chattopadhyay, Swati. 2009. The Art of Automobility. *Journal of Material Culture* 14 (1): 107–39.

Chipkin, Ivor. 2007. *Do South Africans Exist? Nationalism, Democracy and the Identity of the "People."* Johannesburg: University of Witwatersrand Press.

Clifford, James. 1997. *Routes: Travel and Translation in the Late Twentieth Century*. Cambridge, MA: Harvard University Press.

Collins, Elizabeth F. 1997. *Pierced by Murugan's Lance: Ritual, Power and Moral Redemption among Malaysian Hindus*. Chicago: Northern Illinois University Press.

Collins, John F. 2004. "X Marks the Future of Brazil": Protestant Ethics and Bedeviling Mixtures in a Brazilian Cultural Heritage Center. In *Off Stage/On Display: Intimacy and Ethnography in the Age of Public Culture*, ed. Andrew Shryock. Palo Alto, CA: Stanford University Press.

Comaroff, Jean. 1985. *Body of Power, Spirit of Resistance*. Chicago: University of Chicago Press.

Comaroff, Jean, and John L. Comaroff. 1992. *Ethnography and the Historical Imagination*. Boulder, CO: Westview Press.

———. 1997. *Revolution and Revelation: The Dialectics of Modernity on a South African Frontier*. Vol. 2. Chicago: University of Chicago Press.

———, eds. 2001. *Millennial Capitalism and the Culture of Neo-liberalism*. Durham, NC: Duke University Press.

———. 2004. Criminal Obsessions after Foucault: Postcoloniality, Policing and the Metaphysics of Disorder. *Critical Inquiry* 30: 800-824.

———. 2005. Naturing the Nation: Aliens, Apocalypse, and the Postcolonial State. In *Sovereign Bodies: Citizens, Migrants and States in the Postcolonial World*, ed. Thomas Blom Hansen and Finn Stepputat. Princeton: Princeton University Press.

———. 2006. Figuring Crime: Quantifacts and the Production of the Un/Real. *Public Culture* 18 (1): 209–46.

Community Research Unit, Durban. 1986. *Socio-economic Conditions and Household Subsistence Levels in Four Durban Communities: Chatsworth, Newlands East, Phoenix and Wentworth*.

Connolly, William. 2003. *Neuropolitics: Thinking, Culture, Speed (Theory Out of Bounds, Number 23)*. Minneapolis: University of Minnesota Press.

Coombes, Annie. 2003. *History after Apartheid: Visual Culture and Public Memory in Democratic South Africa*. Durham, NC: Duke University Press.

Cooppan, Vilashini. 2009. *Worlds Within: National Narratives and Global Connections in Postcolonial Writing*. Stanford, CA: Stanford University Press.

Critchley, Simon. 2001. *On Humour*. London: Routledge.

Crossley, Nick. 1993. The Politics of the Gaze: Between Foucault and Merleau-Ponty. *Human Studies* 16: 399–416.

Cruikshank, Barbara. 1999. *The Will to Empower: Democratic Citizens and Other Subjects*. Ithaca: Cornell University Press.

Csordas, Thomas. 1994. *The Sacred Self: A Cultural Phenomenology of Charismatic Healing*. Berkeley: University of California Press.

Dangor, Ahmed. 1995. *Sufi Sahib*. Durban: IQRA Publishers.

Das, Veena. 2007. *Life and Words: Violence and the Descent into the Ordinary*. Berkeley: University of California Press.

Davis, Mike. 1990. *City of Quartz*. New York: Vintage Books.

Dayan, Joan. 1995. *Haiti, History and the Gods*. Berkeley: University of California Press.

De Certeau, Michel. 1984. *The Practice of Everyday Life*. Berkeley: University of California Press.

Desai, Ashwin. 1987. *The Origins, Development and Demise of the South African Indian Council, 1964–1983: A Sociological Interpretation*. MA thesis, Rhodes University.

———. 1996. *Arise Ye Coolies: Apartheid and the Indian, 1960–1995*. Durban: Impact Africa.

———. 1999. *South Africa Still Revolting*. Durban: Impact Africa.

———. 2000. *The Poors of Chatsworth: Race, Class and Social Movements in Post-Apartheid South Africa*. Johannesburg: Madiba Publishers.

———. 2002. *Blacks in Whites: A Century of Cricket Struggles in KwaZulu-Natal*. Pietermaritzburg: University of KwaZulu-Natal Press.

———, ed. 2010. *The Race to Transform: Sports in Post-Apartheid South Africa*. Pretoria: Human Sciences Research Council.

Desai, Ashwin, and Goolam Vahed. 2007. *Inside Indenture: A South African Story, 1860–1914*. Johannesburg: Madiba Publishers.

Diesel, Alleyn. 1998. The Empowering Image of the Divine Mother: A South African Hindu Woman Worshipping the Goddess. *Journal of Contemporary Religion* 13 (1): 73–90.

Diesel, Alleyn, and Patrick Maxwell. 1993. *Hinduism in Natal: A Brief Guide*. Pietermaritzburg: University of Natal Press.

Dirks, Nicholas. 2001. *Castes of Mind: Colonialism and the Making of Modern India*. Princeton: Princeton University Press.

Dlamini, Jacob. 2009. *Native Nostalgia*. Johannesburg: Jacana Media.

Donzelot, Jacques. 1977. *The Policing of Families*. Baltimore: Johns Hopkins University Press.

Dubois, Laurent. 2004. *Avengers of the New World: The Story of the Haitian Revolution*. Cambridge, MA: Harvard University Press.

Dubow, Saul. 1995. *Scientific Racism in Modern South Africa*. Cambridge: Cambridge University Press.

Dugard, Jackie. 2001. Drive On? Taxi Wars in South Africa. In *Crime Wave: The South African Underworld and Its Foes*, ed. Jonny Steinberg. Johannesburg: Witwatersrand University Press.

Dumont, Louis. 1981. *Homo Hierarchicus: The Caste System and Its Implications*. Chicago: University of Chicago Press.

Dutton, Michael. 1992. *Policing and Punishment in China: From Patriarchy to "the People."* Cambridge: Cambridge University Press.

———. 1998. *Streetlife China*. Cambridge: Cambridge University Press.

Ebr.-Vally, Rehana. 2001a. Have Culture, Will Travel. In *Culture in the New South Africa*, ed. R. Krieger and A. Zegeye. Johannesburg: Kwela Books.

———. 2001b. *Kala Pani: Caste and Colour in South Africa*. Cape Town: Kwela Books and SA History Online.

Eckert, Julia. 2002. *Governing Laws on the Appropriation and Adaptation of Control in Mumbai*. Working Paper no. 33. Halle, Germany: Max Planck Institute for Social Anthropology Working Papers.

———. 2003. *Charisma of Direct Action: Power, Politics and the Shiv Sena*. New Delhi and New York: Oxford University Press.

———. 2005. *The Trimurti of the State: State Violence and the Promises of Order and Destruction*. Working Paper no. 80. Halle, Germany: Max Planck Institute for Social Anthropology Working Papers.

Edwards, Iain. 1989. *Mkhumbane Our Home: African Life in Cato Manor Farm, 1946-1960.* PhD dissertation, University of Natal.

———. 1996. Cato Manor, June 1959: Men, Women, Crowds, Violence, Politics and History. In *The People's City: African Life in Twentieth Century Durban*, ed. Iain Edwards and Paul Maylam, 102–43. Pietermaritzburg: University of Natal Press.

Eisenlohr, Patrick. 2007. *Little India: Diaspora, Time and Ethnolinguistic Belonging in Hindu Mauritius.* Berkeley: University of California Press.

Engle Merry, Sally. 1988. Urban Danger: Life in a Neighborhood of Strangers. In *Urban Life: Readings in the Anthropology of the City*, ed. George Gmelch and Walter Zenner, 115–25. Long Grove, IL: Waveland Press.

Erlmann, Veit. 1996. *Nightsong: Performance, Power and Practice in South Africa.* Chicago: University of Chicago Press.

Ewing, Katherine. 1997. *Arguing Sainthood: Modernity, Psychoanalysis and Islam.* Durham, NC: Duke University Press.

Fabian, Johannes. 1998. *Moments of Freedom: Anthropology and Popular Culture.* Charlottesville: University of Virginia Press.

Fanon, Frantz. 1967. *Black Skin, White Masks.* Trans. Charles Lam Markmann. New York: Grove Press.

Farred, Grant, and Rita Barnard. 2004. *After the Thrill Is Gone: A Decade of Post-Apartheid South Africa.* Special issue of *South Atlantic Monthly* 103 (4).

Fedida, Pierre. 2003. The Relic and the Work of Mourning. *Journal of Visual Culture* 62 (2): 62-68.

Ferguson, James. 1999. *Expectations of Modernity: Myths and Meanings of Urban Life on the Zambian Copperbelt.* Berkeley: University of California Press.

Foucault, Michel. 1982. The Subject and Power. In *Michel Foucault: Beyond Structuralism and Hermeneutics*, ed. Hubert Dreyfus and Paul Rabinow, 208–26. Chicago: University of Chicago Press.

———. 1983. Discourse and Truth: The Problematization of Parrhesia. Lectures presented at Berkeley, October–November 1983. Posted at http://foucault .info/documents/parrhesia/.

———. 1990. *The History of Sexuality.* Vol. 2, *The Uses of Pleasure.* New York: Vintage.

———. 1994. *Ethics: Subjectivity and Truth (Essential Works of Michel Foucault, 1954-1984).* New York: New Press.

Fox, Richard. 1985. *Lions of Punjab: Culture in the Making.* Berkeley: University of California Press.

Freud, Sigmund. (1905) 1989. *Jokes and Their Relation to the Unconscious.* Trans. and ed. James Strachey. New York: W. W. Norton.

———. (1913) 2001. *Totem and Taboo.* London: Routledge.

———. (1917) 1969. Mourning and Melancholia. In *The Standard Edition of the Complete Psychological Works of Sigmund Freud.* Vol. 14. Trans. and ed. James Strachey. London: Hogarth Press.

———. (1919) 2003. *The Uncanny.* London: Penguin.

———. 1927. Fetishism. In *The Standard Edition.* Vol. 7, 152–59. Penguin: Harmondsworth.

Freund, Bill. 1991. Indian Women and the Changing Character of the Working Class Indian Household in Natal, 1860–1990. *Journal of Southern African Studies* 17 (3).

———. 1995. *Insiders and Outsiders: The Indian Working Class of Durban, 1910–1990*. Portsmouth, NH: Heinemann.

Frisby, David, ed. 1994. *Georg Simmel: Critical Assessments*. Vol. 3. London: Routledge.

Frisby, David, and Mike Featherstone, eds. 1997. *Simmel on Culture: Selected Writings*. London: Sage Publications.

Fuller, Chris, ed. 1996. *Caste Today*. Delhi: Oxford University Press.

Garland, David. 2001. *Culture of Control: Crime and Social Order in Contemporary Society*. Chicago: University of Chicago Press.

Gerwel, Jakes, and Linda Rode, eds. 1998. *Keerpunt: Stories vir'n nuwe Suid-Afrika*. Johannesburg: Kwela Books.

Geschiere, Peter. 2009. *The Perils of Belonging: Autochthony, Citizenship, and Exclusion in Africa and Europe*. Chicago: University of Chicago Press.

Ghai, R. K. 1990. *Shuddhi Movement in India: A Study of Its Socio-political Dimensions*. New Delhi: Commonwealth Publishers.

Gilman, Sander. 1991. *The Jew's Body*. London: Routledge.

———. 1993. *Freud, Race and Gender*. Princeton: Princeton University Press.

Gilroy, Paul. 1993. *The Black Atlantic: Modernity and Double Consciousness*. London: Verso.

———. 2002. *Against Race: Imagining Political Culture beyond the Color Line*. Cambridge, MA: Harvard University Press.

———. 2006. *Postcolonial Melancholia*. New York: Columbia University Press.

Ginsburg, Rebecca. 1996. "Now I Stay in a House": Renovating the Matchbox in Apartheid-era Soweto. *African Studies* 55 (2): 127–39.

Glaser, Clive. 2000. *Bo-Tsotsi: The Youth Gangs of Soweto, 1935–1976*. Cape Town: David Philip.

Glover, William. 2008. *Making Lahore Modern: Constructing and Imagining a Colonial City*. Minneapolis: University of Minnesota Press.

Goffmann, Erving. 1982. *Interaction Ritual: Essays on Face-to-Face Behavior*. New York: Pantheon Books.

Govender, Ronnie. 1978. *The Lahnee's Pleasure*. Johannesburg: Ravan Press.

———. 1996. *At the Edge and Other Cato Manor Stories*. Pretoria: Hibbard.

Green, Nile. 2008. Islam for the Indentured Indian: A Muslim Missionary in Colonial South Africa. *Bulletin of SOAS* 71 (3): 529-53.

Guha, Ramachandra. 1999. *Savaging the Civilized: Verrier Elwin, His Tribals and India*. Chicago: University of Chicago Press.

Guha, Ranajit. 1982. *Elementary Aspects of Peasant Insurgency in Colonial India*. Delhi: Oxford University Press.

———. 2002. *History at the Limit of World-History*. New York: Columbia University Press.

Gunner, Elizabeth. 2000. Wrestling with the Present, Beckoning to the Past: Contemporary Zulu Radio Drama. *Journal of Southern African Studies* 26 (2): 223-37.

Gunner, Elizabeth. 2008. Jacob Zuma, the Social Body, and the Unruly Power of a Song. *African Affairs* 108 (430): 27–48.

Guy, Jeff. 1994. *Destruction of the Zulu Kingdom: Civil War in Zululand, 1879–84.* Durban: University of KwaZulu-Natal Press.

——. 2002. *The View across the River: Harriette Colenso and the Zulu Struggle against Imperialism.* Charlottesville: University of Virginia Press.

——. 2007. *Remembering the Rebellion: The Zulu Uprising of 1906.* Piertermaritzburg: University of KwaZulu-Natal Press.

Hamilton, Carolyn. 1998. *Terrific Majesty: The Powers of Shaka Zulu and the Limits of Historical Invention.* Cambridge, MA: Harvard University Press.

Hansen, Thomas B. 1999. *The Saffron Wave: Democracy and Hindu Nationalism in Modern India.* Princeton: Princeton University Press.

——. 2000. Plays, Politics and Cultural Identity among Indians in Durban. *Journal of Southern African Studies* 26 (2): 255–69.

——. 2001a. Governance and State Mythologies in Mumbai. In *States of Imagination: Ethnographic Explorations of the Postcolonial State.* Durham, NC: Duke University Press.

——. 2001b. *Wages of Violence: Naming and Identity in Postcolonial Bombay.* Princeton: Princeton University Press.

——. 2002. Diasporic Dispositions. *HIMAL* 15 (12): 12–20.

——. 2005. In Search of the Diasporic Self: Bollywood in South Africa. In *Bollyworld: Popular Indian Cinema through a Transnational Lens*, ed. Raminder Kaur and Ajay Sinha. New Delhi: Sage Publications.

——. 2006a. Performers of Sovereignty: On the Privatization of Security in Urban South Africa. *Critique of Anthropology.* Special Issue on State Violence, ed. Toby Kelly and Alpa Shah.

——. 2006b. Where Names Fall Short: Naming and Forgetting in Contemporary South Africa. In *The Anthropology of Naming*, ed. Barbara Bodenhorn and Gabriele vom Bruck, 279–95. Cambridge: Cambridge University Press.

——. 2009. *Cool Passion: The Political Theology of Modern Conviction.* Amsterdam: Amsterdam University Press.

Hart, Keith, and Vishnu Padayachee. 2000. Indian Business in South Africa after Apartheid: New and Old Trajectories. *Comparative Studies in Society and History* 42 (4): 683–712.

Hassim, Shireen. 2009. Democracy's Shadows: Sexual Rights and Gender Politics in the Rape Trial of Jacob Zuma. *African Studies* 68 (1): 57–77.

Hassim, Shireen, Tawana Kupe, and Eric Worby, eds. 2008. *Go Home or Die Here: Violence, Xenophobia and the Reinvention of Difference in South Africa.* Johannesburg: Wits University Press.

Haysom, Nicholas. 1986. *Apartheid's Private Army.* London: CIIR (Catholic Institute of International Relations).

Hegel, G.W.F. (1807) 1977. *Phenomenology of Spirit.* Trans. A. V. Miller. Oxford: Oxford University Press.

Henning, C. G. 1993. *The Indentured Indian in Natal (1860–1917).* New Delhi: Promilla & Co.

Herwitz, Daniel. 2003. *Race and Reconciliation: Essay from the New South Africa.* Minneapolis: University of Minnesota Press.

Herzfeld, Michael. 1997. *Cultural Intimacy: Social Poetics in the Nation State.* London: Routledge.

Hirschkind, Charles. 2006. *The Ethical Soundscape: Cassette Sermons and Islamic Counterpublics.* New York: Columbia University Press.

Hirschman, Albert O. 1977. *The Passions and the Interest: Political Arguments for Capitalism before Its Triumph.* Princeton: Princeton University Press.

Honneth, Axel. 1995. *The Struggle for Recognition: The Moral Grammar of Social Conflicts.* Cambridge: MIT Press.

Hughes, Heather. 1987. Violence in Inanda, August 1985. *Journal of Southern African Studies* 13 (2): 311-54.

Humphrey, Caroline. 1999. Russian Protection Rackets and the Appropriation of Law and Order. In *States and Illegal Practices*, ed. Josiah Heyman, 199-232. Oxford: Berg Publishers.

Hunt, James D. 2005. *An American Looks at Gandhi.* Delhi: Promilla & Co.

Hunt, Lynn. 2007. *Inventing Human Rights.* New York: W. W. Norton.

Hunt, Nancy. 1990. Domesticity and Colonialism in Belgian Africa: Usumbura's Foyer Special, 1946-1960. *Signs* 15: 447-74.

Hunter, Monica. 1936. *Reaction to Conquest.* London: Oxford University Press.

Huq, Rupa. 1996. Asian Kool? Bhangra and Beyond. In *Dis-orienting Rhythms: The Politics of New Asian Dance Music*, ed. Sanjay Sharma, John Hutnyk, and Ashwani Sharma. London: Zed Books.

Indiers en militere opleiding: 'N meningsopname onder Indier-Suid-Afrikaners. 1978. *Instituut vir Sosiologisiese, Demografisie en Kriminologiese Navorsing.* Pretoria.

Innes, Duncan. 1984. *Anglo-American and the Rise of Modern South Africa.* New York: Monthly Review Press.

Isaacs, Marion. 2010. *The Swenkas: Masculinity and Representation in the City of Johannesburg.* Unpublished master's dissertation, Oxford University.

Jacobs, Jane. (1961) 2011. *The Death and Life of Great American Cities.* New York: Modern Library.

Jaffrelot, Christophe. 1996. *The Hindu Nationalist Movement and Indian Politics.* London: Hurst & Co.

Jauregui, Beatrice. 2009. *Shadows of the State, Subalterns of the State: Police and "Law and Order" in Postcolonial India.* PhD dissertation, University of Chicago.

Jensen, Steffen. 2008. *Gangs, Politics and Dignity in Cape Town.* Chicago: University of Chicago Press.

Jensen, Steffen, and Lars Buur. 2004. Introduction: Vigilantism and the Policing of Everyday Life in South Africa. *African Studies* 63: 139-52.

Jeppie, Shamil. 2007. *Language, Identity, Modernity: The Arabic Study Circle of Durban.* Cape Town: Human Sciences Research Council Press.

Jithoo, Sabita. 1975. Fission of the Hindu Joint Family. *Journal of the University of Durban-Westville* 2: 55-62.

———. 1978. Complex Households and Joint Families among Indians in Durban. In *Social Systems and Tradition in Southern Africa*, ed. Eleanor Preston-Whyte and John Argyle, 86-100. Cape Town: Oxford University Press.

Jones, Kenneth. (1976) 1997. *Arya Dharm: Hindu Consciousness in Nineteenth Century Punjab*. Berkeley: University of California Press.

Joosub, H. E. 1972. The Future of the Indian Community. In *South African Dialogue*, ed. N. J. Rhoodie, 424–25. Johannesburg: McGraw-Hill.

Joshi, P. S. 1942. *The Tyranny of Color*. Durban: E. P. and Commercial Printing Company.

Kalyvas, Andreas. 2008. *Democracy and the Politics of the Extraordinary: Max Weber, Carl Schmitt and Hannah Arendt*. Cambridge: Cambridge University Press.

Kant, Immanuel. (1764) 2004. *Observations on the Feeling of the Beautiful and the Sublime*. Trans. John Goldthwait. Berkeley: University of California Press.

——. (1788) 2002. *Critique of Practical Reason*. Trans. Werner Pluhar. Indianapolis: Hackett Publishing Company.

——. 1963. *On History*. Ed. Lewis White Beck. Trans. L. W. Beck, R. Anchir, and E. Fackenheim. Indianapolis: Bobbs-Merrill.

Kapadia, Karen. 1996. Dancing the Goddess: Possession and Class in Tamil South India. *Modern Asian Studies* 30 (2): 423–45.

Kaplan, Lionel. 1997. The Popular Culture of Evil in South India. In *The Anthropology of Evil*, ed. David Parkin, 110–27. London: Blackwell.

Kaviraj, Sudipta. 1995. *The Unhappy Consciousness: Bankimchandra Chattopadhyay and the Formation of Nationalist Discourse in India*. Delhi: Oxford University Press.

Kazi, Durriya. 2002. The Spirited Art of Truck Decoration. *City* 1 (July): 64–74.

Keane, Webb. 2006. *Christian Moderns: Freedom and Fetish in the Mission Encounter*. Berkeley: University of California Press.

Keil, Charles, and Steven Feld. 1994. *Music Grooves: Essays and Dialogues*. Chicago: University of Chicago Press.

Kelly, John. 1991. *A Politics of Virtue: Hinduism, Sexuality and the Countercolonial Discourse in Fiji*. Chicago: Chicago University Press.

Kertzer, David, and Barbagli, eds. 2002. *Family Life in the Twentieth Century: The History of the European Family*. Vol. 3. New Haven: Yale University Press.

Khan, Aisha. 2004. *Callaloo Nation: Metaphors of Race and Religious Identity among South Asians in Trinidad*. Durham, NC: Duke University Press.

——. 2009. Caucasian, Coolie, Black or White? Color and Race in the Indo-Caribbean Diaspora. In *Shades of Difference: Why Color Matters*, ed. by Evelyn Nakano Glenn. Stanford, CA: Stanford University Press.

Khemisi, Phuze. 2004. "Phuze Khemisi." Produced by Damon Heatlie. South African Broadcasting Corporation, Channel 1, June 11.

Khosa, Meshack M. 1992. Changing State Policy and the Black Taxi Industry in Soweto. In *The Apartheid City and Beyond*, ed. D. M. Smith. London: Routledge.

Kirk, S. L. 1983. *The 1949 Durban Riots: A Community in Conflict*. MA thesis, University of Natal.

Kirkwood, K., and C. de B. Webb. 1949. *The Durban Riots and After*. Johannesburg: South African Institute for Race Relations.

Krips, Henry. 1999. *Fetish: An Erotics of Culture*. London: Free Association Books.

Kuper, Hilda. 1960. *Indian People in Natal*. Pietermaritzburg: University of Natal Press.

Lacan, Jacques. 1977. *Ecrits: A Selection.* New York: W. W. Norton.

Ladlau, L. K. 1975. *The Durban Riots (1949).* BA essay, University of Natal.

Lal, Brij V. 1983. *Girmitiyas: The Origins of Fiji Indians.* Canberra: Journal of Pacific History.

———. 1998. Understanding the Indian Indenture Experience. Special issue of *South Asia* 21: 215–37.

———. 2004. *Bittersweet: The Indo-Fijian Experience.* Canberra: Pandanus Books.

Larkin, Brian. 2008. Ahmed Deedat and the Form of Islamic Evangelism. *Social Text* 26 (3): 101–21.

Lasnier, Frank. 2002. *Rickshaw Art in Bangladesh.* Dhaka, Bangladesh: Dhaka University Press.

Latour, Bruno. 2005. From Realpolitik to Dingpolitik, or How to Make Things Public. In *Making Things Public: Atmospheres of Democracy*, ed. Bruno Latour and Peter Weibel, 14–41. Cambridge, MA: MIT Press.

Latour, Bruno, and Peter Weibel, eds. 2005. *Making Things Public: Atmospheres of Democracy.* Boston: MIT Press.

Lee, Rebekah. 2009. *African Women after Apartheid: Migration and Settlement in Urban South Africa.* London: I. B. Tauris.

Lefebvre, Henri. 1947. *Critique of Everyday Life.* Vol. 1. Trans. John Moore. London: Verso, 1991.

———. 2002. *Critique of Everyday Life.* Vol. 2, *Foundations for a Sociology of the Everyday.* London: Verso.

Lehmann, David. 1996. *Struggle for the Spirit: Religious Transformation and Popular Culture in Brazil and Latin America.* Cambridge: Polity Press.

Lerner, Daniel. 1958. *The Passing of Traditional Society.* New York: Free Press.

Louw, Antoinette, and Martin Schönteich. 2001. Playing the Numbers Game: Promises, Policing and Crime Statistics. In *Crime Wave: The South African Underworld and Its Foes*, ed. Jonny Steinberg, 41–49. Johannesburg: University of Witwatersrand Press.

Maasdorp, G. M., and N. Pillay. 1977. *Urban Relocation and Racial Segregation.* Research monograph, Department of Economics, University of Natal, Durban.

MacDonald, Michael. 2006. *Why Race Matters in South Africa.* Durban: University of KwaZulu-Natal Press.

Maharaj, Brij. 2003. Co-operation? Consultation and Consent? The Failure of Voluntary Residential Segregation in Durban in the 1940s. *South African Geographical Journal* 85: 134–43.

Manuel, Peter. 2000. Ethnic Identity, National Identity and Music in Indo-Trinidadian Culture. In *Music and the Racial Imagination*, ed. Ronald Michael Radano and Philip Vilas Bohlman, 318–45. Chicago: University of Chicago Press.

Mare, Gerhard. 1992. *Brothers Born of Warrior Blood: Politics and Ethnicity in South Africa.* Johannesburg: Ravan Press.

Marks, Shula. 1975. The Ambiguities of Dependence: John L. Dube of Natal. *Journal of Southern African Studies* 1 (2): 162–80.

Marks, Shula. 1995. Natal, the Zulu Royal Family and the Ideology of Segregation. In *Segregation and Apartheid in Twentieth Century South Africa*, ed. William Beinart and Saul Dubow, 91–117. London: Routledge.

Marshall, Ruth. 2009. *Political Spiritualities: The Pentecostal Revolution in Nigeria*. Chicago: University of Chicago Press.

Martin, David. 2002. *Pentecostalism: The World Their Parish*. London: Blackwell.

Mason, Jean. 1985. Family Functioning in the South African Indian Community. In *Aspects of Family Life in the South African Indian Community, Occasional Paper No. 20*, 29–49. Durban: Institute for Social and Economic Research.

Masud, Khalid, ed. 2000. *Travelers in Faith: Studies of the Tablighi Jama'at as a Transnational Islamic Movement for Faith Renewal*. Leiden: E. J. Brill.

Mattern, Mark. 1998. *Acting in Concert: Music, Community, and Political Action*. New Brunswick, NJ: Rutgers University Press.

Maynes, Mary Jo. 2002. Class Cultures and Images of Proper Family Life. In *Family Life in the Long Nineteenth Century, 1789–1913*, ed. David Kertzer and Mario Barbagli, 195–228. New Haven: Yale University Press.

Mazzarella, William. 2003. *Shoveling Smoke: Advertising and Globalization in Contemporary India*. Durham, NC: Duke University Press.

Mbembe, Achille. 2008. Passages to Freedom: The Politics of Racial Reconciliation in South Africa. *Public Culture* 20 (1): 5–18.

Mbembe, Achille, and Janet Roitman. 1999. Figures of the Subject in Times of Crisis. In *The Geography of Identity*, ed. Patricia Yaeger, 153–86. Ann Arbor: University of Michigan Press.

Mbembe, Achille, and Sarah Nuttall. 2004. Writing the World from an African Metropolis. *Public Culture* 16: 347–72.

McLeod, John, and Kenneth Robbins, eds. 2006. *African Elites in India*. Ahmedabad: Mapin Publishing.

Meer, Fatima. 1969. *Portrait of South African Indians*. Durban: Avon House.

——. 1976. *Race and Suicide in South Africa*. London: Routledge and Kegan Paul.

——, ed. 1985. *Unrest in Natal Special Report*. Durban: Institute for Black Research.

Meer, Y. S. 1980. *Documents of Indentured Labour in Natal, 1857–1917*. Durban: Institute for Black Research.

Mehta, Deepak, and Roma Chatterji. 2001. Boundaries, Names, Alterities: A Case Study of a "Communal Riot" in Dharavi, Bombay. In *Remaking a World: Violence, Social Suffering and Recovery*, ed. Veena Das, Arthur Kleinman, Margaret Lock, Mamphela Ramphele, and Pamela Reynolds. Berkeley: University of California Press.

Meñez, Herminia. 1988. Jeeprox: The Art and Language of Manila's Jeepney Drivers. *Western Folklore* 47 (1): 38–47.

Merleau-Ponty, Maurice. 1945. *Phenomenology of Perception*. London: Routledge, 2002.

——. 1969. *The Visible and the Invisible*. Chicago: Northwestern University Press.

——. 1995. *La Nature*. Paris: Seuil.

Meshtrie, Rajend. 1991. *Language in Indenture: A Sociolinguistic History of Bhojpuri-Hindi in South Africa*. Johannesburg: Wits University Press.

——. 1992. *English in Language Shift: The History, Structure, and Sociolinguistics of South African Indian English.* Cambridge: Cambridge University Press.

Metcalf, Barbara. 1993a. Living Hadith in the Tablighi Jamaat. *Journal of Asian Studies* 52 (3): 584–603.

——. 1993b. Remaking Ourselves: Islamic Self-fashioning in a Global Movement of Spiritual Renewal. In *Accounting for Fundamentalism*, ed. Martin E. Marty and R. Scott Appleby. Chicago: University of Chicago Press.

Metz, Christian. 1986. *The Imaginary Signifier: Psychoanalysis and the Cinema.* Bloomington: Indiana University Press.

Meyer, Birgit. 1998. "Make a Complete Break with the Past": Memory and Postcolonial Modernity in Ghanaian Pentecostal Discourse. *Journal of Religion in Africa* 27 (3): 316–49.

——. 1999. *Translating the Devil: Religion and Modernity among the Ewe in Ghana.* London: Africa World Press.

Miller, Daniel. 1994. *Modernity, an Ethnographic Approach: Dualism and Mass Consumption in Trinidad.* Oxford: Berg.

——. 2001. Driven Societies. In *Car Cultures*, ed. Daniel Miller. Oxford: Berg.

——, ed. 2005. *Materialities.* Durham, NC: Duke University Press.

Mishra, Vijay. 2007. *The Literature of the Indian Diaspora.* London: Routledge.

Mohapatra, Prabhu. 1995. Restoring the Family: Wife Murders and the Making of a Social Contract for Indian Immigrant Labour in the British Caribbean Colonies, 1860–1920. *Studies in History* 2: 228–60.

Molins Lliteras, Susana. 2009. A Path to Integration: Senegalese Tijanas in Cape Town. *African Studies* 68 (2): 215–33.

Morran, E. S., and L. Schlemmer. 1984. *Faith for the Fearful: An Investigation into New Churches in the Greater Durban Area.* Durban: Centre for Applied Social Sciences, University of Natal.

Mueggler, Erik. 2001. *The Age of Wild Ghosts: Memory, Violence and Place in Southwest China.* Berkeley: University of California Press.

Naidoo, Jay. 1990. *Coolie Location.* Johannesburg: Witwatersrand University Press.

Naidoo, Riason. 2009. *The Indian in Drum Magazine in the 1950s.* Johannesburg: Bell Roberts Publishing.

Naidoo, Thillayvel. 1992. *The Arya Samaj Movement in South Africa.* New Delhi: Motilal Banarsidass Publishers.

Ngcobo, Ndumiso. 2007. *Some of My Best Friends Are White: Subversive Thoughts from an Urban Zulu Warrior.* Cape Town: Schreiber Ford Publications.

Ngema, Mbongeni. 2002. "AmaNdiya." From *Jive Madlokovu!!!* Johannesburg: Universal Music.

Niranjana, Tejaswini. 1997. Left to the Imagination. *Small Axe* 1 (2): 3–19.

——. 2006. *Mobilizing India: Women, Music and Migration between Indian and Trinidad.* Durham, NC: Duke University Press.

Norval, Aletta. 1996. *Deconstructing Apartheid Discourse.* London: Verso.

Oosthuizen, G. C. 1975. *Pentecostal Penetration into the Indian Community in Metropolitan Durban, South Africa.* Pretoria: Human Sciences Research Council.

Oosthuizen, G. C. n.d. *The Meaning of Religious Commitment in an Unstable Society*. Durban: University of Durban-Westville.

Oosthuizen, G. C., and J. H. Hofmeyr. 1981. *A Socio-religious Survey of Chatsworth*. Durban: University of Durban-Westville, Institute for Social and Economic Research.

Pachai, Bridglal. 1971. *The International Aspects of the South African Indian Question, 1860–1971*. Cape Town: C. Struik.

Pachai, Bridglal, and Surendra Bhana, eds. 1984. *A Documentary History of Indian South Africans*. Cape Town: David Philips.

Padayachee, Vishnu, and Robert Morrell. 1991. Indian Merchants and Dukawallahs in the Natal Economy, ca. 1875–1914. *Journal of Southern African Studies* 17 (1): 73–102.

Palmer, Mabel. 1957. *The History of Indians in Natal*. Cape Town: Oxford University Press.

Pasquino, Pasquale. 1991. *Theatrum Politicum*: The Genealogy of Capital; Police and the State of Prosperity. In *The Foucault Effect: Studies in Governmentality*, ed. Graham Burchell, Colin Gordon, and Peter Miller, 105–18. London: Wheatsheaf-Harvester Press.

Pauw, B. A. 1973. *The Second Generation: A Study of Family among Urbanised Bantu in East London*. Cape Town: Oxford University Press.

Pelser, Eric, Johann Schnetler, and Antoinette Louw. 2002. *Not Everybody's Business: Community Policing in the SAP's Priority Areas*. Johannesburg: Institute for Security Studies.

Pietz, William. 1985. The Problem of the Fetish. *Res* 9: 5–17.

——. 1987. The Problem of the Fetish. *Res* 13: 23–45.

——. 1988. The Problem of the Fetish. *Res* 16: 106–23.

Pillay, Govindamma. 1991. *An Investigation into the Caste Attitudes that Prevail amongst Hindus in the Durban Metropolitan Area*. MA thesis, University of Durban-Westville.

Pisarski, Alan. 1999. *Cars, Women and Minorities: The Democratization of Mobility in America*. The Automobility and Freedom Project. Available at http://cei.org/PDFs/pisarski.pdf.

Posel, Deborah. 1991. *The Making of Apartheid, 1948–1961: Conflict and Compromise*. New York: Oxford University Press.

——. 2001. What's in a Name? Racial Categorisations under Apartheid and Their Afterlife. *Transformation* 47: 50–74.

Pritchett, Jack. 1979. Nigerian Truck Art. *African Arts* 12 (2): 27–31.

Profile KwaZulu-Natal. 2001. The Taxi Commission of Inquiry: Cleaning Up the Taxi Industry in KwaZulu-Natal. *Profile KwaZulu-Natal* 1, no. 1.

Rajadhyaksha, Ashish. 2000. Viewership and Democracy in the Cinema. In *Making Meaning in Indian Cinema*, 267–95. New York: Oxford University Press.

Raman, Parvati. 2003. A Resting Place of the Imagination: In Search of the "Authentic" Diasporic Subject. *Himal South Asian* 16 (9):22–30.

Ramasar, P. 1967. Emerging Social Problems among the Indian People of South Africa. In *The Indian South African*, 23–36. Johannesburg: South African Institute of Race Relations.

Ramphal, R. 1989. Social Transition. In *The Indian South Africans: A Contemporary Profile*, ed. A. J. Arkin, K. P. Magyar, and G. P. Pillay, 73-92. Durban: Owen Burgess.

Reddy, D. C. 1992. *The Apostolic Faith Mission in South Africa with Special Reference to Its Rise and Development in the Indian Community*. Master's dissertation, University of Durban-Westville.

Rhoodie, N. J., C. de Kock, and M. Couper. 1985. *Indian Perceptions of the First Election for the House of Delegates: Findings of a Sample Survey Undertaken in June 1985*. Pretoria: Human Sciences Research Council.

Riess, Nancy. 2002. Anthropology and the Everyday: From Comfort to Terror. *New Literary History* 33 (4): 725-42.

Robb, Peter, ed. 1995. *The Concept of Race in South Asia*. New Delhi: Oxford University Press.

Robins, Steven. 2008. *From Revolution to Rights in South Africa: Social Movements, NGOs and Popular Politics after Apartheid*. London: James Currey.

Rose, Nikolas. 1999. *Powers of Freedom: Reframing Political Thought*. Cambridge: Cambridge University Press.

Sadouni, Samadia. 1998. Le minoritaire sud-africain Ahmed Deedat, une figure originale de *da'wa*. *Islam et societies au Sud du Sahara* 12: 149-70.

——. 2009. God Is Not Unemployed: Somali Refugees in Johannesburg. *African Studies* 68 (2): 235-49.

Sahlins, Marshall. 1985. *Islands of History*. Chicago: University of Chicago Press.

Sala-Molins, Louis. 1987. *Le Code Noir, ou le Calvaire du Canaan*. Paris: Presses Universitaire de France.

Sanders, Mark. 2002. *Complicities: The Intellectual and Apartheid*. Durham, NC: Duke University Press.

Sanyal, Usha. 1995. *Devotional Islam and Politics in British India: Ahmad Riza Khan Barelwi and His Movement, 1870-1920*. New York and Delhi: Oxford University Press.

Sarkar, Sumit, and Tanika Sarkar, eds. 2008. *Women and Social Reform in India*. Bloomington: Indiana University Press.

Sartre, Jean-Paul. 1965. *The Philosophy of Jean-Paul Sartre*. Ed. Robert Denoon Cumming. New York: Vintage Books.

Schneider, David M. 1968. *American Kinship: A Cultural Account*. Chicago: University of Chicago Press.

Schönteich, Martin. 2001. The South African Prosecution Service. In *Crime Wave: The South African Underworld and Its Foes*, ed. Jonny Steinberg, 156-74. Johannesburg: University of Witwatersrand Press.

Schoombee, G. F., and E. A. Mantzaris. 1985. Attitudes of South African Indians towards Westernization and Its Effects on Their Family Life. In *Aspects of Family Life in the South African Indian Community, Occasional Paper No. 20*, 51-65. Durban: Institute for Social and Economic Research.

Scott, David. 2004. *Conscripts of Modernity: The Tragedy of Colonial Enlightenment*. Durham, NC: Duke University Press.

Scott, Dianne. 1995. *Communal Space Construction: The Rise and Fall of Clairwood and District*. PhD dissertation, University of Natal.

Seedat, Zubeida. 1973. *The Zanzibaris in Durban: A Social Anthropological Study of the Muslim Descendants of African Freed Slaves Living in the Indian Area of Chatsworth*. MA thesis, University of Natal.

Segal, Lauren, Joy Pelo, and Rampa Pule. 2001. Into the Heart of Darkness: Journeys of the Amagents in Crime, Violence and Death. In *Crime Wave: The South African Underworld and Its Foes*, ed. Jonny Steinberg. Johannesburg: Witwatersrand University Press.

Sennett, Richard. 1990. *The Conscience and the Eye: Design and Social Life of Cities*. New York: W. W. Norton.

Seshadri-Crooks, Kalpana. 1998. The Comedy of Domination: Psychoanalysis and the Conceit of Whiteness. In *The Psychoanalysis of Race*, ed. Christopher Lane, 352–79. New York: Columbia University Press.

Sharma, Sanjay. 1996. Noisy Asians or "Asian Noise"? In *Dis-orienting Rhythms: The Politics of New Asian Dance Music*, ed. Sanjay Sharma, John Hutnyk, and Ashwani Sharma. London: Zed Books.

Shaw, Mark. 2002. *Crime and Policing in Post-Apartheid South Africa*. Bloomington: Indiana University Press.

Sheller, Mimi. 2004. Automotive Emotion: Feeling the Car. *Theory, Culture and Society* 21 (4/5): 221–41.

Shryock, Andrew. 2004. The Double Remoteness of Arab Detroit: Reflections on Ethnography, Culture Work, and the Intimate Disciplines of Americanization. In *Off Stage/On Display: Intimacy and Ethnography in the Age of Public Culture*. ed. Andrew Shryock, 279–314. Palo Alto, CA: Stanford University Press.

Siegel, James. 1998. *The New Criminal Type in Jakarta: Counter-revolution Today*. Durham, NC: Duke University Press.

Simmel, Georg. 1950. *The Sociology of Georg Simmel*. Glencoe: Free Press.

——. 1959a. The Aesthetic Significance of the Face. In *Georg Simmel, 1858–1918: A Collection of Essays*, ed. Kurt Wolff, 276–82. Columbus: Ohio State University Press.

——. 1959b. *Georg Simmel, 1858–1918: A Collection of Essays*, ed. Kurt Wolff. Columbus: Ohio State University Press.

Singh, Anand. 1999. *Perceptions of and Responses to Transformation among People of Indian Origin in Post-apartheid South Africa, 1994–1999*. PhD dissertation, University of Durban-Westville.

——. 2005. *Indians in Post-apartheid South Africa*. New Delhi: Concept Publishing.

Sjöholm, Cecilie. 2001. The Expression of Another in Me. In *Merleau-Ponty, Non-philosophy and Philosophy*, ed. R. Barbaras, M. Carbone, and L. Lawlor, 173–83. Paris: Mimesis.

Skaria, Ajay. 2001. *Hybrid Histories: Forests, Frontiers and Wildness in Western India*. New York: Oxford University Press.

Soske, Jon. 2009. *Wash Me Black Again: African Nationalism, the Indian Diaspora, and KwaZulu-Natal, 1945–79*. PhD dissertation, University of Toronto.

Sparks, Allister. 2003. *Beyond the Miracle: Inside the New South Africa*. Chicago: University of Chicago Press.

Spyer, Patricia. 1998. *Border Fetishisms: Material Objects in Unstable Places*. London: Routledge.

Srinivas, M. N. 1962. *Caste in Modern India and Other Essays*. Bombay: Media Publishers.

Steinberg, Jonny. 2009. *Thin Blue: The Unwritten Rules of South Africa Policing*. Cape Town: Jonathan Ball Publishing.

Stephens, Simon. 1999. Kwaito. In *Senses of Culture: South African Culture Studies*, ed. Sarah Nuttall and Cheryl-Ann Michael. Cape Town: Oxford University Press.

Stoler, Ann. 1995. *Race and the Education of Desire: Michel Foucault's History of Sexuality and the Colonial Order of Things*. Durham, NC: Duke University Press.

———. 2002. *Carnal Knowledge and Imperial Power: Race and the Intimate under Colonial Rule*. Berkeley: University of California Press.

Subramony, Kalviselvum. 1993. *A History of Chatsworth: Impact of Group Areas Act on the Indian Community of Durban, 1958-1975*. MA thesis, University of South Africa.

Swan, Maureen. 1985. *Gandhi: The South African Experience*. Johannesburg: Ravan Press.

Tambiah, Stanley. 1996. *Leveling Crowds: Ethnonationalist Conflicts and Collective Violence in South Asia*. Berkeley: University of California Press.

Taussig, Michael. 2003. *Law in a Lawless Land*. New York: Columbia University Press.

Taylor, Charles. (1989) 1992. *Sources of the Self: The Making of Modern Identity*. Cambridge: Cambridge University Press.

———. 1994. *Examining the Politics of Recognition*. Princeton: Princeton University Press.

Tayob, Abdulkader. 1995. *Islamic Resurgence in South Africa*. Cape Town: UCT Press.

———. 1999. *Islam in South Africa*. Miami: University of Florida Press.

Thrift, Nigel. 2004. Driving in the City. *Theory, Culture and Society* 21 (4–5): 41-59.

Torpey, John. 2000. *The Invention of the Passport: Surveillance, Citizenship and the State*. Cambridge: Cambridge University Press.

Tranberg-Hansen, Karen. 1989. *Distant Companions: Servants and Employers in Zambia, 1900-1985*. Ithaca: Cornell University Press.

———, ed. 1992. *African Encounters with Domesticity*. New Brunswick, NJ: Rutgers University Press.

Trilling, Lionel. 1972. *Sincerity and Authenticity*. Cambridge, MA: Harvard University Press.

Urry, John. 2004. The System of Automobility. *Theory, Culture and Society* 21 (4-5): 25-39.

Vahed, Goolam. 2000. Changing Islamic Traditions and Emerging Identities in South Africa. *Journal of Muslim Minority Affairs* 20 (1): 43-73.

———. 2001a. Constructions of Community and Identity among Indians in Colonial Natal, 1860-1910: The Role of the Muharram Festival. *Journal of African History* 43: 77-93.

———. 2001b. Race or Class? Community and Conflict amongst Indian Municipal Employees in Durban, 1914–49. *Journal of Southern African Studies* 27 (1): 105-25.

Vahed, Goolam. 2003. Contesting Orthodoxy: The Tablighi-Sunni Conflict among South African Muslims in the 1970s and 1980s. *Journal of Muslim Minority Affairs* 23 (2): 314–34.

——. 2005. Passengers, Partnerships, and Promissory Notes: Gujarati Traders in Colonial Natal, 1870–1920. *International Journal of African Historical Studies* 38 (3): 449–79.

——. 2006. "Unhappily Torn by Dissension and Litigations": Durban's Memon Mosque, 1880–1930. *Journal of Religion in Africa* 36 (1): 36–49.

Vaid, Jyotsna. 2009. Fair Enough? Color and the Commodification of Self in Indian Matrimonials. In *Shades of Difference: Why Color Matters*, ed. Evelyn Nakano Glenn. Stanford, CA: Stanford University Press.

Valodia, Farhana. 1987. *Indian Christians in Phoenix.* Honors thesis, University of Durban-Westville.

Van den Heever, F. P. 1949. *Report of the Commission of Enquiry into Riots in Durban.* Pretoria: Union of South Africa, Union Government, 36/1949.

Van der Veer, Peter, ed. 1994a. *Nation and Migration: The Politics of Space in the South Asian Diaspora.* Philadelphia: University of Pennsylvania Press.

——. 1994b. *Religious Nationalism: Hindus and Muslims in India.* Berkeley: University of California Press.

——, ed. 1996. *Conversion to Modernity.* London: Routledge.

——. 2002. *Imperial Encounters: Religion and Modernity in India and Britain.* Princeton: Princeton University Press.

Varma, Pavan. 2006. *Being Indian.* Delhi and London: Penguin.

Vawda, Shahid. 1994. The Emerging Islam in an African Township. *American Journal of Islamic Social Sciences* 11 (4): 532–47.

Vedalankar, Nardev. 1950. *Religious Awakening in South Africa.* Durban: Arya Pratinidhi Sabha.

Veeran, Naresh. 1999. *Orchestral Music Was the Music of the Working Class: Indian Popular Music, Performance Practices, and Identity among Indian South Africans in Durban, 1930–1970.* PhD dissertation, University of Natal.

——. 2007. *31 Million Reasons.* Durban: Niche Media Network.

Vertovec, Steven. 2001. *The Hindu Diaspora: Comparative Patterns.* London: Routledge.

Viljoen, H. G. 1974. Relationship between Stereotypes and Social Distance. *Journal of Social Psychology* 92, 313–14.

Viswanathan, Gauri. 1998. *Outside the Fold.* Princeton: Princeton University Press.

Wade, Peter. 1993. *Blackness and Race Mixture: The Dynamics of Racial Identity in Colombia.* Baltimore: Johns Hopkins University Press.

Waldmeir, Patti. 1998. *Anatomy of a Miracle: The End of Apartheid and the Birth of the New South Africa.* New Jersey: Rutgers University Press.

Warner, Michael. 2002. *Publics and Counterpublics.* New York: Zone Books.

Webb, Maurice, and Kenneth Kirkwood. 1949. *The Durban Riots and After.* South Africa: Institute of Race Relations.

Webster, Eddie. 1977. The 1946 Durban "Riots": A Case Study in Race and Class. In *Working Papers in Southern African Studies*, ed. Phil Bonner. Johannesburg: African Studies Institute Publications.

Wedeen, Lisa. 1999. *The Ambiguities of Domination: Politics, Rhetoric and Symbols in Contemporary Syria*. Chicago: University of Chicago Press.

Westerlund, David. 2003. Ahmed Deedat's Theology of Religion: Apologetics through Polemics. *Journal of Religion in Africa* 33: 263–778.

Western, John. 1981. *Outcast Cape Town*. Berkeley: University of California Press.

White, Hylton. 2010. Outside the Dwelling of Culture: Estrangement and Difference in Postcolonial Zululand. *Anthropological Quarterly* 83 (3): 497–518.

———. 2011. Zumania and Zuluness: Authoritarian Post-Fordism and the Problem of Regression in South Africa. Unpublished paper, Department of Anthropology, University of Witwatersrand.

Willford, Andrew. 2006. *Cage of Freedom: Tamil Identity and the Ethnic Fetish in Malaysia*. Ann Arbor: University of Michigan Press.

Wittgenstein, Ludwig. 1953. *Philosophical Investigations*. London: Blackwell Publishing.

Witz, Leslie. 2003. *Apartheid's Festivals: Contesting South Africa's National Pasts*. Bloomington: Indiana University Press.

Young, Robert. 1995. *Colonial Desire: Hybridity in Theory, Culture and Race*. London: Routledge.

Yurchak, Alexei. 2005. *Everything Was Forever, until It Was No More: The Last Soviet Generation*. Princeton: Princeton University Press.

Žižek, Slavoj. 1989. *The Sublime Object of Ideology*. London: Verso.

———. 1994. *Tarrying with the Negative*. Durham, NC: Duke University Press.

Zupančič, Alenka. 2008. *The Odd One In: On Comedy*. Cambridge: MIT Press.

Index

African National Congress (ANC), 11; affiliated organizations, 106, 108; and beer boycott, 108–109, 315; and cultural unity 20, 290; and development programs, 20, 109; and elections, 51, 129, 130–131, 217; and Gandhi, 100–101; local activists, 102, 264, 323; and police officers, 54, 56; and race, 298; relation of to Indians, 26, 40, 45, 90, 136–137, 140, 161, 163, 165, 167, 210, 308, 311, 314; resistance to, 166–168; and squatter settlements, 130–131; and tensions with Inkatha, 117, 183

African National Congress Youth League, 106–107

African Renaissance, 26

Africans, 125; in Cato Manor, 106–107, 109, 112; in Chatsworth, 285, 287; displacement of, 32, 40, 308; fear of, 6, 22, 51, 53, 111, 116, 126, 130, 134, 172; growing visiblity of, 135–137, 148; as intimate strangers, 46, 116; and "kangaroo courts," 53; and living conditions, 16, 46, 48, 50, 127, 191; and marriage, 115–116, 126; as Muslims, 246, 249, 256, 258–259; perceptions of, 99–101, 113–115, 132; policing of, 47; racism against, 21, 87, 151, 161; and relations with Indians, 21–22, 26, 54, 57–58, 85, 90, 97–99, 100–101, 109–112, 117, 119, 127, 130–131, 133, 136–141, 165–166, 180, 221, 284, 291, 293; and security forces, 47, 302; separation from, 101, 106; and taxi industry, 176–177, 179, 184, 188–189; and townships, 46–49, 59, 68, 86, 107, 186, 190, 195, 198, 285; and urban modernity, 107–108, 122, 198, 300; and urban music, 22, 186–187, 193; and urban riots, 102–104, 187, 193; and urban riots, 102–104,

106–108, 113, 118; and vernaculars, 84; and violence, 10, 18, 118; as workers, 47, 100, 129–130

Afrikaans, 91, 116, 172; as public language, 84; slang in, 187, 306; white speakers of, 139

Afrikaners, 30, 48, 91

AIDS, 87, 134; as a "black thing," 135; and stabbing incidents, 134

Alexandra bus boycott, 176, 315

amaKula, 99–100, 113; Anglo-Zulu Battlefield Tours, 138

antiapartheid movement, 9, 26, 54, 137, 188, 290, 298,

anxiety, 7, 16, 134, 188; and gaze, 15; sexualized, 123; and unknowability, 46, 193

apartheid, 5; and community life, 11, 17, 21, 59, 68, 81, 91, 199; and crime, 47, 194; as part of everyday practice, 10, 17–18, 20; final stages of, 183; government during, 7, 9, 11, 15, 35, 41, 47–48, 200, 298; and Indians, 65, 153–155, 163, 194, 206, 231, 236–237, 259: late phase of, 156; "mature" phase of, 144; and racial division, 6–7, 10, 49, 51, 119, 121, 125, 143, 293; resistance to, 8, 9, 14, 28, 43, 46, 53–54, 142, 153–154, 159, 161, 188; and urban space, 29, 31, 46, 67, 201, 247, 292

apprehensive coexistence, 97, 136

Areas Class Bill of 1922, 29

Aryan Benevolent Home, 163, 230

Arya Pratinidhi Sabha, 229–230

Arya Samaj, 75, 210, 229–230, 232, 319

Asiatic Land Tenure and Indian Representation Act, 31

"Asiatic question," 21, 27–29, 32, 300

automobility, 177, 180; as self expression, 181

GPSR Authorized Representative: Easy Access System Europe - Mustamäe tee
50, 10621 Tallinn, Estonia, gpsr.requests@easproject.com

www.ingramcontent.com/pod-product-compliance
Lightning Source LLC
Chambersburg PA
CBHW022259280326
41932CB00010B/917